METHODOLOGIES FOR THE RHETORIC OF HEALTH & MEDICINE

This volume charts new methodological territories for rhetorical studies and the emerging field of the rhetoric of health & medicine. In offering an expanded, behind-the-scenes view of rhetorical methodologies, it advances the larger goal of differentiating the rhetoric of health & medicine as a distinct but pragmatically multifarious area of study, while providing rhetoricians and allied scholars new ways to approach and explain their research.

Collectively, the volume's 15 chapters:

- Develop, through extended examples of research, creative theories and methodologies for studying and engaging medicine's high-stakes practices.
- Provide thick descriptions of and heuristics for methodological invention and adaptation that meet the needs of new and established researchers.
- Discuss approaches to researching health and medical rhetorics across a range of contexts (e.g., historical, transnational, sociocultural, institutional) and about a range of ethical issues (e.g., agency, social justice, responsiveness).

Lisa Meloncon is Associate Professor of Technical Writing in the Department of English at the University of South Florida. She is the founder and coordinator of the biennial Symposium for the Rhetoric of Health & Medicine. Her research in the rhetoric of health & medicine includes work with disability and embodiment, an historical study of vernacular healing, and understanding the impact of place on healthcare communication.

J. Blake Scott is Professor of Writing and Rhetoric and member of the Texts & Technology PhD faculty at the University of Central Florida. His research in the rhetoric of health & medicine includes studies of HIV testing and prevention practices and of global pharmaceutical policy debates.

Together, Lisa and Blake are cofounders and co-editors of the new journal *Rhetoric of Health & Medicine (RHM)*, published by the University of Florida Press.

METHODOLOGIES FOR THE RHETORIC OF HEALTH & MEDICINE

*Edited by Lisa Meloncon
and J. Blake Scott*

Routledge
Taylor & Francis Group

NEW YORK AND LONDON

First published 2018
by Routledge
711 Third Avenue, New York, NY 10017

and by Routledge
2 Park Square, Milton Park, Abingdon, Oxon OX14 4RN

Routledge is an imprint of the Taylor & Francis Group, an informa business

© 2018 Taylor & Francis

Library of Congress Cataloging-in-Publication Data
Names: Meloncon, Lisa K., editor. | Scott, J. Blake, 1969– editor.
Title: Methodologies for the rhetoric of health & medicine / edited
    by Lisa Meloncon and J. Blake Scott.
Description: New York : Routledge / Taylor & Francis Group, 2017.
Identifiers: LCCN 2017004572 | ISBN 9781138235854 (hbk) |
    ISBN 9781138235861 (pbk) | ISBN 9781315303758 (ebk)
Subjects: LCSH: Communication in medicine. | Rhetoric.
Classification: LCC R118. M48 2017 | DDC 610—dc23
LC record available at https://lccn.loc.gov/2017004572

ISBN: 978-1-138-23585-4 (hbk)
ISBN: 978-1-138-23586-1 (pbk)
ISBN: 978-1-315-30375-8 (ebk)

Typeset in Bembo
by Apex CoVantage, LLC
Printed by CPI on sustainably sourced paper

*We dedicate this book to the memory of Carol Berkenkotter
and the other pioneers of the field of the
Rhetoric of Health & Medicine.*

CONTENTS

ACKNOWLEDGMENTS

We wish to gratefully and thankfully acknowledge the contributors who trusted us with their work and who worked so diligently and with good humor to make it a book we are proud to give to the rhetoric of health & medicine and rhetorical studies.

Lisa wishes to acknowledge The University of Cincinnati's Faculty Development Fund, University of Cincinnati's Office of Research Third Century Grant, and the Charles Phelps Taft Research Center for their financial support for parts of this project.

FIGURES AND TABLES

Figures

Tables

CONTRIBUTORS

Elizabeth L. Angeli is an Assistant Professor of English at Marquette University. At Marquette, she teaches courses in writing and rhetoric. Her current research projects examine how health care professionals manage changing, urgent medical information in unstable medical contexts, including emergency medical services and public health crisis response. Elizabeth also holds an appointment as an Assistant Adjunct Professor at the Medical College of Wisconsin and Clinical and Translational Science Institute.

Kristin Marie Bivens is an Associate Professor of English at Harold Washington College—one of the City Colleges of Chicago. Bivens's scholarly interests range from health care and neonatal intensive care unit communication to environmental engineering communication. Her work has appeared in Harlot, Technical Communication Quarterly, and Health Communication, as well as other journals and collections.

Rachel Bloom-Pojar is an Assistant Professor of English at the University of Wisconsin-Milwaukee. Her research examines the rhetoric of health & medicine at the intersections of transnational health programs, cross-cultural rhetoric, and medical interpretation. Her scholarship and teaching aim to challenge stigma and reduce bias in how patients' discourses of health are perceived by providers and conceptualized in health literacy studies.

Jennifer Edwell is currently a doctoral student at the University of North Carolina-Chapel Hill. Before coming to North Carolina, she attended The Ohio State University, where she received a BA in English, and the Methodist Theological School in Ohio, where she earned a Masters in Theological Studies. Now,

Jen works in rhetoric, composition, and the medical/health humanities. She is particularly interested in the way people tell stories about health and the role of religion in medicine for patients, providers, and health care systems. Jen strives to utilize feminist, intersectional values when using the tools of rhetoric to study these important issues.

Dan Ehrenfeld is a doctoral candidate at the University of Massachusetts Amherst. His areas of interest include public writing pedagogy, digital rhetoric, textual circulation, media theory, genre, basic writing pedagogy, and the rhetoric of health & medicine. He is currently writing a dissertation entitled *rhetorical Investments: Writing, Technology, and the Emerging Logics of the Public Sphere*, in which he argues that a model of public rhetoric based on the metaphor of an "ecology" lays the groundwork for pedagogies that engage developing writers in meaningful reflection about their own practices with genres and technologies.

Catherine C. Gouge is an Associate Professor in the Department of English at West Virginia University. Her recent scholarship has appeared in *Rhetoric Society Quarterly*, the *Journal of Technical Writing and Communication*, and the *Journal of Medical Humanities*. Her research interests include the rhetoric of health & medicine, science and technology studies, writing and editing pedagogy, and technical communication. She is currently working on a book that explores divergent textual and rhetorical practices in health and medicine and elaborates on the possibilities for ethical engagement enabled by them.

David R. Gruber is a Senior Lecturer in the School of English and Media Studies at Massey University, Auckland. His research bridges the rhetoric of science and technology, technical communication, and digital media studies. He has published in *Rhetoric Society Quarterly, Public Understanding of Science, Journal of Medical Humanities*, among other journals. David also works creatively across media and has developed interactive exhibits featured in online journals including *HyperRhiz.net* and *The New Everyday*. Currently, he is embarking on a cross-cultural, multidisciplinary Public Understanding of Neuroscience project funded by The New Zealand Centre at Peking University.

Kelly E. Happe is Associate Professor of Communication Studies and Women's Studies at the University of Georgia and author of the award-winning book *The Material Gene: Gender, Race, and Heredity After the Human Genome Project* (NYU Press). She is coeditor of the forthcoming book *Biocitizenship: Bodies, Health, and Politics*, also with NYU Press. Her current projects address the relationship between scientific models of the body and history; theories of the material in intellectual thought; and the politics of new materialism in the humanities. She teaches in the areas of science studies, environmental communication, and rhetorical theory.

Molly Hartzog is an Assistant Professor in the Department of English and Foreign Languages at Frostburg State University, where she teaches technical and professional writing. She completed her PhD at North Carolina State University in the Communication, Rhetoric, and Digital Media program under the guidance of Carolyn R. Miller. As an NSF-IGERT Fellow in the Genetic Engineering and Society program at NC State, she coauthored a white paper appearing in *Genetic Control of Dengue and Malaria* (Ed: Adelman, 2015). Her research explores the nexus of rhetorical invention and scientific invention, especially in the context of genetic engineering and disease control.

Nathan R. Johnson conducts research and teaches in the areas of public rhetorics, rhetorical theory, and infrastructural studies, exploring how infrastructure, place, and space interact with public discourse. He is particularly interested in how public places change human relationships and how groups who change infrastructure and space can better represent their needs, interests, and communities. Johnson's scholarship has been published in *Poroi*, *Enculturation*, the *Journal of Technical Writing and Communication*, and other journals and edited collections. His forthcoming book project explores how information infrastructures intersect with public memory.

Lisa Meloncon is an Associate Professor of Technical Writing in the Department of English at the University of South Florida. She specializes in the rhetoric of health & medicine and programmatic issues in technical and professional communication. Her award winning research has appeared in journals such as *Technical Communication Quarterly*, *Technical Communication*, and *Journal of Business and Technical Communication*. She is also editor of *Rhetorical Accessability: At the Intersection of Technical Communication and Disability Studies* (2013) and is founding coeditor of the journal *Rhetoric of Health & Medicine*.

Dawn S. Opel is Assistant Professor of Digital Media and User Experience in the Department of Writing, Rhetoric, and American Cultures at Michigan State University. In 2017, she serves as faculty fellow at the Michigan State University/Sparrow Health Center for Innovation and Research. A former lawyer, she researches at the intersection of health care law, policy, technology, and user experience. Her recent work focuses on health care service delivery and payment reform, with specific emphasis on design of communication for care coordination and health care IT interoperability. Recent work has appeared in *connexions: international professional communication journal* and *Communication Design Quarterly*.

Laura Maria Pigozzi PhD is a Lecturer and Director of Graduate Studies of the MS/Certificate Program in the Department of Writing Studies at the University of Minnesota. She is currently a Health Equity Leadership & Mentoring Fellow. Her research site is the immigrant Latino community with a focus on health communication and informed consent, specifically the consent of this community in clinical trials specifically consent by immigrant Latinos being enrolled into clinical trials. Dr. Pigozzi is committed to using participatory research to allow inclusion of the immigrant voice. In 2016 she was presented the Joan Aldous Diversity Grant from her college to study clinical consent, again focusing on the immigrant Latino community.

J. Blake Scott is Professor of Writing & Rhetoric at the University of Central Florida, where he also served as the department's founding associate chair and director of degree programs. With Lisa Meloncon, he is coeditor of the new journal *Rhetoric of Health & Medicine*, to be published by the University of Florida Press. His work in this area has examined public health policy and broader cultural arguments around HIV testing and around transnational pharmaceutical access and regulation.

Nathan Stormer is the Bailey Professor of Speech & Theatre at the University of Maine. His primary line of research is medical rhetoric about abortion in the United States; his secondary line is rhetorical theory. His research can be found in *Quarterly Journal of Speech, Critical/Cultural Studies of Communication, Women's Studies in Communication, Signs: Journal of Women in Culture and Society*, and other outlets. He has two books: *Articulating Life's Memory: US Medical Rhetoric about Abortion in the Nineteenth Century* (2002) and *Sign of Pathology: US Medical Rhetoric on Abortion, 1800s to 1960s*.

Susan Wells is working on a rhetorical analysis of Robert Burton's *Anatomy of Melancholy*. Her most recent book is *Our Bodies, Ourselves and the Work of Writing* (Stanford University Press, 2010). Her interests include rhetorics of science and medicine, critical theory, theories of the public sphere, and feminism. Wells's book on 19th-century women physicians and scientific writing, *Out of the Dead House*, was published by the University of Wisconsin Press in 2001, and won the 2002 W. Ross Winterowd Award for the most outstanding book in composition theory. She has also published *Sweet Reason: Rhetoric and the Discourses of Modernity* (University of Chicago Press, 1996) and *The Dialectics of Representation* (Johns Hopkins University, 1985).

1

MANIFESTING METHODOLOGIES FOR THE RHETORIC OF HEALTH & MEDICINE

J. Blake Scott and Lisa Meloncon

Keywords: methodology, rhetoric, mixed methodologies, theory building, methodological mutability, values, practices

As E. Johanna Hartelius (2009) argues, the rhetoric of medicine, as an area of rhetorical inquiry, "currently finds itself in a sort of sub-disciplinary self-reckoning. It faces a critical exigence of identity, like all inquiries do in their own time" (p. 458). Contributing to this exigence are a number of challenges: accounting for broader health practices; persuading other researchers and practitioners of our work's value; identifying our unique contributions (including methodological) while acknowledging and embracing cross-disciplinary and interdisciplinary influences; and defining our area of inquiry in relation to other scholarly movements, including some that served as our antecedents.

We offer this collection as a contribution to the ongoing, self-reflexive discussion of how we might characterize and advance what we're calling the Rhetoric of Health & Medicine (RHM). Although a number of scholars have begun this discussion around the scope and purposes of what we do, the topics and discursive-material practices we study, and the methodologies we build, adapt, and employ, it is this latter means of characterization that the essays in this volume extend. In attempting to further characterize rather than rigidly define, this collection seeks to keep open questions about our scholarly identity while advancing common threads of concerns, approaches, and contributions. In order to achieve this, we define broadly our key terms of methodology, rhetoric, and health and medicine. We will unpack each of these in sections that follow, but to summarize here, we view methodologies as multidimensional, value-laden frameworks for approaching, studying, and making sense of phenomena (see Sullivan & Porter's [1997] similar characterization, p. 26). We share Burke's expansive notion of rhetoric as the "use of language as a symbolic means of inducing cooperation in beings that by nature respond to symbols" (p. 43; see Segal's [2005] discussion of Burke, 1968, pp. 5, 12). Our view of health and medicine encompasses rhetorical interactions across varied and overlapping cultural spheres, including those related to health and medical research, clinical medicine, health and medical policymaking, consumer health and personal health management, health advocacy, and community-based health practices.

In this introductory chapter and the larger collection, we argue that the RHM can and should be recognized for its methodological contributions (along with other types), contributions that include new or extended concepts, hybrid forms of inquiry and analysis, and self-reflexive forms of engagement. These contributions help to answer Hartelius' (2009) call for what distinguishes RHM, as well as what it can offer back to rhetorical studies, writ large, and other areas. Accordingly, the essays in this collection emphasize questions of why we study health and medicine, the methodological, moves and decisions, resources and challenges, and engagements that shape our research, and what makes our research both rhetorical and potentially useful to a range of stakeholders.

Such methodological questions have framed a number of ongoing discussions about RHM, including those sponsored by the Association of Rhetoricians of Science, Technology, & Medicine (ARSTM) and the Discourses of Health & Medicine Symposium sponsored by the University of Cincinnati. Some of this scholarship has explicitly advanced methodological arguments as part of its primary contributions; examples include Schryer and Spoel's (2005) argument for employing rhetorical genre theory to study professional identity formation through health care discourse; Keränen's (2011) call for biocriticism as the "sustained and rigorous analysis of the artifacts, texts, discursive formations, visual representations, and material practices positioned at the nexus of disease and culture" (p. 225); Bellwoar's (2012) use of cultural-historic activity theory to track the "chains of reception" that shape patients' interpretation and use of health care texts; and Graham's (2015) development of rhetorical-ontological inquiry to study the medical rhetoric around pain medicine. A recent special issue of the *Journal of Medical Humanities* (Keränen, 2014a) develops methodologies for identifying, studying, and engaging health and medicine's publics, and recent special issues of *Communication Design Quarterly* (Meloncon & Frost, 2015) and *Communication Quarterly* (Landau, 2015) explore methodological intersections of RHM with communication design and health communication studies, respectively. It is this thread of methodology-focused scholarship that the current collection most directly extends, in the process advancing the discussion of RHM's identity around how and why we do what we do.

Before we return to a fuller discussion of methodology and a preview of this collection's specific methodological contributions, we want to provide our rationales for calling this emergent scholarly movement a "field of inquiry," for situating it under the umbrella of rhetorical studies, and for calling it the "Rhetoric of Health & Medicine."

Characteristics of RHM

Several scholars, including Hartelius (2009), have characterized RHM as subfield of rhetorical studies. In their entry for the *Oxford Research Encyclopedia of Communication*, Malkowski, Scott, and Keränen (2017) describe it as an "emerging interdisciplinary subfield" (rhetoric itself being interdisciplinary) that "seeks to uncover how symbolic patterns structure thought and action in health and medical texts, discourses, settings, and materials" (n.p.). In their *Communication Design Quarterly* special issue introduction, Meloncon and Frost (2015) go a step further to declare that RHM is an emerged field (and not just an emerging subfield) that is continuing to "build a meaningful, connected" body of work (p. 12).

Regardless of how we classify its degree of development and relation to longer recognized fields, we can now discern a substantial and quickly growing body of scholarship (self) identified as RHM, published since the 1990s, and captured by Meloncon and Frost's comprehensive literature review along with a number of bibliographic essays (Segal, 2005; Eberhard, 2012; Jensen, 2015) and encyclopedia entries (Segal, 2009; Keränen, 2010; Keränen, 2014b; Malkowski et al., 2017). Anchored by rhetoricians in communication studies, rhetoric and composition, and technical/professional communication, this work has appeared in a number of monographs, edited collections, articles and book chapters, and, perhaps most visibly, journal special issues. The latter include *Technical Communication Quarterly* ("Medical Rhetoric," Heifferon & Brown, 2000; "Online Health Communication," Koerber & Still, 2008), the *Journal of Business and Technical Communication* ("The Discourses of Medicine," Barton, 2005), *Written Communication* ("Writing and Medicine," Haas, 2009), *Present Tense* ("Medical, Gender, and Body Rhetorics," Prenosil, 2012), *Poroi* ("Inventing the Future: the Rhetorics of Science, Technology, and Medicine," Keränen, 2013), the *Journal of Medical Humanities* ("Rhetoric and Biomedicine," Lyne, 2001; "Medicine, Health, and Publics," Keränen, 2014a), *Communication Design Quarterly* ("Rhetorics of Health and Medicine," Meloncon & Frost, 2015), and *Communication Quarterly* ("Forum on the Rhetoric of Health & Healing," Landau, 2015). Along with journals and presses, RHM work has been sponsored and supported by a number of professional organizations and forums. These include several ARSTM preconferences focusing on rhetorical studies of medicine, seven Rhetoric Society of America (RSA) Summer Institute seminars and workshops, the Conference on College Composition and Communication (CCCC) Medical Rhetoric standing group, the biennial Discourses of Health & Medicine Symposium, the Rhetoricians of Health and Medicine website (http://medicalrhetoric.com/), and the Flux Facebook group.

Although we are confident in identifying RHM as an emerged movement, we are not as comfortable calling it a disciplinary one, instead preferring to call it a field of inquiry guided by rhetoric but shaped by and drawing upon a range of disciplinary and interdisciplinary bodies of scholarship. Disciplines tend to align and standardize, while fields of inquiry are more likely to advance knowledge in an indeterminate manner. Even while we seek to characterize RHM's collective values, approaches, and contributions, we do not want to lose the methodological flexibility, rich explanatory power, and potential expanded influence gained from bringing together diverse goals, perspectives, and approaches, whether in our own mixed methodologies or our roles in transdisciplinary and/or community-based research ventures. Scott, Segal, and Keränen (2013) capture this goal in calling on the field to stake a "scholarly claim in a way that clarifies our unique contributions" while encouraging methodological collaboration and experimentation, including the merging of critical-analytic and social scientific approaches (p. 2).

We also think it is important to value and extend the various scholarly traditions and conversations (disciplinary, interdisciplinary, and otherwise) that have informed research in our area of inquiry. Rhetoricians of health and medicine have been influenced by and have adapted methodologies, theories, and research findings from (but not limited to) the following: other interdisciplinary areas, such as the medical and health humanities (including narrative medicine), science and technology studies (STS), and cultural studies; various disciplines and subdisciplines, such as rhetoric and composition (including the rhetoric of science and technology), technical and scientific communication, communication studies (especially health communication), anthropology, sociology, philosophy, and history; and various health and medical fields or areas of practice such as public health, clinical medicine, and biomedical research (for overviews of these influences, see Segal, 2005; Meloncon & Frost, 2015; Lynch & Zoller, 2015; Malkowski et al., 2017).

In order to make sense of complex, high-stakes phenomena, RHM scholarship tends to employ mixed methodologies that integrate theories and methods from a number of scholarly traditions and research practices, ranging from cultural and critical theories such as new materialisms to various forms of community engagement and participant observation to software-aided qualitative and quantitative analysis of large data sets. Although we have experienced some tensions among methodological approaches in forums such as ARSTM preconferences and the Discourses of Health and Medicine Symposium, we echo Meloncon and Frost's observation that RHM scholars have embraced the "messiness" of methodological variation. They observe that, "Unlike the debates happening between medical humanities and health humanities about boundaries and territories (see Crawford, Brown, Naker, Tishcler, & Abrams, 2015), the rhetorics of health and medicine are comfortable navigating a myriad of sites and locations and texts" and "working with a host of actors within health care from patients to care givers and nurses to policy makers" (p. 8). Meloncon and Frost go on to explain how the "capaciousness" of rhetoric "affords scholars lots of room to maneuver and find their own voice, while still feeling as though they belong to a specific community. . . . Moreover, the capaciousness of rhetoric and the long standing belief that it is a useful tool in both creating and critiquing discourse helps us to mark the territory of the field" (p. 8).

At the same time that RHM has embraced the usefulness of various methodologies, research sites, and collaborators in knowledge making, we have also brought to bear our expertise in rhetorical theory and *techne* to make unique contributions to the study, understanding, critique, and engagement of health and medicine.

Several scholars have offered useful explanations of such rhetorical contributions. Echoing Burke, Keränen (2012) references our rhetorical expertise about "how specific symbolic patterns structure meaning and action in health and medical contexts and practices" (p. 37). In citing this point, Meloncon and Frost add that rhetoricians can also help explain how "discourses create situations and allow participants and users to act on them" (p. 8). Expanding on these depictions and on that offered by Malkowski et al. (2017), we characterize RHM as having several interrelated qualities:

- It focuses on the persuasive agents and functions of health and medical discourse, asking "who [or what] is persuading whom of what?" and "what are the means of persuasion?" (Derkatch & Segal, 2005, p. 139). In studying such phenomena, our field of inquiry recognizes rhetoric as constitutive action that works with other agents to shape phenomena and knowledge about them, and it draws on various theories of persuasion (from a number of rhetorical traditions, including interdisciplinary ones such as rhetorical-cultural theory) and various analytic approaches (from traditional rhetorical criticism to hybrid approaches that involve rhetorical and other types of analysis, such as qualitative and new materialist).
- Guided by a saturated attunement and responsiveness to the phenomena it studies, RHM is characterized by what we call a "methodological mutability"—a willingness and even obligation to pragmatically and ethically adjust aspects of methodology to changing exigencies, conditions, and relationships. In this volume, for example, both Pigozzi and Bivens discuss how they adjusted their informed consent processes and subsequent data collection methods based on their emergent sensitivity to research subjects' needs and wishes. Experimenting with new forms of mixed methodologies, and undertaking methodologies that involve layers of institutional approval, also sometimes prompt RHM scholars to adjust what they borrow, adapt, and implement as they go along.
- It poses what Segal calls "prior questions" about health and medical discourses and phenomena. Prior questions, Segal (2005) explains, take a step back from the procedural questions typically posed by health and medical experts and practitioners to inquire about what makes certain meanings possible in the first place.[1] In her rhetorical study of complementary

and alternative medicine (CAM), for instance, Derkatch (2016) supplements more common questions around how CAM research might lead to practice applications with the prior questions about how such research "presupposes" particular "models of practice" and thereby poses views of "patients as particular kinds of decision makers" (p. 191).

- It accounts for the mutual conditioning or interanimation of the discursive and material (e.g., forms of embodiment, technologies, objects) dimensions of health and medical practices, including what Hayles (1999) describes as a feedback loop between inscription and incorporation practices.[2] We can see such an accounting in the field's turn to new materialisms, such as Teston's (2016) study of how the "background" lab technologies for direct-to-consumer genetic testing products frame possible understandings and decisions of their users, as well as Graham's (2015) rhetorical-ontological inquiry into the materialization of pain science research, including the institutional "modes of calibration that bring together researchers and practitioners who subscribe to different approaches to pain" (p. 2).

- Relatedly, it resists simple claims about rhetorical agency, instead accounting for its distributed nature and indeterminacy in the face of biopower. We can see examples of such nuanced arguments in Angeli's (2015) study of distributed cognition and memory in emergency medical situations, and in Owen's (2015) discussion of how women's birth plans can be disregarded in institutional birthing settings but still enable a kind of self-educational empowerment.

- It typically examines the discursive-material practices of health and medicine as multilayered, or situated among and along multiple scales of context (e.g., historical, cultural, institutional, local, interpersonal). In *Our Bodies, Ourselves and the Work of Writing*, for example, Wells (2010) interprets the historical changes in and multilayered sponsors of and contributions to the collective's distributed writing practices. Increasingly, as in Bloom-Pojar's chapter in this volume, RHM studies are analyzing interworking transnational and local scales of influence.

- In addition to theories of persuasion and rhetorical analysis, it employs rhetorical *techne*—or the productive art of making and adapting knowledge—to study, make sense of, and in some cases suggest improvements to health and medical discourses. We can see this in Emmons' (2010) call for a "rhetorical care of the self," which encourages us to actively question and dialogue about the ways we are interpellated as self-regulating health consumers (p. 17). We can also see it in Reynolds, Mair, and Fischer's (1995) study of mental health records, presented so that mental health practitioners can better understand, assess, write, and make decisions about such records.

- It is explicitly interested, taking care to articulate the values and ideologies, ameliorative or otherwise, driving the inquiry and its methodologies, including the researcher's relative positionality. This is hardly surprising given that the exigency for much of this work comes from scholars' own experiences with illness and health care.

Segal (2009) references a "rhetorical frame of mind" that comes from a deep and disciplined study of rhetoric, a frame of mind that can attune scholars to pose "prior questions" about discursive practices, explain how they attempt to persuade, and assess their persuasiveness (p. 239). We would add here that for researchers of health and medicine, a rhetorical frame of mind includes being attuned not only to the available means of persuasion in the discourses we study, but also to the available means of inquiry and interpretation offered by various combinations of methods we might employ, based on the specific questions we ask and the concrete challenges of answering them. Unlike Segal (2005), we avoid the argument that rhetoricians of health and medicine necessarily use what has been traditionally identified as "rhetorical theory"; following Meloncon and Frost (2015), we want scholars studying persuasive discourse from a number of perspectives and traditions to feel at home in this field (p. 12). This preference for on viewing RHM scholarship more holistically and broadly allows us to see a fuller constellation of both scalable and mutable contributions to the emerging field, as well as to rhetorical studies and other areas.

Scalability becomes an important component to any emerging or new field because it enables the systematic and cross-pollinating growth of intellectual space, including methodologies. Over the last several years, this growth has already been evident as scholarship has moved into a myriad of new sites and locations to gather data around a vast array of discourses of health and medicine that represent an even broader set of voices, including many voices that had been previously unheard. Although RHM scholars have raised useful starting points for identifying our characteristic or common moves, these will be refined and extended as the field grows, largely through the work of younger scholars such as the ones contributing to this collection.

We believe it is important to include and even foreground the term "health" in RHM. Earlier versions of what might be called "medical rhetoric" scholarship tended to mirror rhetoric of science scholarship in focusing on the rhetorical production and reception of influential texts from biomedical research and clinical medicine. An emphasis on broader health practices foregrounds the myriad of actors (especially flesh-and-blood people) with varying relationships to and stakes in health, illness, and wellness rather than solely focusing on the medical establishment and the medical model of care. Segal (2009) documents how RHM grew from these roots to more broadly cover "health and illness more generally" (p. 227). We have since seen arguments for and examples of studying a "broad array of health publics, their *nomoi*, and their discursive practices, some of which only partially intersect with medical institutions" (Scott et al., 2013, pp. 1–2). In affirming this expansion of our scope to consider health-related practices more broadly, we find helpful Paula Treichler's (1999) analysis of AIDS discourses and constructions as illustrating a "continuum, then, not a dichotomy, between popular and biomedical discourses" (p. 15), and we would add between contexts marked as medical and people's everyday encounters with, experiences of, and negotiations of health and illness.

As we have indicated, the expanded scope of RHM scholars into broader health publics and practices has been accompanied by a proliferation of alternative and hybrid methodologies. We now turn to a more focused discussion of methodology in order to more fully discuss the implications of this development and to offer some modest recommendations for how our scholarship could explicitly address its multiple methodological dimensions.

Dimensions and Discussions of Methodology

Like Rickly (2007), we adopt Harding's (1987) notion of methodology as "a theory and analysis of how research does or should proceed" (p. 3), which Harding distinguishes from the more common notion of method as "a technique for (or way of proceeding in) gathering [and analysis] of evidence" (p. 2). Further, we embrace the importance of "messiness." Drawing on Law's concept of "mess in social science research," Rickly (2007) calls on teachers and scholars in composition, rhetoric, and technical communication to embrace methodologies that are "less static, less rigid, and more malleable" (p. 3). Given the high-stakes discursive-material practices, dynamics of (bio)power, and subjectivities taken up by our research, we think scholars of RHM are uniquely positioned to answer this call.

Scholars in RHM can heed Rickly's call, and the related exhortation by Sullivan and Porter (1997) to treat methodologies as rhetorical constructions and modes of invention (p. 10), by acknowledging and emphasizing in our publications and other accounts the rhetorical aspects of methodology in our research sites, processes, and interactions. Like rhetoric more generally, methodologies, Sullivan and Porter explain, involve three interrelated dimensions: *ideology*, or networks of values, assumptions, and concepts that guide interpretation; *practice*, or "how people actually do constitute their relations" through discourse; and *method*, or the "procedures, heuristics, or tools that people use for inquiry" (p. 10). They go on to point out that traditional discussions of methodology in rhetoric and composition overlook the first two dimensions, in the process de-emphasizing the rhetorical nature of methodology (p. 11).

Like Sullivan and Porter, we want to encourage a more explicit accounting for our methodologies, including their ideological and practice dimensions. One way of doing so is to think in ecological terms. In arguing for an alternative ecological understanding of research in writing studies, Fleckenstein, Spinuzzi, Rickly, and Papper (2008) critique the standard "container" metaphor shaping discussions of methods because it does not provide enough flexibility and attention to the way that research is actually conducted in complex, messy locations that include a number of actors and ideologies. If research is by nature messy, then a researcher's processes should be approached in ways that account for such messiness. The "container" lacks the dynamic and multifaceted nature of research, which is why Fleckenstein et al. argue for ecology "because an ecology, responsive to the ambient environment, evolves with that environment (p. 414). The ecology metaphor can account for the methodological experimentation and responsiveness to the complex phenomena and sites that scholars in RHM may study.

We also draw on Jeffrey Grabill's (2006) adaptation of Sullivan and Porter's framework to call for more discussions of research location and practice (see pp. 153–154). Grabill points to a number of practice-level interactions and negotiations that were at the heart of how he enacted his community-based research but that are "sometimes invisible given the ways we talk about methodology"; these include exigencies for initiating a study, gaining access to people and practices, "studying up" or learning about the issues and stakeholders, building relationships and negotiating power dynamics, facilitating participation of and communication among all those involved, and ensuring sustainable impacts (p. 161). Through such examples of research practices, Grabill suggests a view of methodology not just as a *techne*, or the contextually contingent production of knowledge guided by theories and principles (see Atwill, 1998), but also of *metis*, or the "cunning intelligence" enabling opportunistic and tactical responses to changing conditions (see Detienne & Vernant, 1991). Making our practices more transparent and thinking in terms of various ways to enact knowledge are critical methodological moves for studies in RHM.

Some (though certainly not all) RHM scholarship has conformed to scholarly conventions reinforcing one-dimensional, "cleaned up," "smoothed out," and somewhat detached accounts of methods, practices, and methodologies. This is unfortunate because the richness of such research and the complex problems and practices it engages beg for more robust discussions of guiding values and assumptions and more contextualized, opportunistic, and practice-level enactments and adjustments. At the same time, other rhetoricians (e.g., Fairhurst, 2014; Jacobs, 2012; Teston, 2012) are contributing a growing number of studies that offer richer accounts that uncover the nuances and complexities of research methodologies. For example, although they discuss their community-based fieldwork in Rwanda within such standard process "containers" as research design, data collection, and data analysis, and although they seem largely concerned with arguing for the validity of their approaches, Walton, Zraly, and Mugengana (2015) capture some of the messy contextual factors that led them to make such adjustments as ensuring participant confidentiality, expanding the scope of transcription notes, and experimenting with creative forms of sharing initial findings. We hope this collection contributes to alternative conventions that encourage open and concrete discussions of the how, why, and effects of our messy, context-responsive decision making, such as opportunistic workarounds of access challenges or ethically driven adjustments to participant engagement. For additional models of scholarship attuned to the messiness of research, we can also look to other health-related disciplines. For example, public health scholars Dickson-Swift, James, Kippen, and Liamputtong (2007) interviewed 30 qualitative health researchers to gain a better understanding of the challenges they faced. Their findings indicated a myriad of problems, ranging from building rapport with participants to ethical considerations in coding data to the self-care needed to consistently engage such high-stakes topics.

Too little attention is given to documenting and explaining decisions made during the research process; in studies of health and medicine, where researchers are often faced with unexpected, high-stake, and emotionally challenging situations, this type of vulnerability, reflection, and frankness is perhaps needed more acutely. Yet exposing the values, practices, adjustments, problems, and messiness of research will be crucial to helping rhetoricians of health and medicine, along with any collaborators, enter into and work with complex research sites.

Turn to Mixed Methodologies

Over the past 15 years or so, published RHM studies have increasingly included discussions of and rationales for mixed methodologies—in terms of humanistic and social scientific research practices, guided and grounded research design, indirect and direct engagements of research "subjects," useful and applied research implications, etc. This is not to say that studies drawing more squarely on one disciplinary tradition and methodology have not made important contributions to RHM. But many RHM scholars have found that multiple methodological approaches and methods for collecting, analyzing, and otherwise engaging phenomena and "data" about them are needed to understand and tackle health and medicine's "wicked problems" (i.e., complex and ill-defined problems that resist transferrable and sustained solutions; see Conklin, 2005). Because "meaning and knowledge making can come from traditional (e.g., scientific studies) and nontraditional sources (e.g., online patient communities)" RHM scholars must employ a number of ways of accessing and engaging such sources (Meloncon & Frost, 2015, p. 8).

Meloncon and Frost (2015) point out that many who position their work in RHM view their methodologies as "inter-, cross-, and trans-disciplinary," emphasizing that such work can still contribute to more field-specific conversations and understandings (p. 11). The authors "encourage a more active and critical engagement in both the practice (our teams and in authorship) and in scholarly orientation (reading across boundaries)" of such work (p. 11). In order to answer rhetorical questions about health and medicine's discursive-material practices, RHM scholars have turned to various scholarly traditions—perhaps most notably the rhetoric of science and technology, technical and scientific communication, critical/interpretive health communication, STS, disability studies, and the medical and health humanities. Accordingly, RHM scholars have also incorporated and merged from these traditions a number of approaches to defining scope and foci, accounting for historical and cultural "contexts," identifying and engaging rhetorical actors or actants and their relationships, positioning themselves, collecting and analyzing "data," and presenting their analyses and arguments. We can see different combinations of these approaches—all of which use rhetorical theory to make sense of and explain persuasive practices—in rhetorical historiography (Johnson, 2014), rhetorical-cultural analysis (Scott, 2003), cultural-historical activity theory (Bellwoar, 2012), critical contextualized transnational analysis (Ding, 2014), rhetorical-ontological inquiry (Graham, 2015), feminist methodologies and disability studies (Elmore, 2013; Moeller, 2014), grounded rhetorical-genre analysis (Teston, 2009), genre-based discourse analysis (Schryer, McDougall, Tait, & Lingard, 2012), participatory rhetorical analysis (Lay, 2000; Kuehl & Anderson, 2015), and community-based participatory research (Zoller & Meloncon, 2013). RHM studies can and do define the aims and scope of their research in various ways; collect data through archival, qualitative, quasiethnographic, and/or quantitative methods; and move deductively, inductively, and/or abductively in their analysis.

Grabill argues that attending to the rhetorical nature of methodology can be a "mechanism for rhetorical agency with a research project" (p. 151). We add that fuller accounts of methodology, mixed or otherwise, can similarly promote research agency, particularly for other scholars who seek to understand the how and why of conducting RHM research. Such attention would involve more than a drive-by summary of methods, narrowly defined, but would entail a more thorough and nuanced explanation of the exigencies, values, epistemological assumptions, limitations, affordances, and adaptations of methodology. This would help to contextualize and show the power of RHM scholarship to various audiences, and, just as importantly, it would provide exemplary models for training and teaching other rhetorical scholars.

Another way such studies could broaden their usefulness and agency is by achieving a version of what Barton (2001) calls "disciplined interdisciplinarity." Barton borrows this term from Klein to call for observational studies of medical discourse that contribute to both medicine and language studies and that are guided by the prospective design principles of representativeness and generalizability. We could extrapolate from her call a broader one to integrate (rather than just assemble) different approaches around "points of mutual interest" with the aim of producing knowledge recognizable and valued by the different scholarly areas (p. 314). We add that such contributions might also be recognizable and valued by health publics, health and medical policymakers and practitioners, and other stakeholders involved.

Theory Building as Methodology

Theory building is another way RHM and the studies in this collection can develop sustainable scholarship and advance Leach and Dysart-Gale's (2010) call to form a "corpus of rhetorical analysis in health and medicine for use by scholars and students" (p. 8). A more expansive view of methodology accounts for theory in several ways—as part of an ideological network of interpretation, as a tool for analysis, and as a product of a study, as with methodologies employing grounded theory. We argue that theory building should be recognized as an important methodological goal and practice for RHM scholarship, and that it should not be viewed as antithetical to our area's careful attention to context-specific embodied and material practices. Indeed, without an inventive approach to theory, we lose our ability to notice different things in familiar phenomena and sites, and to make sense of the happenings in less familiar sites. Further, foregrounding theory-building elements of our methodologies can help us avoid too-simplistic assumptions about the roles and limitations of theory in rhetorical analysis, grounded theory, and other approaches, while simultaneously encouraging more specific explanations of such approaches. In other words, theory building gives a necessary force to our existing methodologies that encourages and supports alternative and innovative ways of doing the work of research.

In her discussion of "how to have theory in an epidemic [of AIDS]," Treichler (1999) exhorts scholars to recognize that "[a]t the end of the day, theory is another word for intelligence, that is, for a thoughtful and engaged dialectic between the brain, the body, and the world that the brain and the body inhabit" (p. 6). In this way, she adds, theory is a lens for understanding and interpreting "people's lives" (p. 6), including how signification, representation, persuasion, and other functions of language "facilitate and constrain" our meaning-making and embodied experiences. Theories of rhetoric, or the persuasive use of language, can be especially powerful, given that language "is one of the most significant ways we know reality, experience it, and articulate it" (p. 8). Although he doesn't reference theory building explicitly, Dolmage (2014) goes further to suggest that theory and interpretation are forms of care, stating "to care about the body is to care about how we make meaning" (p. 4).[3] In her review essay arguing for the value of critical affect theory to rhetorical studies, Rice (2008) proposes that such theory can help us tap into and examine "the physical life of social bodies," such as the transmission of anxiety or love among bodies (pp. 202–203), as well as "language beyond official content," or the nonexpressive and nonrepresentational ways that people intimately experience the effects of social language (pp. 208–209). Rather than eliding embodied experience, then, theory can be a means of thoughtfully attending to and caring for it.

Drawing on these observations, we want to advance a view of theory as a framework for thinking, feeling, interpreting, and creating—as a mode of inquiry that can help us pose questions, discern language's functions and impacts, and provisionally help us know. This expands the familiar notion of theory as a "tool to think with" by incorporating affective elements of meaning making and by acknowledging theory-building as a fuller methodology with guiding values. Further, theory—and theory building as a process—can function as frameworks for caring and inventing more beneficial experiences and interactions with health and medicine. In other words, theory building can also be seen as a framework for imagining a better world.

In discussing theory building in empirical rhetoric and composition research, Schriver (1989) foregrounds the ideological dimension of such research, stating that "All empirical work is a subjective and social act, influenced by particular communities' belief systems, work agendas, and assumptions about what is important to study" (p. 273).[4] In casting empirical research as a creative, rhetorical practice, Schriver points out several types of theory-building moves, including the following:

- "Making [and testing] speculations based on existing theory" with new research (i.e., data collection and analysis);
- Developing theory to explain and test a new, surprising observation;
- Reexamining a theoretical framework and its assumptions after "[n]oticing an incongruity in the way an interpretive community conceptualizes" the framework;
- Proposing alternative explanations through different or modified theories, and conducting research "designed to discriminate among the theories";
- Using an analogy or metaphor to explain a phenomenon; and
- Reconsidering "aesthetic issues [e.g., clarity, simplicity] of an existing theory" (pp. 280–281).

We would add these theory-building approaches:

- Noticing and addressing interpretive gaps or "blind spots" of an existing theoretical framework;
- Extending a theoretical concept by fleshing out its nuances and contingencies; and
- Bringing together and relating or merging frameworks or concepts from different theoretical traditions.

We think several of these moves can also apply to RHM scholarship that is not primarily empirical, including historical, rhetorical-cultural, and mixed-method studies. In addition, some studies employ more than one of these theory-building moves, even if they do not explicitly identify such moves.

We want to echo Schriver's caution that theory-building contributions, like those of other methodologies, include "guarded claims and qualified conclusions" that are grounded in the systematic, reflective, and careful examination of discourse and other phenomena, and that avoid exaggerating the interpretive value of a particular theory (p. 274). Molloy (2015) offers a noteworthy example of such methodological care in her field study of the day-to-day social-rhetorical interactions of people with chronic mental illnesses at an outpatient facility. Through thoughtfully designed and adjusted on-site observations and interviews with participants, Molloy developed the notions of "recuperative ethos" and "agile epistemologies" to understand and value the rhetorical performances of outpatients as efforts to recover credibility and "productively disrupt underestimations" of their "rhetorical ability" (p. 144). Instead of only applying classical rhetorical, vernacular, and multiple ontologies theory, she substantively *adapts* it, building new, more nuanced concepts with more specific explanatory power for the interactions under study—not to mention a new understanding of rhetorical agency. In highlighting her values of reducing "stigma's menacing effects," Molloy ends with the modest suggestion that her concepts and focus on overlooked sites of vernacular interactions might be useful to other studies of protected and stigmatized patient populations, but hopes that such studies "sharpen the definitions of these terms and that their continued refinement is informed by everyday talk from diverse participants who would otherwise remain unheard" (p. 160). Another noteworthy example of theory building, and one derived from historical research, is Jensen's (2010) study of sex education rhetoric. As Jensen (2015) explains in a follow-up article to her book, her research examines Progressive Era arguments for "social hygiene" education to "situate and categorize contemporary arguments about sex education curricula" and to qualitatively study such arguments, including the ways they argue for comprehensive sex education using "science-based appeals" (p. 524). By making cross-historical speculations based on existing theories of rhetorical ecologies, and by fleshing out more specific ways rhetorical ecologies function, Jensen develops what she calls a "percolation model" of rhetorical ecologies, which explains how "historical arguments about health percolate up at distinct, chronologically disjointed moments" (p. 524).

Rhetoricians of health and medicine should continue to traffic in a variety of theoretical traditions, whether by testing, extending, adapting, complexifying, merging, distinguishing contributions among, and/or proposing alternatives to theories and concepts. Promising directions for theory building in RHM include but are not limited to the following: ways to identify and engage health and medicine's stakeholders (e.g., Scott, 2014; Lawrence, Hausman, & Dannenberg, 2014; Pigozzi, this volume); ways to explain the rhetorical circulation and transformation of health and medical discourses and practices (e.g., Bellwoar, 2012; Ding, 2014; Johnson, this volume); ways to account for the possibilities and limitations of participants' rhetorical agency in the face of biopower and "rhetorical disability" (e.g., Owens, 2015; Koerber, 2013; Molloy, 2015; Bivens, this volume); ways to account rhetorically for health and medicine's material and affective dimensions (Graham, 2015; McNely, Spinuzzi, & Teston, 2015; Edwell, this volume); and ways to define and attend to the ethics of health and medicine research and practice (see Meloncon & Frost, 2015, p. 11; Opel, this volume). Regardless of its various trajectories in RHM, we hope theory building as a methodology will be approached as continuing rather than having an end point, as pluralistic rather than canon forming, as measured and nuanced rather than universalizing and flattening, and as ethically responsive rather than self-indulgent.

Overview of Chapters

The volume features chapters drawn from larger, ongoing studies by both well-established and younger, emerging scholars. The volume's chapters address a range of methodological questions through which RHM has been shaped, including (but not limited to) questions about

- how to account for the sometimes unpredictable circulation and uptake of health and medical rhetoric;
- how to engage health and medical practices and their stakeholders ethically and responsively;
- how to foreground our contributions in collaborative research involving health and medical professionals and publics; and
- how to build new hybrid concepts with explanatory power for both rhetoric and for health and medicine.

Because each chapter includes an abstract, we will introduce the rest of the collection not by offering chapter summaries but by discussing examples of common methodological and topical threads. Although we attempt to point to a range of examples for each thread, these are meant to be illustrative rather than comprehensive; readers will undoubtedly find additional examples across other chapters.

First, the chapters in this collection *leverage and integrate conversations and methodologies from various traditions*, but in ways that *suit the specific phenomena under study and, often, that extend conversations across multiple domains*. One especially inventive example of this is Gouge's discussion of patient noncompliance, which merges ideas from rhetoric, disability and queer theory, feminist new materialisms, and urban design to argue for valuing and flexibly responding to patients' divergent paths or behaviors as rhetorical responses; her research has implications for RHM scholars but also health care experts working on the wicked problem of noncompliance. Through an extended historical example of how proteins became an important health concept and category, Johnson uses infrastructure theory to explore the "background resources" that shaped the rhetorical knowledge work of nutrition research and nutritional consumer information. Hartzog analyzes how the genetically modified mosquito functions as a rhetorical boundary object for negotiating tensions by malaria researchers; her analysis not only couples the rhetorical notion of *topoi* with the sociological notion of boundary object to understand rhetorical tensions in health-related malaria research, but also serves as a case study for negotiating tensions and forging productive boundary spaces between the RHM and the rhetoric of science and technology (RST). In his chapter, Gruber extends work on neurorhetoric—which "evaluates the potential for new brain findings to contribute to rhetorical theory"—to discuss how rhetoricians might work on cross-disciplinary projects that more playfully "expose alternative material realities ultimately benefitting both neuroscience and rhetoric." In order to reprioritize and reinfuse the material body and embodied experience in RHM research, Meloncon develops the interdisciplinary approach of "performance phenomenology," which integrates phenomenology's emphasis on first-person lived experience with performance theory's emphasis on the actions and relational interactions of embodied beings like patients and providers.

Second, the chapters in this collection attempt to *foreground methodology in its multiple dimensions*. They feature *explanations of research exigencies and the values undergirding their research questions, designs, and interpretations*, with some guided by the social justice concern with ensuring the agency of the most vulnerable. To illustrate this emphasis in terms of research values, Pigozzi, in her discussion of participatory research involving a local Latino/a community, discusses ethical principles and cultural knowledge crucial to negotiating informed consent with participants, particularly when they have "therapeutic misconception" about their potential benefits from participation. Bivens similarly emphasizes the ethics of informed consent, discussing how she watched and listened for "microwithdrawals of consent" by new mothers in neonatal intensive care units. In her compilation of ethical concerns for researching health care in networked digital contexts, Opel emphasizes the values of protecting vulnerable populations, anticipating and defining possible harms contextually, and consulting a number of sources beyond review boards in ethical decision-making. Happe calls on communication scholars (including rhetoricians) researching racial disparities in health to replace starting with "race" as a static analytic concept with accounting for race and racialization as shaped by communication in specific contexts; offering an example of a "prior question," Happe illustrates this shift by preceding the goal of crafting better health campaign messages for different groups of women with the question of how health communication shapes identity-based group membership in the first place.

In addition to foregrounding methodological values, the chapters in this collection *argue for and/or enact exposing the messy, "behind the scenes" decision-making, negotiation, and adjustments of their methodologies in action*. Some chapters go further in also providing new rhetorical *techne* or heuristics for planning and conducting methodological practice. Gruber calls for an approach to neurorhetorics that embraces a playful, wild, or messy methodological pluralism that does not "overlook [or hierarchize] how multiple approaches change what is seen, how it is seen, how it is written, and why." Both Pigozzi and Bivens discuss ways they adjusted their informed consent process and data collection in response to the unique circumstances and needs of their participants. Angeli also foregrounds the ways she adjusted her data collection, in this instance due to the challenges of identifying the most important regulatory stakeholders and getting permission from multiple IRBs to conduct some of her planned observations. In discussing examples of her "assemblage mapping" and offering readers a step-by-step guide for making their own, Angeli also shows how such tools for determining institutional relationships and entry points were created out of and can shape the changing dynamics of research practices. Like Angeli, Edwell offers readers a heuristic to guide methodological practice, in her case around the process of researching "emplaced" rhetoric, including demarcating "site" boundaries and determining modes of experiencing place(s). Beyond the multiple historical lenses they explain, Wells and Stormer offer several strategies and resources for doing historical work which counter the logistical challenges around accessing protected information in archives.

Instead of or in addition to tools for planning and implementing methodological approaches, other chapters *build and contribute revised or new theories or conceptual resources*. Gouge repurposes the urban landscape notion of "desire lines" to theorize patients' divergent responses to treatment plans and protocols as rhetorical enactments of emergent knowledge and agency rather than "things to fix." In his chapter, Ehrenfeld develops the concept of "ecological investment" to capture how the "constituent parts of complex ecologies seem to 'invest' in the maintenance of . . . infrastructures" supporting the circulation of medical rhetoric, and how specific rhetors also invest in these infrastructures, thereby "altering the[ir] embodied, material relations." One of the exigencies for developing this concept, Ehrenfeld explains, was the limitation of existing theories to account for and situate an individual rhetor's contributions to and agency in rhetorical ecologies; another exigency was to historically complicate the too-simple ways that notions of rhetorical ecologies have "functioned as universalizing [rather than historically specific] metaphors." Other examples include Bivens' notion of "microwithdrawals of consent" to capture the embodied signals of participants that require consent to be constantly negotiated, Bloom-Pojar's notion of "vernacular medical terminology" as a way to value the lay translingual discourse of patients and communities, Gruber's notion of "neuro-rhetorical performance" as a cross-disciplinary invention practice, and Johnson's notions of "republication" and "translation" to trace and explain the invisible work of creating or changing an infrastructure to support health knowledge.

Another way the studies in this collection reflect and extend the larger body of RHM work is by *incorporating into their analyses multiple layers and scales of health and medical practices, contexts, and influences*. In his rhetorical-historical study of Dr. Emma Elizabeth Walker's social hygiene lectures in the early 20th century, Ehrenfeld turns to models of ecology and circulation to capture the relationships between Walker's health promotion rhetoric and cultural forces (e.g., "obscenity laws, habitation patterns, utopian movements, professional medical communities") that shaped the ecology in which this rhetoric circulated. In their chapter, Wells and Stormer argue persuasively that, in its increasing focus on contemporary issues, RHM is losing the rich knowledge, conceptual resources, and methodologies that historical studies and historiography offer. In addition to providing resources for making knowledge and persuading from both familiar and strange historical practices, they explain, historiographic methods can "situate the present as a historical moment" by bringing together materialist, axiological, practical, analogical, and cultural viewpoints that enable a dialogue between the present and the past.

Some chapters study local health and medical practices as also having transnational or transcultural dimensions. For example, Bloom-Pojar interprets the translingual health practices of a clinic in the Dominican Republic as transculturally situated, both in terms of the transnational group of providers, translators and other helpers, and patients, but also in terms of the different cultural sites and sources of language-use in and around the locale. Such transcultural dimensions were reflected in the different types of Spanish spoken (e.g., "professional, American, Dominican, campo, and medical"). Bivens explains how her attunement to patients' microwithdrawals of consent in her study of a Danish neonatal intensive care unit prompted her to change the way she negotiated consent in a follow-up study at a similar U.S.-based site. In her analysis of global malaria research, Hartzog analyzes how global malaria researchers "employ strategies of boundary work to demarcate a certain set of behavioral and taxonomic characteristics that they see as relevant to the control of malaria," thereby creating an inventional framework that replaces the more established *topos* of "evolutionary relatedness" of mosquito species with that of "vector capacity." One reason we decided against grouping these chapters into a discrete "global" section was to signal that transnational and transcultural work should be embedded throughout the fabric of RHM rather than existing in a single thread.

A number of chapters *develop new concepts and approaches for studying the mutually conditioning relationships between discursive and material (e.g., forms of embodiment, technologies, environments, objects) constituents of health and medicine*, with several contributors spotlighting embodied subjects and experiences in their studies and methodological arguments. Edwell's methodology for emplaced rhetorics, for example, goes further than contextualizing symbolic representation by making the interaction of bodies in spaces and environments the primary object of study. Bivens' studies carefully attends to the ethics of collecting data in sensitive research spaces and in response to embodied acts of microwithdrawal. As suggested by her title of "Bringing the Body Back," Meloncon's methodology most intensely prioritizes the body and embodied performance in both research practices and publications, particularly at the level of "the small agencies, the small moments, the small feelings." For her part, Happe critiques the material effects of research assumptions and approaches that essentialize race by displacing historical, contextualized communication processes and behaviors.

Finally, a thread of *ethical concerns* is woven through several of the chapters. Opel explains how research ethics need to be updated when moving into online settings. In addition to synthesizing relevant ethical considerations, she offers a case study that illustrates the nuances of an updated orientation to Health 2.0. Both Meloncon and Gouge provide theoretical orientations that include ethical dimensions as major exigencies for theory building. Bivens, Pigozzi, Angeli, and Edwell all explicitly discuss enactments of ethical responsiveness when they describe their methods, practices, and ideologies. In short, this volume provides an up-to-date view on the importance of ethics in RHM research.

Although the volume's chapters have multiple points of convergence, we have ordered them to create the following conversational progression: 1) exploring the roles and forms of historical inquiry (Wells & Stromer; Ehrenfeld; Johnson) since in some ways this has been and should continue to be the foundation of the field; 2) reframing key research concepts, particularly around forms of embodiment (Happe; Meloncon; Gouge); 3) developing more contextually attuned and responsively ethical research practices (Bivens; Edwell; Opel), and including more fully participatory ones (Angeli; Pigozzi; Bloom-Pojar); and 4) positing new relationships between RHM and other fields (Hartzog; Gruber).

Through the various methodological contributions we've been overviewing, the chapters in this collection offer a version of what Hartelius calls "sustainable scholarship," advancing the larger goal of recognizing RHM as a pragmatically multifarious and discernable area of study that can inform rhetorical studies and other areas, such as the medical humanities, medical education, health communication, health policy-making, medical research, and the practice of medicine. Although we believe, and have tried to explain and show how, RHM scholarship has developed a somewhat unique combination of methodological orientations, we also echo Scott et al.'s (2013) hope that our emergent field will "carve out an expansive focus on the exigencies, functions, and impacts of health-related discourse; attend to the movement, surrounding networks, and ecologies of this discourse; and work with other scholars/researchers, both inside and outside disciplinary rhetorical studies, toward a variety of goals" (p. 1). We offer this collection as an advancement of this hope—one that foregrounds methodology in the richness of its multiple dimensions.

Notes

1 We might relate this approach to what Teston (2016), citing Michael Lynch, describes as rhetorical ontography, which "inquires into how, when, and for whom such questions become important or come to be asked in the first place" (n.p.).
2 Hayles (1999) explains that "changes in experiences of embodiment bubble up in language" while, at the same time, "discursive constructions affect how bodies move through space and time" (pp. 206–207).
3 We thank Catherine Gouge for making and sharing this observation with us.
4 Schriver (1989) goes on to mention another aspect of some empirical research that often gets de-emphasized in published overviews of studies' methods—the alternate use of inductive and deductive inferencing, the latter guided by theoretical propositions and concepts (p. 280).

References

Angeli, E. L. (2015). Three types of memory in emergency medical services. *Written Communication, 32*(1), 3–38.

Atwill, J. (1998). *Rhetoric reclaimed: Aristotle and the liberal arts tradition*. Ithaca, NY: Cornell University Press.

Barton, E. (2001). Design in observational research on the discourse of medicine: Toward disciplined interdisciplinarity. *Journal of Business and Technical Communication, 15*(3), 309–332.

Barton, E. (2005). Introduction to the special issue: The discourses of medicine. *Journal of Business and Technical Communication, 19*(3), 245–248.

Bellwoar, H. (2012). Everyday matters: Reception and use as productive design of health-related texts. *Technical Communication Quarterly, 21*(4), 325–345.

Burke, K. (1968). *Language as symbolic action.* Berkeley, CA: University of California Press.

Conklin, J. (2005). *Dialogue mapping: Building shared understanding of wicked problems.* New York, NY: Wiley.

Crawford, P., Brown, B., Naker, C., Tishcler, V., & Abrams, B. (2015). *Health humanities.* Basingstoke, Hampshire: Palgrave Macmillan.

Derkatch, C. (2016). *Bounding biomedicine: Evidence and rhetoric in the new science of alternative medicine.* Chicago, IL: University of Chicago Press.

Derkatch, C., & Segal, J. Z. (2005). Realms of rhetoric in health and medicine. *University of Toronto Medical Journal, 82*(2), 138–142.

Detienne, M., & Vernant, J-P. (1991). *Cunning intelligence in Greek culture and society* (J. Lloyd, Trans.). Chicago, IL: University of Chicago Press.

Dickson-Swift, V., James, E. L., Kippen, S., & Liamputtong, P. (2007). Doing sensitive research: What challenges do qualitative researchers face? *Qualitative Research, 7*(3), 327–353.

Ding, H. (2014). *Rhetoric of a global epidemic.* Carbondale, IL: Southern Illinois University Press.

Dolmage, J. (2014). *Disability rhetoric.* Syracuse, NY: Syracuse University Press.

Eberhard, J. M. (2012). Rhetoric of health & medicine. *Present Tense: A Journal of Rhetoric in Society, 2*(2). Retrieved from www.presenttensejournal.org/volume-2/an-annotated-bibliography-of-literature-on-the-rhetoric-of-health-and-medicine/.

Elmore, K. (2013). Embracing interdependence: Technology developers, autistic users, and technical communicators. In L. Meloncon (Ed.), *Rhetorical accessibility: At the intersections of technical communication and disability studies* (pp. 15–38). Amityville, NY: Baywood.

Emmons, K. (2010). *Black dogs and blue words: Depression and gender in the age of self-care.* New Brunswick, NJ: Rutgers University Press.

Fairhurst, G. T. (2014). Exploring the back alleys of publishing qualitative organizational communication research. *Management Communication Quarterly, 28*(3), 432–439.

Fleckenstein, K. S., Spinuzzi, C., Rickly, R. J., & Papper, C. C. (2008). The importance of harmony: An ecological metaphor for writing research. *College Composition and Communication, 60*(2), 388–419.

Grabill, J. (2006). The study of writing in the social factory: Methodology and rhetorical agency. In J. B. Scott, B. Longo, & K. V. Wills (Eds.), *Critical power tools: Technical communication and cultural studies* (pp. 151–170). Albany, NY: State University of New York Press.

Graham, S. S. (2015). *The politics of pain medicine: A rhetorical-ontological inquiry.* Chicago, IL: University of Chicago Press.

Haas, C. (2009). Writing and medicine [Special issue]. *Written Communication, 26*(3).

Harding, S. (1987). Introduction: Is there a feminist methodology? In S. Harding, (Ed.) *Feminism and methodology: Social science issues* (pp. 1–14). Bloomington, IN: Indiana University Press.

Hartelius, E. J. (2009). Sustainable scholarship and the rhetoric of medicine. *Quarterly Journal of Speech, 95*(4), 457–470. doi:10.1080/00335630903296234.

Hayles, N. K. (1999). *How we became posthuman: Virtual bodies in cybernetics, literature, and informatics.* Chicago, IL: University of Chicago Press.

Heifferon, B., & Brown, S. (2000). Medical rhetoric [Special issue]. *Technical Communication Quarterly, 9*(3).

Jacobs, G. (2012). Troubling research: A field journey through methodological decision making. In K. Powell & P. Takayoshi (Eds.), *Practicing research in writing studies: Reflexive and ethically responsible research* (pp. 331–348). Cresskill, NJ: Hampton Press.

Jensen, R. E. (2010). *Dirty words: The rhetoric of public sex education, 1870–1924*. Urbana-Champaign, IL: University of Illinois Press.

Jensen, R. E. (2015). An ecological turn in rhetoric of health scholarship: Attending to the historical flow and percolation of ideas, assumptions, and arguments. *Communication Quarterly, 63*(5), 522–526.

Johnson, J. (2014). *American lobotomy: A rhetorical history*. Ann Arbor, MI: University of Michigan Press.

Keränen, L. (2010). Rhetoric of medicine. In S. H. Priest (Ed.), *Encyclopedia of science and technology communication* (Vol. 2, pp. 639–642). Thousand Oaks, CA: Sage.

Keränen, L. (2011). Addressing the epidemic of epidemics: Germs, security, and a call for biocriticism. *Quarterly Journal of Speech, 97*(2), 224–244.

Keränen, L. (2012). "This weird, incurable disease": Competing diagnoses in the rhetoric of morgellons. In T. Jones, D. Wear, & L. D. Friedman (Eds.), *Health humanities reader* (pp. 36–49). New Brunswick, NJ: Rutgers University Press.

Keränen, L. (2013). Inventing the future: The rhetorics of science, technology, and medicine [Special issue]. *Poroi, 9*(1).

Keränen, L. (2014a). Medicine, health, and publics [Special issue]. *Journal of Medical Humanities, 35*(2).

Keränen, L. (2014b). Rhetoric of health & medicine. In T. L. Thompson (Ed.), *Encyclopedia of health communication* (Vol. 3, pp. 1174–1175). Thousand Oaks, CA: Sage.

Koerber, A. (2013). *Breast or bottle? Contemporary controversies in infant-feeding policy and practice*. Columbia, SC: University of South Carolina Press.

Koerber, A., & Still, B. (2008). Online health communication [Special issue]. *Technical Communication Quarterly, 17*(3), 259. doi:10.1080/10572250802100329.

Kuehl, R., & Anderson, J. (2015). Designing public communication about doulas: Analyzing presence and absence in promoting a volunteer doula program. *Communication Design Quarterly, 3*(4), 75–84.

Landau, J. (2015). Special section forum on rhetoric and health communication. *Communication Quarterly, 63*(5).

Lawrence, H.Y., Hausman, B. L., & Dannenberg, C. J. (2014). Reframing medicine's publics: The local as a public of vaccine refusal. *Journal of Medical Humanities, 35*(2), 111–129.

Lay, M. M. (2000). *The rhetoric of midwifery: Gender, knowledge, and power*. New Brunswick, NJ: Rutgers University Press.

Leach, J., & Dysart-Gale, D. (Eds.). (2010). *Rhetorical questions of health and medicine*. Lanham, MD: Lexington Books.

Lynch, J. A., & Zoller, H. (2015). Recognizing differences and commonalities: The rhetoric of health & medicine and critical-interpretive health communication. *Communication Quarterly, 63*(5), 498–503.

Lyne, J. (2001). Rhetoric and biomedicine [Special issue]. *Journal of Medical Humanities, 22*(1).

Malkowski, J. A., Scott, J. B., & Keränen, L. (2016). Rhetorical approaches to health and medicine. In *Oxford encyclopedia of communication*. New York, NY: Oxford University Press. doi: 10.1093/acrefore/9780190228613.013.180.

McNely, B., Spinuzzi, C., & Teston, C. (2015). Contemporary research methodologies in technical communication. *Technical Communication Quarterly, 24*(1), 1–13.

Meloncon, L., & Frost, E. A. (2015). Charting an emerging field: The rhetorics of health and medicine and its importance in communication design. *Communication Design Quarterly*, *3*(4), 7–14.

Moeller, M. (2014). Pushing boundaries of normalcy: Employing critical disability studies in analyzing medical advocacy websites. *Communication Design Quarterly*, *2*(2), 52–80.

Molloy, C. (2015). Recuperative ethos and agile epistemologies: Toward a vernacular engagement with mental illness ontologies. *Rhetoric Society Quarterly*, *45*(2), 138–163.

Owens, K. H. (2015). *Writing childbirth: Women's rhetorical agency in labor and online.* Carbondale, IL: Southern Illinois University Press.

Prenosil, J. (2012). Medical, gender, and body rhetorics [Special issue]. *Present Tense*, *2*(2).

Reynolds, J. F., Mair, D. C., & Fischer, P. C. (1995). *Writing and reading mental health records: Issues and analysis in professional writing and scientific rhetoric* (2nd ed.). New York, NY: Routledge.

Rice, J. E. (2008). The new *new*: Making the case for critical affect studies. *Quarterly Journal of Speech*, *94*(2), 200–212.

Rickly, R. J. (2007). Messy contexts: Research as a rhetorical situation. In H. McKee & D. N. Devoss (Eds.), *Digital writing research: Technologies, methodologies, and ethical issues* (pp. 377–397). Cresskill, NJ: Hampton Press.

Schriver, K. (1989). Theory building in rhetoric and composition: The role of empirical scholarship. *Rhetoric Review*, *7*(2), 272–288.

Schryer, C., McDougall, A., Tait, G. R., & Lingard, L. (2012). Creating discursive order at the end of life: The role of genres in palliative care settings. *Written Communication*, *29*(2), 111–141. doi:10.1177/0741088312439877.

Schryer, C. F., & Spoel, P. (2005). Genre theory, health-care discourse, and professional identity formation. *Journal of Business and Technical Communication*, *19*(3), 249–278.

Scott, J. B. (2016). Boundary work and the construction of scientific authority in the vaccines-autism controversy. *Journal of Technical Writing and Communication*, *46*(1), 59–82.

Scott, J. B. (2003). *Risky rhetoric: AIDS and the cultural practices of HIV testing.* Carbondale, IL: Southern Illinois University Press.

Scott, J. B., Segal, J. Z., & Keranen, L. (2013). The rhetorics of health and medicine: Inventional possibilities for scholarship and engaged practice. *Poroi*, *9*(1), Article 17.

Segal, J. Z. (2005). *Health and the rhetoric of medicine.* Carbondale IL: Southern Illinois University Press.

Segal, J. Z. (2009). Rhetoric of health & medicine. In A. Lunsford, R. Eberly, & K. H. Wilson (Eds.), *The Sage handbook of rhetorical studies* (pp. 227–246). Los Angeles, CA: Sage.

Sullivan, P., & Porter, J. E. (1997). *Opening spaces: Writing technologies and critical research practices.* Westport, CT: Ablex Publishing.

Teston, C. (2012). Considering confidentiality in research design: Developing heuristics to chart the un-chartable. In K. M. Powell & P. Takayoshi (Eds.), *Practicing research in writing studies: Reflexive and ethically responsible research* (pp. 307–330). Cresskill, NJ: Hampton Press.

Teston, C. B. (2009). A grounded investigation of genred guidelines in cancer care deliberations. *Written Communication*, *26*(3), 320–348. doi:10.1177/0741088309336937.

Teston, C. (2016, April). Rhetorical ontographies of evidentiary shadow work. Paper presented at Conference on College Composition and Communication, Houston, TX.

Treichler, P. A. (1999). *How to have theory in an epidemic: Cultural chronicles of AIDS.* Durham, NC: Duke University Press.

Walton, R., Zraly, M., & Mugengana, J. P. (2015). Values and validity: Navigating messiness in a community-based research project in Rwanda. *Technical Communication Quarterly*, *24*(1), 45–69.

Wells, S. (2001). *Out of the dead house: Nineteenth century women physicians and the writings of medicine*. Madison, WI: University of Wisconsin Press.

Wells, S. (2010). *Our bodies, ourselves, and the work of writing*. Palo Alto, CA: Stanford University Press.

Zoller, H. M., & Meloncon, L. (2013). The good neighbor campaign: A communication intervention to reduce environmental health disparities. In M. J. Dutta & G. L. Kreps (Eds.), *Reducing health disparities: Communication interventions* (pp. 436–456). New York: Peter Lang.

2

HISTORICAL WORK IN THE DISCOURSES OF HEALTH AND MEDICINE

Susan Wells and Nathan Stormer

Keywords: historiography, archival methods, time, place, rhetorical histories

For students of rhetoric and communication, Kenneth Burke's (1974) image of the parlor is a powerful metaphor:

> Imagine that you enter a parlor. You come late. When you arrive, others have long preceded you, and they are engaged in a heated discussion, a discussion too heated for them to pause and tell you exactly what it is about. In fact, the discussion had already begun long before any of them got there, so that no one present is qualified to retrace for you all the steps that had gone before. You listen for a while, until you decide that you have caught the tenor of the argument; then you put in your oar.
>
> *(pp. 110–111)*

This image is especially powerful for scholars of health and medicine; we have entered a parlor (or a lounge, or a conference room) where health care providers, patients, and members of the public have already settled in. Their conversation about bodies and their vicissitudes is not easy to follow; we fail more than once to put in an oar. But we want to speak and listen in this uncomfortable setting: These are, after all, our bodies that are in question.

In a corner of this room, a quiet side conversation has been going on for a while, a conversation about the history of health and medicine. What rhetorics organized the perceptions of the body in ancient Greece, in 19th century America? From time to time, a Foucault or a Latour drops in to take up these questions, and a small crowd will drift over to the historians' corner; sometimes the historical conversation catches the interest of the big group in the center;

individual historians enter or leave the contemporary conversation. The talk among historians and their sources, all of whom—even the dead ones—have a lot to say to each other, continues, but in our field it continues in more hushed tones, even as the practices of historiography diffuse and are taken up into other forms of research.

This chapter is an attempt to rearrange that space by considering the state of histories and historiography within the study of the discourses of health and medicine. For our purposes, "history" refers to research that investigates the past and "historiography" refers to methods of situating objects in time and space. In what follows, we trace the relative decline of research on previous eras in our field and consider the reasons for it. We discuss the past in terms of what our field might learn from studying medicine before and during its professionalization in the mid-19th century. The abandonment of historical work, we argue, could cut our field off from critical conceptual resources and methodologies. Finally, we describe how some obstacles to historical work are being removed and suggest some ways of incorporating historical work into the ongoing conversations of the rhetoric of health & medicine.

Regarding historiography, we consider its value in framing discourses of health and medicine, which includes what is typically understood as history as well as the employment of historiographic methods to situate the present as a historical moment. We demonstrate not only that rhetorical histories are important works for research on the discourses of health and medicine, but also that the connection between histories and historiography should not be overlooked. It is unwise to borrow historiographic practices without deepening our understanding of the past.

What Has Happened to Historical Work?

The earliest work in science studies focused on the emergence of new sciences in the early modern period, and a lively scholarship in medieval and early modern science continues in the history and philosophy of science. Twentieth-century scholars in science studies, such as Evelyn Fox Keller or Stephen Shapin, were interested in the development of sciences as intellectual practices and social formations in the early modern period, and research projects on those topics continue to be productive in the history and philosophy of science. Within writing and rhetoric studies, archival research into the history of writing practices is an important research method. But research in the rhetorics of health and medicine focuses almost exclusively on relatively recent issues.

To be sure, compelling historical monographs continue to be written. Since 2010, several groundbreaking works have been published: Jennell Johnson's (2014) *American Lobotomy: A Rhetorical History*; Marika Seigel's (2014) *The Rhetoric of Pregnancy*; Nathan Stormer's (2015) *Sign of Pathology: U.S. Medical Rhetoric on Abortion, 1880s-1960s*; and Susan Wells' (2010) *Our Bodies, Ourselves and the Work of Writing*.

Additionally, a number of important studies of contemporary practices and issues, such as T. Kenny Fountain's (2014) *Rhetoric in the Flesh: Trained Vision, Technical Expertise, and the Gross Anatomy Lab*, use historical methods. But when we look at research articles in refereed journals, and consider the relative place of historical research in the field, a different, and more sober, picture emerges.

We can get a handle on this trend by examining a series of special issues related to the rhetoric of health & medicine published between 2000 and 2015. The two earliest special issues—in *Technical Communication Quarterly* (Heifferon & Brown, 2000) and in *Journal of Medical Humanities* (Lyne, 2001)—included articles that explicitly used historical materials. The former special issue featured one historical article, Francoise Salager-Meyer's (2000) analysis of citation practices in French medical journals; the latter special issue included both David Depew's (2001) analysis of the Darwinian tradition and Lisa Keränen's (2001) account of the Hippocratic Oath. In five more recent journal special issues (Barton, 2005; Haas, 2009b; Keränen, 2014; Meloncon & Frost, 2015; Landau, 2015), only one traditionally historical article appears, in *Written Communication* (Haas, 2009b); significantly, this issue's call for papers included a request for "histories of writing within medical contexts" (Haas, 2009a). On the other hand, articles in two of these special issues, those edited by Landau (2015) and by Meloncon and Frost (2015), investigate, deploy, and develop historiographic methods. While focused on contemporary issues—digital drug ads and abstinence education—both essays use historiographic methods, framing objects temporally, and interrogating the ways in which we understand historical change (Mogull & Balzhiser, 2015; Jensen, 2015). While we welcome this interest in historiography as a multidimensional engagement with the practices of the past, we are concerned by the eclipse of historical work, since historical methods offer perspectives that cannot be replaced.

In their introductory essays, editors of these special issues summarized the state of the field and proposed topics for future research. Only Heifferon and Brown (2000) included historical work, and no editor proposed history as an area for future research. This trend extends to health communication research as well. When researchers J. Kim, S. Park, S. Yoo, and H. Shen (2010) made a meticulous inventory of 642 articles published in *Health Communication* over 22 years (1989–2010), coding them by topic, research method, and theoretical frame, historical work appeared nowhere in their account—it was not a topic for research, nor a method of developing knowledge, nor a theoretical frame. The authors of the census made thoughtful recommendations for future research directions, but they did not recommend attention to history. The place of history in the discourses of health and medicine is not, of course, determined by the age of the object being studied, and historical work has appeared outside of these representative venues. But given that historical periods are a convenient marker of the steady diminution of historical work in the field, and that special issues have a programmatic function, especially in an emerging field, we can confidently identify a scholarly emphasis that has shifted to the present. What could account for this change?

What Happened to History?

To be sure, this decline in historical research is not limited to our field. As a whole, liberal arts majors have held steady as a share of all university graduates, but fields that are structured historically—history, of course, but also English literature—have declined, while fields oriented to contemporary production and collaboration—creative writing, anthropology—have prospered (National Center for Educational Statistics, 2014, Table 319.30). However, historical work in health and medicine has faced additional challenges. It was certainly not the intention of the writers of the Health Insurance Portability and Accountability Act (1996) to push researchers out of the archives. But that legislation established the privacy rights of dead people for the first time, and specified no time limits to those rights. Under the original HIPAA regulations, archival medical records could only be made available to researchers after the redaction of some eighteen elements, including the name of any place smaller than a state (Novack, 2003). Not surprisingly, smaller institutions, facing their own exigencies, have often simply barred researchers rather than undertaken the expensive and uncertain work of dis-identification. Even larger institutions engaged in facilitating historical research have restricted access; for example, at the Bernard Becker Library of the Washington University Medical School, a researcher who wanted to use the clinical records of, say, Edmund Alvis, an ophthalmologist who practiced from 1934–1978, could not copy any records, or refer to any individual case, even anonymously. These restrictions have made the close study of language in historical documents very difficult, and there has been little incentive to change them. An institution could be sued or fined for compromising patient privacy, and there is no corresponding payoff for permitting scholarly access.

Even when some institutions have allowed access, they have been reluctant to permit researchers to copy or photograph the texts produced by caregivers or to allow quotations from them in scholarly work. Students who in the early 1990s had been able to use archival materials at sites close to their home institutions now faced a brick wall: Why should a cash-strapped hospital open its 19th century medical records to a pleading dissertator? There are some reports that even previously published texts were declared "private medical information," barring further use of that knowledge. For nearly 15 years, scholars in medical rhetoric have faced barriers that have been most crippling to scholars at the beginning of their research careers. It is no wonder that historical research in medical rhetoric has not kept pace with the growth of the field. One of the authors, Wells, experienced this shift dramatically. At the 2007 Workshop on Medical Rhetoric at the Rhetoric Society of America's Summer Institute, nearly half of the projects presented by participants included a significant historical or archival element. Two years later, at the 2009 workshop, enforcement of the HIPAA rules had become more rigorous, and historical projects were thin on the ground. Graduate students whose dissertations depended on research in local archives were considering changes of topic or method.

New obstacles to work in medical archives, of course, were not the only reasons why fewer researchers did historical work. Researchers in the rhetoric of health & medicine are deeply interested in affecting current practices and changing medical discourses. And some historical documents can be dauntingly resistant to study: they may require a fine-grained historical context or language skills that are hard to reconcile with such demanding academic expectations of continuous publication, grant-supported research, or direct engagement with medical education.

The Persistence and Value of Historiography

All is not lost, however. Interdisciplinary scholarship on the rhetoric of health & medicine includes many perspectives on the historical intersections of healing and discourse. It would be foolish to divvy up this nascent body of work into categories, and also contrary to the spirit of creativity and experimentation evident in the literature. However, several lenses for engaging the discourses associated with health and illness can draw the attention of scholars not only to the kinds of historiographic work being written, but more importantly to the need for more histories. These viewpoints include the materialist, the axiological, the practical, the analogical, and the cultural. Together they highlight an underappreciated bond between the investigation of the past and the effective placement of the present. If historiography is unavoidable and vital to research on the rhetoric of health & medicine generally, then it is all the more important to recognize the interdependence of research on historical periods with the "contemporary history" that predominates scholarship. In other words, the connection between past and contemporary history can be understood through multiple lenses, which adds weight to our call for more attention to seemingly remote times. The present is not a break from the past; it is a dialogue with it.

From a *materialist* point of view, it is impossible to understand medicine *without* historicizing it as a practice. Caring for the sick could be summed up as a complex set of material histories: diagnosis and treatment require a history of things (biota, practices, foods, chemicals, lived spaces—everything, in fact, that touches the body). Embedded in these material histories are a wealth of communicative practices and their attending arrays of rhetorics. In this volume, Nathan Johnson's history of the protein paradigm as a naturalized element of the medical information infrastructure is a case in point. Such work contributes to the material history of medicine, but it can also be read as the analysis of corporeal historicizing, that is, of making patient histories, disease histories, evolutionary histories, technological histories, organic histories, and so on. In a Foucaultian sense, the continuous emergence of new forms of materialistic memory-work within medicine suggests the need for genealogies that trace *how* the healing arts and sciences generate new ways of putting human bodies and societies into history.

For example, rhetorical work on 16th- and 17th-century medical humanism uncovers a distinctive relation between medical discourses, lay discourses, and other cultural practices in producing corporeal histories. Early modern physicians integrated the texts of antiquity into their writing, and lay readers developed new interpretive practices to make sense of the printed medical literature made available to them. The sick body entered early modern history as a literary problem. Illnesses and their remedies existed in the memory made available through language and the visual rhetorics of anatomy and their corresponding, entwined hermeneutics. The practice of addressing physical ailments came to involve reading medical language and the body together as one text, with gradually more refined documentation of physician-patient interactions that fed back into the interpretive practice. Diagnosing and treating the sick became a way of writing history, not just of bodies, but of people and their worlds. The moment in early modern culture when scientific information was both distributed widely in print and available to educated readers in Latin also offers an analogue to the significance of English as a transnational language and of European, scientific medicine as a transcultural vernacular for the body. It might show us that these events are, well, precedented, and prompt questions about how we place ourselves in history today through contemporary medical discourse.

Similarly, in the 18th century, the expansion of imagery in biology and medicine made corporeality newly visual. The visuality offered by words was increasingly connected to images of the heretofore unseen. Enlightenment art and medicine, nourished by new technologies and by each other, were driven "by a compulsion to find an immaterial or supernatural clarity within material or ambiguous phenomena," writes Barbara Maria Stafford (1993, p. 1). Making the invisible visible through such practices as dissection, abstraction, marking, drawing, magnifying, and staining became a critical part of knowing the body though a kind of "palpable demonstration" (p. 17). The body turned inside out and atomized became a central feature of medical empiricism, which also provided a way to place ourselves in the world through visual histories of the body. Medicine could newly document with images the consequences of time and lived conditions on bodies, either as developmental histories of specific patients or as epidemiological histories of populations. Further, certain bodies—especially dark, female, and foreign ones—became observable markers of hidden, medicalized threats to order, health, and morality. The history of a society's infirmity could now be brought before our eyes through the condition and presence of dangerous corporealities. This raised questions about how we tell histories of risk through a visual catalog of contagious, leaky, broken bodies.

From an *axiological* point of view, the evaluative nature of medicine cries out for historical, discursive analysis. George Canghuilhem's (1989) masterwork, *The Normal and the Pathological*, makes the case that definitions of the normal (and so visions of health) are historical responses to changes in physical and mental capacity, to "life gone wrong" (p. 99). Disease is an education of the normal, which means that medicine is a history of pedagogies, of using patients and their diseases as sources of knowledge. If learning (from the world, from each other, from ourselves) is not a fundamental mode of communication, then nothing is. The adaptive and mobile nature of medicine-as-pedagogy calls for a historical investigation of how we've learned so that we might learn better in order to live better. Nothing is more normal to "normalizing" than that.

The work of Bernice Hausman and her associates (2014) is a case in point. Her research on vaccination shows that even the initial smallpox inoculation was met with suspicion. In the hands of her Vaccination Research Group, opposition to vaccination is no longer seen simply as a refusal to believe scientific evidence; it becomes a textured series of responses, argued with varying degrees of scientific responsibility, to a set of specific medical problems. Refusal to vaccinate has not been assuaged by either ridicule or shame, but Hausman's project suggests that engagement with opponents of vaccination, based on an understanding of historical responses to vaccination mandates, might be more fruitful. As a history of how we contest what is normal, vaccination practices can be understood not as a question of medical knowledge versus ignorance, but rather of how efforts to address the relative loss of life and well-being within a community prompted reconsideration of what is pathological and what is healthy. If medical knowledge can only define "health" in relation to pathology, then histories of how pathologies are made knowable can help us understand conflicts over treatments and even over what constitutes being well. Studies of medicine as it was learned and practiced before the advent of professionalization give us perspective on medicine as a pedagogy of the normal that we could not obtain in another way. Because the conversion of abnormalities to visions of normalcy is a rhetorical problem that cannot be adjudicated by the latest medical knowledge, investigation of moments when new regimes of normalcy came into being can shed light on contemporary clashes over health and illness (and perhaps over health citizenship), as useful for their differences as for their similarities.

In a different way, histories of pathologies that go untreated or undertreated such as breast cancer or HIV tell us about the rhetoric of medicine and its function within broader society. The central thesis of Susan Sontag's *Illness as Metaphor* (1989) is that historically, being ill has stood as a commentary on people and their cultures. Kelly Happe's (2013) work on hereditarianism after the Human Genome Project broadly aligns with Sontag and is an excellent example of historiography embedded within a critique of contemporary discourse. Happe demonstrates how research on BRCA breast cancer genes reactivates gendered, racialized ideologies within genetics while drawing on the ideology of personal responsibility to explain risk factors. Pathology produces more than negative images of illness, but also comparative images of health as not living the sick life or in the sick body. Pathology is a critical tool for establishing what it means to lead a good life, to have a good body.

From a completely *practical* point of view, the charge of healing, the obligation to always improve our abilities to heal, mandates an ever-changing matrix
of communicative forms. Historical research on adaptation is as likely to reach
into the future as to study the past. And what's possible medically is conditioned,
situated in a convergent institutional, technological, cultural, and professional
moment. Rhetorical histories of medical communication are histories of medical performance as it has attempted to chart and master the pathological currents of those moments. Such histories expose not only the technical rhetorical
aspects of producing medical knowledge, but also the constitutive praxis by which
medical rhetoric reproduces the apparatus of knowledge-making. These studies
can advance the development of rhetorical theory: For example, Dan Ehrenfeld's
chapter in this volume demonstrates that an analysis of Emma Elizabeth Walker's
"social hygiene" lectures calls into question the conventional understanding of
rhetorical agency as located in individuals, and highlights the need for developed
theoretical study of rhetorical networks and ecologies.

In contemporary history, the production and orientation of communication
around diagnosis is a complex enterprise, a network of interconnected perceptual technologies, instructional practices, interpretive practices, and referencing
practices. Two different ethnographic projects are good examples of how critical
analysis is served by historiography. In *The Politics of Pain Medicine*, Scott Graham
(2015) couples historiography with ethnography to study how rhetoric helps
produce and calibrate different realities of pain within medicine. He traces six pain
ontologies dating from classical Greece, noting that two have become antiquated,
and then analyzes how new ontologies are being constituted in contemporary
clinical practices. Barry Saunders (2008) similarly provides a window on the
complexity of discourse and practice with his ethnography *CT Suite*, which he
describes as a "case study concerning case study," delineating the diagnostic work
of sectional images from a CT scanner. He calls the use of the scanner to hunt
for lesions "noninvasive cutting" in reference to the older art of autopsy (p. 305),
and situates the production of diagnostic evidence and medical expertise within
a web of institutional spaces, relationships, technologies, and acts. The modes of
communication between residents, attending physicians, and CT viewboxes, for
instance, are layered, interactive, and dense. Complicated nodal points like the
gross anatomy lab or the CT suite constitute bodies, experts, clinics, and professions, in part due to the variety of rhetorics immanent to the work of pathology
and diagnosis such as reading, declaring, dictating, interrogating, testifying, and
teaching. All of these practices are historically emergent; they extend and modify
prior forms of medical analysis, some with very long roots.

But the elements of early cultures that are not consonant with contemporary
problems can be even more valuable, demonstrating novel ways of making and
disseminating knowledge, of devising persuasive strategies. We can sharpen our
vision of how medicine constructed knowledges by looking at those that are now
unutterably strange to us. The Galenic "decretal day," a critical point in the course

of an illness that prognosticated its course on a specific subsequent day, suggests a distinct understanding of how disease develops through time, and even of what time is and how it is punctuated by events. What relation between the body and the environment led to Galen's counsel to drink water that had caught the rays of the rising sun? The past is not an alien, unknowable territory, but elements of earlier cultures that have no visible intersection with contemporary problems demonstrate distinctive ways of communicating medical knowledge. Our very estrangement from such strategies makes their persuasive force clear to us, and alerts us to the ways in which knowledges that have become naturalized for us are constructed and disseminated.

Old ways can also provide an inverted view on discourses about health and medicine relative to contemporary times. In *Contracting a Cure*, Gianna Pomata (1998) investigates the legal procedure against a healer who failed to cure an ailment in early modern Bologna. Such procedures existed in Europe from the 13th to the 18th century: patients were promised a cure; payment was connected to success; the contract was legally binding. A patient's subjective sense of not having been cured was the critical evidence of a failed promise by physicians. Pomata's account portrays a physician-patient relationship that reverses the asymmetry of current practices. Before disease had become its own entity and physicians had achieved higher status as interpreters of the body, the statements of patients had far more agency within medical discourses. Historical work can demonstrate that patient voices were prominent and powerful in defining medicine, health, and illness, throwing into sharp relief how heavily confined and framed patient discourse is today.

From an *analogical* point of view, rhetoric and medicine are metaphors of each other, and, in turn, become metaphors for the political. Medical analogies pop up throughout the history of rhetorical theory, particularly when it broaches politics (Plato, Aristotle, Burke are just the headliners, let alone Gorgias who wrote of the druglike effects of persuasion). Rhetoric, medicine, and politics are all practices that analyze a live event in order to change its course, producing some kind of constitutional change. The strange resonance between these forms of thinking—consider the valences of *constitution*—lends itself to many interesting moments within the practice of medicine. Aren't prescriptions wonderfully confused instances in which symbols become the prostheses to treatment and vice versa? And isn't prescribing a remedy a basic way of understanding the politics of acting for the good? If medicine is resolutely historical in its way of being, as politics is, then so is rhetoric. That we study the history of medical rhetoric might be thought of as unavoidable, then, because that is fundamentally what rhetorics and medicines do: They unfold histories across a landscape of ethically and politically embodied interventions.

Part of the analogical similarity of medicine and rhetoric may stem from a shared political concern with the fragility of things and people, in their openness, vulnerability, and mortality. Amy Schmitter (2012) argues that both Descartes and

Spinoza stake fundamental claims on the somatic fragility of humans, which calls for a remedy that allows the full development of human potential while mitigating the risks that come from irrevocable openness to each other and the larger world. For Descartes, such a remedy includes the improvement of medicine as part of "the manipulation of matter, and particularly our own bodies, in ways that promote the good" (p. 154). For Spinoza, the remedy is "to expand one's boundaries, both to incorporate more in the 'interior' of the individual and to better resist what is outside" (p. 158), seeking greater interconnection with nature. Here we can see the complicated tangle of rhetoric, medicine, and politics all stemming from the shared ontological problem of being vulnerable to forces in the world. What Schmitter does not address is that rhetoricity is also an art of managing vulnerabilities: learning to work with changeable materials and people in order to produce changes, always with the danger that rhetoric may produce ill outcomes. Plato's metaphor of the *pharmakon* is most apt here, as is the specter of persuasion in Gorgias's "Encomium on Helen." Schematized between Descartes and Spinoza, medicine is a response to a political problem, politics is a response to a medical problem, and rhetoric is a response to the medico-political problem of responsiveness.

Scholarship on Heideggerian rhetoric provides an alternate lens for investigating the analogies among medicine, rhetoric, and politics. In his 1924 *Lectures on Aristotle's Rhetoric* (2009), Heidegger maintained that rhetoric studied the emerging practices of ancient Greek political life as they developed, day to day, in the spaces of Athenian democracy. For Heidegger, logic, dialectic, and politics were all derived from rhetoric; his rewriting of the ancient quarrel between philosophy and rhetoric was not an act of charity toward our field, but an attempt to reclaim for philosophy issues of ordinary embodied life with all their baggage of impurity and relevance. His historical reconstruction opened new possibilities for philosophy (many of which, sadly, he betrayed) and new ways of understanding rhetoric that we have barely begun to explore.

Rhetoric offered fruitful analogies to the new sciences of the 16th and 17th centuries, including medicine. Questions about proof and evidence, probability and observation could not be resolved by physicians within the traditional Aristotelian framework, but they could be addressed with the tools of rhetoric. There, collectors of observations and designers of experiments found modes of explanation unmoored from the rigidity of the final cause, mobilizing all the resources of *ethos*, *logos*, and *pathos*. They faced rhetorical problems: moving from general rules to particular instances; acting without sufficient information; effecting a change in the state of a client or audience. It was rhetoric that offered ways of thinking these matters through.

One can appreciate the ancient, tangled metaphoric likenesses of rhetoric, medicine, and politics in the accelerating evolution of medical knowledge. Once medical information has been disproved, it becomes largely useless: for the practice of medicine, this type of history really is bunk. But archaic practices of representing the body, long discarded from professional *doxa*, remain active in the professional lexis, and have colonized political discourses, shaping contemporary understandings of both bodily and political health. Just as 19th-century physicians, disabused of humors theory, still spoke of a "sanguine diathesis," images of purity and contamination can still operate simultaneously with framings of disease as inflammation or infection. Controversies over access to care or end of life issues would be better understood through reconstruction of the practices and representations that haunt contemporary medical knowledge and practice. Such representations move fluidly between everyday talk and professional discourse; they can be deeply consequential. Framing AIDS as a plague, mobilizing tropes of divine judgment on deviant populations, surely has cost lives. Rhetoric helps us understand that medicine *is* representational and that both medicine and rhetoric are politically charged and strategic: As Nancy Struever (2005, p. 555) put it, "The strength of rhetoric . . . is that it serves as a treasure-house of the relegated, the great depository of the occasions and strategies of chance, contingency rejected by philosophy as not amenable to method." We might substitute science for philosophy, and concur with Struever's conclusion that "Failure is, indeed, a rhetorical specialty" (p. 555). Rhetoric, medicine, and politics each make sense of the other when their analogical conjunctures are understood historically as part of their ontological kinship.

And similarly, from a *cultural* point of view, medicine is inseparable from society. As Ludwig Fleck (1981) argued, the life of a people is intimately raveled up with the life of their bodies, so that if one wants to understand a society, one needs to understand how it communicates about the disease and health of those bodies. Enemies are diseased, utopias are pure, and how we care for ourselves will always involve medical knowing and doing. The history of medical discourses is a part of the history of a culture, in particular of the terms by which a culture considers itself getting better or worse. Understanding that is of great value.

We can also learn of culture through histories of individual practitioners and patients. Susan Mattern, in *Galen & the Rhetoric of Healing* (2008), offers a careful examination of Galen's rhetoric about medicine, patients, and disease, opening a window on social institutions and cultural practices as they are refracted through the physician's writings. Patient reports are equally revealing, as Barbara Duden shows with her study of the extensive case histories of women patients left by Johann Storch, an 18th-century German physician. She carefully reconstructs a history of the body grounded in the recorded complaints of women, sorting out what can be determined about medical practice in Storch's world and interpreting that culture's perception of the body. The woman's body that emerges from this archive is very different from the transparent, genetic-chemical machine with which we are familiar today, supporting a different place for women in the life of the culture. And we can learn from the patient's testimony, both at some distance from today as Pomata exemplifies, or through contemporary autobiographical work such as S. Lochlann Jain's (2013) *Malignant: How Cancer Becomes Us*. Jain's anthropology of cancer is extraordinary for using memoir to demonstrate how cancer has become a complex bio-social phenomenon, completely integrated into and integrative of culture economically, politically, aesthetically, legally, corporeally, and discursively. The historical continuities and discontinuities between testimony from physicians like Galen, and patients like those discussed by Jain or Storch deserve scrutiny because they embody the intersection of medical rhetoric and culture.

Using approaches that most rhetoricians probably feel more at home with, we can also learn of culture from the forms of language used in medicine. Jennell Johnson (2014) explores the medical and popular history of discourses on lobotomy, for example, showing in particular how lobotomy exists in professional and public writings, journalism, speeches, images, and films. She argues that concepts such gender, psychiatric health, surgery, chemical treatments, and monstrosity both shape and are shaped by the rhetorical history of lobotomy in the United States. The intersection of medical knowledge and public health is inscribed in the language that mediates the movement of knowledge from expert to public audiences, as Robin Jensen (2010) demonstrates with her history of sex education rhetoric in the United States. She traces the gender dynamics and strategic deployment of ambiguity in the language of sex education from the late 19th into the early 20th century, which provides important insights about changing cultures of sexuality and how activists in the public sphere had to negotiate the incorporation of medical discourse in popular political discourse.

To summarize, histories of medical discourse 1) are already part of medicine's material historiographic habit; 2) help us understand how medicine "educates" the way we live; 3) highlight how medicine shifts what it means to heal; 4) mirror medicine itself, diagnosing and developing therapies for troubled social bodies; and 5) help us to broadly understand society, especially the heavily medicalized societies typical of Westernized nations. These points of view are not discrete: all of them are available to any study, depending on its scope and aim. Rhetorical historiography of medicine is, therefore, part and parcel of learning about illness, healing, the body, power, culture, and technology, not to mention the limits of rhetoric, whether that history comes in a more traditional form or it is folded into ethnography, autobiography, or technical analyses. Realizing the persistence and value of rhetorical historiography as a general methodology is an important step for appreciating the need for more research on discourses of health and medicine that inform the present. If one is to situate contemporary medical practices in time and place, then greater inspection of the past is not only rewarding but also necessary. What we need is a great, creative diversity of histories.

Aids for Doing History

In constructing these histories, we can draw on an emerging body of scholarship investigating the role of rhetoric for early modern medicine. This work, originating in the history of ideas and the history of medicine, is a rich resource for our field. We are thinking, first, of the writing of Nancy Struever, whose 40 years of dauntingly good research on the relation between medicine and rhetoric began with her 1976 essay on Vico and led to the electrifying 2012 collection, coedited with Stephen Pender, *Rhetoric and Medicine in Early Modern Europe*. It is a sign of the interdisciplinary nature of the rhetoric of health & medicine that investigations by rhetoricians like Struever and Pender intersect directly with developments within medical history. Nancy Siraisi, widely considered the senior scholar in early modern medical history, has written widely on such topics as the performance of medical orations, the development of correspondence networks among early modern physicians, and the relationship between medicine and rhetoric in early modern learning. Taken together, these bodies of scholarship offer a picture of rhetoric as a practice that integrated science and other forms of culture, a picture we cannot afford to lose sight of.

Equally important to historical work is the loosening of limits on our access to archives, for which we have to thank medical archivists organized as Archivists and Librarians in the History of the Health Sciences (ALHHS). The HIPAA rules requiring onerous redactions of archival documents have been revised by the Office of Civil Rights of the U.S. Department of Health and Human Services. Under the recent 2013 regulations, known (somewhat portentously) as the Final Rule (DHHS, 2013) health information about individuals who have been dead for at least 50 years is no longer legally protected, and archivists have developed rules for providing reasonable access to records of those whose date of death cannot be determined. The ALHHS has developed a set of best practices, including the organization of institutional Privacy Boards that can resolve questions of access and apply the rules to particular cases (Letocha, 2013). Together with the Society of American Archivists, they maintain a helpful HIPAA Information website, including examples of access policies (ALHHS, 2014). Archives such as the Johns Hopkins Medical Archive and the Historical Section of the National Library of Medicine have implemented these policies, allowing full access to records of individuals who can be presumed dead for 50 years—usually records 150 years old or older—and making modest provisions for prepublication review of potentially sensitive materials. These procedures are codified in the Best Practices document compiled by Letocha and Gustainis (2015) and can serve as models for smaller archives.

Such welcome developments are making research on medicine and health in early periods more possible again in this country. Under these best practices, everything up to the Civil War should now be available, and work with early 20th century records of specific patients whose dates of death can be determined should also be supported. Of course, it will always be easier to close archives than to open them, and the Final Rule allows institutions to impose additional limits to access; senior scholars in this field have an obligation to familiarize local archives with the new rules and work with them to develop sustainable procedures.

What Balance of History Do We Need?

If historiography has become a general methodology necessary in many forms of scholarship, but more recognizable kinds of histories have been less frequently developed, then what balance of historical work do we need? We would personally be glad to read any number of them, but we don't expect a spate of essays analyzing the tropes in Harvey's *De motu cordis*. Instead, we hope for a range of engagements with historical materials, from deep research in earlier periods to historical references offered *en passant* in analyses of contemporary issues, placing them in a trans-historical frame. This spectrum would help us develop a sense of history as a part of our disciplinary armamentarium; like the analysis of trope or genre, it is a resource that can be scaled up or down, torqued or modified to deal with new questions.

What would these uses of history look like? The typical image, now, is a book length project, usually on a moment at some distance from the present. This image is too exclusive to capture the landscape of practice. Historiography in other research projects is often passed off as "context" or "background" or simply descriptive information about culture, technology, professions, or institutions. Studies that do not profess themselves as histories still need to incorporate rhetorical historiography because, as we have argued, rhetoric and medicine share an important, frankly unavoidable, historical connection for many reasons. The historical work embedded in other studies—let's call it microhistory—operates as a kind of unacknowledged mixing of methods.

Further, questions of rhetoric, historical or analytic, pop up in any manner of study, from history and public policy to anthropology or sociology. A study principally about a subculture of medicine, for example, may be concerned with how public identities are produced by medical knowledge practices, or how ways of seeing impact not just the health but the relative freedom of different groups (pregnant women are a significant example). Research on rhetoric passes under many different names.

Finally, the scope of the present is too flexible to tolerate a permanent sense of rupture from the past. One could legitimately argue that we are still in the same moment that initially gave us scientific medicine because of the optical rhetorics that drive knowledge production. Or one could just as easily mark a break with postgenomic medicine due to the kind of lab science that is currently underway. Or that any work in digital communication of health and medicine demands skills that adapt archival methods to the collection and analysis of these texts, with their deep temporal location. The upshot of setting aside any predisposition to when history becomes history is that research on contemporary rhetorics of health and medicine can be placed into productive historical conversation with those that look at barber-surgeons a half a millennium ago.

In a recent proposal, Blake Scott, Judy Segal, and Lisa Keränen (2013) suggest that our field should adopt the name "rhetorics of health and medicine" and consider "modeling our collaboration after the viruses that some of us study, seeking openings to infect, mutate, and transform larger projects" (p. 2). We would suggest that rhetoric's relation to historiography defines our contribution to the understanding of medicine and health uniquely: We are the only field that studies the language, imagery, and practices that constitute health and medicine as complex, historical discourses.

Putting all of these elements together—micro- to macrohistories, rhetoric by other names, and an indefinite threshold of "the historical"—one can see that historiography is an indispensable element of research in the rhetoric of health & medicine. What historians of rhetoric offer is a focalizing of interest, an intensification of inquiry into shared questions which is of benefit to all, given that historicizing medical discourse is a common problem distributed unevenly across a wide range of specialties and research programs. Yet, that common problem maintains a complicated relation with the past, which makes it all the more important that scholars who study discourses of health and medicine realize both their dependence on historiography and the significance of a full investment in history. If scholars unduly limit themselves to work on issues in the 20th and 21st centuries, the loss would be profound because rhetoric and medicine are ancient, inseparable practices whose present relationship is understandable only in light of that long entanglement. It is not hard to imagine inviting our ancient friends back into Burke's parlor, and it is vitally important that we do just that.

References

Archivists and Librarians in the History of Health Sciences. (2014). *HIPAA resource page.* www.alhhs.org/

Barton, E. (Ed.). (2005). The discourses of medicine [Special issue]. *Journal of Business and Technical Communication, 19*(3).

Burke, K. (1974). *The philosophy of literary form.* Berkeley, CA: University of California Press.

Canghuilhem, C. (1989). *The normal and the pathological.* Brooklyn, NY: Zone Books.

Department of Health and Human Services. (2013). 45 CFR parts 160 and 164: Modifications to the HIPAA privacy, security, enforcement, and breach notification rules . . . final rule. *Federal Register, 78*(17), 5565–5702.

Depew, D. (2001). Genetic biotechnology and evolutionary theory: Some unsolicited advice to rhetors. *Journal of Medical Humanities, 22*(1), 15–28.

Fleck, L. (1981). *Genesis and development of a scientific fact* (T. J. Trenn & R. K. Merton, Eds., F. Bradley & T. J. Trenn, Trans.). Chicago, IL: University of Chicago Press.

Fountain, T. K. (2014). *Rhetoric in the flesh: Trained vision, technical expertise, and the gross anatomy lab.* New York, NY: Routledge.

Graham, S. S. (2015). *The politics of pain medicine: A rhetorical-ontological inquiry.* Chicago, IL: University of Chicago Press.

Haas, C. (Ed.). (2009a). Special issue call for papers: Writing and medicine. *Written Communication, 26*(2), 210–211.

Haas, C. (Ed.). (2009b). Writing and medicine [Special issue]. *Written Communication, 26*(3).

Happe, K. (2013). *The material gene: Gender, race, and heredity after the Human Genome Project.* New York, NY: New York University Press.

Hausman, B. L., Ghebremichael, M., Hayek, P., & Mack, E. (2014). "Poisonous, filthy, loathsome, damnable stuff": The rhetorical ecology of vaccination concern. *The Yale Journal of Biology and Medicine, 87*(4), 403–416.

Heidegger, M. (2009). *Basic concepts of Aristotelian philosophy* (R. D. Metcalf & M. B. Tanzer, Trans.). Bloomington, IN: Indiana University Press.

Heifferon, B., & Brown, S. (Eds.). (2000). Medical rhetoric [Special issue]. *Technical Communication Quarterly, 9*(3).

Jain, S. L. (2013). *Malignant: How cancer becomes us.* Berkeley, CA: University of California Press.

Jensen, R. (2010). *Dirty words: The rhetoric of public sex education, 1870–1924.* Urbana Champaign, IL: University of Illinois Press.

Jensen, R. (2015). An ecological turn in rhetoric of health scholarship: Attending to the historical flow and percolation of ideas, assumptions, and arguments. *Communication Quarterly, 63*(5), 522–526.

Johnson, J. (2014). *American lobotomy: A rhetorical history.* Ann Arbor, MI: University of Michigan Press.

Keränen, L. (2001). The Hippocratic oath as epideictic rhetoric: Reanimating medicine's past for its future. *Journal of Medical Humanities, 22*(1), 55–68.

Keränen, L. (Ed.). (2014). Public engagements with health and medicine. *Journal of Medical Humanities, 35*(2), 103–109.

Kim, J., Park, S., Yoo, S., & Shen, H. (2010). Mapping health communication scholarship: Breadth, depth, and agenda of published research in health communication. *Health Communication, 25*, 487–503.

Landau, J. (2015). Special section forum on rhetoric and health communication. *Communication Quarterly, 63*(5), 495–532.

Letocha, P. (2013). Recent changes to the HIPAA privacy rule. *The Watermark, 36*(2), 10–19.

Letocha, P., & Gusainis, E. (2015). Recommended practices for enabling access to manuscript and archival collections containing health information about individuals. *Medical Heritage Library.* www.medicalheritage.org/2015/02/now-available-recommended-practices-for-enabling-access-to-manuscript-and-archival-collections-containing-health-information-about-individuals/

Lyne, J. (2001). Rhetoric and biomedicine [Special issue]. *Journal of Medical Humanities, 22*(1).

Mattern, S. (2008). *Galen & the rhetoric of healing.* Baltimore, MD: Johns Hopkins University Press.

Meloncon, L., & Frost, E. A. (Eds.). (2015). The rhetorics of health and medicine [Special issue]. *Communication Design Quarterly, 3*(4).

Mogull, S., & Balzhiser, D. (2015). Pharmaceutical companies are writing the script for health consumerism. *Communication Design Quarterly, 3*(4), 35–49.

National Center for Educational Statistics. (2014). *Digest of educational statistics.* Retrieved from https://nces.ed.gov/programs/digest/d13/tables/dt13_318.20.asp.

Novack, S. (2003). The health insurance portability and accountability act of 1996: Its implications for history of medicine collections. *The Watermark, 26*(3), 1–4.

Pender, S., & Struever, N. (2012). *Rhetoric and medicine in early modern Europe.* Burlington, VT: Ashgate.

Pomata, G. (1998). *Contracting a cure: Patients, healers, and the law in early modern Bologna* (G. Pomata, R. Foy, & A. Taraboletti-Segre, Trans.). Baltimore, MD: Johns Hopkins University Press.

Salager-Meyer, F. (2000). Debate-creating vs. accounting references in French medical journals. *Technical Communication Quarterly, 9*(3), 291–310.

Saunders, B. (2008). *CT suite: The work of diagnosis in the age of noninvasive cutting.* Durham, NC: Duke University Press.

Schmitter, A. (2012). Responses to vulnerability: Medicine, politics and the body in Descartes and Spinoza. In S. Pender & N. Struever (Eds.), *Rhetoric and medicine in early modern Europe* (pp. 147–172). Farnham, UK: Ashgate.

Scott, B., Segal, J., & Keränen, L. (2013). The rhetorics of health and medicine: Inventional possibilities for scholarship and engaged practice. *Poroi, 9*(1), 1–6.

Seigel, M. (2014). *The rhetoric of pregnancy.* Chicago, IL: University of Chicago Press.

Sontag, S. (1989). *Illness as metaphor and AIDS and its metaphors.* New York, NY: Doubleday.

Stafford, B. (1993). *Body criticism: Imaging the unseen in enlightenment art and medicine.* Cambridge, MA: MIT Press.

Stormer, N. (2015). *Sign of pathology: US medical rhetoric on abortion, 1880s–1960s.* University Park, PA: Pennsylvania State University Press.

Struever, N. (1976). Vico, Valla, and the logic of humanist inquiry. In G. Tagliacozzo & D. P. Verene (Eds.), *Giambattista Vico's science of humanity* (pp. 173–185). Baltimore, MD: Johns Hopkins University Press.

Struever, N. (2005). Historical priorities. *Journal of the History of Ideas, 66*(4), 541–556. doi:10.1353/jhi.2005.0059.

Wells, S. (2010). *Our bodies, ourselves and the work of writing.* Palo Alto, CA: Stanford University Press.

3

ECOLOGICAL INVESTMENTS AND THE CIRCULATION OF RHETORIC

Studying the "Saving Knowledge" of Dr. Emma Walker's Social Hygiene Lectures

Dan Ehrenfeld

Keywords: sex education, rhetoric, circulation, ecology, methodology, chronotope, health, medicine, social hygiene, infrastructures

In recent years, rhetoric and composition scholars have demonstrated renewed interest in the concept of circulation. From revisions of the classical canon of delivery (Trimbur, 2000; Buchanan, 2002; Rude, 2004; Yancey, 2006; Porter, 2009; Ridolfo, 2012; McCorkle, 2012) to ecological models of interconnectedness (Spinuzzi & Zachry, 2000; Bawarshi, 2001; Edbauer, 2005; Chaput, 2010; Rivers & Weber, 2011; Shepley, 2013), from engagements with complexity theory, systems theory, and actor-network theory (Syverson, 1999; Rickert, 2004; Hawk, 2007; Dobrin, 2011; Cooper, 2011; Jung, 2014; Gries, 2015; Ridolfo, 2015, Pflugfelder, 2015) to the adoption of network theory (Brooke, 2009; Brouwer & Asen, 2010; Dingo, 2012), we have continually redefined the contexts within which rhetoric moves and the dynamics of its movement.

In this chapter, I consider the methodological implications of this burgeoning subfield of circulation studies (Gries, 2011), focusing especially on how an "ecological" tendency in this body of scholarship might resonate with the work of rhetoricians of health and medicine. As Robin Jensen (2015) has written, emerging ecological models of rhetorical circulation offer us "a path relatively untrodden and underdeveloped yet teaming [sic] with the potential to help decipher the moving target that is 'health' and its related constructs" (p. 523). Along with Jensen, I welcome this ecological turn. I value, as she does, how ecological models have compelled us to question static mappings of the public, private, and technical spheres, focusing our attention instead on "the transformative nature of discourse as it flows across fields, actors, and rhetorical-cultural networks" (p. 524).[1] In this chapter, however, I argue that ecological models have not yet yielded research methodologies that enable rhetoricians to adequately consider the complex material-semiotic infrastructures that are central to the study of circulating health and medical knowledge. While ecological models have complicated our atomized understandings of rhetoric and its contexts, they haven't helped us fully account for the distinct temporal and spatial logics that animate these contexts in particular times and places.

Rhetoricians of health and medicine, I argue, can contribute to the development of research methodologies more attuned to these distinct logics. In order to lay the groundwork for such methodologies, this chapter proposes the metaphor of "investment." A methodology that helps us better account for the ways that complex ecologies seem to "invest" in the circulation of rhetoric might enable us to more fully consider the reflexive relationships that exist between rhetorical practices and the material-semiotic infrastructures that undergird complex ecologies of circulation.

To explore the productive potential of such a methodology, I examine the rhetoric of Emma Elizabeth Walker, a doctor whose "social hygiene" lectures aimed to distribute knowledge about sex and bodies to a lay public of girls and young women in the early 1900s. Tracing the circulation of Dr. Walker's "saving knowledge"—from its production at the confluence of multiple overlapping (and often conflicting) networks of stakeholders to its eventual circulation in more public contexts—this case study draws upon Mikhail Bakhtin's (1981) concept of the *chronotope* and Paul Prior and Julie Hengst's (2010) concept of *semiotic remediation* to articulate a methodology that helps us better account for the building and maintenance of the infrastructures through which health and medical knowledge circulates.

An Ecological Model of Rhetorical Circulation

In 1968, Lloyd Bitzer coined the term *rhetorical situation* to refer to "a natural context of persons, events, objects, relations, and an exigence which strongly invites utterance" (p. 5). In recent decades, scholarship in rhetoric and composition studies has revised this model of context, moving away from Bitzer's situational model and toward "ecological" models that consider not only the relationships that exist between the elements of a rhetorical situation but also the complex webs of influence and interdependence that link one rhetorical situation to another.

According to ecological models of rhetorical circulation, a complex system—whether it be an insect swarm, a social network, a street protest, or an academic discipline—follows the logic of "a web, in which anything that affects one strand of the web vibrates throughout the whole" (Cooper, 1986, p. 370). Byron Hawk (2007) uses another metaphor, borrowed from Mark C. Taylor, when he writes, "Like ants, writers are a 'colony of writers' caught up in the larger evolutionary flows of other networks" (p. 194). And Jenny Edbauer (2005), proposing the concept of *rhetorical ecologies*, argues that rhetoric moves and transforms as an "*amalgam of processes*, . . . encounters and actions" (p. 12), overlapping "through a kind of *shared contagion*" (p. 18) and spreading through "affective channels" that are always already structured by traces of experience and mood (p. 21).

Drawing upon the "posthumanism" of Giles Deleuze, Bruno Latour, Mark C. Taylor, Jane Bennett, and others, ecological models of rhetorical circulation focus our attention not on the rhetorical practices of individual rhetors but instead on the emergent properties of crowds, networks, and flows. This ecological perspective productively decenters the study of rhetoric, challenging the autonomy of the individual agent by exposing the radically interconnected nature of the contexts that she inhabits. As Laurie Gries (2011) writes, an ecological perspective encourages us to "realize that this entire web of life is actually a dynamic dance in which people, discourse, technologies, other entities and our environments intra-act to co-construct our daily materialities" (p. 88).

Ecological models ask us, in other words, to see agents as nodes within larger "constellations of humans and nonhumans" (Pflugfelder, 2015, p. 124), and ultimately as "indistinguishable from the system itself" (Dobrin, 2011, p. 133). A paradigm shift of this kind challenges instrumental models of rhetoric, which locate agency in the interplay between the will of the rhetor and the constraints that particular audiences and situations present. In contrast, ecological models of rhetorical circulation stress the fact that systems cocreate with rhetors (Ridolfo, 2015) in ways that are rarely fully evident to rhetors themselves. As Margaret Syverson (1999) writes, quoting William Paulson, a complex ecology is characterized by "a discontinuity in knowledge between the parts and the whole" (p. 4). Elaborating upon Mark C. Taylor's metaphor of a "colony of writers," Byron Hawk (2007) explains that, "[E]ach ant reacts only to its immediate neighboring ants and circumstances, but the larger flow of the colony nevertheless has a coherent, complex movement" (p. 183). A system, in other words, evolves as if it has a mind of its own. Yet the constituents of the system remain unable to consciously monitor or contribute to its evolution. Essentially, ecological models of rhetorical circulation are premised upon the idea that an agent's rhetorical acts can do little more than help her adapt to the shifting dynamics of fundamentally unpredictable systems.

To some, this paradigm shift may appear to diminish—or even invalidate—the field of rhetorical studies, which remains deeply invested in theorizing the agentive practices of individuals. Rhetoricians, however, are not ready to pack it up just yet. As Syverson (1999) writes, "[I]t would be an error to assume that an ecological theory of composing negates the significance of the individual in favor of the 'system' simply because the theory situates individuals within networks of physical and social structures and processes" (p. 201). As she writes, complex systems operate "at various levels of scale" (p. 5). But developing a methodology that enables us to study both the lifelike dynamics of complex systems and the rhetorical practices of individuals has necessitated a reconceptualization of human agency. Rather than defining agency as an individual's ability to predict and enact instrumental action on a large scale, ecological models have theorized agency in terms of rhetors' ongoing processes of attunement, adaptation, and cultivation. Noah Roderick (2012), for example, writes that "the writer's agency in a complex ecology depends upon her ability to successfully adapt to new settings by making analogies to her experience of prior settings" (Consequences for Composition Studies section, para. 3). Syverson (1999) writes that agents are constantly "moving into coordination with each other and their environment" (p. 68) by using "internal structures" (p. 6) to make predictions about situations. Hawk (2007) claims that being able to anticipate and coadapt with a moment is a "vital rhetorical skill" that one can develop over time (p. 185). And Thomas Rickert (2004) proposes that we see both a writer and her environment as unified when they "mutually tak[e] part in" the singular moment of the present situation, an unrepeatable, unfolding, coadaptative amalgamation that he terms an "ambience" (p. 916).

As I hope that this brief discussion has demonstrated, our "ecological turn" has enabled us to theorize the relatively diminished rhetorical agency of our "posthuman" world. We know, according to ecological models, that rhetoric happens within a complex web of interrelations between humans, nonhumans, the discursive, and the material. And we know—if we extend Cooper's metaphor—some of the many ways that rhetors might participate in the spinning and respinning of this web. Yet while this "ecological turn" has helped us productively theorize the limits of human agency, it has not yet offered rhetoricians and compositionists research methodologies that enable us to consider the relationships between individual rhetorical acts and the durable logics that dominate ecologies in particular times and places. Ecological models, in other words, have failed to illuminate the *infrastructural* nature of rhetorical circulation.

Because terms such as "ecology," "network," and "system" have functioned as universalizing metaphors, rhetoricians and compositionists have neglected to consider the many ways that the nodes of a web might be linked, amalgamated, and assembled. In turn, we have failed to consider the many ways that rhetorical acts might ripple and reverberate through the ecologies that we inhabit. Without a methodology that enables us to consider the historically distinct dynamics of circulation infrastructures, I argue that we lack the means to theorize the power dynamics that animate complex ecologies and the politics of practicing rhetoric within them.[2]

This lack of attention to historical specificity is compounded by the fact that rhetoricians and compositionists have rarely applied ecological models of rhetorical circulation to real-world case studies. In theory, ecological models help us consider the implications of practicing rhetoric in contexts characterized by radical relationality and inexorable flux. In practice, however, these models have not yet enabled us to consider the varied contexts within which discourse circulates.[3] As a result, our claims about the ecological dynamics of rhetorical circulation have remained broad and theoretical. I want to claim, however, that rhetoricians of health and medicine have something to contribute to the next phase of our ecological turn. Rhetoricians of health and medicine have provided thick qualitative descriptions of the complex contexts that we study—contexts which are both material and discursive, which are shot through with power relations, mediated by technologies, and composed of institutions, publics, bodies, pathogens, regimes of knowledge production, and material infrastructures. Studying the shifting dynamics of this complex terrain, rhetoricians of health and medicine have done much to articulate how actual—not hypothetical—bodies are impacted by the dynamics of complex systems.

Hence, rhetoricians of health and medicine are uniquely positioned to contribute to—and benefit from—research methodologies that illuminate 1) how the constituents of material ecologies seem to "invest" in the building and maintenance of circulation infrastructures, and 2) how rhetors and their semiotic resources become implicated in these ecologies, altering the embodied, material relations of the circulation infrastructures within which they are enmeshed. Writing about the related framework of assemblage theory, Elizabeth L. Angeli (this volume) writes that medical rhetoricians should attend to "dynamic relations among the components involved in an assemblage" (p. 238). Doing so, she argues, enables us to better account for the complex networks of stakeholders within which our research sites are situated. My own research has considered how the material, semiotic, and embodied constituents of an ecology invested—without conscious coordination—in the circulation infrastructures of New York City in the early 1900s. Though the far-flung constituents of this complex ecology did not—in a literal sense—invest in the building and maintenance of the city's circulation infrastructures, my work explores a process of *ecological investment* that occurs in such a system.[4] In order to develop a research methodology that attunes us to this process of ecological investment, I devote the remainder of this chapter to an examination of the medical lectures of Dr. Emma Elizabeth Walker. My primary goal is to develop a research methodology that enables rhetoricians and compositionists to investigate how rhetors—in particular times and places—come to shape, reinforce, subvert, and reinvent the logics of the ecologies within which they are enmeshed.

The "Saving Knowledge" of Dr. Emma Elizabeth Walker

In 1902, a congress composed of medical professionals from around the world convened in Brussels to consider strategies for the prevention of venereal disease. Concerned that questions of purity had not been dealt with adequately, the Brussels congress declared that "the whole question should be studied anew from a broader standpoint, and with special reference to the social conditions involved in the causation of these diseases" ("Social Purity," n.d.). This prescription was the inspiration behind the establishment of a worldwide network of Societies of Social and Moral Prophylaxis, including a U.S. branch founded in New York City where Dr. Emma Elizabeth Walker—the subject of this study—began working as a lecturer ("Social Purity," n.d.).[5]

Addressing audiences of medical professionals, mothers, and school-aged girls, Dr. Walker delivered lectures about the dangers of venereal disease and the taboo realities of sexual health. She was a passionate proponent of a movement that came to be known as the "social hygiene" movement. During the first decades of the 20th century, the social hygiene movement championed the spread of knowledge about sex and bodies. As Walker lamented in an address to a meeting of mothers, a "conspiracy of silence" had made important health information inaccessible to those who needed it. Millions of dollars were spent on "defectives"—children affected by venereal disease—while no money at all was set aside for "the spread of saving knowledge" (Walker, n.d.). The American Public Health Association agreed with this assessment, announcing that a primary goal should be to surmount "the hysteria and lack of balance which has too often characterized earlier interest in this problem" ("The Social Hygiene Movement," 1913, p. 1157). At the turn of the century, didactic lectures had failed. Social hygienists began calling for new methods to reach populations of young women who, more and more, seemed beyond the guiding influence of their families. From the middle-class "New Woman" to the parentless immigrant, a young woman in New York City was more likely to live alone than in previous generations, and was tied more and more to the public arena, where many engaged in heterosocial leisure rituals that tested the sexual mores of the era. Practices of "petting" and "treating" blurred the boundaries between work and leisure, and the issue of prostitution, once considered an inevitable feature of every American city, was becoming a hotly debated public issue (Peiss, 1986, pp. 165–185).

It was within this cultural context that Walker emphasized the urgent need to present information "scientifically, definitely, plainly, and wholesomely" (Walker, n.d.). Two of her lectures from this period end with a quotation from Professor Max Mueller that embodies this mission: "All truth is safe, and nothing else is safe, and he who keeps back the truth or withholds it as a matter of expediency is either a coward, a criminal, or both" (Walker, n.d.). As these quotations demonstrate, Dr. Walker's lectures were emblematic of an ongoing struggle to provide accurate information about sex and bodies to the public. Walker believed that young women and wives were especially vulnerable to the ravages of venereal disease, and that the most effective way to protect the most vulnerable members of society was to break taboos surrounding the discussion of disease transmission.

Yet her lectures reveal an interesting tension. On the one hand, she espouses the view that knowledge is fungible, a currency that might spread freely if liberated from the imposition of unnatural Puritan mores. On the other hand, however, her lectures insist that knowledge about sex and bodies should circulate in very particular ways—in face-to-face encounters between experts and nonexperts that mimic the roles of the domestic sphere. Critiquing the didactic talks and extended horticultural metaphors that characterized the sex education efforts of previous eras, Walker recommends "modeling the isolated lecture as far as may be after the ideal method of a mother with her child" (Walker, n.d.). She speaks of the importance of conveying "deep sympathy with them in their lives," the kind of "mutual confidence" that one experiences when a message passes "from one family member to another" (Walker, n.d.). Explaining this model of sex education to other medical professionals, Walker quotes Patterson Du Bois's insight that education is "less a matter of direct teaching and preaching than atmospheric influence—example, suggestion, pure speech, gentle manner, sweet temper, strong handling, firm stepping in virtue" (Walker, n.d.). In other words, Walker's lectures highlight the embodied, situated, and affective dimensions of knowledge work— as one Professor James put it, the potential to "make our nervous system our ally instead of our enemy" (Walker, n.d.). According to this "atmospheric" model, a social worker, teacher, school administrator, settlement worker, clubwoman, or doctor might take on the role of "the foster father and mother" (Peiss, 1986, p. 179) for young urban women whose families were absent or seen as unfit to deliver instruction about sex and bodies.

It is tempting, with the advantage of hindsight, to view Dr. Walker's mother-daughter rhetoric as a strategic success; positioning herself as a foster mother of sorts, Walker repurposed the generic conventions of the domestic sphere in ways that enabled her to smuggle controversial medical knowledge into a prudish, regressive public sphere. Reading her lectures according to this agent-centered model of rhetorical practice, the mother-daughter tropes that Dr. Walker deploys were simply semiotic resources that she operationalized at an opportune moment. We might imagine, in other words, that this domestic genre offered Walker a familiar role that she could play, and that this role provided her with a convenient means of circulating her "saving knowledge" without censure. A theoretical-methodological orientation of this kind might illuminate how an individual rhetor cleverly repurposed semiotic resources in order to enact her private intentions. Yet it would also assure that our gaze remain narrowly focused on an individual rhetor and the constraints that she faced. According to this agent-centered methodology, the constituent parts of the wider ecology would only be studied to account for the ways that they helped or hindered Dr. Walker's attempts to enact her private intentions.

In order to ask broader questions about how Dr. Walker and her semiotic resources became enmeshed in a far-flung circulation infrastructure that encompassed much more than her own rhetorical situation, I suggest that we develop research methodologies that are ecological in nature. In particular, I argue that we should develop research methodologies that pay close attention to the relationships between individual rhetorical practices and historically distinct ecologies.

In the following section, I begin to articulate a methodology that has enabled me to investigate these ecological processes. Drawing upon Mikhail Bakhtin's (1981) concept of the *chronotope* and Prior and Hengst's (2010) concept of *semiotic remediation*, I consider the ways in which Dr. Walker's local rhetorical work was related to larger "investments" in circulation infrastructures, the lasting channels through which rhetoric circulates. Specifically, I consider 1) how Dr. Walker's rhetorical action was shaped by the temporal and spatial logics that animated these circulation infrastructures and 2) how her semiotic resources become integral to the building and maintenance of these infrastructures.

Bakhtin's Embodied-Representational Chronotope

Bakhtin (1981) defines the chronotope as "the intrinsic connectedness of temporal and spatial relationships that are artistically expressed in literature" (p. 84). A chronotope is, in other words, a time-space logic embedded in a genre. Though Bakhtin articulated the concept of the chronotope through an analysis of "various histories of generic heterogeneity in the European novel" (p. 85), chronotopic analysis has not been limited to artistic or literary texts. Bakhtin's concept of the chronotope has been adapted for the study of rhetorical genres (Schryer, 1999; Schryer, 2002; Crossley, 2007; Artemeva, 2008), electronic discourse (Bostad, 2004), and the spatiotemporal frames that delimit debate and action in the public sphere (Jack, 2006). It has been leveraged not only for descriptive purposes but also to analyze the ideological assumptions embedded in discourse—in particular, to analyze the ways that enacted logics of time and space regulate the contours of the social world. Like Walter Ong's (1975) "fictional" audience and Lisa Ede and Andrea Lunsford's (2011) "audience invoked," Bakhtin's concept of the chronotope encourages us to consider how rhetoric orients senders and receivers in relation to one another within the intersubjective "space" of discourse.

Paul Prior and Jody Shipka (2003), however, argue that we might pursue a reading of Bakhtin's later work that expands the scope of chronotopic analysis to include the embodied relationships of the social, material world. According to this reading of Bakhtin, the concept of the chronotope troubles an all-too-common assumption about discourse—that it occurs in a disembodied, virtual, immaterial realm somehow separate from the one that we inhabit. They write:

> [R]epresentational chronotopes (those on paper, in talk, and in the mind) co-evolve with embodied chronotopes, the actual concrete times, places, and events of life. Or perhaps it would be best to say that Bakhtin came to view all chronotopes as embodied-representational—with concrete time-place-events deeply furrowed with, and constructed through, representations and with representations always deeply rooted in chains of concrete historical events.
>
> *(p. 186)*

I argue that seeing a chronotope as simultaneously representational and embodied provides us with a useful means of considering how the interactional logics embedded in our semiotic resources and materialized through our rhetoric do more than create "imagined" or "invoked" textual dramas in the minds of audiences. Embodied-representational chronotopes undergird our social worlds,

positioning and repositioning bodies according to sedimented interactional logics that we continually reproduce through rhetorical practices. Seeing a chronotope as simultaneously representational and embodied means recognizing that our
rhetoric and its larger material contexts are not linked in simple, causal ways, but
are instead knotted together according to temporal and spatial logics that defy
the binary between the material and the discursive. Thus, Jan Blommaert (2015)
can speak of the fundamentally chronotopic nature of social identities, which
are always constrained by "roles, discourses, modes of interaction, dress, codes of
conduct, criteria for judgment of appropriate versus inappropriate behavior, and
so forth" (p. 3). And Chelsea Milbourne and Sarah Hallenbeck (2013) can apply
Bakhtin's concept of the chronotope to the gendered history of the microscope,
considering how this material object has carried with it "a spatio-temporal user
orientation produced and stabilized through users' routinized and embodied performances" (p. 403). The temporal and spatial logics of particular chronotopes, in
other words, are constantly materialized, subverted, repurposed, and reinforced not
in a textual world that is somehow separate from our own but in the imminently
material world that our bodies inhabit. As such, an analysis of the temporal and
spatial logics that undergird complex ecologies is an inherently political analysis
of how people, things, technologies, and environments are continually positioned
and repositioned in relation to one another. And rhetoric, far from being merely
a means of attuning oneself to these dynamics, is seen to play a significant role in
shaping the logics that underlie these processes of positioning and repositioning.

In order to consider how Dr. Walker's social hygiene lectures might have played
a role in positioning and repositioning the constituents of the ecology within
which she was enmeshed, and to consider as well how networks of stakeholders
might have "invested" in this infrastructural work, we can begin by analyzing her
rhetoric in terms of the embodied-representational logics that animated it. To do
so, we must first consider the assumptions about time and space embedded in the
mother-daughter chronotope that Walker repurposed in her lectures.

What do we know about the recurring "scene" of a mother figure teaching
her daughter about reproduction and the body? Repurposed from a domestic
context, the mother-daughter chronotope positions participants in hierarchical
relationships based on differing levels of expertise and knowledge. According
to the temporal and spatial conventions of this chronotope, a daughter holds
"latent" questions about sex and the body. Approached by her mother, she enters
into an open-ended process of asking and answering through which she receives
guidance. Curiosities are satisfied, vague and undefined questions come into
focus, and competing versions of the truth are evaluated in light of a parent's
authoritative knowledge. The medium is speech, not writing. Participants are
always face-to-face, together in a private setting, bound to each other in a relationship of mutual confidence. In essence, the mother and daughter establish an
exclusive channel of circulation, one that no one else will ever access, and discuss
things that might be considered unacceptable or embarrassing in other contexts.

A circulation infrastructure of this kind supports a young woman in her attempts to validate or invalidate contradictory knowledge acquired in multiple contexts, setting the stage for a "scene" that can recur indefinitely.

Though many would argue that this mother-daughter chronotope serves an obvious purpose in a domestic context—its recurring time-space logics enable mothers to share taboo information with their daughters through an ongoing, open-ended process of private discussion—its function in a public lecture hall merits critical analysis. Walker's assertions that "an ounce of mother is worth a pound of doctor" and that girls have "latent" painful questions that should be turned into "clean, honest and reputable questions" (Walker, n.d.) in a "proper and discrete manner" ("Social Purity," n.d.) aren't just extended metaphors about motherly pedagogy. They are, I want to claim, temporal and spatial orientations that delimit the ways that actors can be positioned in relation to one another, how they act in response to one another, the tenor of their interactions, the public/private nature of their positioning in material space, and how their interactions interface (or not) with the wider ecology that we might call the public sphere.

Paul Prior and Julie Hengst's (2010) concept of *semiotic remediation* helps us theorize how Dr. Walker repurposed the logics of one context for use in a new context. Prior and Hengst write that semiotic remediation "points to ways that activity is (re)mediated—not mediated anew in each act—through taking up the materials at hand, putting them to present use, and thereby producing altered conditions for future action" (p. 1). Borrowed from the domestic sphere (or some idealized version of it), what function did the time-space logics of Dr. Walker's mother-daughter chronotope serve in the public contexts in which she delivered her lectures? Seen through the lens of semiotic remediation, Dr. Walker's mother-daughter chronotope was not simply a rhetorical frame that she deployed in order to navigate the constraints of a complex rhetorical situation. It was, instead, an entire lifeworld that was activated at a moment when it could play a crucial role in the building and maintenance of the circulation infrastructures of the city. To understand how Dr. Walker, her semiotic resources, and the complex ecology of New York City in the early 1900s became knotted together through the use of this mother-daughter chronotope, we need to consider how a far-flung network of stakeholders continually "invested" in the circulation infrastructures within which this chronotope was deployed. Who invested in the building and maintenance of these circulation infrastructures? And what kinds of infrastructural changes did these stakeholders invest in?

There were a number of stakeholders who invested directly in the work of Dr. Walker. In the early 1900s, when Dr. Walker delivered her first public lectures, she was already enmeshed within a complex network of health advocates, institutions, community organizations, and medical societies. She was a physician and member of the American Medical Association, the New York Academy of Medicine, the Women's Medical Society of New York State, the Medical Society of the County of New York, the Medical Society of the State of New York, and the Society of Sanitary and Moral Prophylaxis; she was also a published author of books and articles, a lecturer for the City of New York's Department of Education, and later—during WWI—an employee of the YWCA's War Work Council. Throughout her career, interconnected networks of stakeholders provided Dr. Walker with invitations to lecture, to publish, to collaborate, and to contribute to discussions about the future of social and moral hygiene initiatives.

These interconnected networks invested in the work of Dr. Walker in very concrete, direct ways. But by focusing our attention on how the constituents of an ecology supported or constrained Walker's work, we again risk overemphasizing the intentional acts of an individual rhetor. An ecological methodology, on the other hand, encourages us to consider how a far-flung network of constituents is always already animated by temporal and spatial logics that are much larger and more diffuse than the rhetorical situations that individual rhetors navigate. Studying the lectures of Dr. Walker using an ecological methodology of this kind, we might consider how her lectures were bound to other constituents—even those who weren't in direct contact with her—by nature of the fact that they were embedded together in the larger circulation infrastructures of the city.

Drawing upon Bakhtin's concept of the embodied-representational chronotope, we can better consider the ways that rhetors—enmeshed within circulation infrastructures—shape the temporal and spatial logics of these infrastructures in meaningful, somewhat lasting ways. We might say, in fact, that the temporal and spatial logics of an ecology are constantly being sedimented, and that the temporal and spatial logics of our rhetorical practices contribute to this ongoing process of sedimentation. The term "infrastructure," in other words, captures a duality that characterizes ecologies of rhetorical circulation—they are both durable and perpetually under construction.[6] Through a process of *ecological investment*, these circulation infrastructures are built and maintained, perpetually creating and recreating the conditions under which others become rhetorical. In other words, the temporal and spatial logics according to which rhetors become relational with one another are delimited by the temporal and spatial logics that have been laid down before their arrival. At the same time, rhetors invest themselves in rhetorical work in very personal ways. In doing so, they also "invest"—along with innumerable others, often unwittingly—in the maintenance of the very circulation infrastructures within which they enact rhetorical work.

For example, when Dr. Walker invested herself in the circulation of knowledge about sex and bodies, she didn't do so independently. Her attempts to disseminate knowledge throughout New York City were shaped, through and through, by the temporal and spatial logics laid down by constituents who had "invested" in the city's circulation infrastructures through myriad dispersed actions. The concept of ecological investment enables us to consider how a print shop selling pornography out of a basement on Warren Street might be related—chronotopically—to Dr. Walker's decision to conduct her sex education lectures through the medium of speech. It was in that basement that Anthony Comstock began his personal campaign against the circulation of indecent materials in New York City, a campaign which in 1873 was codified into law through the Comstock Law. Based on "elusive" definitions of obscenity, Comstock prosecuted more than 3,800 people, disproportionately from working class and immigrant backgrounds, for the selling of contraceptives, literature about sex, and even medical tracts (Jensen, 2010). How did the suppression of material that was thought to corrupt the minds of viewers set up a particular temporal and spatial orientation toward printed works—a chronotope—that had enduring effects on the circulation of texts in New York City? Attention to the temporal and spatial logics underlying the Comstock Law might enable us to consider how Anthony Comstock came to "invest" in circulation infrastructures that outlasted his crusade in ways that he could not have planned or predicted.

In addition, an ecological methodology might enable us to consider how the diverging branches of the social hygiene movement itself contributed to the building and maintenance of the circulation infrastructures of New York City in the early 1900s. In the November 1913 issue of the *American Journal of Public Health*, an editorial about the future of social hygiene painted a daunting picture of the task ahead of the movement. To survive, it would need to "weld together a large number of diversified and, even, antagonistic elements" ("Social Hygiene," p. 1155). The movement included those who believed that moral education was the only path to righteousness, those who advocated direct clinical work with victims of venereal disease, those who saw social hygiene as the public arm of a burgeoning eugenics movement, those who were working to eradicate red-light districts, those who pushed for the ethical regulation of prostitution, and those who believed that only domestic instruction would have any effect at all. The social hygiene movement witnessed uneasy alliances between the last vestiges of the social purity movement and more scientifically minded reformers, among them eugenicists (Pivar, 2002). One can see, then, how the production of knowledge about sex and bodies was bound, under the umbrella of "social hygiene," to a multitude of campaigns for moral, domestic, urban, and racial purity. Yet the development of circulation infrastructures that would support the kind of standardization necessary for a coordinated national effort was delayed by the unbridgeable divergences that characterized the movement's "investments." We can imagine how an ecological methodology might help us illuminate the extent to which Walker's mother-daughter chronotope became felicitous within a circulation infrastructure shaped by the strange convergences and divergences of varied professional agendas. An ecological methodology might also enable us to consider how this chronotope continued to shape the infrastructures within which it was deployed.

In addition, considering the circulation of knowledge about sex and bodies in all of its complexity means considering how Dr. Walker's lectures were ecologically bound to circulation infrastructures that fell outside of the professional medical communities that she belonged to. A methodology that highlights how ecologies "invest" in the temporal and spatial logics of circulation infrastructures might encourage us to examine how competing circulation infrastructures interfered with the social hygiene movement's attempts to standardize health and medical knowledge. As I have discussed, Walker's attempts to position herself as a mother to young urban women materialized a "scene" whose temporal and spatial logics played a role in the ongoing regulation of the ways that knowledge moved between the technical sphere and the public sphere. According to this scene, an expert authoritatively dispels myths that have *previously* circulated and responds to "latent" questions *before* these questions can be addressed via competing circulation infrastructures. The mother-daughter chronotope appears to reinforce an exclusive channel of circulation that serves to consolidate and reconcile the seemingly incompatible factions of the social hygiene movement while simultaneously discouraging girls from seeking information about sex and bodies via the unauthorized circulation infrastructures of the public sphere. Dr. Walker warned, in one of her lectures delivered to the Society of Sanitary and Moral Prophylaxis, that in the absence of "the right information" and "giving information rightly," young women would "gather knowledge in a haphazard way, from companions, books, and in other ways" (Walker, n.d.). Similarly, in a 1908 lecture to the American Society of Sanitary and Moral Prophylaxis, F.N. Seerly spoke of how the "instruction of the street" poisons minds with "stories which are told in shops, on the streets, the pictures on the bill-boards, in newspapers, or sold by thought-to-be reputable newsdealers, books and pamphlets sold or given away, some of them advertisements of museums or quack doctors" (*Transactions*, 1910, p. 5). Attention to these street-level circulation infrastructures, with their "haphazard" temporal and spatial logics, calls attention to the fact that any effort to build and maintain a circulation infrastructure is also an effort to occlude alternative circulation infrastructures. In his study of food labels, for example, Nathan R. Johnson (this volume) considers how the repetition of information and formats contributes to the development of dominant information infrastructures that support particular ways of seeing. "When rhetoricians attend to information infrastructure," he writes, "they can identify important rhetorical traffic that pushes health and medicine to attend to some knowledge regimes instead of others" (p. 76).

Seen in this light, Emma Walker's lectures can be understood not only as vehicles for the dissemination of information but also as technologies that enabled her to enact the very political work of building and maintaining circulation infrastructures. Walker's attempts to standardize an exclusive channel of circulation become especially interesting when we consider her role as a "foster mother" for young women whose family structures conflicted with the domestic ideals that she championed. Inspired by a "cult of domesticity" that positioned the mother as custodian of the health and longevity of the American nation and the white race, many social hygienists were concerned not only with rising rates of venereal infection but also with the independence of young women who were moving to cities and finding themselves suddenly unmoored from traditional family structures (Pivar, 2002). Though Dr. Walker believed that a mother was the ideal teacher for a young woman, she was of the opinion that the social hygiene movement could not entrust this responsibility to "the large majority of mothers as we [see] them here in New York" (*Transactions*, 1910, p. 33). Such a description carried, at the time, classed and raced overtones about the families of new immigrants (both foreign and domestic) to New York City.

The circulation infrastructures of New York City in the early 1900s were, as this discussion has demonstrated, in flux. And they were shaped by paradoxical investments. From obscenity laws to pulp novels to purity movements to migration and habitation patterns, myriad "investors" shaped the circulation infrastructures through which Dr. Walker spread her "saving knowledge." In shaping the temporal and spatial logics of circulation in New York City, how did the constituent parts of this ecology shape the conditions within which Dr. Walker could enact her own work? And how might Dr. Walker's mother-daughter chronotope have shaped the circulation of rhetoric in lasting ways that could be described as "infrastructural"?

We might speculate, for example, about the fact that Dr. Walker used the medium of speech, as opposed to writing, to circulate knowledge about sex and bodies. Walker was a widely published author, but her published work focused on noncontroversial subjects such as beauty, hair care, and bathing. It would be quite right, I think, to argue that the Comstock laws operated as very direct constraints on Dr. Walker, limiting her ability to publish material about sex and bodies. An agent-centered model of this kind, which considers how situational constraints prevented Dr. Walker from enacting her personal intentions, certainly yields important insights. Working in this vein, Robin Jensen (2010) suggests that social hygienists of the early 1900s deployed an "ambiguous discourse" in order to achieve their goals without interference. One only has to consider the name of the movement itself ("social hygiene" was a euphemism designed to avoid censure) to understand the value of strategic language choices (Jensen, 2010, p. 18). But focusing solely on how the Comstock laws *directly* constrained Dr. Walker lead us to neglect the complex ecological processes according to which Dr. Walker, the Comstock laws, and innumerable other "investors" shaped the circulation infrastructures of New York City.

Using a methodology based on the concept of ecological investment, one can see how the temporal and spatial logics that animated Walker's mother-daughter chronotope were particularly suited to enact infrastructural work in a time and place in which the future of these infrastructures was contested. In this case study, such a methodology raises the following questions: To what extent did the temporal and spatial logics of the mother-daughter chronotope—which emphasized face-to-face interactions that left no trace of their existence—align with a circulation infrastructure within which the dissemination and possession of medical tracts was actively prosecuted? To what extent did this chronotope enable Walker to reinforce the logics of authorized circulation infrastructures at the expense of contested, marginalized infrastructures? And to what extent did this chronotope serve to regulate not only the circulation of particular kinds of information but also the gendered, classed, and raced dynamics of the city itself?

Conclusion

I have argued that the mother–daughter chronotope that animated Dr. Walker's public lectures did much more than aid in the dissemination of information. By remediating temporal and spatial logics from the domestic sphere into the public sphere, Walker linked scores of young women to the authorized networks of the social hygiene movement and its related medical communities. This chronotope positioned people in relation to one another in distinct ways, in the process shaping the temporal and spatial logics of circulation infrastructures in accordance with the "investments" of a much larger ecology. We can see, then, that Dr. Walker's mother–daughter chronotope shaped circulation infrastructures primarily through the positioning and repositioning of people themselves, who became central to the circulation of health and medical knowledge during the Progressive Era. In other words, because people themselves—along with built environments, matter, discourse, and other constituent parts—constituted the very substance of the era's circulation infrastructures, one could not invest in these infrastructures without investing in the relational dynamics of the social world.

Though my discussion of this ecology has been brief and necessarily incomplete, I have highlighted a few of the "investors" that participated in the building and maintenance of the circulation infrastructures within which Dr. Walker worked. As I have demonstrated, an ecological methodology can be used to help us draw conclusions from a flux of endlessly interrelated networks of constituents. In our attempts to draw these conclusions, however, we run up against the limitations of our conceptual tools, which are rooted in human causal logic. Hence, terms such as "invest," which anthropomorphize complex ecological processes and ascribe to them an intentionality that we know they lack, must be awkwardly couched in quotation marks. Philip Ball (2015), discussing the challenge of articulating the dynamics of complex systems using our narrative instincts, writes "[A] complex system [is] one in which many agents interact with one another simultaneously . . . [I]t might be quite wrong to tell such a story in terms of *this* small-scale action leading to *that* large-scale effect" (para. 29).

Despite this challenge, I argue that we should continue to develop methodologies that help us tell ecological stories. Rhetoricians of health and medicine can benefit from the systemic perspectives that ecological models provide. But we can also contribute to the wider field of rhetorical studies by sharing what we know about how rhetoric operates in complex contexts. In studying obscenity laws, habitation patterns, utopian movements, professional medical communities, pamphlets, billboards, pulp novels, stories, circulating tropes, and built environments, I have widened my definition of a stakeholder, coming to see various stakeholders not as the *causes* of Emma Elizabeth Walker's rhetorical action or the *constraints* that she worked around but instead as "investors"—along with Dr. Walker herself—in the circulation infrastructures of the city.

Though an agent-centered methodology might explain the mother-daughter tropes that animated her lectures as primarily strategic rhetorical choices, the ecological methodology that I have developed can illuminate how the embodied-representational chronotope that Walker remediated from a private, domestic context to the relatively public context of a lecture hall did a particular kind of *work* in a particular time and place. Such a methodology illuminates how rhetors participate in the building and maintenance of circulation infrastructures that are always already conditioned by the "investments" of a larger ecology. Focusing on the temporal and spatial logics that animate circulation infrastructures encourages us to think not only in terms of how rhetors shape or adapt to their surroundings but also in terms of how their rhetorical practices contribute to the unending reorganization of the complex contexts within which they are enmeshed.

Like Susan Wells and Nathan Stormer (this volume), I believe that the present is a dialogue with the past, not a break from it. "If one is to situate contemporary medical practices in time and place," Wells and Stormer write, "then greater inspection of the past is not only rewarding but also necessary" (p. 35). My study of Dr. Emma Elizabeth Walker's life trajectory contributes to such a goal, offering a lesson in the organization and reorganization of the ecologies that rhetors inhabit. When WWI began, the social hygiene movement was suddenly animated by a new set of ideals—namely, the protection of our fighting forces from venereal disease (*Social Hygiene*, 1918). Dr. Walker found herself enmeshed within a changed circulation infrastructure. The U.S. government took a more active role in shaping the movement, asking Walker to lecture in multiple contexts throughout the war. Others also tapped her rhetorical experience. Walker's collected documents tell a story about not only her rhetorical performances but also the ways in which her semiotic resources were reshaped in different contexts and operationalized for varied purposes throughout her lifespan.

In 1924, late in her career, Walker wrote to the YWCA's Education and Research Division for information about how she might refer to herself when composing a resumé. They informed Walker that she should be referred to as "a lecturer on the staff of the Bureau of Lecturers of the Committee on Social Morality, War Work Council of the Young Women's Christian Associations" and added, "That sounds very lengthy but is apparently the only accurate way of stating it" (Walker, n.d.). Walker's title, a Frankenstein's monster of institutional mergers, incorporations, and consolidations offers a hint of the enormous transformations that circulation infrastructures can undergo when systems of power invest in their rearticulation. But we should continually remind ourselves, when studying how the world invests in the circulation of rhetoric, that these investments come not only in the form of direct support but also in "ecological" forms of investment that are less visible but undoubtedly more complex.

Notes

1 For recent work in the rhetorics of health and medicine that explores ecological models of rhetorical circulation, see the *Journal of Medical Humanities* special issue titled "Medicine, Health, and Publics" (Keränen, 2014).

2 Ecological models have rarely considered the issue of power dynamics. Exceptions include Margaret Syverson, who in 1999 asked, "[H]ow do some agents—particular readers, writers, or texts, for instance—come to have a greater influence on such systems and why? How is that influence situated and exerted? Where complex systems do take a hierarchical form, how is the hierarchy structured and maintained—and at what costs and benefits to the system?" (p. 202). Collin Gifford Brooke's recent work (2015) has considered the hierarchical nature of networks. Noah Roderick (2012), too, has written that our engagements with complexity science and network theory need not champion a "post-political project that naturalizes status-quo neoliberal capitalism" (opening section, para. 5). And John Trimbur's (2000) work, though it doesn't draw upon the ecology metaphor, offers a valuable model for understanding the historical specificity of the "delivery systems" through which texts and capital circulate.

3 Exceptions include Spinuzzi and Zachry (2000) and Syverson (1999). These works, however, develop ecological models of rhetorical circulation in order to theorize relatively bounded systems of workplaces and composition classrooms, respectively. For an in-depth study of rhetoric as it circulates within and across institutions, media, and built environments, see Gries (2015).

4 I draw upon the metaphor of "investment" because it evokes two things. First, that circulation infrastructures are never simply designed and built; they are always created through the collective "investments" of far-flung constituents. This financial metaphor hints at the cooperative yet often anonymous nature of ecological interconnectedness. Second, the metaphor references the ways that we invest ourselves—emotionally, intellectually, physically—in the work that we do as individuals. Far from being simply byproducts of ecological dynamics, our rhetorical acts are personal commitments. Investment, then, is a concept that hints at the radically "posthuman" nature of rhetorical circulation as well as the fundamentally human ways that we commit ourselves to local projects that we care about. In addition, my use of the term has been influenced by the work of Deborah Brandt (2009), who considers the ways that literacy sponsors consciously or unconsciously "enable, support, teach, model, as well as recruit, regulate, suppress, or withhold literacy—and gain advantage by it in some way" (p. 25).

5 This archival case study is based upon lectures and lecture notes from the Emma Elizabeth Walker papers, held in Smith College's Sophia Smith Collection. Among these is a lecture addressed to social hygienists that discusses strategies for educating young women.

6 My use of the term *infrastructures* builds upon the work of J. Blake Scott (2014) and Nathan R. Johnson (2012), two rhetoricians who use the concept to consider the circulation of health and medical knowledge.

References

American Social Hygiene Association. (1918). *Social hygiene: Volume 4*. New York, NY: Author.

Artemeva, N. (2008). Toward a unified social theory of genre learning. *Journal of Business and Technical Communication, 22*(2), 160–185.

Bakhtin, M. M. (1981). Forms of time and of the chronotope in the novel. In M. Holquist & C. Emerson (Trans.), *The dialogic imagination: Four essays* (pp. 84–258). Austin, TX: University of Texas Press. (Original Work Published 1975)

Ball, P. (2015, November 12). The story trap. *Aeon*. Retrieved from https://aeon.co/essays/why-story-is-used-to-explain-symphonies-and-sport-matches-alike.

Bawarshi, A. (2001). The ecology of genre. In S. Dobrin & C. Weisser (Eds.), *Ecocomposition: Theoretical and pedagogical approaches* (pp. 69–80). Albany, NY: SUNY Press.

Bitzer, B. (1968). The rhetorical situation. *Philosophy and Rhetoric, 1*(1), 1–14.

Blommaert, J. (2015). Chronotopic identities. *Working Papers in Urban Language and Literacies*. London, UK: King's College London, Centre for Language, Discourse, and Communication.

Bostad, F. (2004). Dialogue in electronic public space: The semiotics of time, space and the Internet. In F. Bostad, C. Brandist, L. S. Evensen, & H. C. Faber (Eds.), *Bakhtinian perspectives on language and culture* (pp. 167–184). New York, NY: Palgrave Macmillan.

Brooke, C. G. (2009). *Lingua fracta: What we teach when we teach about literacy*. Cresskill, NJ: Hampton Press.

Brooke, C. G. (2015, April 3). *Entropics of discourse: Post/human rhetorics amidst the networks (Speaker Series 2015)* [Video file]. Retrieved from www.youtube.com/watch?v=UskVL36kph8&feature=youtu.be.

Brouwer, D., & Asen, R. (2010). *Public modalities: Rhetoric, culture, media, and the shape of public life*. Tuscaloosa, AL: University of Alabama Press.

Buchanan, L. (2002). Regendering delivery: The fifth canon and the maternal rhetor. *Rhetoric Society Quarterly, 32*(4), 51–73.

Chaput, C. (2010). Rhetorical circulation in late capitalism: Neoliberalism and the overdetermination of affective energy. *Philosophy and Rhetoric, 43*(1), 1–25.

Cooper, M. (1986). The ecology of writing. *College English, 48*(4), 364–375.

Cooper, M. (2011). Rhetorical agency as emergent and enacted. *College Composition and Communication, 62*(3), 420–449.

Crossley, S. (2007). A chronotopic approach to genre analysis: An exploratory study. *English for Specific Purposes, 26*(1), 4–24.

Dingo, R. (2012). *Networking arguments: Rhetoric, transnational feminism, and public policy writing*. Pittsburgh, PA: University of Pittsburgh Press.

Dobrin, S. (2011). *Postcomposition*. Carbondale, IL: Southern Illinois University Press.

Edbauer, J. (2005). Unframing models of public distribution: From rhetorical situation to rhetorical ecologies. *Rhetoric Society Quarterly, 35*(4), 5–24.

Ede, L., & Lunsford, A. (2011). Audience addressed/audience invoked: The role of audience in composition theory and pedagogy. In V. Villanueva & K. Arola (Eds.), *Cross-talk in comp theory* (3rd ed., pp. 77–95). Urbana, IL: National Council of Teachers of English.

Gries, L. (2011). Agential matters: Tumbleweed, women-pens, citizens-hope, and rhetorical actancy. In S. Dobrin (Ed.), *Ecology, writing theory, and new media* (pp. 67–91). London, UK: Routledge.

Gries, L. (2015). *Still life with rhetoric: A new materialist approach for visual rhetoric*. Logan, UT: Utah State University Press.

Hawk, B. (2007). *A counter-history of composition: Toward methodologies of complexity*. Pitts-burgh, PA: University of Pittsburgh Press.

Jack, J. (2006). Chronotopes: Forms of time in rhetorical arguments. *College English, 69*(1), 52–73.

Jensen, R. E. (2010). *Dirty words: The rhetoric of public sex education, 1870–1924*. Urbana, IL: University of Illinois Press.

Jensen, R. E. (2015). An ecological turn in rhetoric of health scholarship: Attending to the historical flow and percolation of ideas, assumptions, and arguments. *Communication Quarterly, 63*(5), 522–526.

Johnson, N. R. (2012). Information infrastructure as rhetoric: Tools for analysis. *Poroi, 8*(1), Article 10.

Jung, J. (2014, April 7). Systems rhetoric: A dynamic coupling of explanation and description. *Enculturation*. Retrieved from www.enculturation.net/systems-rhetoric.

Keränen, L. (Ed.). (2014). Medicine, health, and publics [Special issue]. *Journal of Medical Humanities, 35*(2).

McCorkle, B. (2012). *Rhetorical delivery as technological discourse*. Carbondale, IL: Southern Illinois University Press.

Milbourne, C., & Hallenbeck, S. (2013). Gender, material chronotopes, and the emergence of the eighteenth-century microscope. *Rhetoric Society Quarterly, 43*(5), 401–424.

Ong, W. J. (1975). The writer's audience is always a fiction. *PMLA, 90*(1), 9–21.

Peiss, K. L. (1986). *Cheap amusements: Working women and leisure in turn-of-the-century New York*. Philadelphia, PA: Temple University Press.

Pflugfelder, E. H. (2015). Is no one at the wheel? Nonhuman agency and agentive move-ment. In P. Lynch & N. Rivers (Eds.), *Thinking with Bruno Latour in rhetoric and composi-tion* (pp. 176–200). Carbondale, IL: Southern Illinois University Press.

Pivar, D. (2002). *Purity and hygiene: Women, prostitution, and the "American Plan," 1900–1930*. Westport, CT: Greenwood.

Porter, J. (2009). Recovering delivery for digital rhetoric. *Computers and Composition, 26*(4), 207–224.

Prior, P., & Hengst, J. (2010). Introduction: Exploring semiotic remediation. In P. Prior & J. Hengst (Eds.), *Exploring semiotic remediation as discourse practice* (pp. 1–23). New York, NY: Palgrave Macmillan.

Prior, P., & Shipka, J. (2003). Chronotopic lamination: Tracing the contours of literate activity. In C. Bazerman & D. Russell (Eds.), *Writing selves/writing societies* (pp. 180–238). Fort Collins, CO: The WAC Clearinghouse.

Rickert, T. (2004). In the house of doing: Rhetoric and the kairos of ambience. *JAC, 24*(4), 901–927.

Ridolfo, J. (2012). Rhetorical delivery as strategy: Rebuilding the fifth canon from practi-tioner stories. *Rhetoric Review, 31*(2), 117–129.

Ridolfo, J. (2015). Rethinking human and non-human actors as a strategy for rhetori-cal delivery. In S. Dobrin (Ed.), *Writing posthumanism, posthuman writing* (pp. 174–191). Anderson, SC: Parlor Press.

Rivers, N., & Weber, R. (2011). Ecological, pedagogical, public rhetoric. *College Composi-tion and Communication, 63*(2), 187–219.

Roderick, N. R. (2012). Analogize this! The politics of scale and the problem of substance in complexity-based composition. *Composition Forum, 25*. Retrieved from http://com positionforum.com/issue/25/scale-substance-complexity.php.

Rude, C. (2004). Toward an expanded concept of rhetorical delivery: The uses of reports in public policy debates. *Technical Communication Quarterly, 13*(3), 271–288.

Schryer, C. F. (1999). Genre time=space: Chronotopic strategies in the experimental article. *JAC, 19*(1), 81–89.

Schryer, C. F. (2002). Genre and power: A chronotopic analysis. In R. Coe, L. Lingard, & T. Teslenko (Eds.), *The rhetoric and ideology of genre: Strategies for stability and change* (pp. 73–102). Cresskill, NJ: Hampton.

Scott, J. B. (2014). Afterword: Elaborating health and medicine's publics. *Journal of Medical Humanities, 35*(2), 229–235.

Shepley, N. (2013, February 28). Rhetorical-ecological links in composition history. *Enculturation*. Retrieved from http://enculturation.net/rhetorical-ecological-links.

The social hygiene movement [Editorial]. (1913, November). *American Journal of Public Health, 3*(11), 1154–1157.

Social purity is discussed (n.d.). *Newburgh Daily Journal*. Emma Elizabeth Walker papers, Sophia Smith Collection, Smith College, Northampton, MA.

Spinuzzi, C., & Zachry, M. (2000). Genre ecologies: An open-system approach to understanding and constructing documentation. *Journal of Computer Documentation, 24*(3), 169–181.

Syverson, M. A. (1999). *The wealth of reality: An ecology of composition*. Carbondale, IL: Southern Illinois University Press.

New York Social Hygiene Society. (1910). *Transactions of the American society of sanitary and moral prophylaxis: Vol. I*. New York, NY: Author.

New York Social Hygiene Society. (1910). *Transactions of the American society of sanitary and moral prophylaxis: Vol. III*. New York, NY: Author.

Trimbur, J. (2000). Composition and the circulation of writing. *College Composition and Communication, 52*(2), 188–219.

Walker, E. E. (n.d.). Untitled lectures, Emma Elizabeth Walker papers, Sophia Smith Collection, Smith College, Northampton, MA.

Yancey, K. B. (2006). *Delivering college composition: The fifth canon*. Portsmouth, NH: Boynton/ Cook.

4

INFRASTRUCTURAL METHODOLOGY

A Case in Protein as Public Health

Nathan R. Johnson

Keywords: information infrastructure, ploche, protein, boundary objects, methodology

In this chapter I describe an infrastructural approach to rhetoric in health and medicine. An infrastructural approach explores how shared, background resources politicize the knowledge work of health and medicine. This kind of approach gives insight into how organizational techniques like layout design of medical records, classifications used in pain assessment charts, or the organizational blueprints of hospital areas, for instance, change how health and medicine are imagined and practiced. In this chapter, the infrastructural approach described provides a set of conceptual tools. These tools provide a lens that needs to be accompanied by other research techniques, so to illustrate I draw on the rhetorical tradition to perform a rhetorical-historical study of protein classifications. More specifically, after describing an infrastructural approach, I illustrate it by looking at how "protein" became an object of concern that was built into classification systems of modern nutrition and health, identifying how work done to popularize protein as a health intervention in the 19th and 20th centuries generated several distinctive epistemic regimes influential in contemporary public health.

A Modern Practice of Protein Health

In 2009 Ethan Brown founded Beyond Meat, an organization that sells vegetarian facsimiles of meat products (Foster, 2013). Beyond Meat's line of alternative products includes genetically modified foods like "beast burgers" and "beyond chicken tenders," assembled primarily with pea protein. Brown and many others like him maintain that consuming fewer animal products helps with "improving human health, positively impacting climate change, conserving natural resources and respecting animal welfare" (Beyond Meat, 2015). Organizations like Beyond Meat act as just one vehicle of the abundant number of public movements to raise awareness about environmentally conscious forms of protein.

Alternative meat sources are contentious territory, though. Early advocates of animal-free diets often equated health and vegetarianism with religious devotion (Spencer, 1996, pp. 65–80). Antimeat groups have long defended the rights of animals on principle, an early case being that of the Greek mathematician Pythagoras who suggested that meat eating was wrong because animals, like their human counterparts, had souls (Spencer, 1996, pp. 39–47). Still, Ethan Brown's contemporary claims for meatless meat are compelling for reasons not always put forward in arguments for meat alternatives. He compares the environmental sustainability of pea protein to animal protein. According to Brown, it can take 7.5 pounds of dry feed and 30 liters of water to produce one pound of boneless chicken breast, but it only takes 1.1 pounds of ingredients and two liters of water to produce a pound of Beyond Meat (Foster, 2013). In comparing proteins instead of foodstuffs, Brown convincingly argues that he is simply doing what industrialized farm factories already do: reconstituting vital nutrients through intensive production methods. It's just that Brown's pea protein requires far fewer natural resources than farm-factory chicken. Given previous cultural, religious, and health concerns, his comparison places a tremendous emphasis on understanding animal foods as mostly strings of hydrogens, carbons, oxygens, and nitrogens linked together as an amino acid.

Comparing foodstuffs in terms of proteins requires significant infrastructural work. By suggesting one type of amino acid—one found in animal flesh—is like another—one found in vegetable matter—Brown draws attention away from the provenance, culture, and sociology of food, and he forwards a food culture that prioritizes proteins and sustainability. Unmistakably, in some sense a piece of chicken processed through farm factory methods is not the same as a petri dish of protein that had been assembled from peas. But Brown's argument necessitates that his audience willingly go along with his translation of food into amino acid, and it's not even possible to make this argument and see a "protein" without the background work of scientific infrastructure. Brown's comparison depends on a long-established health information infrastructure to provide the backing for his advocacy.

What Is Information Infrastructure?

Information infrastructure consists of shared, pervasive resources of knowledge work (Bowker, Baker, Millerand, & Ribes, 2007). Infrastructures are embodied in standards, classifications, protocols, and algorithms (Johnson, 2012; Star & Ruhleder, 1996). They are often palpable through an ever-shifting list of materials: computers, databases, classification systems, field data, archival data, etc. Although those materials aren't infrastructure on their own, they connect users with the shared networks of standards, classifications, protocols, and algorithms that provide the dependable background of knowledge work.

Often, the most critical components of information infrastructure are the most mundane. They are embedded into social practices and become the material of everyday life (Star & Ruhleder, 1996, p. 113). While the glimmering medical information infrastructure of today consists of the technologies supporting electronic medical records and evidence-based techniques, more foundational technologies—classifications for disease and regimented techniques of patient care—are more fundamental for doing the everyday work of health and medicine (Bowker & Star, 1999; Bowker, Timmermans, & Star, 1996). The more mundane parts sink into the environment, becoming more embedded in use and providing support for newer components. For instance, without a good disease classification, it's difficult to fill out the diagnosis box in an electronic medical record.

When infrastructures are working well, their components work together seamlessly and are unnoticed. Indeed, the hallmark of a working infrastructure is that it is invisible. Ironically, infrastructures are most visible when they are in the midst of breakdown and crisis. When infrastructural technologies break, they cause massive interruptions in knowledge work. The more foundational and global the infrastructure, the more likely it can cause global, catastrophic problems. Electronic medical records aren't yet globally adopted, and if the software that ran them ceased to work, it would be less of a problem than if all access to the International Classification of Diseases (ICD) disappeared. Either way, when infrastructure stops working or breaks down, it causes big problems for users. Notably, some infrastructure breakdowns may only affect specific user groups, like when an Internet provider's service goes down for a subset of its clients.

Even though information infrastructure aids knowledge work, its components are often noninformational. For instance, the electrical grid is one of the most important components of today's medical infrastructure. Without it, computers that run hospital databases, life support devices keeping patients alive, and digital diagnostic equipment fail. The importance of the grid becomes recognizable when it ceases to work. It's during breakdown that the infrastructural devices of health and medicine cease to seem like "natural" parts of the environment. And if you've ever witnessed the work that it takes to keep the power grid producing energy, you witnessed that it takes an enormous amount of hidden labor to sustain infrastructures that support everyday knowledge work. That work makes it easy to take infrastructure for granted by making information infrastructure seem natural.

Two techniques that establish infrastructure as natural are its embedded materiality and its anticipation of audiences' needs. Consider the ICD for example. The ICD is the World Health Organization's diagnostic tool for medical diagnosis. Medical and health care providers use it to classify diseases for use in patient records, and it's important in the work of many groups that practice knowledge for health and medicine. The ICD stabilizes a vocabulary of diseases and distributes them in a reproducible form, both print and electronic.

Copies (both print and digital) of the ICD have become so important for medical work, that it's nearly impossible to perform some tasks without them. The embedded distribution of the ICD makes it seem like the diseases it names are natural and recognizable parts of the medical world. Yet because infrastructure must meet the diverging needs of different audiences, those diseases are much less straightforward than they may seem. Infrastructural technologies like the ICD bridge relationships between several groups that have different information needs. Statisticians, interested in identifying generalizable themes of disease, are not particularly concerned with a classification that allows doctors to diagnose rare instances of disease. Indeed, an overly verbose ICD makes their quantitative analysis more time-consuming, because it means there is more data to clean (Bowker & Star, 1999, p. 114). Meanwhile, public health officials want every disease documented as meticulously as possible to ward off potential pandemics. Oftentimes, especially when services are unregulated, the groups with the most financial clout have the greatest influence over infrastructure development.

The ICD's contents accommodate many groups, and consequently its classifications become a compromise in objectivity. In working infrastructure, the conflicting needs of various groups are consolidated into shared resources. Powerful groups get more of their interests represented in infrastructure, while less powerful groups have less influence over its articulation. In practice, with a technology like the ICD, this means that a few types of cholera strains might be lumped into one classification to meet the needs of statisticians while different types of flu are split meticulously to head off potentially serious and deadly diseases. To cite another example, many groups are currently advocating for electronic health records (EHRs) as an infrastructural technology that will bolster quality and efficiency in medical practice. These technologies often are harder for smaller institutions to adapt because they require a standardized network infrastructure. Computer problems can bring a small medical practice to a halt. Yet insurance providers are frequently the most interested in EHR adoption because this technology makes it easier to bill patients (Blumenthal & Glaser, 2007). Successful infrastructural technology anticipates the needs of the groups and entities most likely to benefit from its use.

All of that background difference disappears in the materialized, embedded versions of infrastructure like the ICD. In everyday use, the ICD simply looks like a long list of diseases. The primary user groups and their needs aren't written into its pages, and it underrepresents the needs of less powerful groups who might benefit from a similar tool. For instance, tropical diseases are underrepresented because the classification primarily caters to medical labor in the industrialized world and its climates (Bowker & Star, 1999, p. 114). Infrastructure is important for many, but its pervasive work is often invisible until it doesn't work, which depends not only on whether it's technically breaking down, but also for whom it isn't working. Consequently, identifying potential infrastructural breakdowns and underserved groups becomes important for providing equitable access to health and medical care.

Infrastructural Method

Because the imbalances of infrastructure often remain hidden, it can be difficult to identify how some ways of knowing are legitimized over others. This is one reason an infrastructural methodology aided by rhetoric can be particularly illuminating and practical. Working infrastructure often stays invisible (Star & Ruhleder, 1996). It often fades into the background and becomes transparent (Bowker & Star, 1999, p. 34). A rhetorical approach gets at the invisibility of infrastructure by taking advantage of tools that rhetoricians have developed for identifying how symbols and materials exert influence through argument.[1] For instance, rhetoricians may be particularly adept at identifying key metaphors important for an infrastructure's classification system. In this volume, Ehrenfeld notes how discursive forms are sustained through ecological investments in material infrastructures. While Ehrenfeld focuses on evolving infrastructures, in this chapter I locate how rhetoric works to create closure in health infrastructures. As such, I see these two approaches as complementary. Rhetorical analyses like Ehrenfeld's and the one offered here help to further understand infrastructure and rhetoric.

The two facets of infrastructure described above—embedded materiality and anticipation of audience needs—provide starting points for an infrastructural approach to health and medicine, especially when paired with rhetorical figures. In the following historical case I remix these two facets of infrastructure with the rhetorical concepts of ploche and metonymy. When ploche, which provides emphasis by invoking the same concept repeatedly, is synthesized with infrastructure's embedded materiality, it becomes a rhetorical concept that I call a *republication*. When metonymy, which transfers aspects of one idea to another, is synthesized with infrastructural references to audience, it becomes a rhetorical concept I refer to as an infrastructural *translation*. These infrastructure/rhetoric pairings are discriminating tools for investigating rhetoric in the infrastructure of health and medicine. These pairings are not exhaustive of all possible infrastructural approaches, but they are two components that contribute to a larger methodological suite targeting the rhetorical work of infrastructure (Johnson, forthcoming).

Infrastructural Republications and Translations

Republications are infrastructural objects that are replicated and distributed in multiple places and times. Republications happen when information or objects supporting informational practices are duplicated to provide reliable experiences in different environments. They share theoretical kinship with two concepts from

Science and Technology Studies (STS): immutable mobiles and boundary objects (Latour, 1986, p. 198; Star & Griesemer, 1989; Wilson & Herndl, 2007). Immutable mobiles are physically durable meaning-making objects that can be moved from one location to another (Latour, 1986, pp. 10–11). Microscopes are good examples of immutable mobiles since they can easily be moved and generate meaning in new contexts (Latour, 1987, pp. 122–123). Printed books are also good examples, as they perform similar functions. Books are moved from one location to another while maintaining their physical properties (Latour, 1986, p. 11).

Boundary objects act as a more specific type of immutable mobile (Star & Griesemer, 1989, p. 411). They are durable like immutable mobiles, but are more flexibly interpreted (Star, 2010). Different groups use boundary objects for diverging purposes even though the object has the same physical durability. Books, again, are a good example of a boundary object as well as an immutable mobile, since they can be interpreted in multiple ways even though they share duplicate physical characteristics. One reader will take away different ideas from the same print source. Readers will share the same resource, although it may have a different meaning to each of them. Maps are also good examples of boundary objects because they can be used for a variety of different purposes: finding locations, identifying routes, or measuring area (Star & Griesemer, 1989, pp. 408–412). When immutable mobiles can be flexibly interpreted, they take on the characteristics of boundary objects.

Immutable mobiles and boundary objects are complicated when they can easily be duplicated and distributed, because surrogate objects seem to maintain durability of an "original" even when distributed. Consequently, immutable mobiles and boundary objects are more complex in networked spaces, like information infrastructures, which specialize in duplication and distribution of multiple copies. In the Industrial Age, boundary objects could be turned into legions of physical copies. In the Electronic Age, the technical logic of digital communication could quickly produce numerous electronic copies of boundary objects. More recently, 3-D printing is now bringing the same speed and travel of digital communication to three-dimensional objects.

Placing duplicate copies of objects in separate locations changes their perceived time and space (Latour, 1986, p. 11). They create a feeling omnitopia, which "represents the construction and performance of geographically distinct spaces as perceptually ubiquitous" even though omnitopia "does not appear as a singular . . . but as a matrix" (Wood, 2003, pp. 325–326). While omnitopia often refers to place, it also refers to information within places. For instance, the ability to read a webpage on a work computer and then on a tablet at home makes it seem as though web information is ubiquitous, regardless of space, even though it takes significant background technology and labor to continually serve webpages of the same information. That infrastructural work provides a sense of ubiquity. When informational materials are distributed through infrastructure, they become omnitopical, infrastructural republications. Infrastructure deploys information while also replicating multiple copies and technologies in different times and spaces. The protein case discussed in the next section looks at how food labels act as republications that distribute ubiquitous knowledge.

Health and medical infrastructures rely on republications to sustain knowledge practices. As an example, consider the ICD, which is reproduced and distributed across multiple work environments and used during medical diagnosis. Whether in digital or printed form, it would be difficult, if not impossible, to diagnose a disease if access to the ICD was lost. Very little and arguably no long-term diagnostic knowledge work could be conducted without the ICD's overwhelming number of descriptions of disease. Republications do not just consist of textual materials like the ICD, but also more invisibly through equipment that hardwires algorithms and measurements. For instance, EEG tests provide sensors and measurement scales that enable diagnosticians to measure electrical patterns in the brain. Without the measurement techniques hardwired into EEG technology, it would be incredibly difficult to reproduce practices or conduct tests that diagnose diseases like epilepsy. Republications materialize background information and make it seem like natural phenomena. Republications distribute material evidence that users need to conduct more complicated medical practice.

Republications frequently work in tandem with infrastructural translations. Again, the STS concept of boundary objects is helpful here. Translations project some audience needs from one epistemic community into another through a shared infrastructural object, simultaneously legitimizing and interpellating those needs into new audiences. The flexible interpretation associated with boundary objects metonymically traffics some user needs into new communities. For example, translations occur when the ICD's list of diseases allows diagnoses that wouldn't have been as likely in the past; the inclusion of ICD diagnosis code F90.9 for attention-deficit hyperactivity disorder now allows subjects across the globe to be classified as hyperactive, regardless of how appropriate this diagnosis is in a specific case. Translations spread user needs into multiple groups. Reframing these STS concepts has the benefit of foregrounding the material constraints of rhetorical action. In the following case, as language about science techniques has become more embodied in public technologies of health such as nutrition labels, it has become more difficult to deploy alternate models without some recourse to popular ones.

Here, I deploy translations and republications as sensitizing concepts, a term used by sociologist Harold Blumer (1954). Blumer writes that sensitizing concepts "lack precise reference and have no bench marks which allow a clean-cut identification of a specific instance and of its content" (1954, p. 7). Rather, sensitizing concepts provide researchers with a direction to look. Thus, Blumer contrasts sensitizing concepts with definite ones, explaining that the latter have benchmarks or fixed attributes and that the former point to more abstract ideas, like "culture, institutions, social structure, mores, and personality" (1954, p. 7). Sensitizing concepts are useful for alerting researchers to concepts that are hidden among more noticeable action. This is a central reason why sensitizing concepts are useful for identifying rhetoric in infrastructure. Rhetoric is often adept at staying hidden. Unrecognized metaphors often exert great conceptual force during communication. And simultaneously, infrastructure often remains hidden until it doesn't work for someone.

Sensitizing concepts are flexible in that they lend themselves to a number of collection, coding, and production strategies for research. They are often generated with the coding procedures of grounded theory (Bowen, 2006). In the following case, I developed the sensitizing concepts by combining key ideas from rhetoric and infrastructure. Translations were developed by recognizing how messages are adapted to audiences and how infrastructures bridge multiple audiences. Republications were developed by recognizing how standardized infrastructure repeats some of its most important parts to provide a sense of consistency across space and time.

In the next section, I describe a historical case study exploring the multiple discursive registers surrounding protein as a public health concept in the 19th, 20th, and 21st centuries. Although the history is significant as a study of public health, this paper forwards the two methodological concepts for rhetoricians of medicine: translations and republications. These two concepts are infrastructural rhetorics—the epistemological and sociotechnical supports of disciplined knowing. Translations and reproductions are one part of a large methodological apparatus for investigating infrastructure in the sciences (Johnson, forthcoming). Investigating infrastructural rhetorics helps to investigate why scientists, engineers, technologists, and medical practitioners frame problems and how their solutions can be interpreted among different audiences.

My case study used the sensitizing concepts to interpret archival documents. By specifically reading for moments of translation and republication, I was able to better understand how the logic of a protein infrastructure had developed over the past several centuries. Because of this, sensitizing concepts were used in combination with more established archival methods and especially informed by recent material approaches within rhetoric and composition (Clary-Lemon, 2014; Ramsey, Sharer, L'Eplattenier, & Mastrangelo, 2010). This study was prompted because I wanted to better understand why a company that produces a frankenfood promotes its use of protein. I was intrigued by Beyond Meat, a company promoting sustainability through "protein." More than that, after reading several stories about Beyond Meat, I was curious about the rhetorical constraints of nutrition labels as advertising techniques. Elsewhere in this volume, Wells and Stormer identify this as an axiological approach to history in the rhetoric of health & medicine, an approach that helps to highlight how notions of health come to be normalized.

Protein as Public Technology

The history of modern nutrition science includes an important touchstone in mid-19th century Germany. In 1838, the Dutch physician Gerrit Mulder used previous chemistry research to create a new component of foods that he called "protein." According to Mulder, these foods contained the same underlying "protein" radical characterized by a consistent ratio of nitrogen to other elements $(C_{40}H_{62}N_{10}O_{12})$. Mulder was self-taught as a chemist—his formal training was actually in medicine. In a letter to Swedish chemist Jacob Berzelius, he described how he trained himself to get reliable lab results by analyzing cane sugar samples hundreds of times. Each analysis took over seven hours (Brouwer, 1952). His protein research showed that the foods egg albumin, serum albumin, fibrin, and gluten all contained the same proportion of nitrogen, carbon, hydrogen, and oxygen, the only difference being the amount of phosphorous and sulfur attached to molecules of different foods. As he explains, Mulder chose the word "protein" from the Greek word for "primary,"—proteios—indicating that he thought it the root substance of animal nutrition:

> I chose to derive from the Greek word πρωτεοδ (proteios), because it appears to be the fundamental or primary substance of animal nutrition which plants prepare for herbivores, and whole in turn supply it to the carnivores.
>
> *(Carpenter, 1994a, p. 43)*

Until that point, the foods Mulder grouped together were considered separate substances with different properties—related to be sure, but very different in terms of their uses and properties. Mulder's primary contribution to chemistry was to impose a new type of order on the foods with a disciplinary term.

Mulder's protein radical caught on as an idea in the chemistry community. After his early work, many other chemists came to believe that fundamental problems of life could be explained by the concept of protein even as Mulder himself was skeptical of the extent of his findings (Brouwer, 1952). Many came to regard Mulder's protein radical as the elementary building block of animal and plant life. Famed German chemist Justus von Liebig, for example, was one of the primary supporters of the protein research, and even went as far as to suggest that the protein radical was the *only* nutritional substance. For him, "the function of the carbohydrates and fats in foods was reduced to their reacting with oxygen in the lungs, which protected the tissues from a toxic level of oxygen, and as a result, they served also as a source of animal heat" (Carpenter, 1986). In following, Liebig and his students developed precise, replicable techniques for analyzing protein. These techniques were oriented toward analysis of substances during periods when they were not interacting with human bodies; measuring nitrogen in food and in urine was a popular technique, for instance. Chemists apparently preferred to do their work without the messiness of the human body, and hence created Latourian black boxes (1987, pp. 1–20) for the research community of the time.

A set of socioanalytic transformations was happening in the Liebig camp and its supporters. These were infrastructural translations, and Bruno Latour's (1999) descriptions of soil science research are useful for clarifying these transformations (pp. 49–51). Latour notes that deploying equipment that allows soil to be stripped from the ground generates scientific evidence that can be studied as samples rather than as part of an embedded context. The resulting science can make generalizations about the soils with reference to provenance. Strings of inferences are built into the resulting soil findings. Black boxed inferences warrant some ways of knowing while delegitimizing others.

Hence, primary research in organic chemistry on animal nutrition defined health and nutrition in terms of proteins, carbohydrates, and fats, terms still in public circulation today. Yet modern chemists rarely deal with the macronutrients or engage in public discourse on health. Chemistry as a discipline doesn't add much to public health conversations. Today, public health advocacy on nutrition is left largely to scholars in nutrition sciences, physiology, kinesiology, and dietetics. And these fields tend to organize their health-related research questions with other concepts: amino acids, vitamins, or whole foods. The macronutrients aren't a popular technical vocabulary in "scientific" research today (Ahuja, Moshfegh, Holden, & Harris, 2013; Haytowitz, Pehrsson, & Holden, 2008). They really weren't *ever* very popular within the field of physiology, which focuses on animals in their environment. However, macronutrient discourse related to protein *is* circulated through quasiexperts, government legislation, or the lay public.

Here's a little more background to how this happened. In the late 19th century, chemists began to shift their focus from macronutrient profiling to practical problems related to human diseases—scurvy, beriberi, and kwashiorkor. Early attempts to "cure" these diseases had been conducted under the protein paradigm but were largely unsuccessful. Health historian Kenneth Carpenter (1994a) suggests that protein had become the popular theoretical basis in animal chemistry but that early attempts to cure these diseases under that paradigm were either unproductive or coincidental (for example, the introduction of a "high protein" diet coincided with an overall larger variety and more foods). It wasn't until other chemists identified objects like vitamins that any progress was made for treating the malnutrition diseases of the time.

This protein logic in chemistry also started weakening because of studies that measured nitrogen in human waste. Because nitrogen was a basic component of "proteins," some chemists ran experiments monitoring the amount of nitrogen they ate in foods and compared it to the amount that left their body in feces and urine, during sedentary and active periods. They noted no difference in nitrogen going in versus coming out regardless of how active they were, which weakened the idea that protein was as important as the German school suggested. The most famous experiment of this type involved two chemists who measured nitrogen in their urine as they walked up and down a Swiss mountain. Theirs was a crude study, but it provided evidence to rethink the protein paradigm.

Others challenged the protein paradigm by running experiments with international populations, third world countries, or by doing short-term clinical experiments with low protein diets. American chemist Russell Chittenden is notable for challenging the protein paradigm. His research was conducted with the typical scientific rigor associated with modern science: replicability and reliability (Taylor, 1991). He took his own daily dietary and urine histories to determine nitrogen excretion and protein utilization while recording his own body weight for nine months. Although his weight decreased from 65 to 58 kg, his daily protein intake was one third of what Voit recommended to maintain nitrogen equilibrium, and his health remained excellent without compromising physical vigor or muscular tone.

In a follow up, yearlong study, he put athletic men in excellent health on a low protein diet (less than 1 gram per kg daily) with similar results. Chittenden's data showed that, even without a large protein intake, individuals could maintain their health and fitness (Carpenter, 1994a; Katch, 1998; Vickery, 1945). He published pictures of his men to circulate new evidence. There are also pictures of Chittenden conducting the research on himself in order to smash the protein paradigm.

The Germans responsible for the protein paradigm resisted adopting a different perspective. Nutrition historians have noted that Liebig, Voit, and Rubner personally conducted experiments that showed that protein wasn't as important as they suggested, but they simply ignored the results or reinterpreted them to fit their theoretical lens.

In other scientific fields like physiology, the protein paradigm was never really accepted because of the types of inferences chemists made. Chemists didn't like touching human bodies; they liked measuring food with chemical processes. Physiologists didn't believe that *human* health could be adequately discussed without addressing *human* or at least *animal* bodies (Carpenter, 1994a). The few experiments of the time record how dogs were fed diets of only sugar as a way of seeing whether protein was essential. The dogs frequently died, which provided the *pathos* and *logos* to fortify that protein was a component of animal health. At no point during this time did the chemists hypothesize that by cutting off some of a food supply, they were concomitantly cutting off other major parts. These types of experiments ended up being a huge part of the reason that some chemists suggested at one point that protein was the only essential nutrient, while others remained skeptical. So, when chemistry studies were done on animals, they usually consisted of feeding dogs starvation diets while assuming they simply weren't eating enough protein.

There is further evidence of how the protein paradigm was lodged in contemporary public concerns, and I'll be touching on that later, but first, I want to clarify the argument. It's not that these early insights were incorrect, exactly, just that the creation and circulation of the terms pushed early research efforts and funding in a particular direction. When the "protein" concept was put into circulation, basic research in chemistry aimed to describe food components by breaking it into smaller components. Scholars familiar with the rhetorical tradition instantly recognize this as one of the classical Greek *topoi*—division—specifically the trope of *merismus*, which generates discursive force by dividing wholes into parts and emphasizing the part/whole relationship. This *merismus* was then used to make inferences about nutritional health.

Division *topoi* were a piece of what it meant to do organic chemistry, and this was built into a number of technical and analytical lenses of the time. For example, the technical work of assaying proteins involved heating substances with dilute caustic soda. Chemists would also wet flour to separate out gluten protein to provide a foundation for higher order work focused on how food interacts with other phenomena. This procedure divides gestalt foods into smaller categories of analysis, serving as one of the fundamental lenses of chemistry science. Divide. Divide. Divide. Chemistry was, and still occasionally is, a descriptive science of classification and division. The protein techniques of the time highlighted substances that look like protein at the gestalt level of analysis. The procedures filtered out other whole food components, and this is likely one of the reasons why vitamins weren't discovered until later. A fundamental substance of later chemistry literally washed out.

Thus, division *topoi* became a piece of what it meant to do organic chemistry, informing the scientific, technical and analytical lenses of the time. Carl Voit became famous for the analytical techniques he devised to do consistent food analysis. These techniques and tools could then be transported into other spheres. The chemistry work foregrounded macronutrients while backgrounding other concepts of food.

This division is a translation, one of the infrastructural rhetorics described above. In this case, the translation is the *merismus* from gestalt foodstuffs to protein/carbohydrate/fat subcategories and the translation from food structure to human health. Working to translate a phenomenon into a different set of terms, translations also metonymically transfer objects of infrastructure into new spaces. They can be identified by comparing the unifications and divisions of old and new terminologies. Translations are infrastructural rhetorics because they depend on and sustain regimes of knowing. They are like bricks in a wall; the bricks depend on the support below them while simultaneously holding up the work above them. A translation is simultaneously a discursive act and the conceptual support that enables a discursive event and is supported by a previous conceptual apparatus. Translations fortify some epistemic agendas while occluding others.

Despite disagreement over the role of protein, the early German chemists had fortified a research agenda built around a set of macronutrient vocabularies. After identifying protein in foods, Germans Carl Voit and Max Rubner advocated protein intakes of between 118 and 127 grams a day, based primarily on what they observed robust citizens of Germany eating. The reasoning was a little more complicated, but they essentially measured healthy populations and assumed they were naturally eating "correct" amounts of protein. Their "correct" amounts were enabled because of the emergence of protein as a conceptual component of health.

This discourse generated in Germany was decisive for U.S. public health. Wilbur Atwater, the inventor of the respiratory calorimeter, was trained by Justus Liebig. Atwater returned from his chemistry training in protein-crazed Germany espousing the ideas of his teachers. Food historian Andrew Smith (2009) notes that Atwater remained beholden to the high-protein paradigm for the rest of his life. In fact, he escalated the discourse by suggesting that Americans needed even more protein than Germans because they worked harder. The moralizing of his Protestant background combined with the language of protein combined both scientific and religious discourses. He wrote multiple popular articles about nutrition, protein, and health. One of his notable popular articles was called "What the Church can do toward improving the nutrition of the masses."

Atwater was a renowned chemist in America at the time, and his recommendations for eating a specific amount of protein were taken seriously. Decisively, he was instrumental in several important pieces of nutrition research and legislation that would set the tempo of public health infrastructure. First he published tables of protein in relation to health. These tables were circulated as institutionalized government documents of health, published with the same gravitas of today's FDA reports.

These tables are evidence of a classic infrastructural bootstrapping issue, in which the categories of an information infrastructure need to simultaneously constitute what the infrastructure can support without knowing what it will ultimately support (Bowker, 1994). As Atwater worked to turn protein into a category of health, he simultaneously worked to define health in terms of protein, regardless of what type of health it created. In this case, foods that could be classified as protein were then classified as "health" foods. Health foods were then sold and adopted by publics who were being convinced that they were supporting their health. You can imagine all the frankenfoods currently being manufactured as protein foods today.[2]

In the subsequent decades, the protein discourse was popularized and disseminated in the larger public sphere because of several social issues and events that highlighted a lack of food rather than an overabundance. More naturally seemed better than less. Protein was scientifically identified as one of the god terms of nutritional discourse in the public sphere, simultaneously situated amongst carbohydrates, fats, and calories as the cluster of health terms.

Much more happened in between Atwater's work and today's modern protein infrastructure. After the protein paradigm, a number of significant social events occurred that lodged protein in public discourse. Although covering the entire infrastructural history of modern protein is outside the scope of this overview of methodology, some of the major events included:

1. Passage of the Morrill Land Grant Act (1857) that provided University funding for Agricultural and Mechanical Arts.
2. Creation of the Department of Agriculture (1862) by Lincoln as a health policy organism.
3. Passage of the Hatch Act (1887) that provided federal funding of agricultural experiment stations. Atwater informally made sure that each station conducted nutrition research (Smith, 2009).
4. Beginning of publication of USDA food composition tables (1892) instigated by Atwater and documenting water, protein, fat, total carbohydrates and ash, calories, and refuse.
5. World War I (1914–1918), which foregrounded soldier nutrition as a national issue.
6. The Smith-Lever Act (1914) that funded cooperative extension services in each state to teach agriculture, home economics, and related subjects to the public, educating the public on protein health.
7. The Great Depression (1929–1939), which foregrounded poverty and hunger as a national problem.
8. World War II (1939–1945), which foregrounded a need to feed troop populations.
9. Creation of Recommended Dietary Allowances (RDA; 1941) as response to World War II.
10. Continuation of RDA through Reference Dietary Intakes (1968).
11. The creation of a national database based on Atwater's work—USDA National Nutrient Database for Standard Reference (1980)—which standardized the nutrient values of foods and is used for assessing food today.
12. Passage of Nutrition Labeling and Education Act (1990), which standardized nutrients on labels stamped on food products.

The passage of the Nutrition Labeling and Education Act standardized and produced a modern day infrastructural republication that Americans are now familiar with: the USDA mandated food label that divides up carbohydrates, fats, and proteins. These labels are reproduced on every package and legitimize a way of understanding that projects a particular category of health into the American diet. To be clear, I'm not arguing that protein is erroneously being identified in food, just that the identification foregrounds one area of health concern while backgrounding other factors, although vitamins are also on labels. In addition, it's important to note that some contemporary scientific communities produce competing discourses that focus on concepts that occlude protein as chief concept of nutrition and public health. The standardized food label generates a regime of health infrastructure that continually reminds the public of one notion of health.

In this case, look what is not foregrounded—the actual whole food as well as other categories that are considered important parts of health discourse today. These include other concepts like amino acids, RNA strands, geographical provenance, and pesticide use. The standardized label universalizes human health and synthesizes it as a classificatory regime that motivates publics. This is the work of a second part of my methodology—republications, the rhetorical transformation that occurs through repetition.

To review this aspect of an infrastructural method, recall that republications show how discourse is amplified through its continued and standardized repetition in information infrastructures, and in this case, food labels. This concept dovetails with previous work from Jeanne Fahnestock (1999) who has identified the Greek scheme *ploche*—repetition—as one of the key figures that organizes scientific discourse today. *Ploche*, originally the bang-the-listener-over-the-head repetition of orators, is similar to the repetition of label genres like those appearing in public spaces as part of health information infrastructure. It is similar to the recurrence of any health symbol that organizes a larger vocabulary—nutrition labels, standardized exercise routines, or standardized measurement technologies like Fitbits. When *ploche* is standardized and repeated throughout infrastructure, it becomes a republication. Republication bombards public discourse by repeating the same information in the same format over and over again across times, spaces, and people, lending credibility to a knowledge regime. As such, republications provide the background work enabling knowledge-making about health and medicine. They continually compel audiences to their legitimacy because they are so prevalent.

Where does this leave work in rhetoric of health of medicine? I suggest that scholars can identify and intervene in moments of translation and republication, asking questions about how and why infrastructure was produced, and how it is thereafter deployed. I suggest that medical rhetoricians may also be useful for retranslating infrastructure for the particular situations of individuals and groups. This case presents three possible moments of methodological intervention. First, describing a conceptual history of medical infrastructure produces a better understanding of why infrastructures have emerged in particular ways, and that awareness can provide grounds for advocating change. In this specific case, I suggested that the transformation of food into protein has generated a health regime that highlights knowledge of personal health instead of environmental sustainability. Second, sensitizing concepts highlight points where minor changes can make a big difference in infrastructure. In this case, I suggest that locating moments of translation and republication highlight points for change. A medical rhetorician may be attuned to the importance of particular gatekeepers whose decisions make differences across infrastructure. In this case, I would suggest that important points of infrastructural rhetoric include label designers and policy advocates. Infrastructural change has large-scale effects, and this bleeds into a third point for rhetoricians. Translations and republications are types of rhetoric that can inform argument. Rhetoricians of medicine can develop translations and republications to change infrastructure and large-scale practices. When rhetoricians attend to information infrastructure, they can identify important rhetorical traffic that pushes health and medicine to privilege some knowledge regimes over others.

Legitimizing Protein Through Infrastructural Rhetorics

Back to Ethan Brown and Beyond Meat. If meat substitutes are to be accepted, it is important to compare them to animal products in the consumer marketplace. In this chapter I have explored some of the infrastructural rhetorics that have gone into making that transition. Significant background work has generated sustained infrastructural rhetorics that allow food products to be seen in terms of their protein macronutrients. Indeed, without the intervention of a few chemists interested in nitrogen and urine, we may never have witnessed any advocacy for the protein frankenfoods of today.

Today's discussions about genetically modified foods are heated and contentious. An infrastructural approach like the one above can help highlight the important background work that supports the historically situated evidence of foodstuffs as protein. That same work draws attention away from other important reasons for adopting or rejecting vegetarian alternatives to meat, like those related to provenance, religious affiliation, or views on GMOs. More significantly, an infrastructural approach to rhetoric in health and medicine highlights invisible labor that sustains the taken-for-granted background of health and medicine. It highlights the groups that have been put at a disadvantage, sustainability advocates like Ethan Brown for example, because their ways of seeing aren't supported by dominant infrastructures of health and medicine.

Notes

1 In this volume, Angeli uncovers invisibility by mapping assemblages during observational research. A mixed methods approach that employs both her perspective and this historical one could be a formidable methodological suite that would more richly address the multiple concerns (materialist, axiological, practical, analogical, and cultural) raised by Wells and Stormer in their chapter on historiography.
2 As an aside, Atwater also did the same thing with alcohol. He ran an experiment that showed that liquor fulfilled fundamental nutrition needs for the population (Carpenter, 1994a). The alcohol industry ate this up and began marketing liquor as a health food. We still do this with wine today. Paradoxically, members of Atwater's Protestant faith— teetotalers—got really upset with him for advocating alcohol as a health food.

References

Ahuja, J. K. C., Moshfegh, A. J., Holden, J. M., & Harris, E. (2013). USDA food and nutrient databases provide the infrastructure for food and nutrition research, policy, and practice. *Journal of Nutrition, 143*(2), 241S–249S.

Beyond Meat. (2015). *Beyond Meat: Our mission* [Commercial Website]. Retrieved November 28, 2015, from http://beyondmeat.com/about

Blumenthal, D., & Glaser, J. P. (2007). Information technology comes to medicine. *The New England Journal of Medicine, 356*(24), 2527–2534.

Blumer, H. (1954). What is wrong with social theory? *American Sociological Review, 19*(1), 3–10.

Bowen, G. A. (2006). Grounded theory and sensitizing concepts. *International Journal of Qualitative Methods, 5*(3), 12–23.

Bowker, G. C. (1994). *Science on the run: Information management and industrial geophysics at Schlumberger, 1920–1940.* Cambridge, MA: MIT Press.

Bowker, G. C., Baker, K., Millerand, F., & Ribes, D. (2007). Toward information infrastructure studies: Ways of knowing in a networked environment. In J. Hunsinger, L. Klastrup, & M. Allen (Eds.), *International handbook of Internet research* (pp. 97–118). New York, NY: Springer Verlag.

Bowker, G. C., & Star, S. L. (1999). *Sorting things out: Classification and its consequences.* Cambridge, MA: MIT Press.

Bowker, G. C., Timmermans, S., & Star, S. L. (1996). Infrastructure and organizational transformation: Classifying nurses' work. In W. J. Orlikowski (Ed.), *Information technology and changes in organizational work* (pp. 344–370). London, UK: Chapman & Hall.

Brouwer, E. (1952). Gerrit Jan Mulder (1802–1880). *The Journal of Nutrition, 46*(1), 1–11.

Carpenter, K. J. (1986). *The history of scurvy and vitamin C.* Cambridge, UK: Cambridge University Press.

Carpenter, K. J. (1994a). *Protein and energy: A study of changing ideas in nutrition.* Cambridge, UK: Cambridge University Press.

Clary-Lemon, J. (2014). Archival research processes: A case for material methods. *Rhetoric Review, 33*(4), 381–402.

Fahnestock, J. (1999). *Rhetorical figures in science.* New York, NY: Oxford University Press.

Foster, T. (2013, November 18). Can artificial meat save the world? *Popular Science.* Retrieved from www.popsci.com/article/science/can-artificial-meat-save-world.

Haytowitz, D. B., Pehrsson, P. R., & Holden, J. M. (2008). The national food and nutrient analysis program: A decade of progress. *Journal of Food Composition and Analysis, 21*(S1), S94–S102.

Johnson, N. R. (2012). Information infrastructure as rhetoric: Tools for analysis. *Poroi, 8*(1), 1–3.

Katch, F. I. (1998). Russel Henry Chittenden (1856–1943). *Sports Science, 2*(4). Retrieved from www.sportsci.org/1998/4/index.html.

Latour, B. (1986). Visualization and cognition: Thinking with eyes and hands. *Knowledge and Society: Studies in the Sociology of Culture Past and Present, 6,* 1–40.

Latour, B. (1987). *Science in action: How to follow scientists and engineers through society.* Cambridge, MA: Harvard University Press.

Latour, B. (1999). *Pandora's hope: Essays on the reality of science studies.* Cambridge, MA: Harvard University Press.

Ramsey, A. E., Sharer, W. B., L'Eplattenier, B., & Mastrangelo, L. (Eds.). (2010). *Working in the archives practical research methods for rhetoric and composition.* Carbondale, IL: Southern Illinois University Press.

Smith, A. F. (2009). *Eating history: 30 turning points in the making of American cuisine.* New York, NY: Columbia University Press.

Spencer, C. (1996). *The heretic's feast: A history of vegetarianism.* Hanover, NH: University Press of New England.

Star, S. L. (2010). This is not a boundary object: Reflections on the origin of a concept. *Science, Technology & Human Values, 35*(5), 601–617.

Star, S. L., & Griesemer, J. R. (1989). Institutional ecology, "translations" and boundary objects: Amateurs and professionals in Berkeley's Museum of Vertebrate Zoology, 1907–1939. *Social Studies of Science, 19*(3), 387–420.

Star, S. L., & Ruhleder, K. (1996). Steps toward an ecology of infrastructure: Design and access for large information spaces. *Information Systems Research, 7*(1), 111–134.

Taylor, C. A. (1991). Defining the scientific community: A rhetorical perspective on demarcation. *Communication Monographs, 58*(4), 402–420.

Vickery, H. B. (1945). Biographical memoir of Russell Henry Chittenden, 1856–1943. In *National Academy of Sciences* (pp. 57–104). Washington, DC: National Academy of Sciences. Retrieved from www.nasonline.org/publications/biographical-memoirs/memoir-pdfs/chittenden-russell-h-1.pdf.

Wilson, G., & Herndl, C. G. (2007). Boundary objects as rhetorical exigence: Knowledge mapping and interdisciplinary cooperation at the Los Alamos National Laboratory. *Journal of Business and Technical Communication, 21*(2), 129–154.

Wood, A. (2003). A rhetoric of ubiquity: Terminal space as omnitopia. *Communication Theory, 13*(3), 324–344.

5

HEALTH COMMUNICATION METHODOLOGY AND RACE

Kelly E. Happe

Keywords: health disparities, race, critical research

In the fall of 2013, I attended an interdisciplinary conference of communication scholars that brought together both humanists and social scientists around the shared topic of discourses of health and medicine. At one point, the question of health disparities research came up, at which time I raised the question of whether we should look critically at how the race concept is operationalized in health disparities research and whether or not, as rhetorically oriented communication scholars, we might have something to contribute to the debate about its efficacy (and indeed, whether we had an ethical obligation to do so given the stakes). The responses I received, both publicly and privately, were not surprising, although no less discouraging: Was I really suggesting, asked my interlocutors, that we question our methodologies when *lives were at stake*?

To frame the debate in such terms—critique or life—brought to mind Paula Treichler's (1999) book *How to Have Theory in an Epidemic* in which she takes on the unenviable task of theorizing power, subjectivity, and social constructions of the normal and pathological within the context of the HIV/AIDS crisis. The book argues that communication about the disease is as much a site of interpretation and contestation as bodies themselves. Indeed, the one research question cannot be separated from the other, since particular communication practices have had both positive and devastating effects on bodies constructed as "risky" or "not risky"—a process inextricably bound with long-standing cultural norms.

The "critique or life" binary raised similar questions for me: How, as communication scholars, do we take seriously the abundance of scholarly work criticizing the use of race in biomedicine and public health? This is all the more pressing since several scholars have argued that health disparities research might actually *deflect* attention from the role of racism in the production of those very disparities. As rhetoric and communication scholars, are we not uniquely positioned to think critically about the terms used in communication about health? This is not simply a matter of pragmatic considerations—although this is important as well, since our goal is effective communication about health—it is also a question of the relationship between our methodologies and social justice.[1]

Taking the critique of health disparities as its starting point, this chapter argues for a reevaluation of race in health communication (including critical/ interpretive) and, by extension, related scholarship. In particular, I put forward the claim that the existence of racially differentiated health disparities does not, *ipso facto*, necessitate health communication messages based on racial identity. There are two reasons for this: First, the "discourse of disparity" that sometimes frames epidemiological and health communication research contributes to a broader discursive field in which attention is deflected from the historical-material conditions giving rise to the disparities themselves. The rhetoric of disparity also contributes to the implicit belief that disparities are a durable, biological feature of the racialized body. Second, the use of identity as a basis for effective health communication should be critically evaluated and possibly jettisoned. In so doing, communication scholars will bring to the study of health disparities a much needed rhetorical-critical-historical perspective on race and racialization and be better able to evaluate whether racial categories have the analytic force and explanatory power they are otherwise assumed to possess.

But first, on what methodological grounds are health disparities research critiqued by public health and critical race scholars? As recent research suggests that health disparities in disease diagnosis are growing (Gnagey, 2015), the limitations of this research are worth reflecting upon.

The Critique of Health Disparities Research

The use of the race concept in the biological and social sciences is hotly contested and has been since the early part of the 20th century (e.g., Montagu, 1964). What is not as well known is that the use of the race concept in health disparities research—research specifically aimed at challenging the notion that race is biological and offering instead evidence that disparities are an index of institutional racism—is also controversial, albeit for more nuanced reasons. In 2011, historian and public health scholar Merlin Chowkwanyun published an essay in the *DuBois Review* in which he made the case for critically evaluating the state of health disparities research. Speaking to an audience of both historians and social scientists, Chowkwanyun's major claim revolves around what he calls the "strange disappearance" of history from this area of health research. Although the rigorously collected and analyzed quantitative data upon which health disparities research relies is important to consider, what is missing, says Chowkwanyun,

> is a deeper understanding of how and why these social determinants of racial health disparities matter so much, the long-term *process* through which they came into being, and how they might have been avoided. I argue, then, that the major shortcoming in racial health disparities research is an absence of historical perspective that would enable exploration of historically rooted "fundamental causes." This analytical lacuna, in turn, may become a major pitfall, hampering fuller understanding of causal dynamics at exactly the moment when interest in racial health disparities has reached unprecedented levels.
>
> *(2011, p. 254)*

"Putting the past back in," Chowkwanyn (2011, p. 254) explains, would include examination of such factors as housing policy, demographic shifts, employment and labor trends, economic development initiatives, as well as the sundry and varied institutional mechanisms whereby these policies and initiatives are implemented, enforced, and/or undermined. Such a perspective, Chowkwanyun (2011) persuasively argues, allows, conceptually, for the possibility of change: such detail and specificity historical analyses afford not only tell us how the present came to be (an underappreciated benefit) but also when and how different choices could have been made with different results.

One could of course counter his critique by noting that epidemiology's goal is to document how institutional racism compromises an individual's *health*, but this goal is not, on its face, incompatible with the historical research Chowkwanyun (2011) says is necessary for elaborating root causes. There are, in fact, examples of critically and historically minded epidemiological projects that examine the connection between effects of geographically specific racism (such as social isolation experienced in present-day Chicago) and adverse health events (such as elevated glucocortisoid levels). Chowkwanyun's point is not that epidemiology is without significant use value, but that it unwittingly undermines the very critical perspective it purports to embrace. This outcome is the result of the particularities of quantitative research methods, in particular. As Chowkwanyun shows, in quantitative social science health disparities research, "race" is a static variable against which factors associated with health disparities are studied. Although for epidemiologists race is socially constructed, not a natural attribute of the human body, when race is a static variable in social scientific research, it starts to lose its status as a social construction.[2] This is because "race" is not subject to investigation as a concept that changes over time but instead, as an independent variable, takes on the attributes of an immutable, naturalized feature of the human body, whether understood as biology or behavior.[3] Use of the race concept in health disparities research ultimately results in findings that, at best, may not hold sufficient analytical force:

> But to the extent quantitative methodology—and its language of variables and associations—becomes predominant, its practitioners can unwittingly narrow the scope of analysis. Questions and their explanations become constricted by quantitative categories that can reduce complex social processes into variables for models. Moreover, explanation can take on a rather mechanical cause-effect form. Such a form then focuses heavily on individual-level characteristics or behaviors and how much they predict life chances in the larger social structure—but far less attention is given to how transformations of the latter can alter the former.
>
> *(Chowkwanyun, 2011, p. 258–259)*

Janet Shim (2002) advances a similar argument, noting that in epidemiology, accepted and routinized models (specifically, the multifactorial model of disease) require that the social reality of race be measured at the individual level. "This kind of devolution," she writes, "simplifies a complex world into smaller, presumably independent units of observation" (p. 132). Researchers choose those variables "closest" to the observed outcome (disease), and these "typically translate to the direct biological risks or causes of disease and/or to the lifestyles or behaviours addressable at the individual level" (p. 132). Inclusion of racial categories (inclusion that is often mandated by federal funding agencies)[4] allows epidemiologists the political advantage of claiming to address health disparities even though their data do not shed light on what it actually means for race to explain health—it is, in practice, merely assumed. The result has been disparities research that, for the most part, merely documents and describes the disparities themselves. Thus, one implication of the use of quantitative methodologies is that the disparities will persist, largely because the individual becomes, by default, solely responsible for societal-level causes.

The other implication is equally serious, and that is by continuing to operationalize race as an unexamined causal force, researchers surreptitiously insert biologistic thinking into epidemiological health research which then circulates among other fields of inquiry and the public sphere once their research findings are publicized. This biologistic thinking is the result of the rhetorical effect of these research findings: The repeated observation of the existence of race-based health disparities constitutes what Reed and Chowkwanyun (2012) term a "discourse of racial disparity" in which race and racism become a historical phenomenon that then "straitjackets research and tempts researchers, in Ian Shapiro's words, to 'load the dice in favor of one type of description,'" in this case, characterizing disparities as "racial" rather than the outcome of racialization "embedded in multiple social relations" including racialization, economic relations, and how the two variably intersect (pp. 150–151).[5]

Taking as their point of departure observations about the differential impact of the 2008–2009 economic crisis, and particularly the ways in which blacks were harder hit by the dramatic downturn, Reed and Chowkwanyun (2012) pay close attention to the collection of studies that serve as founding narratives of racialized economic disparity. Even when purporting to show the historical reasons for enduring disparities, these foundational studies nevertheless assume that "history powerfully exerts its effects at all times, from the creation of racial wealth gaps through their persistence to the present" (p. 161). Also central to the argument advanced by Reed and Chowkwanyun is that a sole focus on racial disparity does not have as much explanatory force as would appear given its inattention to political economy, class, and stages of capitalism—an inattention that reflects in turn "a class position tied programmatically to the articulation of a metric of social justice compatible with neoliberalism" (p. 169). Such a metric will at best fail to realize the necessary policy and regulatory reform and at worst enable a "strain of stigmatizing behavioural argument" (p. 166).

In health disparities research, historical conditions of something like psychosocial stress (which is thought to play a role in adverse health outcomes), conditions that would include capitalist-driven economic policy, become the rarified matter of racialized bodies. Put another way, historical specificity becomes transhistorical biological evidence, and a racialized form of biological evidence at that. Reed and Chowkwanyun (2012) counter that although injustices of the past are surely relevant to any historicization of disparity (of which race classifications matter), what is even more important is documenting precisely how the material conditions of the past may or may not be the historical conditions of the present. Meanings of race and racialization are thus reconceived to be the *result* of periodized intersections of unemployment, uneven economic redevelopment, maldistribution of wealth, and the like—not their cause.

Rhetoric and health communication scholars whose aim is to effectively reach those populations classified under the category "health disparities" can reproduce the very problematic logics of epidemiological research described above. For one, they rhetorically enact a "discourse of disparity" when they justify their studies on the basis of race-based differences in health outcomes alone. Like their counterparts in epidemiology and related fields, the goal is not to explain the disparities so as to intervene at the level of public policy, but to observe the disparities, acknowledge that racism is likely a key causal factor (amounting to what Reed and Chowkwanyun [2012, p. 163] describe as rhetorical "genuflection"), and set about the pragmatic task of communicating the existence of said disparities. More significantly, health communication research may exacerbate the individualizing, privatizing effects of disparities discourse insofar as messages are designed to alter "racial" behavior as a way to maximize health. Methodologically, this takes the form of employing racial identity as both a cause of health outcomes and the basis for particularized communication practices. As I will argue in the following section, however, it is not at all clear that the existence of health disparities necessitates recourse to *identity* as an analytic category. Furthermore, unreflexively employing the category of racial identity risks reifiying race when other categories of analysis will likely provide much greater explanatory power.

Methodology in Health Communication: Moving Beyond Rhetorics of Disparity and Identity

Health disparities communication research generally falls into two distinct yet overlapping categories: 1) health campaigns and outreach to underserved publics and 2) construction of culturally appropriate and thus more effective health messages. Both categories of research assume that biomedical and public health information plays a key role in exacerbating or ameliorating health disparities (information dissemination itself constitutes one such disparity) and that communication cannot be employed using a "one size fits all" model. As such, health communication research can be a crucial link between data about health disparities and a broader swath of persons, therefore enabling effective preventative and palliative care.

Regarding the first category, researchers rightly assume that members of underrepresented groups are unaware of particular threats to health and well-being and/or are unaware of or willing to seek preventive and palliative care due to lack of access, perceived lack of access, or prior experience with racist medical and public health practices. However, it is not clear whether outreach messaging must include observation of race-based disparities to be effective. In other words, there is a difference between communicating the need for regular health check-ups to underserved groups and communicating the need for check-ups based on the observation that African Americans, on the whole, are more likely to be diagnosed or to die from a particular disease. Some research, in fact, shows that including statements about race-based population level statistics may have the opposite effect intended. For example, in 2015, researchers reported that risk communication that includes information about race-based disparities can elicit angry responses that disincentivize action (Landrine and Corral, 2015).[6] Beyond the possibility that an implicit discourse of disparity can exact the opposite effect intended is the added likelihood that such a rhetoric will further add to the perception that black bodies are more susceptible to disease and therefore biologically different and inferior. "Disparity" does not imply that biological difference plays a role in disease outcomes; but the language of social science can enact this very slippage.

For example, Allicock, Graves, Gray, and Troester (2013) conducted an analysis of focus groups with African-American women ages 18–49. This study was important in many respects, most notably in the methodological decision to study just African-American women (as opposed to comparing them with white women),[7] thus reducing the chance that their conclusions would flatten out and/ or ignore completely the diverse communication needs of those women labeled or self-identified as African American. Nevertheless, the study's authors engage in unnecessary and potentially dangerous racial thinking when it comes to the fact of disparity. For example, Allicock et al. state that "race" is a risk factor for breast cancer based on statistical data but do not explain what they mean by this (it should be noted that other groups of women are not, to my knowledge, told that their risk has anything to do with their "race"). The authors further conclude that because their respondents wrongly perceived breast cancer to be a "white" disease, "communications should include race-specific and culturally appropriate images and messages" (p. 764). But there is no justification for this leap—it does not necessarily make sense to frame breast cancer as a "black" disease (by emphasizing disparity data and by framing the greater incidence of basal-like breast cancer as a "racial" phenomenon) in response to the misperception that it is a "white" disease. To do so would be to answer one categorical mistake with another or, put another way, to counter one problematic rhetoric of disparity with another (and I should note that researchers employing racial thinking and a rhetoric of disparity only when it comes to African-American women, not white women).

Regarding the second category of health communication research, the construction of culturally appropriate messages, the methodological stakes are more complex. The assumption underlying this research is that racial health disparities themselves necessitate race-based messaging. But upon further examination, it is not at all clear that this logical leap is justified or necessary. For one thing, at its most fundamental level, health disparities research documents the existence of the health effects of social, political, and economic material conditions. Its aspirational goal, in other words, is to collect population-level data regarding health outcomes as well as document how a phenomenon (e.g., elevated glucocortisoid levels) is causally connected to the lived experience of racialization. If anything, this research calls for raising awareness of the lived experience of racism and ensuring that all persons are aware of the risk of acute and chronic illness. This research does not imply that members of underrepresented groups communicate differently about health or do so to a degree that would warrant racial profiling in health communication messaging. While it may be the case that health disparities are exacerbated by the reluctance or inability of African Americans to seek preventative and palliative care, the move from racism to culture is neither warranted nor necessary. What seems to have occurred is that health communication scholars have substituted *identity* for *positionality*. I will address the concept of positionality later in the chapter but first want to take up the question of whether identity is a problematic category at all.

Rogers Brubaker and Frederick Cooper's (2000) critique of the use of identity in sociological research offers a helpful model for developing criteria that can be used to evaluate the way in which "race" is used in health communication research and whether its use has the explanatory power we think or hope that it does. Brubaker and Cooper argue that when social scientists pose their research questions, they should first ask themselves whether "identity" is even necessary to answer the questions posed. If there is a way to conduct the research without recourse to identity, they argue, then researchers should make the effort to do so without this category. Their reasoning is that sociologists run the risk of reifying the meaning of identity, rendering it something akin to essence or substance and therefore carrying with it an implicit biologism.[8] They write,

> The argument of this article is that the social sciences and humanities have surrendered to the word "identity"; that this has both intellectual and political costs; and that we can do better. "Identity," we argue, tends to mean too much (when understood in a strong sense), or nothing at all (because of its sheer ambiguity). We take stock of the conceptual and theoretical work "identity" is supposed to do and suggest that this work might be done better by other terms, less ambiguous, and unencumbered by the reifying connotations of "identity."
>
> *(p. 1)*

If identity is used to describe entire groups of persons, they argue, it risks flattening out differences within those very groups. If, on the other hand, identity is untethered from its essentialist foundation and qualified as multiple, contingent, fluid, hybrid, and the like, it raises the question of why it is used at all. The implication of the claim that scholars in the social sciences and the humanities have "surrendered to the word" is that the term "identity" should be an object of study rather than an unexamined causal force (similar to what I referred to earlier as the need to consider how "race" is the result of social forces, not their cause).

What scholars tend to do, say Brubaker and Cooper (2000), is confuse—sometimes unintentionally—categories of practice for categories of analysis. Identity is, of course, a practice that is a materially real, and significant, phenomenon. But that does not necessarily mean it is a required category of *analysis* by social scientists. Taking the example of "nation," they show that although "nation talk" is a practice with real material outcomes, one does not have to assume "nations" exist (as in real communities of persons) in order to develop a theory of nationalism with any explanatory power. Equally so with race: one does not have to assume "race" exists in order to understand "race talk" as a practice with material consequences. Why is this distinction important? It is important, say Brubaker and Cooper, to avoid the reification of identity, which would have potentially serious consequences given the abiding existence and force of racism.

To take an example from the health communication literature, Kline (2007) assessed breast cancer pamphlets for cultural sensitivity to determine whether they were likely to encourage African-American women to seek out preventive screening and care. This study had notable strengths, including integrating rhetorical criticism and social science research methods, incorporating background research that mammogram uptake rates are nearly the same among white and black women (which suggests that other factors are at work to explain why black women are more likely to die from breast cancer), and analyzing the kinds of messages generated by African-American organizations that diversifies our understanding of what counts as persuasive and therefore effective messaging. Nevertheless, she uses the terms "culture" and "race" interchangeably, a slippage that suggests that they are one and the same when talking about African-American women as an audience. Furthermore, she unreflexively labels some risk factors "racial," a biologistic connotation that has its roots in epidemiology (see Happe, 2013b) but is no less problematic. Kline writes that "mounting evidence indicates the breast cancer risk profile for African American women may differ from that of White women. In spite of this, references to risk factors that increase a woman's susceptibility to breast cancer generally were not specific to African American women—as one text (inaccurately) noted, 'Race is not considered a factor that might increase a woman's chance of getting breast cancer'" (p. 90). Kline makes it clear that she implicitly considers race to have some existence in biology when she writes (citing a popular, general audience book on breast cancer), "Moreover, higher death rates experienced by African American women may be a function of physiological variations that produce more aggressive tumors, a fact acknowledged in only two pamphlets without reference to the implications for reducing the threat" (2007, p. 90). Reference to "physiological variations" is dangerously vague at best, biologistic at worst, since the term "variation" is common in genomics parlance to describe the relationship between ancestry and inherited susceptibility to breast cancer. Put simply "race" is not a risk factor for breast cancer (although in some cases, ancestry can be), and is therefore an unlikely explanation for the existence of health disparities made possible by social and economic structures.[9]

In addition to the question of whether or not "racial" risk should be considered a "culturally-sensitive" message, I want to call into question the widely accepted premise that African-American women have specific cultural needs necessitating messages that Kline says should include references to religion and spirituality, community-based decision making, and distrust of medical authorities. We should question the scholarly and intellectual basis of the premise that cultural interventions (such as identity-based messaging) should be the response to institutionally driven health outcomes; Kline herself acknowledges that even when black women avail themselves of mammography, obstacles to effective prevention remain. While it is important to document and evaluate a variety of messages and scripts, research that may initially stem from a focus on an exclusive group of racially identified women, it does not then follow that these messages should be targeted to racially defined groups. For example, for black women who are atheists, it may be ineffective or even offensive to frame prevention in religious terms (and may miss the opportunity to use religion effectively among other racially-identified women). And regarding skepticism of the medical establishment, women have legitimate reasons for noncompliance, especially in refusing to undergo mammography imaging.[10] There is, for example, much conflicting evidence as to whether or not mammography saves lives.[11] And as Dorothy Roberts

(1997) long ago argued, essentializing African American's relationship with the medical system (e.g., the well-worn proclamation that blacks are skeptical or distrustful and therefore need to be educated about the benefits of medical intervention) masks what are in fact nuanced, context-based, and historical perspectives on particular practices resulting in justifiable skepticism about some (e.g., genetic testing) but the enthusiastic embrace of others (e.g., emergency procedures to extend life).[12]

To be fair, it is not surprising that health communication scholars would gravitate toward culturally coded behaviors (behaviors that are further linked to racial identity), given that generally speaking, epidemiological research itself privileges behavior. Take, for example, the well-rehearsed risk factors for breast cancer such as diet, lifestyle, reproductive history, and body-mass index. Even if it were the case that a racial group may exhibit any one risk factor to a greater degree than another racial group, the documentation of a generally greater propensity is not in and of itself meaningful (and really, if you compare two racial groups, you are bound to find some difference) and more specifically does not necessarily warrant racial profiling in medical care.[13] If, say, diet is a risk factor for breast cancer, it is a risk factor for all women, at least to some degree. It makes little pragmatic sense to profile women based on assumed racial identity or self-identity. Profiling based on differential risk factors means targeting one group of women above and beyond all others, even though there is as much variability within groups as there are across them regarding breast cancer risk. It can be argued, in fact, that racial profiling has resulted in some race-based health disparities, in much the same way that sex profiling led to unnecessary heart disease–related deaths among women when physicians wrongly assumed that heart attacks were a "men's issue."[14]

Returning to the question of health communication methodology, it similarly doesn't make sense to compare black and white women in terms of their communication practices and then recommend racial profiling of women in terms of the messages they receive regarding health care. Indeed, what health communication scholars *are* shedding light on is the link between practices (e.g., food consumption, exercise), geography (e.g., living near toxic waste), and access (e.g., to medical care, medical information, and the like). Whether the research need *begin* from the assumption of identity-based practice (understood as racial identity) or even whether the target of messages related to these practices needs to be racially-identifiable groups is not necessarily given. On the other hand, rhetoric and health communication research that is problem-driven rather than identity-driven would open up the possibility that studying diverse women can add to our understanding of the breadth and variability of communication practices. For example, if religious affiliation should be part and parcel of health outreach (a result of research that included more diverse populations of study subjects, including African-American women), that finding can be applied across the board, regardless of racial identity.

Another concern about higher rates of mortality from breast cancer stem from the fact that the disease is not detected early enough for effective treatment. This discrepancy in detection and mortality rates is the result of many factors, including lack of awareness of the availability of diagnostic services and treatments and the reluctance of black women to engage what has historically been a racist, dismissive health care system. In this example, more effective communication practices are absolutely critical to reducing breast cancer disparities in addition to the reform of health insurance and medical education. But in terms of communication, racial identity may not be the issue here; again, thinking racially might actually be the problem when it comes to reaching and offering diagnostic and treatment interventions to black women who should be as concerned with dying from breast cancer as their white counterparts. In other words, racial profiling could be one reason for the lack of adequate care of black women with regard to breast cancer. It should be noted that there have never been breast cancer health campaigns explicitly targeting "white" women.[15] In other words, campaigns to increase prevention are aimed at changing particular behaviors, not at composing messages that will appeal to the ways in which "white" women talk about health.

Beyond the pragmatic benefit of disarticulating race from risk factors in our operating assumptions about communication is the possibility of theorizing racial identity as complex, historical, and dynamic, an approach that Brubaker and Cooper (2000) compellingly describe when they write,

> The question remains whether we can address the complexity of history—including the changing ways in which external categorizations have both stigmatized and humiliated people and given them an enabling and empowering sense of collective selfhood—in more supple and differentiated language. If the real contribution of constructivist social analysis—that affinities, categories, and subjectivities develop and change over time—is to be taken seriously, and not reduced to a presentist, teleological account of the construction of currently existing "groups," then bounded groupness must be understood as a contingent, emergent property, not an axiomatic given.
>
> *(p. 31)*

While Brubaker and Cooper do not use the word "positionality" as an alternative to identity, their description of groupness as a "contingent, emergent property, not an axiomatic given" lends itself to such a conceptualization. Race understood as positionality shifts it from a diachronic to synchronic register.[16] From a communication perspective in particular, it is worth revisiting the now famous "ideograph" essay by rhetorical scholar Michael McGee (1980). Although the essay is mostly known for introducing a rhetorical understanding of ideology (thus bringing together rhetorical studies and Marxism), what has been less discussed is the methodology that McGee says ideographic analysis calls for: diachronic analyses of ideographs ("race" would be one such ideograph) that map and describe changing meaning over time, and synchronic analyses of ideographs that map and describe the discursive forces that animate an ideograph within a particular historical moment. For the latter in particular, what "race" means with regard to health disparities depends upon the intersection of a variety of social and economic forces at a given point in history—the historical approach advanced by Chowkwanyun (2010) and Reed and Chowkwanyun (2012). From this perspective, the preponderance of health disparities is what gives race meaning in a given spatial and temporal context, and not the other way around. Rhetorically inflected methodologies such as critical-interpretative health communication are particularly well-suited to approach race in this way, since unlike other approaches to health communication such as public relations, social marketing, and mass communication, they are more likely to incorporate critical-rhetorical understandings of language by analyzing the role of power, values, and interests in the development of communication theories and in demonstrating the ways in which communication practices constitute racial identity and not the other way around.[17]

While the notion of racial identity may capture the everyday practices of those living within the complex force fields of racialization and economic social relations (and pragmatically, can help identify and secure the participation of persons in health communication research studies), it does not explain the health disparities themselves. Thus, the problem of using "race" to recruit study subjects and then link their behavior back to said racial category is that it reifies race while offering no clear explanation of how race has anything to do with health. For instance, the relationship between something like diet and race should be understood to be a dynamic and multifaceted one, a relationship that involves multiple factors such as geographic location, political economy of food systems, and cultural practices (but not reduced to the latter).[18] Such an approach capitalizes on the well-founded and not particularly controversial notion that communication itself is constitutive of racial identity, a rhetorical notion seemingly absent in much health communication research. African Americans should not be addressed as a monolithic group, but as persons who occupy a shared racialized positionality with regard to social processes of racialization and access to material resources but who nevertheless have different needs, desires, and cultures. Karla Scott's scholarship (e.g., 2013) on African-American women and communication does not compare blacks and whites (an important methodological choice), but rather, studies an underrepresented, understudied group (black women) so as to explain and theorize a diverse set of communication needs and practices. Her approach takes shared positionality—specifically, the experience of black women's lives as racialized subjects—in which African Americans engage in various institutional contexts. Her methodology does not essentialize black women, but rather theorizes and analyzes the relationship between identity and communication as historically and contextually variable yet always already in shared relation to dominant institutional practices and ideologies.

Conclusion

What I have hoped to show in this essay is the powerful hold of racial thinking when the existence of health disparities is taken to be evidence of culture difference in behavior—behavior that is then tied to race-based identity categories. It is a telling example of what Barbara Fields (1990) has described as racial ideology: when race stands in for racism in our accounting of material inequalities, a displacement that I have described in earlier work as a rhetorical one (Happe, 2013a).

Racial thinking takes hold in two ways in health communication scholarship. First, when health communication scholars merely repeat the observation that race-based disparities exist without any explanation of how they came to be and how social science research can play a productive role in their amelioration, they enact what Reed and Chowkwanyun (2012) call "a discourse of racial disparity," one that contributes to a broader social field in which the biology of racialized bodies come to matter more than their complex social, economic, and political contexts. Second, when health communication scholars assume that the existence of disparities, documented by population-wide statistics of differential rates of diagnoses and mortality, in turn are grounds for culturally-coded messages in campaigns targeting black women, they mistake racial identity for racism—a displacement that, at best, fails to explain the cause of the disparities and how to effectively do something about them, and at worst, takes "race" to be what explains the disparities, a rhetorical event that can have significant consequences in the context of widespread institutional racism.

As Scott and Meloncon write in the introduction of this volume, our methodologies are never value-free, but rather reflect interests and desires by the researchers who enact them and in turn have broader social impacts when knowledge claims circulate among other disciplines and in the broader public sphere. Rhetoric and health communication scholars have an ethical obligation to think critically about their role, inadvertent or not, in perpetuating beliefs about race when they employ racial categories in their research. As Jacqueline Stevens (2008) has warned, "racial categorization is not the same as racism, but racial categorization never happens without also producing racial hierarchies . . . The evidence from history, current large-scale medical studies, and clinical studies shows that race causes racism and racism causes adverse health outcomes" (pp. 324–325). Stevens' claim is made in the context of genomics research that purports to explain health disparities (and the need for the NIH to develop criteria that would deny funding to the bulk of such proposals), but the tenor of her argument is nevertheless relevant here: that researchers have an ethical obligation to scrutinize both their methodologies and stated aims not only for their scientific merit but also for their potential social and economic impact.

At the very least, then, health communication scholars should think critically about whether they are calling attention to race-based health disparities because they feel obligated to do so (in part because of the requirement by funding agencies that race be taken into account) or because it is a necessary component to the crafting of meaningful research questions. Closely tied to this is the question of whether the target audiences of health messages need to be informed of the disease itself or whether disease rates should be framed as evidence of racial disparity. As I mentioned above, some evidence suggests that conveying disease risk as race-based disparity can elicit angry responses that disincentivize action, and other researchers are showing that conveying risk in other terms may be as effective, if not more effective. Health campaigns can convey the importance of regular screening (e.g., in the case of breast cancer prevention) without making such appeals *race-based*, even if the target audience is African-American women.

This holds true to the crafting of culturally appropriate messages. When researchers make the leap (without any explanation) from observing race-based health disparities to calling for cultural-specific messages, they mistake racial identity for racism, betraying the hold racial thinking has on biomedical and social scientific research. "Culture," in the examples I have included, really means "race." We can see this more clearly when we consider the fact that although white women are as differentially affected by breast cancer as other groups (e.g., in higher rates of diagnosis), we do not see calls for "culturally appropriate" messages that would target these women as a *racial* group. Health communication scholarship, therefore, should rethink its reliance on race-based identity categories and instead begin with the identification of problematic behaviors. These behaviors can then be studied as having some basis in, among other things, culture, geography, class, age, and the like. The goal would be to determine exactly what, if anything, racial identity has to do with the observed communicative behavior in order to avoid rendering such identity static that at best fails to explain the role of communication in health disparities and at worse, perpetuates the false, and racialist, assumption that cultural differences are so distinct as to demarcate hard and fast lines between the so-called "races." As I argue above, culture more often than not acts as a placeholder or alibi for biologistic notions of race, notions that are all the more problematic in a context in which racialization can have life or death consequences.

To be clear, I am not advocating that racial categories never be used in health communication research. What I am suggesting is that we think critically about if and when racial categories are necessary to improve health. Specifically, we need to rethink "identity," since in health communication research race functions, more often than not, as an umbrella term for a range of behaviors and experiences that can exacerbate health disparities and raise sometimes insurmountable barriers to effective intervention. And we need to be open to the possibilities that race alone cannot explain disparities. Returning to the Reed and Chowkwanyun (2012) excerpts earlier in the chapter, our research much take into consideration that what "race" and "racialization" mean will change depending on the historical periodization. This is as true for rhetoric and health communication research as it is for epidemiology and public health. Quantitative methodologies, I have argued in this essay, render race a static, transhistorical category, one that seems to exert a causal, explanatory force and that, in turn, forecloses the possibility of considering how what "race" means in any given historical moment is the result of the embodiment of health disparities, embodiment that is the result of many intersecting material realities none of which can be reduced to racial identity.

Rather than commit the categorical and ideological mistake of confusing race for racism, rhetoric and communication scholars are well suited to produce theoretically innovative and methodologically rigorous scholarship that allows for investigation of how, and whether, racial identity changes over time, how such identity is the result of our communication practices and not the other way around, and how to craft effective health messages that communicate risk and effective intervention strategies in ways attentive to the goals of social, economic, and racial justice. We must strive for no less.

Notes

1 See Scott and Meloncon (this volume) for the argument that we must consider the role of values and interests in the construction and application of communication methodology.
2 As Barbara Fields (1990) shows, this can be a problem with historical research as well.
3 See, for example, Happe (2013a).
4 For a history of this requirement, see Epstein (2007).
5 As Donald Lowe (1995) notes, race and capital are distinct forces that are nevertheless materially interwoven. Race is "neither a monolith, nor an isolatable variable. . . . Therefore, let us abandon the search for an isolatable racism which, in effect, frees all other variables from any responsibility," for economic interests are often secured by exploiting "existing racial stratification and racism" (p. 109). Reed and Chowkwanyun (2012) make a similar argument in their critique of liberal analyses of disparities in wealth and access to other vital material resources.
6 Sanders Thompson et al. (2008) also found that race- and ethnic-specific statistical data as well as disparity data can have positive and negative effects and conclude that if data specific to African Americans is communicated, it should not be presented in comparison to data about whites.
7 I thank Karla Scott of St. Louis University for raising this methodological point on a panel on African-American women, breast cancer, and media at the annual National Communication Association conference, San Antonio, TX, November 2006.
8 This is analogous to the long-standing feminist critique of identitarianism. See, for example, Butler (1990).
9 This is a common, but no less problematic mistake. For example, on the Susan G. Komen website, on the page titled "Breast Cancer Disparities," the writers note that white women exhibit a higher rate of incidence of breast cancer, but they do not explain why that might be the case. With regard to African-American/black women, they take stock of "biological" factors such as predisposition to certain tumors and elevated hormone levels to explain higher mortality rates. See http://ww5.komen. org/BCDisparities.html. For the argument that embodiment should be accounted for in health research methodology, see Meloncon (this volume).

10 See Gouge (this volume) for a provocative and much needed theoretical engagement with the practice of noncompliance.
11 For an overview of the debate, see Aschmanden (2015).
12 See Roberts (1997).
13 See Epstein (2007) for an excellent overview and critique of racial profiling in medicine. I would add that profiling in the context of public health is equally problematic.
14 For a foundational study in the unintended consequences of race-focused biomedical research and outreach, see Duster (1990).
15 This is not to deny that white women disproportionately benefit from breast cancer awareness campaigns, rather, it is to point out that race seems to be salient only when discussing and addressing women from underrepresented groups such as African-American women. See Happe (2013b) for an elaboration of the implications of this selective attention to race in breast cancer genomics research.
16 Stevens (2008) uses the terms diachronic and synchronic to discuss how race is operationalized in biomedical research (genomics in particular), which I have found immensely useful for thinking critically about epidemiology as well.
17 Examples of this scholarship include Shugart (2011) and Striley and Field-Springer (2014, 2016).
18 Another example would be the study of the prevalence of sexually transmitted diseases among African-American women. As my colleague and health communication scholar Jennifer Monahan pointed out to me, the problem has nothing to do with "black women" but has everything to do with soaring rates of incarceration of black men. Conversation with author, January 26, 2016.

References

Allicock, M., Graves, N., Gray, K., & Troester, M. (2013). African American women's perspectives on breast cancer: Implications for communicating risk of basal-like breast cancer. *Journal of Health Care for the Poor and Underserved, 24*(2): 753–767.

Aschmanden, C. (2015, October 20). Science won't settle the mammogram debate. *FiveThirtyEight.com.* Retrieved from http://fivethirtyeight.com/features/science-wont-settle-the-mammogram-debate/.

Brubaker, R., & Cooper, F. (2000). Beyond "identity." *Theory and Society, 29*(1), 1–47.

Butler, J. (1990). *Gender trouble: Feminism and the subversion of identity.* New York, NY: Routledge.

Chowkwanyun, M. (2011). The strange disappearance of history from racial health disparities research. *Du Bois Review, 8*(1), 253–270.

Duster, T. (1990). *Backdoor to eugenics.* New York, NY: Routledge.

Epstein, S. (2007). *Inclusion: The politics of difference in medical research.* Chicago, IL: University of Chicago Press.

Fields, B. (1990). Slavery, race, and ideology in the United States of America. *New Left Review, 1*(181), 95–118.

Gnagey, L. T. (2015, December 7). Life expectancy decline overstated, but health inequality has worsened. *Michigan News.* Retrieved from https://record.umich.edu/articles/life-expectancy-decline-slows-health-inequality-has-worsened.

Happe, K. E. (2013a). The body of race: Toward a rhetorical understanding of racial ideology. *Quarterly Journal of Speech, 99*(2), 131–155.

Happe, K. E. (2013b). *The material gene: Gender, race, and heredity after the human genome project.* New York, NY: New York University Press.

Kline, K. N. (2007). Cultural sensitivity and health promotion: Assessing breast cancer education pamphlets designed for African American women. *Health Communication, 21*(1), 85–96.

Landrine, H., & Corral, I. (2015). Targeting cancer information to African Americans: The trouble with talking about disparities. *Journal of Health Communication, 20*(2): 196–203.

Lowe, D. M. (1995). *The body in late-capitalist USA.* Durham, NC: Duke University Press.

McGee, M. (1980). The "ideograph": A link between rhetoric and ideology. *Quarterly Journal of Speech, 66*(1), 1–16.

Montagu, A. (1964). *The concept of race.* New York, NY: Free Press.

Reed, A., Jr., & Chowkwanyun, M. (2012). Race, class, and crisis: The discourse of racial disparity and its analytical discontents. *Socialist Register, 48*, 149–175.

Roberts, D. (1997). The nature of blacks' skepticism about genetic testing. *Seton Hall Law Review, 27*, 971–979.

Sanders Thompson, V. L., Cavazos-Rehg, P. A., Jupka, K., Gratzke, J., Tate, K. Y., Deshpande, A., & Kreuter, M. W. (2008). Evidential preferences: Cultural appropriateness strategies in health communications. *Health Education Research, 23*(3), 549–559.

Scott, K. D. (2013). Communication strategies across cultural borders: Dispelling stereotypes, performing competence, and redefining black womanhood. *Women's Studies in Communication, 36*(3), 312–329.

Shim, J. K. (2002). Understanding the routinized inclusion of race, socioeconomic status and sex in epidemiology: The utility of concepts from technoscience studies. *Sociology of Health & Illness, 24*(2), 129–150.

Shugart, H. A. (2011). Shifting the balance: The contemporary narrative of obesity. *Health Communication, 26*(1), 37–47.

Stevens, J. (2008). The feasibility of government oversight of NIH-funded population genetics. In B. A. Koenig, S. S-J. Lee, & S. S. Richardson (Eds.), *Revisiting race in a genomic age* (pp. 320–341). New Brunswick, NJ: Rutgers University Press.

Striley, K. M., & Field-Springer, K. (2014). The bad mother police: Theorizing risk orders in the discourse of infant feeding practices. *Health Communication, 29*(6): 552–562.

Striley, K., & Field-Springer, K. (2016). When it's good to be a bad nurse: Expanding risk orders theory to explore nurses' experiences of moral, social and identity risks in obstetrics units. *Health, Risk and Society, 18n*(1–2), 77–96.

Treichler, P. (1999). *How to have theory in an epidemic: Cultural chronicles of AIDS.* Durham, NC: Duke University Press.

6

BRINGING THE BODY BACK THROUGH PERFORMATIVE PHENOMENOLOGY

Lisa Meloncon

Keywords: embodiment, theory, performance, phenomenology

We were in the local library. It was cold and snowy outside, and for a while I thought the participants in our focus group would stand us up.[1] One by one, however, they all made it. We settled in around a table in the coziness of the space, and with a recorder on the table and some notecards, we started talking. We had been talking for almost an hour and by then, everyone in the group had relaxed into the experience, and we were having a good conversation.

But, then something happened. The woman at the other end of the table directly in front of me leaned forward across the table, half standing and half sitting. It was as if she wanted to make sure we all noticed her and heard what she was about to say: "I just wish folks around here could, you know, think outside of the box." And to emphasize her point as she was talking, she drew an invisible box in the air with her forefingers while her fists were clenched tight. "Yeah, out of the box," she repeated in almost a whisper as she rocked backward and returned to her chair. No one else spoke. They simply nodded in assent.

I have thought of this moment often in the last five years. It has haunted me in some ways because I keep returning to it—seeing her and feeling the tension of her movements and her body's positioning. None of the embodied actions are captured on the recorder, and there is only a hastily written note where I wrote, "she almost stood and drew box in air." But I cannot forget the emphatic nature of that box she drew and the way her bodily movements added force to that box. I also cannot forget the quiet, yet fully embodied, assent of the others at the table.

A distinguishing feature of the rhetoric of health & medicine (RHM) as a field of inquiry is its emphasis on humanistic scholarship (Meloncon & Frost, 2015), even if that scholarship takes on remarkably different forms. Foregrounding humanistic allows researchers the latitude to discuss people and their experiences, and, as a community of scholars, we have tacitly agreed to the supposition that we carry the responsibility of ensuring that their experiences are accurately represented. As rhetoricians of health and medicine expand their research into field sites and interact more directly with research participants (such as patients, doctors, caregivers, administrative staff, and various stakeholders in community-based projects), important theoretical questions are raised about the place of the human, and especially the place of the body. Pushing the boundaries of rhetorical criticism and analysis to more often engage with and from an embodied and participatory orientation requires the shifting of research methods and methodologies.

Our research should place the body "in direct relations with the flows and particles of other bodies and things" (Grosz, 1994, p. 168) as a way to understand how the body experiences health and illness individually and/or within larger systems. This chapter, then, theorizes the methodological orientation of what I call "performative phenomenology." Merging performance theory[2] (e.g., Conquergood, 2002; Madison, 1999; Roach, 1996) and phenomenology (e.g., Ahmed, 2006; Aho & Aho, 2008; Merleau-Ponty, 2009/1962) affords rhetoricians of health and medicine a way to more concretely and acutely focus on the embodied experiences of research participants. Throughout I will alternately refer to those who participate in our studies as either participants or simply people because they may or may not be patients.

In what follows, I provide a brief overview of both theoretical orientations and then connect them through their mutual dependence on embodiment and experience into performative phenomenology. I then discuss how this methodology can be done and its importance to advancing research methodologies. As a methodology, performative phenomenology captures or records embodied experience in a way that accounts for past and present associations between participants and the multicontextual, multidimensional nature of health care. What performative phenomenology adds to the RHM is a way to push back against traditional methodologies that have too long put the primary emphasis on texts or that have too often erased or minimized the body when writing to develop more complex and nuanced approaches to embodiment that highlight the lived experiences of research participants. In other words, it brings the body back.

Understanding Embodiment and Experience

> Whatever the implications of an attitude, as a kind of incipient future action, it must be by some means grounded in the set of the body. . . .
>
> (Burke, 2003, p. 147)

As Burke reminds us in the epigram of this section, the body shapes how we understand the world. Coming from a variety of fields (e.g., Butler, 1993; De Lauretis, 1987; Scarry, 1985), body studies (see Hawhee, 2004, p. 10) ensures that the recent emphasis on posthumanism and materiality doesn't forget about the living, breathing body since "the body and its specific behavior is where the power system stops being abstract and becomes material. The body is where it succeeds or fails, where it acceded to or struggled against" (Fiske, 1992, p. 162). Following other disciplines and intellectual thought, rhetorical studies writ large has embraced body studies. With a number of works that take an expansive view (e.g., Haas & Witte, 2001; Hawhee, 2009; Selzer & Crowley, 1999) and others a more specific, topical focus (e.g., Dolmage, 2014; Lay et al., 2000; Sauer, 2003; Walters, 2014), these works try to complicate the notions of an unproblematic and disembodied body.

Further, as Crowley (2002) asserts, "body studies also contribute to rhetorical theory because of its habit of pointing up the interestedness of boundary drawing and distinction making. Distinctions and boundaries are never disinterested. . . . And that's why this work is central to rhetorical studies . . ." (p. 186). Despite this recognition of the body's importance in rhetorical theory, locating an embodied subject in much RHM research can be difficult. Ironically, although the work we do is so often focused on people's embodied experiences as they engage some aspect of the health care system, the body is often inadequately recognized through the research process and write-up. Often, by the time research is published, few bodies exist. Current research has left me wanting because I keep looking for and not finding a vibrant and nuanced portrayal of the embodied, living, breathing person and all they are experiencing. Even in research that reports on patient uncertainty (e.g., Donovan et al., 2014); engages with patients in a participatory fashion (e.g., Kuehl & Anderson, 2015); or chronicles the engagement of a person's experiences (e.g., Bellwoar, 2012), the research is reported in such a way that it subjects seem disembodied. For example, in Bellwoar's excellent study, the tracing of the participant's activities does not get at the lived, embodied experience of the participant. Instead, Bellwoar maintains an emphasis on the texts and the interpretation of those texts in light of the everyday. While textual and rhetorical analysis will remain a hallmark of RHM, Bellwoar's study points to my concern about the disembodying the bodies, that is, her study never describes the actual effects on the participant's body, instead treating the body in an abstract sense. Even in the few studies where we get glimpses of embodiment (e.g., Segal, 2012), they are not consistent or in-depth enough to shift the research or discussion to fully understand people's embodied experiences and potentially intervene to improve them. Something has to give; we need to bring the body back throughout our research—in both the study design and in the resulting publication. Part of what I want to answer here is an extension of the question that Perry and Medina (2015) asked: "How we might grant the body its (well-theorized) status in the practice and representation of research?" (p. 5) and, in doing so, provide RHM researchers ways to reembody their research in meaningful ways.

While the studies mentioned above provide valuable insights, RHM needs to better account for the various ideologies that are embedded within our methodologies. What does it say to those who may read RHM research that the actual person and their lived experience is often minimized? Methodologies, as Sullivan and Porter (1997) argued, have ideologies that tend to value specific ways of knowing and knowledge making. For RHM to overlook embodiment as a site of knowledge limits our approaches to methodologies. Research studies in the RHM "need an embodied discourse, one that interprets body as neither a passive *tabula rasa* on which meanings are inscribed nor an inescapable animal that must be subdued before pure knowing can be achieved" (Fleckenstein, 1999, p. 281). So how to move toward an embodied discourse that can bring the body back, that can effectively highlight and pay attention to the nuances such as those in the opening story?

To begin, we need a definition of embodiment, and here I use two definitions together because they get at the importance of embodiment within research methodology: "Embodiment is all the many and various ways that we (self and other) accomplish relations to being in possession of the bodies that we are" (Titchkosky, 2007, p. 13) and, also, embodiment "is contextual, enmeshed within specifics of place, times, physiology, and culture, which together compose enactment," (Hayles, 1999, pp. 196). Seeing embodiment in this way as relational, contextual, and performative provides the opening for performative phenomenology.

Following Crowley's (2002) belief that body studies and embodiment are important to rhetorical theory, I found myself wondering how to account for or capture the experience I described in the opening vignette, particularly considering the problems I was having with existing research. I repeatedly asked myself, "How can we embody experience theoretically?" My dilemma was that I needed a conceptual framework that would make sense of the embodied aspects of research. Neither "body studies" nor rhetoric seemed to provide the depth and nuance I desired. I needed a methodology that could help me understand how my working definition of embodiment could be researched and also help me account for the multidimensions of those bodies beyond discourse. Moreover, I needed a methodology that could move toward the building of theory, a new way of seeing and doing and performing research. In the next two sections, I provide introductions to the methodological orientations of phenomenology and of performance because they both value embodiment.

Phenomenology

> What is discourse, if not a narrative interweaving of experience born of practical perceptual activity?
>
> (Ingold, 2000, p. 286)

Ingold's epigram resonates because his words highlight the important of narratives, experiences, and perceptual activity. These three things drive the phenomenological inquiry. The study of phenomena or spatiotemporal occurrences that are known through sensory experience, phenomenology comes out of philosophy and most prominently the work of Edmund Husserl (1964) and then Martin Heidegger (1962) and Maurice Merleau-Ponty (2009/1962). What drew me to phenomenology was the emphasis on embodiment, and, as importantly, the primacy of lived experiences.[3]

> Phenomenology privileges the first-person experience, thus challenging the medical world's objective, third-person account of disease. The importance phenomenology places on a person's own experience, on the thoroughly human environment of everyday life, presents a novel view of illness . . . it sees illness as a way of living, experiencing the world and interacting with other people.
>
> *(Carel, 2008, p. 8)*

In other words, phenomenology is a theoretical and methodological way of privileging the living and being of people. Or: it is a way of bringing the body back.

While Carel limits her description of phenomenology to those with illness, my interpretation expands it to all those who participate in health care, from patients to caregivers to staff in medical facilities to insurance agents, and my expansion of phenomenology more explicitly addresses what Merleau-Ponty (2009/1962) refers to as the coupling of organism and environment, which would include material places, technologies, and discourse produced (see Hansen, 2006; Meloncon, 2013). This expansion ensures that "the phenomenologist . . . is studying how a particular phenomenon manifests and appears" (Vagle, 2014, p. 23). The research process, then, must provide a sense of structure to those experiences and give voice to how people involved interpret and inhabit the everyday world. For example, in the opening story, the embodied actions of the woman and other participants were not fully captured at the time. Had the moment not been so important within the focus group, it would have been completely lost. Developing a methodology that captures such embodiment moments is critical to RHM scholarship.

A phenomenological description must "go back to the things themselves" (Husserl, 1964). Remember the box that the participant drew in the air? That box—that thing—came into being because as she was sharing those experiences; her entire body, her movements, her words, her physical force, all became phenomena that when described together illustrate the lived experience and relationality of that experience to the other participants, the research study, the industry in the town, and the changes she wanted to happen. One of the ongoing critiques of RHM scholarship is that it is hard to generalize since each participant is different and has different experiences. However, "a powerful phenomenological text thrives on a certain irrevocable tension between what is unique and what is shared, between immanent and transcendent meaning, and between reflective and the prereflective spheres of the lifeworld" (van Manen, 1990, p. 68).

When rich and detailed descriptions from other participants are added together, researchers can potentially "[uncover] and [see] through the presumptions and suppositions that shape our understanding of the world and understanding of life" (van Manen, 1990, p. 55) and point to new ways of understanding lived experiences and embodied meaning.

While phenomenology provides the depth of the lived experiences with a richness of detail focused on the senses and the participants' relationships with other people and things, it is often criticized because it "seeks only to describe how things concretely manifest or reveal themselves to and through people" (Aho & Aho, 2008, p. 10), and it has limited application in answering "what" and "when" questions. Further, part of what keeps phenomenology from "widespread acceptance in contemporary research circles is a lack of clarity concerning the conversion of theory into practice" (Kozel, 2007, 48). Enter performance.

Performance

Performance studies addresses many of the critiques leveled at phenomenology and ensures that singular lived experiences are actually parts of larger relationships, while also providing a way into praxis.[4] According to Richard Schechner (2006), "To treat any object, work or product 'as' performance . . . means to investigate what that object does, how it interacts with other objects or beings, and how it relates to other objects or beings" (p. 30). In this case, it means examining the *what* and *when* of the phenomenological experience.

Performance is about existing in an emergent state (waiting on the next moment of our lived experience), and performance draws on and repeats past associations, which can directly relate to living in-between sick and well states; one is always emerging from the other. Emergence ensures a dynamic relationship between the performers and situation, and illustrates the intimacy and necessity of relationships. Schechner's (2006) definitional statement that "Performance exists as actions, interactions, and relationships" (p. 30) complements Condit's (2010) view that communication (and rhetoric) are relational. Relationality is a key concept within performance (and phenomenology) because it can "help remind us that a relationship is not a discrete, state entity but rather a process of the interaction of forces" (p. 6). Relationships and their interactions are dependent on social roles and how the particular individual or research participant interacts with others. In other words, the relationality of performance directly connects to the lived experience in a way that encourages the force to move it forward. "Phenomenology has tried to pull humans . . . into the intentional relations that always already exist" (Vagle, 2014, p. 28), but what phenomenology has lacked in these relations is some type of force to move it forward. For me, performance becomes the "the active energy [that] does precisely the pushing that is necessary" (Vagle, 2014, p. 28).

When I speak of performance, I use Schechner's (2006) oft-quoted definition, which is an extension of Goffman's *The Social Presentation of the Self in Everyday Life* (1959):

> Performances . . . are 'restored behaviors,' 'twice-behaved behaviors,' performed actions that people train for and rehearse . . . everyday life also involved years of training and practice, of learning appropriate culturally specific bits of behavior, of adjusting and performing one's life roles in relation to special and personal circumstance.
>
> *(pp. 28–29)*

Performance is not simply twice-behaved behavior. It is a ritual and routine. It is acting and doing these rituals in accepted ways, as cultural codes. Rhetoricians of health and medicine can easily identify any number of performances enacted through interfaces with the health care system, from the obvious such as physical therapy and taking medication to the less obvious such as the process of diagnostic tests (e.g., x-rays or blood work) and the telling of patient stories during a clinical visit or the retelling of the visit to family and friends.

When viewed as performances, such experiences incorporate more than the discourses associated with them and enable the capturing of other important and telling aspects of the health and/or medical encounter. Much like the need to capture the embodied moment in the opening story, performance studies insists on recording these other details and asking the hard questions about how the corporeal body moves through time and space, as performs. "It is attention, perception, and thought set in motion in such a way as to kindle or ignite, the space for change" (Kozel, 2007, p. 71), and in the case of the RHM, this space for change is typically the participant's interaction within the health care system.

Many may most likely associate performance with creative endeavors through theatre or speech, and rhetoricians may immediately think of Burke's "dramas of living" with the oft-used dramatist pentad (1945/1969). Performance, however, is much more than that, and as a discipline, it has a much richer and longer history. That history, of course, is not without its contestations and differences, but performance studies scholars agree that the "performance" is the object of inquiry and performance is a collection of doing things such as actions and events. In this way, performance broadens phenomenology to include the lived experience of the research participant(s) within an event or set of actions.

For example, consider a typical office visit to a primary care physician. In the United States (and many Western countries such as Canada, Britain, or France), the same behaviors are expected and occur in both general preventive visits as well as those focused on more acute ailments. Patients check in at a main desk, insurance is verified, and then they are seated to wait. Even emergent situations follow performance rituals. While many of us would not have initially characterized these interactions as performances, thinking of them as such allows researchers to record characteristics of those performances and the experiences and affects of the bodies involved. Incorporating phenomenology keeps performance in the present and focused on the action, actors, and context.

Performance "represents one powerful way in which cultures set about the necessary business of remembering who and what they are" (Roach, 1998, p. 49). This is important to the RHM since people's embodied health and responses to it shift. Health and healing are constantly in motion, constantly being performed and made by a variety of actors.

Performance's insistence and focus on the body as it changes throughout an illness is a useful framework because it allows the researcher the opportunity to identify changing identities (from the moment a participant may get sick all the way through the moment they are well) and begin to understand them within the larger contexts of care, especially from the patient perspective. It helps to capture additional aspects of embodied experience that are outside the usual realms of discourse because unlike texts (even recordings or oral conversations), "performances are ephemeral. They create their effects and then they are gone" (Schieffelin, 1998, p. 198). But in recording these ephemeral aspects we gain important insights into the lived experiences of research participants. As Phelan (1998) makes clear,

> Part of what performance knows is the impossibility of maintaining the distinction between temporal tenses, between an absolutely singular beginning and ending, between living and dying. What performance studies learns most from performance is the generative force of these 'betweens.'
>
> *(p. 8)*

When Mol (2002) talks about multiple bodies, performance studies enables a more in-depth analysis of those bodies. Patients, in particular, are performing two identities simultaneously—the body that is sick and the body that is well, echoing Sontag's (1997) declaration that we all have a dual citizenship. It is true that most of us when healthy are only waiting for the moment that we may encounter some virus or bug and move from the kingdom of the well to that of the sick (see Moeller, 2014). Even for patients with chronic disease, the dual identities become variations of quality of life and how well they are managing their disease at any given moment.

Thinking of health care as performative opens up a space for different performances—different lived experiences—to be studied. Schechner (1993) writes that, in any of these varieties, "Performance's subject [is] transformation: the startling ability of human beings to create themselves, to change, to become—for worse or better—what they ordinarily are not" (p. 1). As this viewpoint unfolds, one can capture the experiences of moving from body state to another.

The researcher can better understand these transformations and performances by merging this active view of performance with the lived experience of phenomenology. In this we move closer to a more critical understanding of, and multidimensional representations of bodies, texts, communities, and contexts.

Performative Phenomenology

The focus on the experience (phenomenology) and the doing or action (performance) allows researchers in RHM to capture the full engagement or interaction of health care. Performative phenomenology concerns itself with events as they are experienced. This makes it a vehicle that works most effectively in participatory settings (see McKinnon et al., 2016; Middleton et al., 2015). By focusing on the embodied present, this methodology provides a means to capture the many layers in play in doing fieldwork. One of the questions that I asked myself originally was what could something new add to what the field was already doing?

Take for example the explanation of Fleckenstein et al. (2008) who do not advocate for a singular method but urge research to include all the "feedback pathways constituting the phenomenon" (p. 398). While their advice begins to move in the right direction because it illustrates how "what is constant is not a kind of context but the act of circumscribing a boundary" (p. 399), it still emphasizes the system or the limits of the research situation rather than focusing on specific people and their experiences within and through the system. On a first read this may look like a semantic switcheroo, but it's an important distinction of emphasis, particularly in the data-gathering phase. Invoking Phaedra Pezzullo's *Toxic Tourism* (2007), in some areas of my hometown you can taste the air on some days, feel it burn your nostrils, and see the haze hang on the horizon. Watching the children play on a playground with one of the largest petrochemical plants in the world looming in the background affords an image that is distinctly embodied for both those children and for the observer/researcher. This aspect of performative phenomenology takes into account more than the "story"—it gives a depth and dimension to people's participation and daily lived experiences that goes beyond what may appear in a textually based narrative. Moreover, it can remind researchers that the data and statistics they read, which often mask the humanity behind those numbers, have actual real bodies attached to each data point about air quality and health outcomes. As Bleeker, Sherman, and Nedelkopoulou (2015) argue, "Phenomenology and performance posit an approach that can account for consciousness and experience from the relationship between action, perception, and environment" (p. 6).

Moreover, the merging of performance with phenomenology gives rhetoricians of health and medicine the opportunity to do important critical work. While it is true that phenomenology can describe relations of power, it does not do so forcefully enough. Performance "works from the ground up as it situates us in the everyday. Through this it works to reconfigure relations of power. It works against dominant conceptions of knowledge by locating itself in and theorizing through the body" in action (Calafell, 2013, p. 116). Thus, performance gives phenomenology the critical edge needed in RHM research. Performative phenomenology further has the potential to expose and even shift some power relationships by giving voice to patients or research participants in different and more forceful ways, while unsettling the power of the doctors.

Performative phenomenology is an inductive theory building approach where a series of experiences can shed light on specific phenomena. Performative phenomenology has the potential to be an applied theory building methodology because it merges existing knowledge with the participants' lived experience. The individual's embodied experience as it is embedded in a specific context becomes a series of data. These data points allow us to see how health care works. As performance artist Susan Kozel (2007) remarks, "phenomenology is fundamentally how we receive a work" (p. 71). This view merges the implied performance and its embodied reception. For the RHM, this reception is an active process that connects bodies, performance, and experience in the research process.

Performative phenomenology, then, affords multiple frameworks for the study and practice of health care and the experience of health, illness, pain, and disability. Performative phenomenology isn't designed to provide conclusive answers to any research question. It is meant to get researchers and research participants closer to understanding the phenomenon, and it directs our attention back to the importance of methodologies that can account for the complexity and the nuance of understanding people's experiences in the health and medical encounter, including their encounters with technologies. No two patients will experience illness in the same way; no two doctors deliver care in the same way; no two health care representatives will welcome patients and their families into an office the same way. Performative phenomenology enables us to record "how people are connected meaningfully with the things of the world" (Vagle, 2014, p. 27) and to capture the how through their interactions—their performances—with those things in the world; it captures the becoming.

Implications

In what follows I further unpack some of the most important implications for using this methodological orientation in the RHM.

Builds theory: Phenomenology creates a theoretical language that explains the importance of lived experiences, the performances, of health and medicine. Using the language associated with the combined methods, I can better describe and articulate the importance of embodiment and embodied actions. When combined with rhetorical analysis of related texts and discourses, performative phenomenology rises to the challenge of capturing the complexity of the work rhetoricians of health and medicine do because it not only accounts for the context but it affords new ways to consider embedded ideological, political, social, and economic structures and how those structures implicate the bodies within them.

Working in online spaces (see Opel, this volume; De Hertogh, 2015; Moeller, 2014) brings its own set of complications, particularly about identity and the lines between public and private. Performative phenomenology enables researchers to work through these issues and better grasp what it means to do the RHM in online spaces. For me, interviewing those who use online health information and analyzing this information (around mental health for teens and information-seeking behaviors) has meant that, once again, I needed a more robust set of tools. What performative phenomenology brought to my research process was the ability to see how those people participating in online spaces were trying to unsettle their own identities in one way or another. Their lived experiences in the different spaces of their lives (home, work, doctor's office, online community) reflected the different identities they performed. Examining online patient and caregiver communities and social media discourse through the lens of performative phenomenology allowed me to see the ongoing performances necessary in different spaces. For example, the mother of a child with a chronic life threatening condition explained her intense need and desire to participate in these online spaces because it gave her strength to perform the different roles that she needed to on a daily basis. She goes to the forums to get advice on how to deal with an acute situation or to commiserate and share her feelings with parents of other children with these same type of conditions. Performative phenomenology brought to the forefront her embodied performances throughout these daily experiences in which social media played a large role. Her experience tweeting, blogging, and using online forums became material, performative instantiations of her role as mother and caregiver. The ongoing emotional toll of managing her child's care in relation to a resistant health care system meant she longed to experience her role as caregiver differently so that she could feel more in control; in doing so she became differently embodied, which my research needed to capture.

Enhances active and participatory research methodologies: Performative phenomenology matches well with active research methodologies such as participatory action research and community-based participatory research. When researching with rather than just about a community, in particular, it is crucial to gain insights into the experiences and feelings of people in the community, keeping in mind how the "intentionality" of the research can affect the "the directional shape of experience" (Ihde, 2012, p. 24). In active and participatory research contexts, participants have an embodied investment in the research study that can manifest through various embodied performances. For example, the opening story was a small part of a research project that involved getting the perceptions of people in the community. This meant that I conducted a series of focus groups to ask community members what they knew about epigenetics. Part of that discussion focused on community participation and what it would take to get people to participate. Something that is often not recorded or discussed in our focus group literature is what the participants do with their bodies during the events. Performance is inherently intentional. From the words that are said to the movements that are made, there is an intention with each no matter whether it is conscious or subconscious. Intentionality and its intimate connection to relationality are key currents that bind together performance and phenomenology. Researchers can use intentionality as a key aspect of the research process by tracing the intentions between relations and how these eventually play out, including their own relationships to the research participants and the research subject.

Focuses on all of the senses: Embodied actions and sensory experiences should be analyzed with the same attention we have given texts. Performative phenomenology complements a growing emphasis on exploring the connections between rhetoric and sensation (e.g., Hawhee, 2015; Ott & Keeling, 2011; Rice, 2015, Rickert, 2013, Walters, 2014) and on methodologies from other fields that focus on multisensory methods (e.g., Pink, 2015; Powell, 2010). Performative phenomenology combines the researcher's senses with the participants into an experience that exposes the lived everydayness and the bits and pieces, smells, and feelings that articulate those experiences.

Sensations would simply be part of the performative phenomenologists toolkit, that is, they would be something that a researcher would be attuned to recognizing and asking about. In technical and professional communication, Beverly Sauer's (2003) work on risk communication in mines illustrates the need to take into account alternative forms of information as valid and credible. In Sauer's case, she incorporated the multitude of oral dimensions that played key roles in the risk communication, but she also included other sensorial aspects, such as the sounds and smells that workers reported and the amount of dust on emergency routes. In this way, Sauer's work points to the importance of performative phenomenology and provides an early model of the kinds of impacts that it can make. As Verbeek (2005) argues, "Giving due attention to the sensorial dimensions of the use of objects will make their materiality relevant again. The sensorial dimension forms a tangent plane between human beings and world in a way that brings this material aesthetics in direct connection with mediation" (p. 235).

Movement is also another dimension of the senses. Take note of how bodies interact within the spaces and with each other, and approach relationships between bodies and other things (e.g., information, see Mitchell & Thurtle, 2003) as porous and ripe for exploration. Embodied participants in health care phenomena are constantly in motion, from the movement to get to and from medical appointments to the movement of our bodies at the gym to the mobility of information we carry in our smart phones. The methodology described here accounts for that. It takes into consideration the mobile contexts that play a role in health care and in our research.

Emphasizes affect: Many health experiences are difficult to explain and laden with affect. Take for a moment the concept of pain and how difficult it may be to adequately relay that experience. The affective dimensions of experiencing pain are thoroughly embodied. In the recent "affective turn," scholars have tended to emphasize the importance of neuroscience, the body, and emotions in the cocreation of meaning and in the experience of the world (e.g., Gregg & Seigworth, 2010; Leys, 2011; Massumi, 2002). Borrowing from Edbauer Rice (2008), the "physical life of social bodies" and "language beyond official content" are affective *topoi* that researchers in the RHM might adapt and study.

As Sara Ahmed (2004) explains, "knowledge cannot be separated from the bodily world of feeling and sensation; knowledge is bound up with what makes us sweat, shudder, tremble, all those feelings that are crucially felt on the bodily surface," (p. 171) which is particularly true in health and medical encounters and the commonplaces found across participant experiences. What makes performative phenomenology successful is that participants do feel as though they have a voice and role. "Affect is found in those intensities that pass body to body . . . in those resonances that circulate about, between, and sometimes stick to bodies and world, and in the very passages and variations between those intensities and resonances themselves" (Seigworth & Gregg, 2010, p. 1). Attending to the affective dimensions sheds light on the importance of such embodied intensities and resonances at various scales.

Highlights context: This methodological orientation provides researchers the ability to take into consideration in more critical ways the contexts of people's experiences and performances. For example, if a researcher is viewing context as including the place of the delivery of care and the ideologies and power embedded in those places, a clinic located in a working-class neighborhood that delivers free care is quite different than that of a physician's office in an upper-class suburb. The shifting in place and context is not a backdrop to the research, but an important aspect that must be documented and described. The participants in these two locations will have different relationships with those providing care and the places themselves. According to Ahmed (2006), "Phenomenology reminds us that spaces are not exterior to the bodies; instead spaces are like a second skin that unfolds in the folds of the body" (p. 9). This unfolding can be seen through performative phenomenology as the lived experiences that are embedded within and enacted through sites and locations and then described during the research process.

Work in the RHM that has attempted to bring lived bodies and experiences into the research practice, such as Koerber's examination of breastfeeding practices (2013), offers first phase examples of the impact performative phenomenology can have. Her discussion (specifically in chapter 5) offers a way to see performative, context-specific acts of embodied resistance as it relates to breastfeeding practices. Through a more deliberate and conscious examination of the bodies in actions in specific locations, researchers can move beyond simple "procedural utility" and instead realize that the research practice is knowledge producing (Grabill, 2006,

p. 166). In other words, much like the political orientation of Ahmed's (2006) merging of phenomenology with queer studies, performative phenomenology opens a larger space for critical orientations into power and culture. Performative phenomenology opens new ways of approaching and researching some of our long-standing questions about and challenges with health and medicine.

A hallmark of performative phenomenology is that it cannot be completed quickly because it forces a much-needed reflexive and reflective practice. This is especially important to our research because of its potential to impact people's lives. Taking time with our research can help us pay attention in more directed and focused ways and not rush to conclusions, which brings to mind Kathleen Stewart's (2007) plea to slow down the pace of our analytic thinking "to find something to say about ordinary affects by performing some of the intensity and texture that makes them habitable and animate" (p. 4). Slow thinking and slow becoming harkens to the theorizing of one of the first phenomenologists, Martin Heidegger (1962), when he advocated for "being there" (p. 135). The "there-ness" for both research and participant must be accounted for throughout the research project. In recording the lived experience with an emphasis on embodiment, performative phenomenology shows the "being-Possible" (Heidegger, 1962, p. 139) for participants. Possibility can be powerful for those with an illness or chronic condition, and it is also powerful for those wanting to maintain their health status. Slowing down ensures we don't miss the possibility by allowing the study to develop and shed light on what the implications truly are. We can't lose sight of this in RHM—too much is at stake.

Conclusion

> The body, then, brings us full circle—it reminds us of how experience is connected to the physical and cultural world.
>
> (Smith, Flowers & Larkin, 2009 p. 199)

This new method/ology ensures that research, particularly research in health and medicine, does not forget the body. It also gives primacy to research participants' contextualized experiences. As this volume's introduction notes, several distinguishing characteristics differentiate the RHM from other areas of rhetoric and other fields that study health and medicine; these include its focus on the creation and critique of discourses attached to the health and medical experience. Discourses, however, are enacted and mediated by people and things, and existing research methodologies do not adequately foreground bodies—imperfect, hurting, diseased, bleeding, disabled, infected, chronic, well, fat, thin. Incorporating performative phenomenology moves us closer to capturing the instantiations and multiplicity of those bodies. This approach can also help us attend to the *what* and *why* of the multidimensional contexts that affect those bodies.

Performative phenomenology grounds the matters of health in the daily performances of experiencing it. This methodology gives rhetoricians of health and medicine another tool to explicate research sites and better understand the lived experiences of participants in those sites by paying close attention to the descriptions, relations, and intentions of the participants. Performative phenomenology provides insights into the becoming of the lived experiences, the becoming of the bodies' changes through illness and wellness. The woman in my focus group who insisted on thinking outside of the box was the inspiration for this methodology, and it stands as my own attempt to think outside of the methodological box. More so, it brings the body back.

Notes

1 The scene described here was part of a research project that has been partially described in Fullencamp, Haynes, Meloncon, Succop, and Nebert (2013). However, the in-depth results of the focus group where this moment occurred have not yet been published.
2 Throughout this chapter, I will be setting aside the distinctions between performance and performativity (see Butler) in order to keep the discussion clear and manageable. Instead, I am using a broader interpretation of performance where it represents the acting and the doing. See note three and the Performance section for more details.
3 Here I want to focus on the primacy of the lived experience, which is generally experienced by a patient and/or their caregivers. Because of that, other research methods and theories more commonly used in rhetoric and RHM, such as actor-network theory (ANT), are not appropriate. I am less interested in "following" the actors than in understanding what happens when actors interact in specific, concrete encounters. Other methodologies that may come to mind, such as ethnography, are also not doing what performative phenomenology does. For example, ethnography is more concerned with the cultural ramifications or aspects of the research question. While those concerns are not lost in performative phenomenology, they are not the primary focus. Finally, the lived experiences I describe are not to be confused with the lived experiences found in narrative medicine and medical humanities made known by Arthur Frank et al. (2015) and Rita Charon (2006), and rightfully critiqued by Woods (2013).
4 Scholarly literature on performance is vast since it is both a field of study and a research methodology. I ground my discussion with Schechner (2006) since his performance studies book is a foundational text that clearly describes the methodological aspects of performance.

References

Ahmed, S. (2004). *The cultural politics of emotion.* New York, NY: Routledge.
Ahmed, S. (2006). *Queer phenomenology: Orientations, objects, others.* Durham, NC: Duke University Press.
Aho, J., & Aho, K. (2008). *Body matters: A phenomenology of sickness, disease, and illness.* Lanham, MD: Rowman & Littlefield.
Bellwoar, H. (2012). Everyday matters: Reception and use as productive design of health-related texts. *Technical Communication Quarterly, 21,* 325–345.

Bleeker, M., Sherman, J. F., & Nedelkopoulou, E. (2015). Introduction. In M. Bleeker, J. F. Sherman, & E. Nedelkopoulou (Eds.), *Performance and phenomenology: Traditions and transformations* (pp. 1–19). London, UK: Routledge.

Burke, K. (2003). *On human nature: A gathering while everything flows, 1967-1984*. Berkeley, CA: University of California Press.

Butler, J. (1993). *Bodies that matter: On the discursive limits of sex*. New York, NY: Routledge.

Calafell, B. M. (2013). Performance: Keeping rhetoric honest. *Text and Performance Quarterly, 34*(1), 115–117.

Carel, H. (2008). *Illness: The cry of the flesh*. Stoskville, UK: Acumen.

Charon, R. (2006). *Narrative medicine: Honoring the stories of illness*. New York, NY: Oxford University Press.

Condit, C. (2010). Communication as relationality. In G. J. Shepherd, J. St. John, & T. Striphas (Eds.), *Communication as . . .: Perspectives on theory* (pp. 3–12). Thousand Oaks, CA: Sage.

Conquergood, D. (2002). Performance studies: Interventions and radical research. *Drama Review, 46*(2), 145–156.

Crowley, S. (2002). Body studies in rhetoric and composition. In G. A. Olson (Ed.), *Rhetoric and composition as intellectual work* (pp. 177–187). Carbondale, IL: Southern Illinois University Press.

De Hertogh, L. B. (2015). Reinscribing a new normal: Pregnancy, disability, and health 2.0 in the online natural birthing community, birth without fear. *Ada: A Journal of Gender, New Media, and Technology, 7*, n.p.

De Lauretis, T. (1987). *Technologies of gender: Essays on theory, film, and fiction*. Bloomington, IN: Indiana University Press.

Dolmage, J. (2014). *Disability rhetoric*. Syracuse, NY: Syracuse University Press.

Donovan, E. E., Crook, B., Brown, L. E., Pastorek, A. E., Hall, C. A., Mackert, M. S., & Stephens, K. K. (2014). An experimental test of medical disclosure and consent documentation: Assessing patient comprehension, self-efficacy, and uncertainty. *Communication Monographs, 81*(2), 239–260.

Fiske, J. (1992). Cultural studies and the culture of everyday life. In L. Grossberg, C. Nelson, & P. Treichler (Eds.), *Cultural Studies* (pp. 154–174). New York, NY: Routledge.

Fleckenstein, K. S. (1999). Writing bodies: Somatic mind in composition studies. *College English, 61*, 281–306.

Fleckenstein, K. S., Spinuzzi, C., Rickly, R. J., & Papper, C. C. (2008). The importance of harmony: An ecological metaphor for writing research. *College Composition and Communication, 60*(2), 388–419.

Fullencamp, A., Haynes, E., Meloncon, L., Succop, P., & Nebert, D. (2013). Perceptions of genetic research in three rural Appalachian Ohio communities. *Journal of Community Genetics, 4*(1), 9–17.

Goffman, E. (1959). *The social presentation of the self in everyday life*. New York, NY: Anchor Books.

Grabill, J. (2006). The study of writing in the social factory: Methodology and rhetorical agency. In J. B. Scott, B. Longo, & K. V. Wills (Eds.), *Critical Power tools: Technical communication and cultural studies* (pp. 151–170). Albany, NY: State University of New York Press.

Gregg, M., & Seigworth, G. J. (Eds.). (2010). *The affect theory reader*. Durham, NC: Duke University Press.

Grosz, E. (1994). *Volatile bodies: Toward a corporeal feminism*. Bloomington, IN: Indiana University Press.

Haas, C., & Witte, S. P. (2001). Writing as an embodied practice: The case of engineering standards. *Journal of Business and Technical Communication, 15*(4), 413–457.

Hansen, M. B. N. (2006). *Bodies in code: Interfaces with digital media.* New York, NY: Routledge.

Hawhee, D. (2004). *Bodily arts: Rhetoric and athletics in ancient Greece.* Austin, TX: University of Texas Press.

Hawhee, D. (2009). *Moving bodies: Kenneth Burke at the edges of language.* Columbia, SC: University of South Carolina Press.

Hawhee, D. (2015). Rhetoric's sensorium. *Quarterly Journal of Speech, 101*(1), 2–17.

Hayles, N. K. (1999). *How we became posthuman: Virtual bodies in cybernetics, literature, and informatics.* Chicago, IL: University of Chicago Press.

Heidegger, M. (1962). *Being and time* (J. Macquarrie & E. Robinson, Trans.). New York, NY: HarperCollins.

Husserl, E. (1964). *The idea of phenomenology* (W. P. Alston & G. Nakhnikian, Trans.). The Hague: Nijhoff.

Ihde, D. (2012). *Experimental phenomenology: Multistabilities* (2nd ed.). Albany, NY: SUNY Press.

Ingold, T. (2000). *The perception of the environment.* London, UK: Routledge.

Koerber, A. (2013). *Breast or bottle: Contemporary controversies in infant-feeding policy and practice.* Columbia, SC: University of South Carolina Press.

Kozel, S. (2007). *Closer: Performance, technologies, phenomenology.* Cambridge, MA: MIT Press.

Kuehl, R., & Anderson, J. (2015). Designing public communication about doulas: Analyzing presence and absence in promoting a volunteer doula program. *Communication Design Quarterly, 3*(4), 75–84.

Lay, M. M., Gurak, L. J., Gravon, C., & Myntti, C. (Eds.). (2000). *Body talk: Rhetoric, technology, reproduction.* Madison WI: University of Wisconsin Press.

Leys, R. (2011). The turn to affect: A critique. *Critical Inquiry, 37*, 434–472.

Madison, D. S. (1999). Performing theory/embodied writing. *Text and Performance Quarterly, 19*(2), 107–124. doi:10.1080/10462939909366254.

Manen, M. van. (1990). *Researching lived experience: Human science for an action sensitive pedagogy.* London, UK: Althouse.

Massumi, B. (2002). *Parables of the virtual: Movement, affect, sensation.* Durham, NC: Duke University Press.

McKinnon, S. L., Asen, R., Chavez, K., & Howard, R. G. (Eds.). (2016). *text+field: Innovation in rhetorical method.* University Park, PA: The Pennsylvania State University Press.

Meloncon, L. (2013). Technological embodiments. In L. Meloncon (Ed.), *Rhetorical accessability: At the intersection of technical communication and disability studies* (pp. 67–81). Amityville, NY: Baywood.

Meloncon, L., & Frost, E. A. (2015). Charting an emerging field: The rhetorics of health and medicine and its importance in communication design. *Communication Design Quarterly, 3*(4), 7–14.

Merleau-Ponty, M. (2009/1962). *Phenomenology of perception* (C. Smith, Trans.). London, UK: Routledge.

Middleton, M. K., Hess, A., Endres, D., & Senda-Cook, S. (2015). *Participatory critical rhetoric: Theoretical and methodological foundations for studying rhetoric in situ.* Lanham. MD: Lexington.

Mitchell, R., & Thurtle, P. (Eds.). (2003). *Data made flesh: Embodying information.* New York, NY: Routledge.

Moeller, M. (2014). Pushing boundaries of normalcy: Employing critical disability studies in analyzing medical advocacy websites. *Communication Design Quarterly, 2*(2), 52–80.

Mol, A. (2002). *The body multiple: Ontology in medical practice*. Durham, NC: Duke University Press.

Ott, B. L., & Keeling, D. M. (2011). Cinema and choric connection: Lost in translation as sensual experience. *Quarterly Journal of Speech, 97*(4), 363–386.

Perry, M., & Medina, C. L. (2015). Introduction: Working through the contradictory terrain of the body in qualitative research. In M. Perry & C. L. Medina (Eds.), *Methodologies of embodiment: Inscribing bodies in qualitative research* (pp. 1–13). New York, NY: Routledge.

Pezzullo, P. C. (2007). *Toxic tourism: Rhetorics of pollution, travel and environmental justice*. Tuscaloosa, AL: University of Alabama Press.

Phelan, P. (1998). Introduction: The ends of performance. In P. Phelan (Ed.), *The ends of performance* (pp. 1–19). New York, NY: New York University Press.

Pink, S. (2015). *Doing sensory ethnography* (2nd ed.). London, UK: Sage.

Powell, K. (2010). Making sense of place: Mapping as a multisensory research method. *Qualitative Inquiry, 16*(7), 539–555.

Rice, J. (2008). The new "new": Making a case for critical affect studies. *Quarterly Journal of Speech, 94*(2), 200–212.

Rice, J. (2015). Pathologia. *Quarterly Journal of Speech, 101*(1), 34–45.

Rickert, T. (2013). *Ambient rhetoric: The attunements of rhetorical being*. Pittsburgh, PA: University of Pittsburgh Press.

Roach, J. (1996). *Cities of the dead: Circum-Atlantic performance*. New York, NY: Columbia University Press.

Roach, J. (1998). Slave spectacles and tragic octoroons: A cultural genealogy of antebellum performance. In D. Pollock (Ed.), *Exceptional spaces: Essays in performance and history* (pp. 49–76). Raleigh, NC: The University of North Carolina Press.

Sauer, B. (2003). *Rhetoric of risk: Technical documentation in hazardous environments*. Mahwah, NJ: Lawrence Erlbaum Associates.

Scarry, E. (1985). *The body in pain: The making and unmaking of the world*. New York, NY: Oxford University Press.

Schechner, R. (1993). *The future of the ritual: Writings on culture and performance*. New York, NY: Routledge.

Schechner, R. (2006). *Performance studies: An introduction* (2nd ed.). New York, NY: Routledge.

Schieffelin, E. L. (1998). Problematizing performance. In R. H. Freeland (Ed.), *Ritual, performance, media* (pp. 194–207). London, UK: Routledge.

Segal, J. Z. (2012). Breast cancer and its narration: An accidental study. *Literature and Medicine, 30*(2), 268–294.

Seigworth, G. J., & Gregg, M. (2010). An inventory of shimmers. In M. Gregg & G. J. Seigworth (Eds.), *The affect theory reader* (pp. 1–25). Durham, NC: Duke University Press.

Selzer, J., & Crowley, S. (Eds.). (1999). *Rhetorical bodies*. Madison, WI: University of Wisconsin Press.

Smith, J. A., Flowers, P., & Larkin, M. (2009). *Interpretive phenomenological analysis*. London, UK: Sage.

Sontag, S. (1977). *Illness as metaphor*. New York, NY: Farrar, Straus, and Giroux.

Stewart, K. (2007). *Ordinary affects*. Durham, NC: Duke University Press.

Sullivan, P., & Porter, K. (1997). *Opening spaces: Writing technologies and critical research practices.* Westport, CT: Ablex Publishing.

Titchkosky, T. (2007). *Reading and writing disability differently: The textured life of embodiment.* Toronto, ON: University of Toronto Press.

Vagle, M. D. (2014). *Crafting phenomenological research.* Walnut Creek, CA: Left Coast Press.

Verbeek, P.-P. (2005). *What things do: Philosophical reflections on technology, agency, and design.* University Park, PA: The Pennsylvania State University Press.

Walters, S. (2014). *Rhetorical touch: Disability, identification, haptics.* Columbia, SC: University of South Carolina Press.

Woods, A. (2013). Beyond the wounded storyteller: Rethinking narrativity, illness and the embodied self-experience. In H. Carel & R. Cooper (Eds.), *Health, illness, and disease: Philosophical essays* (pp. 113–128). Abingdon, UK: Routledge.

7

"NO SINGLE PATH"

Desire Lines and Divergent Pathographies in Health and Medicine

Catherine C. Gouge

Keywords: divergence, agency, knowledge, design, desire lines, noncompliance, nonadherence

> There is no single path for all of us. [. . .] Let us celebrate the spirit of non-compliance that is the self struggling to survive. Let us celebrate the unbowed head, the heart that still dreams, the voice that refuses to be silent.
>
> (Chamberlain, 2013)

On August 22, 1930, 19-year-old Eula Sharp, a recently recovered tuberculosis patient and the poet laureate of the Eastern Oklahoma Tuberculosis Sanatorium, had her picture taken for her doctor outside of the newly constructed Patient Pavilion. In the background behind her, a paved walkway traverses the grass and leads to a set of double doors. In the foreground, smiling and dressed in white in the middle of a lush grassy area, Eula uses her body to draw attention to a small sign staked in the ground that reads, "KEEP OFF THE GRASS." On the back of the photograph, a short message penned and signed by Eula declares, "Dear Dr. Baker, This is the way I want you to remember me." (See https://eots.omeka.net/items/show/11.)

With this image and inscription[1]—in asking Dr. Baker to remember her, perhaps once again and one final time, as disobeying the rules of the sanatorium—Eula draws attention to the fact that her rebellious spirit has survived the highly regimented treatment she received during her stay at the sanatorium intact, that she remains a woman who refuses to play by the rules, a woman who forges her own path, even (or perhaps especially) when posted signs ask her not to. In so doing, she appears to be celebrating "the spirit of non-compliance," her "unbowed head," and her "voice that refuses to be silent" (Chamberlain, 2013). In the context of the history of the preantibiotic treatment of tuberculosis, capturing this act of rebellion in a photograph can be understood as more than just a taunt or an inside joke between doctor and patient—it is an inspired creative and critical act.

In urban design and landscape architecture, the divergence from paved walkways of the sort that Eula Sharp draws attention to in this photograph is that which is said to form a "desire path" or "desire line," and the user-generated traces that constitute such paths (usually across green spaces) have been studied in these disciplines as critical feedback that can support the modification or redesign of spaces. Though their existence is not always celebrated by designers—for example, when they result in the "trampling" of valuable plant life—these paths are recognized as indexing the preferences, goals, and means of users. This chapter leverages this concept of "desire lines" to reorient our attention to divergence in a way that can help us pay more productive attention to the divergent paths of health care participants, paths that trace behaviors often considered to be "noncompliant" or "nonadherent." This reorientation can further help us to be more thoughtful about what Hunter (1991) has called the "epistemological pathways" that we forge and construct in and about health and medicine.

More than this, though, this reorientation is meant to offer a methodology of divergence for health and medicine that does for divergent practices of all kinds what Dolmage (2014) and other disability and justice-oriented scholars have worked to support: an affirmative approach to understanding non-normative embodied orientations that does not "disqualify" those who are divergent "from rhetorical opportunity and efficacy" (Dolmage & Lewiecki-Wilson, 2010) but that foregrounds the rhetorical possibility of divergent acts, of "excess" and "being-more" (Grosz, 2004, p. 104). In so doing, this chapter picks up Segal's (2005) proposal that "noncompliance does not need to be obsessively measured and it does not need to be rejigged out of existence. The actions of patients need to be studied not mechanistically but with an appropriately complex theory of human persuasion and human judgment: a theory of rhetoric" (p. 151). Informed by interdisciplinary scholarship in medical rhetoric, anthropology, disability and queer studies, bioethics, new materialist feminist theory in science studies, and design studies, this chapter articulates an approach to paying attention to and crafting divergent pathographies for health and medicine that can help us contemplate and expand our engagement with divergent practices.

Because compliance or adherence is still so widely considered to be the ethical response to treatment advice, the possibility of making sense of noncompliance/adherence as anything other than a problem to be solved is often foreclosed. This chapter proposes that we think of noncompliance/adherence first and foremost as divergence that, like desire lines, registers the preferences, goals, and means of health care participants in particular contexts. To reorient us to divergence as useful feedback in this way, I offer a series of theses and wind (somewhat divergently) through several examples that illustrate the value of paying attention to the rhetoricity of divergent behaviors. The reorientation I propose is meant, in part, to offer a way of acknowledging and working with the "messiness" that—as Scott and Meloncon argue in the first chapter of this collection—scholars of the rhetoric of health & medicine ought to find a way of accounting for in our approaches to the work we do. But my hope more broadly is that the work enabled by this reorientation will encourage a wide range of heterogeneous stakeholders (not just scholars but health care participants of all kinds) to recognize and craft divergent pathographies in, of, and about health and medicine, pathographies that can disclose valuable alternatives to conventional care practices.

I came to this study inspired by observations made while researching patient communication—in particular, communication with patients when they are discharged from hospitals. As I looked through the studies by health communication and other critical medical studies scholars, I noticed a tension or ambivalence in much of the scholarship about how to address patient compliance or adherence as a factor in communication design (see Gouge, 2016a and Gouge, 2016b): I noticed, for example, that some explicitly patient-centered texts that advocate for patient perspectives in communication and several studies designed to evaluate the effectiveness of patient discharge communication (PDC) have used patient compliance or adherence as a metric for effective PDCs (Engel et al., 2009; Makaryus & Friedman, 2005; Polack & Avtgis, 2011; Waisman, Siegal, & Chemo, 2003). Such studies, while explicitly recognizing the importance of valuing engaged patients who take an active role in their own care, nonetheless index an ambivalence about the role of patients in clinical encounters that I found both interesting and concerning.

Recalling Segal's (2005) prompt that we explore the rhetoricity of noncompliance and Bellwoar's (2012) proposal that researchers ought to do more to explicitly recognize the unofficial uses of medical documents as legitimate and valid literate activity,[2] I started to wonder about how we might make sense of the noncompliance or divergence of health care participants as not just (or even first) something to fix or, alternately, ignore but as powerfully rhetorical and vital articulations of the experiences of health care participants and, therefore, important to pay more and different attention to in the design of communication and other practices meant to support care. After reading broadly in the interdisciplinary conversation about compliance and divergence[3] to consider the ways that scholars with different disciplinary emphases have approached the methods for and stakes of studying these issues, I identified the following five theses as critical to reorienting our attention to the divergence of health care participants.

These theses might be thought of as coordinates for projects that aim to take divergent behaviors in health and medicine seriously, treating them as vital and productive parts of processes, engagements with texts, and interactions among health care participants and systems:

- **Thesis I:** An understanding of divergence primarily as a problem to fix has been costly for modern medicine.
- **Thesis II:** Divergent behaviors in health and medicine are rhetorical and trace desire lines.
- **Thesis III:** Divergent pathographies trace the "storied" divergence of health care participants and, in so doing, underscore the ways that agency is rhetorical—situated, agile, and emergent.
- **Thesis IV:** Divergent pathographies treat as significant that knowledge and expertise in health and medicine are contingent, defined by our orientation in particular moments.
- **Thesis V:** Divergent pathographies draw attention to opportunities for flexible, responsive care practices that meet participants where they are.

The first two theses are the foundational premises for what I propose we call "divergent pathographies": accounts that treat divergence as rhetorical—influential material-discursive articulations of the desires, goals, and means of participants. Theses III and IV address the critical shifts in our approaches to thinking about agency, knowledge, and expertise that distinguish divergent pathographies from conventional compliance-oriented accounts of divergence in health and medicine. And Thesis V identifies the value of divergent pathographies to practices, processes, and texts meant to support care practices. As a collection, my hope is that these theses provide an important reorientation to divergent behaviors, a corrective to the pervasive compliance frameworks that continue to influence critical practices and attitudes in health and medicine.

Thesis I: An Understanding of Divergence Primarily as a Problem to Fix Has Been Costly for Modern Medicine

> Something is wrong with an expensive system of service delivery in which one of its primary products, advice, so often remains unused.
>
> (DiMatteo, 2004, p. 207)

We know that unpredictability is a part of the experience and treatment of illness. We know that "progress" in health and medicine is rarely, if ever, a straight, linear path towards an ideal health goal. Wellness paths zig-zag and divert from established routes and expectations; they have ups and down, and sometimes, they even loop back around. How people "make progress" with regard to their wellness goals is determined by their relationship to and experiences with a wide variety of phenomena in their contexts for care relating to health care professionals, spaces, buildings, documents, home and work life experiences, obligations, and more. People face obstacles—both anticipated and unanticipated, emergent and designed—and resources for care are not always available or consistent. Time, energy, money, support, and access to other resources are variable and, for many, scarce. Because of this, even when patients wish to be compliant, not everyone has the resources to do so,[4] and in fact, many adherence protocols are not patient-centered at all. Instead, they are often physician-centered or organized around institutional structures, timetables, financial interests, and legal concerns (Kenney, 2011). Because logics of compliance so often influence approaches to and expectations of those who seek care from health and medical professionals and because, as Duffy and Yergeau (2011) write, "a function of the rhetoric scholar is to identify [. . .] powerfully shaping instruments and their effects on individuals" (n.p.), it is critical that scholars of rhetoric and health and medicine recognize the privilege and ableism woven into compliance and adherence expectations.

The "problem of noncompliance," as this essay identifies it, is not that divergent behaviors exist—which prefigures that the only logical way to respond to them is to correct or minimize them—but that biomedicine has not found a way to productively engage with them. Biomedicine has historically alternated between a blame- and shame-oriented preoccupation with diagnosing divergence and selectively ignoring its existence in the design of critical processes.[5] Such narrow preoccupations with and minoritizing views of divergence have made it much harder to appreciate the rhetorical nature of divergent acts. Some even cite this lack of rhetorical understanding as one of the key factors contributing to noncompliance because it leads to what Hunter (1991) calls "the poorly returned narrative" (p. 142) or a restorying of the patient experience that reflects the incommensurability of patient accounts of illness and "the medical version" (p. 123).

Most participating in the conversation about compliance agree on one thing: "noncompliance" is undesirable. For practitioners, acts of noncompliance are seen as often frustrating barriers to improving patient health (Hall, 2003; Montori, 2010); for payers, noncompliance is seen as generating waste in the form of unused treatment advice and untaken medications (Gottlieb, 2000; Tanner, Foster, & Kim, 2014); and for patient advocates, the word "noncompliance" is undesirable because it reflects and sometimes reinforces the persistent overvaluing of physician eminence in clinical encounters (Lester, 2014; Malpani, 2014). And yet, what counts as "care" inside of compliance frameworks is usually limited to that which supports progress along a clinically prescribed path. And because divergent behaviors have been assessed against the ideal of compliance, "noncompliance"— not following treatment advice, not taking medications as directed—continues to be understood by primarily as some *thing* to fix.

As I have argued elsewhere (Gouge, in press), there are at least two versions of compliance expectations in modern medicine that constitute the frameworks for such understanding and each are tied to historically dominant models for knowing the body. Alongside the "standardized body" as a way of identifying normal and pathological states and before the recognition of chronic disease as *the* major public health concern, early compliance expectations—what I call "Compliance 1.0"—primarily positioned patients in the "sick role" (Parsons, 1951) of responding to diagnoses by obeying treatment regimes. Finding a way to tolerate and comply with the strict rules for the rest cure, as Eula Sharp would have been expected to have done, is an example of Compliance 1.0. More recently, as the digitized "data-body" has become more accessible via gene-mapping and medical sensing technologies, a new version of compliance expectations, Compliance 2.0, has emerged. Compliance 2.0 is in effect even before we experience illness: It defines patient agency and care as proactive and assesses the extent to which we (some more than others) consent to our construction as "at risk," medicalized subjects. Examples of Compliance 2.0 expectations include preventative practices, treatments, or medications, such as blood thinners to prevent a stroke, diet and exercise to forestall heart disease or type 2 diabetes, or a mastectomy to reduce the chance of developing breast cancer for those with the BRCA gene mutation.

Compliance frameworks operate as part of a fantasy of what Mol (2006) calls the "logic of choice." According to this logic, an "actor" in health and medicine is "someone who makes decisions" (Mol, 2006, p. 92), and an ethical actor is someone who makes the "right" decisions for their own health—decisions that are concordant with expert knowledge and instructions. With both Compliance 1.0 and 2.0, our agency as patients is circumscribed by a willingness and ability to function as a vehicle biomedicine can use to make us "better." This approach to accountability has been costly for modern medicine and has directed attention away from some conclusions and towards others.[6]

For example, a large-scale antiretroviral FEM PrEP (preexposure prophylaxis) study known as "VOICE," for Vaginal and Oral Interventions to Control the Epidemic, was determined to have failed in 2013, leading the funding agency to withdraw support after five years of work and over $94 million dollars were invested. VOICE, which had followed more than 5,000 women in several southern African countries testing the comparative effectiveness of multiple retroviral medications, was cancelled when those conducting the study found that, though 95% of the women participating were showing up for their appointments to receive medication and though 70% reported taking the medication as they were instructed, according to blood work only 25% were actually taking the medication as prescribed (McNeil, 2013). Early reports of the study cancellation noted that those who conducted the study didn't know why the women were noncompliant but speculated that it was likely because the women did not fully understand the risks of HIV transmission. Later reports noted that the women did not adhere to the study protocol they had agreed to for many reasons[7]— because they never intended to take the medications and had only signed up for the study to get access to free medical exams and birth control, because of mistrust of those conducting the study, because of the unacceptable side effects of the powerful medications, and, according to some, because participants had shared the medication with women who they thought to be at a higher risk for contracting the virus.[8]

The most common conclusions I have seen in these follow-up studies are calls for more adherence counseling during studies and better screening—eliminating patients who are likely to be nonadherent with study protocol. However, as Haynes, Taylor, and Sackett (1979) note in their early book-length study of compliance, not including a representative sample of those whom the study is meant to benefit, including those less likely to be compliant, would undermine a study's value. Further, while adherence counseling and screening might help reduce some noncompliance during the course of a study, such an approach presumes that compliance is the responsibility of individuals asked to follow circumscribed paths. It therefore misses critical opportunities for attunement and fit, such as meeting participants where they are—not just in terms of disease knowledge but in terms of access to basic medical care and other critical resources—and crafting more suitable and enabling paths.

Outside of compliance frameworks, health care participant behaviors that can count as doing the "right thing" are not predetermined, because care and doing the right thing are about attunement among individuals, contexts for care, and care practices and therefore are not the sole purview or responsibility of individuals. Further, outside of logics of compliance that prefigure divergence as requiring correction, the divergent paths of health care participants acting in ways that are not coincident with study designs, protocol, plans, and prescriptions present opportunities for learning more about where individuals are, how they are oriented and why, where they are going, and what they need. What those of us who are invested in improving systems of care need, then, is a reorientation toward divergence in health and medicine of all kinds—divergent behaviors, bodies, processes, texts, and more. And to read the embodied rhetorical potential in the divergent paths of health care participants, we must make sense of them another way.

Thesis II: Divergent Behaviors in Health and Medicine Are Rhetorical and Trace Desire Lines

> The patient has decided, in effect, to test a counter hypothesis.
>
> (Haynes et al., 1979, p. 313)

> Proceeding along a path, every inhabitant lays a trail.
>
> (Ingold, 2011, p. 148)

Our practices and behaviors as health care participants—whether we are patients, providers, at-home caregivers, administrators, staff, study participants, or some combination of these—are rhetorical and should be read as such. As we move through the world, as we engage with and respond to multiple stakeholders, purposes, and contexts, the rhetoricity of our engagements emerges as a condition of our being of and in the world. Given this, our behaviors ought to be thought of as a series of deliberative, embodied encounters with constellations of variables that influence courses of action, decision-making processes, texts, and protocols.

The reasons why people diverge from official paths in health and medicine and the motivations to diverge that influence the trajectory our paths are many: because the prescribed paths do not lead to participants' actual (rather than assumed) goals for well-being; because they are oriented in ways other than those designed or preferred by biomedicine and/or contain obstacles preventing participants from being able to follow them; because they are not marked clearly enough or in a manner participants understand; because they are counterintuitive, require resources to navigate environments that are unavailable to participants; and more. As those who have had great success working to improve systems of care have found (Kenney, 2011), sometimes the paths patients are asked to follow are divergent in ways that reflect poorly designed institutional processes or poor attunement to participant needs and means. This was the case, for example, when patients at the Virginia Mason Outpatient Cancer Service in Washington State—people with cancer who often came to the center tired, stressed, or in pain—were asked to travel long distances and navigate circuitous routes to access offices, specialists, diagnostic machines, and other components of their treatment (Kenney, 2011).

In urban design and landscape architecture, when people depart or diverge from prescribed pathways, they are often thought of as tracing "desire lines" or "desire paths." These neologisms have been used for over 100 years to refer to the impressions recorded by traffic patterns and by wear across green spaces or in snow, paths that diverge from those paved or otherwise designed for "official" use (Throgmorton & Eckstein, 2000). Though responses to these paths vary, they are considered to be evidence of motivated use and their content (their direction, width, degree of wear) is often considered feedback that ought to be taken seriously in future modification of or designs for the spaces they inhabit. Sometimes the feedback gathered from observing these paths is used to redesign in a way that enables user-identified paths, as in public park management in Finland and the United States (Lubell, 2007); sometimes it is used to identify places where guidance is needed to prevent soil erosion, as in "trampling studies" (Marion & Reid, 2001); and sometimes it is used to identify places where obstacles need to be remediated or erected to redirect traffic (Hampton & Cole, 1988).

In health care environments, desire lines are impressions formed by the activity of health care participants who are oriented in ways that might both diverge from and, at times, converge with official, prescribed pathways. These impressions or traces can be recognized in a wide variety of pathographies, or accounts of individuals' experiences of illness, well-being, institutional processes, protocol, and systems of care. They are recorded by health care professionals in patient charts; they are noted in interviews or follow-up queries after failed clinical trials; they are documented in images and other visual representations, like the picture Eula asked to have taken for her doctor; they are authored in narrative accounts shared online, in printed texts, or face-to-face; and they are accounted for as case studies in medical journals or in cautionary tales that health care participants tell each other. But always, they are "storied," as people's behaviors are registered and made sense of in relation to different kinds of knowledges (scientific, anecdotal, authorized, and unauthorized). Approaching divergent behaviors in health and medicine as rhetorical practices that trace desire lines offers us one way of productively and more ethically recognizing the confluence of different agencies, bodies, knowledges, and contexts. Rather than assuming the role of care providers is primarily to persuade path-switching or "better," stronger discipline (resisting one's own inclinations) in order to adhere to a plan of care, making sense of divergent practices as desire lines can help us be more attuned to the orientations, goals, and means of participants; to craft more enabling paths; and to design care practices that connect with where participants are when they need support.

Two cases illustrate what this might look like. First, in 2008, a care team at the Benrath Senior Center in Dusseldorf, Germany responded to the occasional "escape" of its residents with dementia or Alzheimer's—events that both caregivers and patients in the Center found very stressful and upsetting because caregivers would often try to restrain residents and residents would frequently attempt to travel to former homes only to be found much later, scared and disoriented and sometimes physically harmed (see Kuang, 2010). Instead of identifying this issue as one requiring more behavioral correction or coercion, the Center came up with a solution that met the residents where they were, a response that has since been adopted by other senior centers around the world: They installed "fake" bus stops and, essentially, invited residents who wished to leave to wait for a bus that would never arrive to take them to their previous homes. Tracing the desire lines of their residents and making sense of the impressions left by them, the care team observed the ways that the residents who felt compelled to leave both moved (physically) and were moved (affectively). Following the divergent paths of its residents in this way, the care team at Benrath noted that residents attempting to leave the facility had to do so at first on foot and then via public transportation. They thought about where the Center residents were going, how they were getting there, why they were trying to leave, what needs those departures addressed for the residents; and they decided to experiment with creating a place of rest instead. According to those at Benrath Senior Center and elsewhere where this solution has been implemented, there is much less distress now when these episodes occur for all involved, and the residents are safer. They can now follow the path they feel compelled to follow out of the Center, and while they wait at the bus stop, caregivers can join them and wait with them until the moment passes (as it apparently always does) and they are ready to return to the Center.

Second, in what has become known as the "blue yarn experiment," a team at the Virginia Mason Outpatient Cancer Center in 2001 used yarn to trace the many paths that participants and objects were asked to travel in order to identify and improve the care experience of people who came for treatment at the Center. In the words of the Virginia Mason team, they followed the "flow of patients, providers, family and relationships, medications, supplies, equipment, and information, [and] the yarn kept getting longer and longer and more complicated and twisting and turning in its journey" (p. 37). And what they found astounded them: The forced "meandering journey" required of patients—"to the lab on six, radiology up on five, up to fourteen for the clinic, down to the infusion center on twelve, then across to radiation"—was radically undermining care for patients. "For someone with cancer," one of the team members noted, "time is the most precious commodity they have" (p. 35) and "the facility itself was not the kind of healing, comforting environment our patients needed" (p. 34). It was also costly and inefficient for Virginia Mason as well and revealed that "the work of nurses and doctors was overlapping at nearly every step in the process [and that] communication among nurses, doctors, schedulers, and others was so poor that it required constant checking and rechecking, interruption, and rework" (p. 36). This process of tracing the forced (in this case) divergent paths of patients and the flow of other participants and materials led to a redesign process that involved multiple stakeholders (including patients and staff) and the remarkable decision to bring all of the services to some patients instead of asking them to go anywhere after their arrival at the center.

While the paths of patients at Virginia Mason would have gone unrecognized if those trying to improve processes and systems more broadly had not made a conscious decision to trace them with the blue yarn experiment, with the VOICE study and the Benrath and Virginia Mason Center examples, multiple individual divergent acts of health care participants made impressions that persuaded radical changes. The divergent actions of residents trying to leave the Benrath Senior Center and the women participating in the VOICE study registered because they worked against the will of health care professionals. In the VOICE study, the divergence of participants was understood as a sign of unresolvable failure, prompting the funding agency to withdrawal support and halt the study. In contrast, recognizing the paths of residents as desire lines enabled the Benrath Center to work with the affective, embodied states of residents and to appreciate the ways in which the divergent, previously "troublesome" departures of residents were "storied" for both residents and those working there. People, things, their actions and movements are always storied, Ingold writes, because they never exist in isolation, separate from their relations to other things: "They *are* their relations" (2011, p. 70).

For this reason, we think of the "desire" of the desire lines of health care participants as storied, rhetorical engagements that disclose relations and orientations to other beings, objects, and contexts for care. "Desire," as Ahmed explains it, "orientates the subject toward some others [. . .] by establishing a line or direction" (2006, p. 70), and "willing over time and in time creates the very impression of 'the will'" (2014, p. 31). In this way, every impression of willfulness is a desire line that traces engagement with the world around us, and divergent pathographies capture these impressions with the goal of making sense of the orientations they disclose.[9] As willful impressions formed by our rhetorical engagements with the world, desire lines emerge in response to all of the variables active in particular moments in health and medicine—from architectural designs to document designs, from individual affective states to societal and procedural contexts, from diagnostic criteria to power differentials. Making sense of the divergent paths of health care participants as rhetorical and as "desire lines" prior to judgment is a way of recognizing the situated rhetorical work of behaviors that otherwise, and certainly inside of conventional ongoing compliance frameworks, are prefigured and oversimplified as *obstacles to*, rather than *opportunities for*, care.

Thesis III: Divergent Pathographies Trace the "Storied" Divergence of Health Care Participants and, in So Doing, Underscore the Ways That Agency is Rhetorical—Situated, Agile, and Emergent

> Between the "no longer" and the "not yet," desire traces the possible patterns of becoming.
>
> (Braidotti, 2012, p. 32)

We are presumed by the logics of compliance to possess agency, to be animated by it, and to animate the world around us with it in a series of deliberated (as opposed to deliberative) acts. Agency in this sense has conventionally been thought of as the property of autonomous subjects who engage in the intentional, strategic deployment of energy in a chosen direction—and this is often how rhetoric has been considered to have the opportunity to intervene (Miller, 1994): by persuading choices about animation of the "right" kind, according to those authorized by biomedicine to give the most informed, expert advice.

In the VOICE study, a focus on divergent behavior as wholly attributable to individual agents, an understanding of agency as possessed, fixed, and unidirectional (of people making choices now to act in a certain way in the future), and the apparent inflexibility of the study design prevented the researchers from seeing the broader potential for formative feedback in the divergence of the study participants. Spending more time prior to the study getting to know the participants and their reasons for joining the study, paying attention to the complex contexts for the women's lives, and finding a way to incorporate that knowledge into a study design that was a better fit for the population being studied might have saved both money and years of work; and it might have led to more information about the effectiveness of the retrovirals being studied. Several women have since reported in follow-up studies, for example, that because their partners travel for work, they were only taking the medications during those times when they were sexually active, one or two weekends a month. If, when it was discovered that so many of the women were not taking the medications as prescribed, those conducting the study had not adopted a minoritizing view of divergence as the avoidable exception, they might have been more prepared to use the women's divergence as a source of critical information that could lead to better study design rather than as a sign of failure attributable to be the willful deceit and ignorance of individual study participants.

Contrary to its figuration in compliance frameworks, agency in health care is not a solitary, controlled, and calculable energy but a contingent, embodied engagement with a wide range of variables that develops in the context of other emergent actors—both human and nonhuman. Recalling Scott's (2006) account of agency in the context of risk in health and medicine, agency is not about seizing control, as some have accounted for it, because it "gets its rhetorical force from a future trajectory" (p. 138). Trajectory here might be understood as the projection derived from a present embodied orientation, from a directed movement of becoming, from a desire line. This does not mean there is no causal relationship between our current intra-actively[10] produced agencies and future consequences, nor that there should be no accountability; quite the contrary, Barad's (2007) theory of agential realism and account of intra-activity are meant, in part, to help us rethink causality in a more nuanced way that can account for uneven orientations, contributions, and accountabilities. Indeed, because accountability is a critical part of recognizing that agency is distributed and attributable to a variety of materially and discursively entangled contributions, too often a focus on an agency as a choice and as thing "possessed" by individuals confuses the issue and leads to ineffective definitions of problems and solutions, as it does when solutions are focused on adherence counseling rather than redesign of systems and processes where that might be more appropriate and effective.

With divergent pathographies—storied accounts of the divergence of health care participants—agency, action, and being are understood to express and invent possibilities for present and future action kairotically[11] and intra-actively— through the process by which "different material-discursive practices produce different material configurations of the world" (Barad, 2007, p. 184). Accordingly, divergent pathographies do not assume that health care participants are autonomous subjects directing outcomes; rather, they see subjects as "flexible, resilient actors" (Mol, 2006, p. 116)—coping, managing fit, and flowing throughout and, at the same time, crafting a textured, meshwork of paths in multiple contexts for care. Divergent pathographies recognize the ongoing disclosure of our willing that constitutes our participation in health and medicine—the *doing* and *becoming*, rather than *being* once and for all. They are about both what Hawhee (2009) calls the "story-ing of motion" (p. 157) and what Braidotti (2011) identifies as the "ethical imperative to engage with the present" (p. 16). As such, divergent pathographies "trace the possible patterns of becoming" (Braidotti, 2012, p. 32) and take seriously emergent opportunities for action.

Accounts of divergence such as those I propose for divergent pathographies are valuable to the study of health and medicine because they can help us elaborate on this acknowledgment that agency, like doing, is both rhetorical and storied. The emphasis on agency as agile, situated, and emergent can help form the basis of a more nuanced—and, perhaps, honest—understanding of divergent behaviors as rhetorical acts of becoming; of the limitations of narrow, oversimplified ideas of agentic action; and of the ableist, mastery-and-control models of agency to which compliance expectations are bound (Davis, 2013; Garland-Thomson, 1997, 2007). Divergent pathographies have the potential to disclose to those engaging with them that agency—even in health and medicine, where the stakes are arguably as high as they can get—is not something we possess; rather, it emerges intra-actively through our involvement with other phenomena in our contexts of care—texts, care practices, people, bodies, technologies. In so doing, divergent pathographies explore the many ways that agency is embodied, oriented, produced, and distributed. In creating divergent pathographies—by tracing and following the desire lines and paths of divergent practices in health and medicine—we ask, following Ahmed (2014), "not what is willfulness, but rather what is willfulness doing? . . . Where do we tend to find willfulness? When does willfulness come up? Who is attributed as willful?" (p. 17).

Thesis IV: Divergent Pathographies Take Seriously the Ways That Knowledge and Expertise in Health and Medicine Are Produced by Orientations in Particular Moments

> Thinking is about tracing lines of flight and zigzagging patterns . . .
>
> (Braidotti, 2011, p. 2)

Desire lines in health and medicine form impressions of the incorporation and enactment of knowledge that is, at once, material and discursive. Depending on the environment and who else is present, we might be considered to be varying degrees of novices and/or experts. The multiple, changing orientations that we live with and through (moment to moment, movement to movement) determine to what extent and in what ways we develop and are considered to have the knowledge that matters. In practice, expertise is accordingly often determined by where we do what we do, how, and (sometimes) why—from what constellation of orientations—not necessarily by our "official" credentials. For example, sometimes, to the great frustration of our professional caregivers, we seek out differently or unconventionally authorized lay-experts in online forums to discuss our experiences of conditions, injuries, illnesses, and disabilities because others living with similar symptoms and conditions are the experts we seek: those who have developed ways of managing, coping, and thriving in everyday life and reconciling that with medical advice; those who can help us generate ways of coping with the complexities of the many challenges, demands, and obstacles of others we consider to be "like us" (Montori, 2010).[12]

Knowledge in divergent pathographies is accordingly not most productively thought of as "a greater accumulation of mental content"; rather, "movement is knowing [and] the integration of knowledge [is understood to] take place 'along' the paths that take people from place to place" (Ingold, 2011, p. 161). Similarly, expertise is recognized by divergent pathographies as variable in our lived experiences, attributable to those who, in particular moments, we consider to have a "greater capacity to respond" to our needs "with judgment and precision" (Ingold, 2011, p. 161). Expertise is defined, in other words, by a person's perceived orientation to us and to what matters most to us in that moment. Different environments and phenomenal contexts, different needs, different calls to action authorize different experts. And because health care participants are differently situated and constituted in different moments, orienting oneself to or aligning oneself with someone determined to be an expert in the situation, condition, or set of variables we seek to manage calls for flexibility, adaptation, and experimentation. This is critical to our understanding of expertise and agency in divergent pathographies because any act of improvisation enacts the formation of a new path or a new means of travelling along a familiar path. In divergent pathographies, intra-active, emergent, divergent willfulness is valued for the knowledge such movement brings. As individuals make their respective ways through new landscapes or by way of new means that are appropriate to their current states and the landscape features they must navigate, they must continue to improvise, and with this improvisation comes new vectors of understanding and expertise.

In divergent pathographies, intra-active, emergent, divergent willfulness is valued for the knowledge such movement through the world brings. In that sense, divergent pathographies are a celebration of *metis* characterized by sideways and sometimes backwards movement (Dolmage, 2014, p. 5). Such adaptive intelligence is recognized as critical, as are the intuitive behaviors we develop in response to this way of knowing (responses that require that every plan that is enacted be improvised to some extent). Seeking care or any kind of support in a divergent pathography is not presumed to be about following directions, complying, or adhering; rather, it is seen as an opportunity to develop new orientations that we think will help us in some way. It is about developing what Braidotti has called a "nomadic subjectivity" (2014) and Ahmed (2006), a "migrant orientation"—an orientation that "might be described as facing at least two directions" (p. 110). A multiply oriented, nomadic subjectivity in a divergent pathography can be thought of as openness to multiple orientations, to turning, and to exploration of additional fields in response to our environments and all that they disclose to us.

Thesis V: Divergent Pathographies Draw Attention to Opportunities for Flexible, Responsive Care Practices That Meet Participants Where They Are

> I never read leaflets before. A close family member does, and he gets all the complaints. He experiences every symptom that is named in the information leaflet. So, you have to learn not to read the leaflet before.

> I have to use [the medications] anyhow, so why do I need information? . . . in the end, you have to swallow everything anyhow. So I don't need information.
> Patient comments (Borgsteede, Karapinar-Çarkit, Hoffmann, Zoer, and van den Bemt, 2011, p. 25)

Approaching behaviors in health and medicine as desire lines expressing and impressing the willful behavior of embodied participants has much to teach us about the design of care practices. First, rather than treating these practices and processes (e.g., communication, treatment plans, drug protocol, and clinical studies) primarily as opportunities for control, coercion, or unidirectional transmission of knowledge, divergent pathographies facilitate care practices that are flexible, exploratory, and improvisational. Such accounts take seriously that, as both the VOICE study and Benrath Senior Center cases illustrate, for example, more adherence counseling is not the only—or necessarily the most productive—way to respond to the divergent behaviors of participants; indeed, some patients do not want or feel that they need medication information or explanation about the reasons for treatment recommendations (Borgsteede et al., 2011).

When we design care practices, just like when we enact or respond to them, we are inevitably rhetorical. Sometimes, we make lines or paths we hope others might follow, focusing on ways to make those paths more prominent, clear, or enabling. As experts in communication design, doing this might involve following the methods for crafting lines that others have created for us in the form of clearly articulated, well-reasoned and broadly recognized design principles. And sometimes, like those who came up with the blue yarn experiment or bus stop solution, we might depart from these lines—conventional practices, our most trusted design strategies—and experiment with something new. If we observe users heavily modifying procedural documents, for example, we might consider ways those documents can or should facilitate impromptu adjustments in order to serve the processes they are meant to support as opposed to fixing the delivery more—crafting more developed, clearly identified lines and paths. This, too, is rhetorical.

To design with divergent pathographies is not about insisting that people stay on specific pathways with a fixed, circumscribed end point. It is about meeting participants where they are and helping them navigate resources and modify or craft paths to be more enabling. Models of design are agile, participatory, compassionate (Crawford, Brown, Naker, Tishcler, & Abrams, 2015), speculative (Rivers & Soderlund, 2016), and open to modifications like the universal design modification to usability proposed by Dolmage (2009). Instead of problems, divergent responses are seen as opportunities for "ensuring quality and accessible design" (Meloncon, 2013, p. 89). By committing careful attention to behavior that exceeds what might have been hoped for or expected, designers who take divergent pathographies seriously are better equipped to facilitate attuned and supportive relationships in context for care.

Because divergence in health and medicine is not always visible to designers, responding to it can require directed attention from multiple stakeholders (not just professionals or those otherwise identified as leaders or experts). Indeed, in order for designers to identify emergent solutions based on desire lines, the enactment of these paths must be invited, welcomed, documented, and made sense of openly and broadly, by participants of all areas of interest, identifications, and expertise.[13] For communication designers, attention to divergent activity cannot preempt the possibility of changing more than the delivery of warnings and information about consequences. Modifications can happen, in other words, if the conclusions drawn from such observations are not primarily judgment and correction, leading to a reiteration of what to do and more warnings about consequences. And yet, this is too often the conclusion drawn in health and medicine as with some of the retroactive analyses of VOICE that reasserted the importance of improving their adherence screening and counseling for future studies.

The bus stop at the Benrath Senior Center and the blue yarn experiment at Virginia Mason's Outpatient Cancer Center were not focused on finding ways to ensure or coerce resident adherence. Instead, they privileged the safety and comfort of participants by meeting them where they were. Thoughtful consideration of the desire lines of their participants and objects of significance led to unconventional and effective solutions that they might never have come up with if they had continued to define the problem as one requiring more behavioral correction or increased expectations of individuals. Because it required identifying the desire of residents to leave as part of the solution rather than the problem, the bus stop response is not one that could have come out of a problem-solving framework premised on compliance expectations. Significant improvements have been noted by those involved in these experiments. At Virginia Mason, patient and staff satisfaction levels have gone up significantly (into the 93rd percentile), the center has increased the number of patients it treats (from 1,100 to 14,927) with no increase in the number of employees, and some patients when they first see the set-up there reportedly refer to new facility appreciatively as the "cancer spa" (p. 41). According to one Benrath account, the benefits have also been dramatic for all involved: "That single idea," one team member reports, "has since changed care at the senior center. The nurses now lead patients back from 'other worlds' by allowing them to explore the conceit, rather than trying to convince them otherwise" (Kuang, 2010).

Reading Desire Lines, Crafting Divergent Pathologies

> Hope is like a path in the countryside. Originally, there is nothing—but as people walk this way again and again, a path appears.
>
> (Lu Xun, 1921, ctd. in Kristof & WuDunn)

Though there are, of course, differences in the content and contexts for the impressions made, divergent pathographies are exercises in empathy and rhetorical understanding—listening for and directing attention to people's motivated behavior in specific contexts for care. They are about thinking through the ways in which people who veer off of prescribed wellness paths are surviving, managing, coping, and sometimes thriving, even if they are not meeting up with prescribed points on authorized pathways we have paved for them. Accordingly, my aim in this chapter has been, in part, to reorient us to divergent subjects as pathmakers, foragers, 'wayfarers' (Ingold, 2011) and to reorient noncompliance and adherence in a more positive, constructive, rhetorical way. I do so to make room for and call for new pathographies of divergence in health and medicine that can more productively explore the divergent movements of those who stray from prescribed pathways. In this way, the divergent pathographies I call for are *metis* pathographies, "stories [about paths] that are most contested, and offer divergent means of engaging" (Dolmage, 2014, p. 6).

Crafting a divergent pathography requires listening for and identifying divergence as it is expressed and/or responded to in rhetorical practices and texts of as wide a variety as possible: habits and first-person accounts of health care participants of all kinds—both formal and informal; articles, monographs, case studies, clinical studies, and patient charts; procedures; observational studies; and more. This ameliorative work requires becoming familiar with people's actual paths, the specific ways in which and reasons why they depart from the plan designed *for* and sometimes *with* them. Whether the divergence is a "micro withdrawal of consent" (Bivens, this volume) or not following agreed upon study protocol, care practices that take divergence seriously must be invested in and willing to meet people where they are to help them identify and overcome obstacles and, sometimes, to redesign paths and networks of paths that can enable and work with the actual trajectories that people are on and must navigate.

As you become aware of divergence you would like to follow and divergent pathographies you would like to craft or chart, these questions might be useful to seeing divergent acts and their desire lines as rhetorical and to exploring critical aspects of them:

- Where has a work-around, walk-around, or short-cut been attempted, tested, explored, or responded to? Where has an impression been made and by whom or what? What divergent practices (even textual ones) are inspiring, troubling, or confusing stakeholders?
- How and by whom has accountability been assigned or cause and effect been established—explicitly or implicitly? What do the solutions or elaborations on existing practices suggest about assumptions being made about who can and should take action?
- What knowledge is put forward as valid and important to improving the situation? Where and how is that knowledge located? To whom is it attributed?
- When stakeholders are asked about the divergence you have observed, how do they respond? In what genres and with what kinds of appeals? To whom are these addressed? What reasons for inspiration or concern do they cite? What do those citations suggest about the values and priorities of those stakeholders?

In some instances, divergent acts go unnoticed or there is no discernable trace of concern. These instances are also important and might prompt questions about why such divergence is ignored or quietly accepted when other divergent acts are not. In such cases, the following questions might be useful:

- What characterizes or distinguishes those divergent acts that prompt major restructuring or reform and what characterizes those that do not provoke such responses? Are there recognizable differences between the divergent actor(s) and/or contexts for action that are overlooked and those that are not?
- When stakeholders are asked about the divergence observed but about which no concern has been expressed, how do they respond? What reasons for their lack of concern do they offer, and what do these reasons suggest about the values and priorities of those stakeholders?

These questions can provide productive starting points for collecting, mapping, and analyzing observations about divergence that might then be used to improve practices and systems of care.

The divergent pathographies for which I call are "premised on hope: the hope that those who wander away from the paths they are supposed to follow leave their footprints behind" (Ahmed, p. 21). This is not to say that divergence is necessarily moral (the antivaccine movement is a great challenge to the idea that it is), nor that designed responses following from the reorientation I offer are necessarily ethical. The Benrath Center bus stop illustrates the ethical complexity of meeting people where they are. Willfulness, as Ahmed writes, "does not provide our action with a moral ground" (Ahmed, 2014, p. 20), but divergent pathographies following from the theses I propose in this chapter do strive to provide caregivers a more ethical *orientation* towards the divergence of health care participants.

The larger goal of paying attention to noncompliance/adherence with divergent pathographies is to make room for a "prior" (Segal, 2005) and broader understanding of divergence in health and medicine. Paying attention to—not avoiding, dismissing, or minimizing—divergent behavior in health and medicine is critical to effective and ethical care. Divergent pathographies endeavor to encourage health care participants of all kinds (those who treat; those who seek, do not seek, or refuse treatment; and those who design studies and systems) to explore why divergence exists as it does prior to judgment, to better understand the importance of and to try to make sense of the relationship among contexts for care, texts and processes, goals, agency, and actionable knowledge prior to assessing divergent behavior as a negative and undesirable problem to solve. Because a divergent pathography is an account that, by definition, values divergence as emergent storied rhetorical practices, it can help us think through how we manage and cope and care for ourselves and each other in the face of the complex, multivariate challenges posed by wellness and illness while living lives connected to socioeconomic and historically specific contexts. Following from Mol's discussion of the "logic of care" (which she identifies as a better alternative to a "logic of choice"), divergent pathographies support an ethic of care that recognizes that "care is not a well-delineated product, but an open-ended process" (Mol, 2006, p. 22). If care is not a well-delineated "thing," it cannot be some *thing* that is being disregarded unethically or irresponsibly by those who diverge. And so, when we consider the image of Eula Sharp described in this essay's opening, an image of a woman drawing attention to herself as someone who survived not just tuberculosis but the tuberculosis sanatorium with her apparently rebellious spirit intact, we might think of the act captured in the image as asking her doctor to recognize that not all who survive—indeed, not all who thrive—are compliant.

Notes

1 In 1930, the treatment for TB was the "tuberculosis routine" or the "rest cure," essentially an intensely restrictive, prolonged bed rest. Most patients had to submit to the tuberculosis routine for years before they were discharged home, but the rules for women were much more strict since they were thought to be more susceptible to excitement from reading and writing, and tensions between those struggling with TB and the rest cure and those caring for them were not uncommon.

2 "This rethinking," Bellowar writes, "of everyday matters of reception offers a different cultural frame, one which patients' practices are considered as tactical and perceptive rather than passive or noncompliant" (p. 325).

3 I found interesting and relevant discussion about divergence, deviance, and compliance issues in fields such as Rhetoric; Health Communication; Bioethics; Medical Anthropology; Psychology; Philosophy; Narrative Medicine; Complexity Theory; and Disability, Feminist, and Queer Studies.

4 Although this essay focuses on those health care participants who are either patients or clinical trial participants, my aim is to develop a methodology that can be helpful for understanding the divergent rhetorical practices of any health care participant. Consider, for example, when those giving flu shots break with protocol by not putting on gloves before removing the delicate, identifying sticker from the syringe and pasting it onto a patient's consent form—because the logistics of doing it gloved are too difficult.

5 The new ICD-10-CM codes, for example, include over 15 ways of citing nonadherence and noncompliance as secondary billable diagnoses under section Z91.19, "Personal risk factors, not elsewhere classified."

6 It has also directed attention away from identifying appropriate drug protocol for smokers who are diagnosed with cancer but who do not adhere to postdiagnosis recommendations to quit smoking (see Gouge, in press).

7 Indeed, as I write, new studies continue to emerge (e.g., Corneli et al., 2015) that account for the reasons study participants are willing to share about their divergent behavior.

8 This is an instance in which paying attention to noncompliance, rather than dismissing it as the cause of a study failure, could lead to the discovery of divergent paths that may turn out to be a form of "positive deviance" (Pascale, Sternin, & Sternin, 2010)—but only if the conversation is open enough to accommodate an acknowledgement of it.

9 There is an important distinction to be made here between the "desire" as "willfulness" as I account for it here (via Ahmed) and the attribution of responsibility to individuals that I note is a negative consequence of compliance frameworks. Compliance frameworks treat "self-willed" behaviors or willfulness as reasonable justification for blame; divergent pathographies do not. Further, divergent pathographies do not see traces of willfulness as indexing critical information just about individuals; rather, they understand the traces of desire or willfulness, prior to judgement, as indexing an individual's dynamic relationship to contextual affordances and constraints.

10 As Barad (2007) defines it, intra-activity is the process by which "different material-discursive practices produce different material configurations of the world" (p. 184) and the intra-actions in any given moment "not only reconfigure spacetimematter but reconfigure what is possible (p. 182).

11 Because it is not just about the when or duration, as with *chronos*, but about the "force" of a moment, according to Hawhee (2004), "*kairos* is . . . rhetoric's timing, for the quality, direction, and movement of discursive encounters depend more on forces at work on and at a particular moment" (p. 66).

12 Victor Montori is a physician who specializes in diabetes care and is the founder of "Minimally Disruptive Medicine" which, in response to modern medicine having taken the "complexity" of treatment and "push[ed] it to the patient" (10:20 in video, 2010), aims to come up with "healthcare delivery designed to reduce the burden of treatment on patients while pursuing patient goals" (at about 12:30 in video).

13 Amazon.com, for example, has actively sought the desire lines of its visitors by allowing voting on reviews—and this is immediately useful as a feedback mechanism, allowing subsequent visitors to sort the reviews they read by most to least recommended if they opt to do so. Many industries fail, according to Myhill (2004), because they don't leave a way for desire lines to leave an impression.

References

Ahmed, S. (2006). *Queer phenomenology: Orientations, objects, others*. Durham, NC: Duke University Press.

Ahmed, S. (2014). *Willful subjects*. Durham, NC: Duke University Press.

Barad, K. (2007). *Meeting the universe halfway: Quantum physics and the entanglement of matter and meaning.* Durham, NC: Duke University Press.

Bellwoar, H. (2012). Everyday matters: Reception and use as productive design of health-related texts. *Technical Communication Quarterly, 21*(4), 325–345.

Borgsteede, S. D., Karapinar-Çarkit, F., Hoffmann, E., Zoer, J., & van den Bemt, P. M. (2011). Information needs about medication according to patients discharged from a general hospital. *Patient Education and Counseling, 83*(1), 22–28.

Braidotti, R. (2011). *Nomadic subjects: Embodiment and sexual difference in contemporary feminist theory.* New York, NY: Columbia University Press.

Braidotti, R. (2012). The notion of univocity of Being or single matter positions difference as a verb or process of becoming at the heart of the matter. In R. Dolphijn & I. van der Tuin (Eds.), *New materialism: Interviews and cartographies.* Open Humanities Press. Retrieved from http://quod.lib.umich.edu/o/ohp/11515701.0001.001/1:4.1/-new-materialism-interviews-cartographies?rgn=div2;view=fulltext.

Braidotti, R. (2014). *Thinking as a nomadic subject* [Video]. Retrieved from www.ici-berlin.org/event/620/.

Chamberlain, J. (2013). Confessions of a non-compliant patient. *National Empowerment Center.* Retrieved from www.power2u.org/articles/recovery/confessions.html.

Corneli, A. L., McKenna, K., Perry, B., Ahmed, K., Agot, K., Malamatsho, F., & Van Damme, L. (2015). The science of being a study participant: FEM-PrEP participants' explanations for overreporting adherence to the study pills and the whereabouts of unused pills. *JAIDS Journal of Acquired Immune Deficiency Syndromes, 68*(5), 578–584.

Crawford, P., Brown, B., Baker, C., Tischler, V., & Abrams, B. (2015). *Health humanities.* London, UK: Palgrave Macmillan.

Davis, L. (2013). *The end of normal: Identity in a biocultural era.* Ann Arbor, MI: University of Michigan Press.

DiMatteo, M. R. (2004). Variations in patients' adherence to medical recommendations: A quantitative review of 50 years of research. *Medical Care, 42*(3), 200–209.

Dolmage, J. (2009). Disability, usability, universal design. In S. M. Cochran & R. L. Rodrigo (Eds.), *Rhetorically thinking usability: Theories, practices, and methodologies* (pp. 167–190). Cresskill, NJ: Hampton Press.

Dolmage, J. (2014). *Disability rhetoric.* Syracuse, NY: Syracuse University Press.

Dolmage, J., & Lewiecki-Wilson, C. (2010). Refiguring rhetorica: Linking feminist rhetoric and disability studies. In E. E. Schell & K. J. Fawson (Eds.), *Rhetorica in motion: Feminist rhetorical methods and methodologies* (pp. 23–38). Pittsburgh, PA: University of Pittsburgh Press.

Duffy, J., & Yergeau, M. (2011). Disability and rhetoric [Special issue]. *Disability Studies Quarterly, 31*(3).

Engel, K. G., Heiser, M., Smith, D. M., Robinson, C. H., Forman, J. H., & Ubel, P. A. 2009. Patient comprehension of emergency department care instructions: Are patients aware of when they do not understand? *Annals of Emergency Medicine, 53*, 454–461.

Eula Sharp—1930. Eastern Oklahoma Tuberculosis Sanatorium. Retrieved from https://eots.omeka.net/items/show/11.

Garland-Thomson, R. (1997). *Extraordinary bodies: Figuring physical disability in American culture and literature.* New York, NY: Columbia University Press.

Garland-Thomson, R. (2007). Integrating disability, transforming feminist theory. In K. Hall (Ed.), *Feminist disability studies* (pp. 13–47). Bloomington, IN: Indiana University Press.

Gottlieb, H. (2000). Medication nonadherence: Finding solutions to a costly problem. *Drug Benefits Trends, 12*(6), 57–62.

Gouge, C. (2016a). "Getting the knowledge right": Patient communication, agency, and knowledge. *Journal of Medical Humanities*, 1–17. doi:10.1007/s10912-016-9389-1.

Gouge, C. (2016b). Improving patient discharge communication. *Journal of Technical Writing and Communication*. doi:10.1177/0047281616646749.

Gouge, C. (in press). The "inconvenience of meeting you": Rereading non/compliance, enabling care. In J. Jung & A. Booher (Eds.), *Feminist rhetorical science studies*. Carbondale, IL: Southern Illinois University Press.

Grosz, E. (2004). *The nick of time: Politics, evolution, and the untimely*. Durham, NC: Duke University Press.

Hall, J. (2003). Facilitating improved compliance among patients with diabetes. *Podiatry Today, 9*(6). Retrieved from http://www.podiatrytoday.com/article/5555#sthash.4V1ewO81. dpuf.

Hampton, B. & Cole, B. (1988). *Soft paths*. Harrisburg, PA: Stackpole Books.

Hawhee, D. (2004). *Bodily arts: Rhetoric and athletics in ancient Greece*. Austin, TX: University of Texas Press.

Hawhee, D. (2009). *Moving bodies: Kenneth Burke at the edges of language*. Columbia, SC: University of South Carolina Press.

Haynes, R. B., Taylor, D. W., & Sackett, D. L. (1979). *Compliance in health care*. Baltimore, MD: Johns Hopkins University Press

Hunter, K. M. (1991). *Doctors' stories: The narrative structure of medical knowledge*. Princeton, NJ: Princeton University Press.

Ingold, T. (2011). *Being alive: Essays on movement, knowledge and description*. New York, NY: Routledge.

Kenney, C. (2011). *Transforming health care: Virginia Mason Medical Center's pursuit of the perfect patient experience*. London, UK: CRC Press.

Kim, S.-H., Tanner, A., Foster, C., & Kim, S. Y. (2015). Talking about healthcare: News framing of who is responsible for rising healthcare costs in the United States. *Journal of Health Communication, 20*(2), 123–133.

Kristof, N. D., & WuDunn, S. (2015). *A path appears: Transforming lives, creating opportunity*. New York, NY: Vintage Books.

Kuang, C. (2010). Uncommon act of design: Fake bus stop helps Alzheimer's patients. *Fast Company*. Retrieved from www.fastcompany.com/1598472/uncommon-act-design-fake-bus-stop-helps-alzheimers-patients.

Lester, R. (2014). Health as moral failing: Medication restriction among women with eating disorders. *Anthropology & Medicine, 21*(2): 241–250.

Lubell, M. (2007). Lecture 9: National Park for ESP172, University of California, Davis. Retrieved from http://www.des.ucdavis.edu/faculty/lubell/Teaching/ESP172/Lecture9Parks.pdf.

Makaryus, A. N., & Friedman, E. A. 2005. Patient understanding of their treatment plans and diagnosis at discharge. *Mayo Clinic Proceedings, 80*, 991–994.

Malpani, A. (2014, March 22). "The noncompliant doctor." Dr. Malpini's Blog: Helping doctors and patients talk to each other! (Blog post). Retrieved from http://blog.drmalpani.com/.

Marion, J. L., & Reid, S. (2001). Development of the U.S. leave no trace program: An historical perspective. Leave No Trace: Center for Outdoor Ethics, Boulder, CO.

McNeil, D. G. (2013, March 4). African trial of H.I.V. drugs fails. The New York Times. Retrieved December 18, 2014, from http://www.nytimes.com/2013/03/05/health/african-trial-of-hiv-drugs-fails.htm?_r=0.

Meloncon, L. (Ed.). (2013). *Rhetorical accessability: At the intersection of technical communication and disability studies.* Amityville, NY: Baywood Publishing.

Miller, C. R. (1994). Opportunity, opportunism, and progress: Kairos in the rhetoric of technology. *Argumentation, 8*(1), 81–96.

Mol, A. (2006). *The logic of care: Health and the problem of patient choice.* New York, NY: Routledge.

Montori, V. (2010). *Noncompliance: Presentation at the Mayo Clinic* [Video]. Retrieved December 15, 2014, from www.youtube.com/watch?v=flcRKdoaiVk.

Myhill, C. (2004). Commercial success by looking for desire lines. *Computer Human Interaction Lecture Notes in Computer Science, 3101,* pp. 293–304. doi:10.1007/978-973-540-27795-27798_30.

Parsons, T. (1951). *The social system.* Glencoe, IL: The Free Press.

Pascale, R., Sternin, J., & Sternin, M. (2010). *The power of positive deviance: How unlikely innovators solve the world's toughest problems.* Boston, MA: Harvard Business Press.

Polack, E. P., & Avtgis, T. (2011). *Medical communication: Defining the discipline.* Dubuque, IA: Kendal Hunt.

Scott, J. B. (2006). Kairos as indeterminate risk management: The pharmaceutical industry's response to bioterrorism. *Quarterly Journal of Speech, 92*(2), 115–143.

Segal, J. (2005). *Health and the rhetoric of medicine.* Carbondale, IL: Southern Illinois University Press.

Throgmorton, J. A., & Eckstein, B. (2000). *Desire lines: The Chicago area transportation study and the paradox of self in post-war America.* Retrieved from www.nottingham.ac.uk/3cities/throgeck.htm.

Waisman, Y., Siegal, N., & Chemo, M. (2003). Do parents understand emergency department discharge instructions? A survey analysis. *1st Medical Association Journal, 5,* 567–570.

8

RHETORICALLY LISTENING FOR MICROWITHDRAWALS OF CONSENT IN RESEARCH PRACTICE

Kristin Marie Bivens

Keywords: rhetorical listening; microwithdrawals of consent; emotional labor; health care communication research; medical rhetoric; NICU communication

A Flat Bicycle Tire in Copenhagen

After a day of data collection that began with a flat bicycle tire and ended with a participant withdrawing consent, I concluded that field research in health care communication was even more challenging than I had originally anticipated. I was completing the final day of data collection, observations, and interviews at the first of two research sites: the University of Copenhagen (KU) Rigshospitalet's Neonatalklinikken in Denmark. The previous day my nurse contact, Louise,[1] had identified a mother of twin boys who had consented to participate in my study. My project explored communication between nurses and the parents (and other legal caregivers) of premature infants. When I arrived at the Neonatalklinikken, or neonatal intensive care unit (NICU), I found the charge nurse, who took me to the room where the mother, Cora, and her babies were housed. I introduced myself to Cora and her babies' nurses and sat down near the door to begin observations.

Shortly thereafter, Cora withdrew her consent to participate in the interview portion of my study. She told a nurse I could continue to observe, but she was not interested in being interviewed. When the nurse told me Cora explicitly withdrew her consent to be interviewed, I became dejected; and what had started out as a challenging morning was turning into a bad day. Eventually, I decided to stop observing Cora even though she stated I could continue. I identify this phenomenon as a *microwithdrawal of consent*, defined as the implied or partial halt of a person's willingness to participate in one or more aspects of the research process and the researcher's awareness of that withdrawal.

Unbeknownst to her, Cora provided the impetus for a methodological reflection that transformed my research practice. The methodological reflection offered in this chapter explores the ethical and rhetorical orientations which led me to determine that Cora had implicitly withdrawn her consent to be observed when she explicitly withdrew her consent to be interviewed—a halt in her willingness to participate in one or more aspects of the research process and my awareness of that withdrawal. Additionally, I contend that recognizing and responding to microwithdrawals of consent is a necessary part of ethically engaging with research participants in sensitive research spaces, like NICUs.

Thankfully, I realized how I could more ethically engage research participants before I began the same study at a second site: a NICU in the United States. Between Denmark and the United States, in a temporal distance of nine months, I reflexively examined my research practices. The ethical and rhetorical frameworks I used to engage research participants shifted and adjusted and changed because of Cora's microwithdrawal of consent, and I became aware that the absence of "no" is not the presence of "yes." Importantly, I realized more fully that assent—a person's willingness to participate in research—can change at any point during the data collection process, and that I must be aware and willing to notice microwithdrawals of consent (and the absence of assent). Adjusting my research practices are moments of what Scott and Meloncon (in this volume) refer to as "methodological mutability" (p. 5)—an asset and quality of the rhetoric of health & medicine (RHM).

I use my research experience in Denmark with Cora as the catalyst for the methodological reflection in this chapter. In the sections that follow, I examine several key orientations previewed here to conceptually frame and physically recognize microwithdrawals of consent. In the remainder of the chapter, I 1) contend informed consent is a constantly negotiated practice; 2) show opportunities to exceed Institutional Review Board (IRB) ethical expectations in health and medical research contexts; 3) suggest classical and contemporary rhetorical concepts are helpful to provide explanations of field research experience; 4) present rhetorical listening as a conceptual and methodological contribution; 5) propose vulnerability as essential emotional labor before accessing sensitive research spaces in medical and health care contexts; and finally, 6) offer pragmatic suggestions for recognizing participants' microwithdrawals of consent.

Informed Consent as a Constantly Negotiated Practice

Before I arrived in Denmark to conduct research, I was granted permission from the Danish Data Protection Agency (DPA) and the local IRB[2] at my university to conduct my research study. Prior to arriving in Denmark, I provided Louise informed consents in two languages: Danish and English. The informed consents were based on IRB requirements and included the study title, my contact information, an explanation of data collection, and space to sign the informed consent. Based on my local IRB experience, my impression was that a study like mine had not been attempted before. After minor copyedits to the informed consent, the IRB approval process concluded. I categorized this IRB experience as relatively simple and swift. Prior to starting my field research, my nurse contact at the Rigshospitalet posted recruiting materials around the unit for potential participants (nurses, parents, and other legal caregivers). The recruiting materials included the informed consent (in both languages), as well as digital access, via a quick reference code (QR code), to my full research proposal.

Returning to the opening anecdote, Cora was the mother of twin boys who explicitly withdrew her consent to be interviewed. Originally, Cora had verbally consented when I spoke to her about the study, and she also consented when she signed the IRB-approved and DPA-exempted informed consent in English. Cora's sons had been in the NICU for about a month when I observed. As I understood it, babies are not allowed to be held for extended periods of time until they weigh 1 kilogram or 2.2 pounds. On this day, one of the twins reached the 1 kilogram threshold, so Cora was able to hold her son through skin-to-skin contact (known as kangaroo or k-care in the United States).

It was quiet in the room while two nurses, both women, expertly and patiently transferred Cora's son to her chest for skin-to-skin contact. Cora laid on her hospital bed in the room; it was still, silent in fact. The room was only occupied by Cora, two nurses, her sons (one son in an incubator across the room and one lying on her chest), and me. The door to her private room where Cora slept alongside her babies was shut to the outside hall. The two nurses were attentive and supportive of both the baby and Cora during the process, which lasted almost an hour. As I understood it, this was the first time Cora was able to have skin-to-skin contact with her son. All eyes were on Cora and her son, including mine.

After about an hour, during my observation of Cora and the silent communication with her nurses, the nurses were satisfied that the baby was tolerating the skin-to-skin contact, and they left Cora's bedside and walked toward me on their way out of the room to the hallway. As the second nurse passed, though, she stopped by me, lowered her voice, and said, "Mom says you can stay and observe, but she does not want to be interviewed." I shook my head as an acknowledgement that I heard her. And I understood Cora had, through her nurse, explicitly withdrew her consent to be interviewed. Of course, I knew any participant at any time could withdraw their consent, and I was prepared for it, I thought, until it happened.

After the nurses left, the quiet persisted. When I glanced toward Cora, she had her eyes closed and appeared to be sleeping while her son also slept on her chest. It was after a few more minutes that I decided I should leave—I felt like I was intruding on a special moment between Cora and her child; in fact, in retrospect, I know I was intruding. NICUs are special and specialized spaces, as well as sensitive ones. I was frustrated because I knew babies' conditions can change so quickly in a NICU setting. A heart rate can go up and blood pressure can go down, and I need to be invisible. I may not be able to help in those instances, but I surely do not want to interfere or cause harm in them either—emotionally or otherwise.

Essentially, navigating my concerns and knowing things can change so quickly did not prepare me for when they did. Cora, as I saw it, used her rhetorical agency—her ability to make decisions about her participation—to overtly withdraw her consent to be interviewed. After I left the hospital that day, bike-less as I had a flat tire and had to walk, I started to wonder why I left feeling so unsettled, so intrusive, so awkward about the research experience with Cora that day. At that time, I was becoming aware of the emotional labor required to research in a sensitive research space like a NICU. However, it was not until months later, while considering Ratcliffe's (2005) ideas about rhetorical listening as a code of cross cultural conduct and critically, ethically, and rhetorically examining my research practices, that I realized Cora had renegotiated her consent, and perhaps other research participants had done the same, but not so overtly. I was shaken by the thought that I might have overlooked similar microwithdrawals of consent.

In his chapter from *Critical Power Tools*, Grabill (2006) calls upon researchers to scrutinize "largely unarticulated research practices" to "address deep problems in rhetorical agency" (p. 151). Research practices, according to Grabill, are "knowledge rich" and "tactical" (p. 160). He argues that tactical practices and the values guiding them are important but underexamined aspects of critical research methodologies. Critically examining my research practices— and feeling through and around my discomfort with Cora's withdrawal of consent—brings to light microwithdrawals of consent as participants enacting rhetorical agency, often in ways that are not overt or even explicit. My response to Cora also illustrated how microwithdrawals of consent involve the responsive agency of the researcher, too. Young et al. (2010) defined rhetorical agency as a "discourse that indicates the individual's ability to recognize and understand options, identify resources as well as barriers, and make purposeful decisions" (p. 629). Through attending to my emotional discomfort, focusing attention on why I eventually stopped observing and left Cora alone with her sons, and later examining the informed consent process critically and rhetorically, I realized informed consent is a constantly negotiated decision-making process for participants and, by extension, researchers, and should be acknowledged in our enactments and discussions of our methodologies. In doing so, we offer research participants opportunities to act with rhetorical agency and negotiate the terms of their participation in our research practices, and we foreground for ourselves and other researchers ethical guidance for our tactical research practices that is not adequately addressed by IRB standards.

Exceeding Institutional Review Boards' Ethical Standards for Research Conduct

Unfortunately, some research practices and related institutional and organizational mechanisms and complexities can limit participants' rhetorical agency, as some medical rhetoricians have discussed. Barton and Eggly (2009) have noted the role of persuasion as an element in recruiting participants for clinical trials. Barton (2008) used linguistic discourse analysis to examine the language of decision-making in interactions between biomedical and behavioral research studies' recruiters and potential participants. Ultimately, she suggested that the binary between a principle-based ethics of rights and the context-based ethics of care is falsely appropriated. She proposed a more complex and problematized ethical research situation when viewed within these frameworks. Although Barton focused on recruitment, retaining participants could be a logical extension of the discussion about recruitment, participation, and decision-making in research practice. In other words, we might further attend and adjust to any indications of a participant's changing commitment to participate over the course of data collection.

Informed consent on paper is not the same as informed consent in practice. Once information about a research study is shared and an informed consent is signed by a participant (especially after the ink dries), a researcher should continually be aware of microwithdrawals of consent during data collection in the field. A microwithdrawal of consent hinges on the researcher's awareness that informed consent is a constantly negotiated practice and involves the participants' continuous assent or willingness to participate in the research process. Since consent is a constantly negotiated practice, participants might implicitly or partially withdraw their consent through gestures, actions, and other methods, like Cora in the Danish NICU.

IRBs are tasked with protecting human subjects around the principles of the Belmont Report (1979) but also preventing litigation that could arise from research practices that violate these principles. The essence of the Belmont Report is to protect human participants in research by respecting persons, doing no harm, and acting justly. However, IRBs can only do so much to protect participants, researchers, and institutions. When participants withdraw consent to participate in an online survey or paper questionnaire, they might just close the screen or throw away the survey—the participant can, in some cases, do this freely, without a researcher next to them when it happens. Mechanisms for withdrawing consent can be less obvious, less available, and more challenging in sensitive research spaces like a NICU, however, and attending to such differences can be challenging for the field researcher.

Before beginning research with human participants, a researcher must complete several steps to gain the legal and ethical clearance to proceed. When asking for permission to access highly sensitive and specialized hospital spaces, the gate-keepers (e.g., nurses and nurse administrators in Denmark and the United States) want to ensure that people who are involved with the research are protected, too. And since access to one of my research sites extended beyond the borders of the United States, I also had to engage with the human research governing body in Denmark—the DPA. The process entailed gaining permissions at the unit (NICU) and hospital administration-levels, as well as from the Danish DPA. Once I had gained the requisite approvals and my research design and protocol had been reviewed and approved by the DPA (followed by my institution's local IRB), I was able to begin my field research in Denmark.

A salient difference between the two processes was my perception of trust from the IRB in the United States and the DPA in Denmark. In Denmark, the DPA granted my study exempt status, with the restriction to not collect sensitive and private information (e.g., union status) from participants. In total, it took two weeks to garner the DPA's approval. And once in the field at the Rigshospitalet's Neonataklinikken, I was on my own—I only checked in with the charge nurse or my contact upon arrival. I felt trusted to conduct this research; I was committed to upholding the principles of the Belmont Report and acting with integrity, but there was literally no one checking up on me.

On the other hand, gaining research approval for the United States NICU was different and not as straightforward. A difference for this site included engaging a third human protection research board: the health sciences IRB, not the local IRB. During the proposal drafting and feedback process for the IRB proposal, I found myself answering questions about how many participants I would observe and interview, which was problematic: if participants (or "subjects") are only included if they consent after being informed about the study, then how could I possibly know in advance how many participants I would observe and interview? Questions like these suggested incommensurability and prioritizing the institution's process, not the people (King, Bivens, Pumroy, Rauch, & Koerber, forthcoming). I could only provide the health sciences IRB with a range of the number of participants. I found myself frustrated with the health science's IRB process. In the United States the layer of litigious considerations designed to protect both subjects and institutions can encumber the researcher, even in her ethical planning. After the IRB's approval of my research project, I questioned how the needs of participants were prioritized in the IRB process (even based on subject/participant terminology). If I only followed the protocols and approvals by my institution's IRB, I could effectively gain consent but not actively looking for microwithdrawals of consent. My awareness of Cora's microwithdrawal of consent exceeded both the local IRB's and the health science's IRB's ethical standards of research conduct. But beyond attending to my emotional discomfort and thinking reflexively about my research encounter with Cora, how could I explain, using familiar, rhetorical disciplinary concepts and frameworks, a microwithdrawal of consent to others?

Understanding Rhetorical Actions: *Kairos, Decorum,* Rhetorical Listening, and Gestures

On a different day of data collection in a United States NICU over a year later, a mother of a baby, Barbara, consented to participate in the same study. When I asked if she had questions before she signed the IRB-approved informed consent, she replied, "no." However, after she signed the consent, she asked if her name would be used in any of the resultant publications. I said, "No, only pseudonyms will be used." It was a few moments later that she returned back to care for her baby and closed the privacy curtain that surrounded her baby's bed space. Barbara closed the curtain and did not make eye contact with me for the next three days as she went about the care of her baby. On the days that I observed, when Barbara was at her baby's bedside, she kept the privacy curtains closed.

In my observations over the next few days, Barbara only emerged from behind the closed curtains to clean her electric breast pump parts at the sink. When she washed the breast pump parts at the sink, which was on the other side of the curtain, I could see her, although she did not make eye contact with me. Her nonverbal communication, like Cora's closed eyes as she held her son during skin-to-skin contact, suggested to me that she had withdrawn her consent to participate. Barbara never explicitly or verbally withdrew her consent; however, it was clear that, even though she had been informed about the study and had signed the consent, she did not wish to participate (in any capacity) any longer. Legally and ethically, it would have been permissible for me to approach her and ask her if I could observe, but it was clear, since she closed the curtain, she did not want to be observed. I did not think it wise or ethical to do so—she had withdrawn her consent. I recognized her microwithdrawal of consent through a series of Barbara's actions and gestures.

Kairos

If you have ever thought that you should ask just one more question during an interview (or, conversely, stop an interview), or if you have ever thought that it was a good time to approach a participant (or, conversely, not approach a participant), then you have tacitly acknowledged the role that *kairos*—appropriate timing or opportunity—plays in the research process during data collection in the field. Both Miller (1994) and Kinneavy (1986) discuss *kairos* as opportunity or timing, with the latter defining it as the "right or opportune time to do something, or right measure in doing something" (p. 80). More recently, Segal (2005) discusses *kairos* in terms of contingency and fit for a specific situation. *Kairos* is an awareness of appropriate timing and opportunity. *Kairos*, as a rhetorical concept, needs attending to in research practices in sensitive health care and medical contexts—it can provide a helpful conceptual means to consider these emotionally unsettling moments or research practices that give us cause to pause and reflect.

In the Danish NICU, parents were allowed to be with their babies, almost without exception, 24 hours a day. In fact, there were hospital beds for parents right next to their baby's beds. Conversely, the United States NICU limited the times parents and other legal caregivers could visit to 20 hours a day. For example, visitors (including parents) were not allowed in the NICU between 6:00–8:00 am and pm. There were no beds available for parents or other legal caregivers to sleep on in the United States NICU. I learned rather quickly that most of the communication between nurses and the parents of these premature babies occurred around feeding times. During feeding times, diapers were changed and body temperatures were taken to cluster the scheduled care for these infants and limit interruptions to their sleep. During these times, nurses and parents were at the baby's bedsides, talking about the care of the baby. In other words, I learned that feeding times were the most appropriate, opportune times to observe, but not to interview. Why would I ask a parent or a nurse to be interviewed when their time and attention was focused on a baby? The rhetorical concept *kairos* provided the framework to know the clustered care schedule was ripe for observation, but inappropriate for interview.

Decorum

As a component of *kairos*, Miller (1994) suggests, "Decorum asks us to judge discourse according to whether it is fitting, or appropriate, to a particular moment" (p. 83). The fit or appropriateness also includes constraints, including the needs, relationships, and values of those involved. Ericsson (2003) reminds us that attending to *decorum* involves recognizing that not all audience's needs in particular moments and spaces are the same. Recognizing timing and the fitness to a particular contextualized occasion creates a "dynamic interplay" (Miller, 1994, p. 83) to which rhetors—and researchers—should attend. The rhetorical concept *decorum* incorporates and applies appropriateness to timing and to opportunity. In other words, it might be the right time for one audience (e.g., the researcher to observe a phenomenon), but is it the right *and* appropriate time for all audiences (e.g., the researcher and the participants)?

I did not immediately recognize the importance of timing and sensitivity to context until I experienced several, compounded challenges while collecting data in the field. Lanham (1991) argues that *decorum* is a "test of acculturation" (p. 46), which suggests a particular awareness or, when deployed within a research context, a set of dispositions and skills only gained via experience. Tending to our research experiences, such as Gouge's (this volume) call to acknowledge divergent or "noncompliant" practices, presents opportunities to "give meaning to the actions and actors of health care" (Edwell, this collection, p. 157). First, my implicit attention to *decorum* was essentially why I did not continue researching after Cora withdrew her consent to be interviewed: Staying seemed convenient for me but inconvenient and undesirable for Cora and therefore improper, inappropriate, and *untimely*. I knew I was observing something sensitive and intimate—something unusual and private. My unsettled feelings suggested the time was not appropriate for all involved. Further, coupling Cora's explicit withdrawal of consent with my emotional displeasure exposed an act of rhetorical agency via noncompliant behavior. Conceptually, *decorum* provided the rhetorical framework to explicate my unsettled feelings and give meaning to Cora's action (and inaction). And attention to *decorum* provided a framework to explain my unsettled feelings—feelings that diverged from my norm—and acknowledge it was not appropriate to continue with research in any capacity.

Second, awareness of timing helped me recognize that it would be best to ask a nurse, a parent, or other legal caregiver to be interviewed after feeding time, but *decorum* provided a second filter to determine if it was appropriate to ask such a participant to be interviewed in a particular context. For example, Molly was the mother of twins in the United States NICU. After the scheduled clustered care and feeding time for her twins, Molly held each one for as long as she was able (she had four other children at home); as far as I could ascertain, this was the only time she was "available" for an interview. She consented to participate, yet I did not interview her until she asked me if I wanted to. *Decorum* suggested to me, since her time with her babies was both precious and limited, it would not be appropriate to interfere or interview her during those times. In the process, Molly willingly reassented to participate in my research study, as well as flexed her rhetorical agency to participate. Conceptually, *decorum* provides the framework to "focus on the embodied experiences of research participants" (Meloncon, this volume, p. 97). In health care and medical contexts, how does the researcher note divergences and noncompliance? How does the researcher provide space for a participant's rhetorical agency? *Kairos* and *decorum* conceptually provide structure, but how can researchers in health care and medical contexts practice and deploy these rhetorical concepts in the field? To answer, next I suggest an attention to rhetorical listening to bring awareness back to the researcher's body before exploring embodied gestures as participants' signals to researchers of microwithdrawals of consent.

Rhetorical Listening

Meloncon (this volume) suggests, "the body is often inadequately recognized through the research process" (p. 98). I agree and want to extend this to argue that both researchers' and participants' bodies provide sensory feedback to interrogate. To begin, I suggest researchers practicing rhetorical listening. Extending some of Kenneth Burke's ideas about persuasion and identification, Ratcliffe (2005) develops a theory of and methodology for rhetorical listening. Burke claims that identification precedes persuasion. In other words, in order to be persuaded, one must first identify with the person who is acting persuasively. As a methodology for "interpretive invention," Ratcliffe describes rhetorical listening as a "stance of openness that a person may choose to assume in relation to any person, text, or culture" (p. 17) "to cultivate conscious identifications in ways that promote pro-ductive communication, especially but not solely cross-culturally" (p. 25). More simply, rhetorical listening is listening for intent, not with intent. As a research practice, rhetorical listening conceptually presents an approach for reflexivity and attending to sensorial experience in research practice.

Rhetorical listening connects to *decorum*. Young et al. (1997) argue for the importance of being heard when discussions include disparate views, interests, and values; I suggest adding participants' needs to this list. Ericsson (2003) elaborates, "Not only does *decorum* allow for an analytical awareness of how complicated *being heard* actually is, it also provides guidance on how to *be heard*" (p. 7). Rhetori-cal listening prepares researchers to listen to those who want to be heard (even if they are silent). Infusing rhetorical listening with *decorum* provides opportuni-ties for researchers in health and medical contexts to be aware of participants' discrete needs. Sometimes the listener must enable the speaker to be heard, in part by adopting a listening stance. In practice, then, researchers can enter and work within health and medical contexts with an awareness of the opportunity rhetorical listening provides to more fully engage with research participants and their needs.

The four nonlinear moves that rhetorical listening entails operationalize *deco-rum*. According to Ratcliffe, these four moves, or dimensions, entail the following:

1. Promoting an *understanding* of self and other.
2. Proceeding with an *accountability* logic.
3. Locating identifications across *commonalities* and *differences*.
4. Analyzing *claims* as well as the *cultural logics* where these claims function. (p. 26)

An understanding of self and others includes listening "with intent, not just for intent" (p. 26); an accountability logic is situated in a specific place and recog-nizes that cultural responsibility is not partaking in blame; locating identifications encourages the exploration of areas of sameness and of difference; and cultural logics aim to reveal the system or cultural roots where assumptions and claims are made. These four moves help the researcher to conceptually shift the "subject" to agential participant, think about the needs and motivations of participants in research practice, and prioritize the bodily experiences of both researcher and participants in consent.

The first rhetorical listening move I used was promoting an understanding of self and others. When I embarked on my research project, I wanted to understand participants. I wanted to hear them beyond the framework of my intent and currently held notions or perceptions about communication in NICUs. Earlier, I discussed how the questions asked by the local health sciences IRB (e.g., "how many participants will your study include?") frustrated me; however, I was able to examine the source of that frustration. In other words, I was able to examine the assumptions that informed my research practices that, until then, had been invisible to me. Now, I can clearly trace how readings about unethical research practices, or "standing under discourses" (Ratcliffe, p. 28), that did not inform participants or allow participants an opportunity to consent, like the Tuskegee Syphilis Trials and the Bikini Islanders' Relocation, figured into my research practices. Ratcliffe's "standing under discourses" includes "discourses that surround us and others while consciously acknowledging all our particular—and very fluid—standpoints. Standing under discourses means letting discourses wash over, through, and around us and then letting them lie there to inform our politics and ethics" (p. 28). I wanted to make sincere, valid attempts to do better than what the IRB process seemed to value: securing documented consent and preventing potential litigation.

In order to make a sincere and a valid attempt to obtain informed consent from participants in my project, I promoted an understanding of myself and participants. Doing so helped me sift through my emotional discomfort after Cora withdrew her consent to be interviewed. Further, filtering through my emotional discomfort revealed my values as a researcher: ethically engaging participants and listening to their needs throughout the research process. Through rhetorical listening, we can recognize microwithdrawals of consent—the implied or partial halt of a participant's willingness to participate in one or more aspects of the research process. Without such critical research practices, researchers can unintentionally harm and restrict the agency of those they study. In RHM fieldwork, listening rhetorically ensures that participants offer informed, full, and persistent consent—a research practice I could identify after applying rhetorical listening's first move to critically examine my research experience with Cora.

Rhetorical listening also helps attend to the principles of the Belmont Report. Proceeding from a logic of accountability, one of Ratcliffe's four moves, I do not condemn or blame the health sciences IRB. Instead, I chose to do better in my own research practice by actively looking for microwithdrawals of consent, like Barbara avoiding eye contact and closing the curtain. These were more than simple gestures. Attending to the closed curtain respected Barbara's ability to choose to participate, and I held myself accountable for seeing this gesture. My research agenda cannot be ethically promoted without an adherence to my participants' involvement and their rhetorical agency in continually assenting to participate. As researchers, practicing rhetorical listening with an ear for microwithdrawals of consent allow researchers to empower participants and enact their rhetorical agency.

Ratcliffe's concept of rhetorical listening can be reoriented as an RHM researcher's methodological stance and approach to respecting persons and providing ongoing opportunities for participants to assent. I turn to the classical rhetorical canon delivery, specifically voice and gestures, to discuss physical cues for knowing when to listen rhetorically and how to attend to embodied communication.

Gestures as Embodied Rhetoric

Gestures, as rhetorical movements, have long been considered an important part of the cannon of delivery (Lanham, 1991). Examining Burke's connections between language, bodies, and communication, Hawhee (2009) explains that, "Bodies, for Burke, enable critical reflection on meaning-making from an anti-Cartesian, noncognitive, nonrational perspective—that is, from a perspective that does not begin by privileging reason or conscious thought" (p. 2). By turning our attention from our minds to bodies, we resituate the body as a critical component of communication—a movement that is embodied and pinned down to a physical location. Haas and Witte (2001) emphasize the contextualized and intuitive nature of embodied actions (p. 416). Embodied actions or embodied movements may be second nature and coexpressed with language, but importantly, body language can be observed and rhetorically listened to.

Once again, I return to Barbara. When she closed the curtain, she was creating a boundary between herself and her baby and everyone else, including me. It was a clear gesture to remove herself from the eyesight of all. Barbara did not speak to withdraw her consent; the gesture represented her microwithdrawal of consent, in effect conveying, "I do not want you to observe me." In the absence of a shared language, as with Cora, if one wants to know the time, usually a person can point to their wrist as an indication that they seek the time: a gesture. A pointing gesture, like pointing to a wrist, is known, in rhetorical terminology, as a deictic gesture. Deictic gestures point and provide focus or clarification. In the Danish NICU, I noticed that deictic gesturing is not only done with hands, but also, as part of nonverbal communication, done with eyes to indicate, for example, the speaker's focus. In particular, I recall interviewing a Danish mother, Alice, in English in a room adjacent to the one where her son was housed in the NICU. During our interview, she heard movement and voices in her son's room, so she looked in that direction. Then after hearing the surgeon speak, she broke off her interview response and said, "It's the surgeon, so I'll just go up." Temporarily, she focused her attention elsewhere; I stopped recording the interview at that point because I knew she was gesturing, or looking, where she wanted to be (and temporarily withdrawing her consent to be interviewed).

Ratcliffe explains that rhetorically listening involves the researcher shifting from one bodily organ—the eyes—to another bodily organ: the ears. I suggest another shift to gestures as embodied movements that communicate consent. Basically, there is a role for acknowledging gestures via rhetorical listening when studying communication in health care and medical contexts. If gesture and speech are viewed as coexpressed, which is an accepted factual phenomenon in this chapter, then listening to embodied movements can present a space to rhetorically listen— as it did for me in the NICUs referenced in this chapter. By critically examining my research practices and operationalizing the concept of rhetorical listening, I was able to ascertain that gestures can also signify microwithdrawals of consent, which might include pulling a curtain or temporarily stopping an interview.

Vulnerability as Essential Emotional Labor

I remember the first time I saw an infant with gastroschisis, a condition when a baby is born with her organs outside her body. When I walked into that NICU nursery (not one of the research sites referenced in this chapter), I glanced at the parents who looked shocked and scared and confused. I listened to their silent reactions and recognized I did not belong in the nursery. In the same NICU, I remember the first time I saw the withdrawal of life support following a Do Not Resuscitate (DNR) order. The baby was extremely premature (fewer than 24 weeks gestation), and I watched as the baby's tiny body, when comforted by a registered nurse's (RN) hands, responded with an increased heart rate. Meanwhile, the parents were letting go of this baby's life. I could see the loss on their understandably grief-stricken and heartbroken faces. The RN's caring hands stimulated the dying baby and prolonged the baby's death. I watched as the RN internally struggled with a decision to console the baby by touch and honor the parents' DNR wish. Hours later, I saw the body of the recently deceased baby. It is an image I think of every time I enter a NICU: the tiny baby who died that day and the RN's emotionally gut-wrenching struggle.

Before I started to research in Denmark, I knew the inherent nature of the NICU as emotionally charged spaces. Ratcliffe suggests rhetorical listening is helpful to listen across cultures "to cultivate conscious identifications in ways that promote productive communication, especially . . . cross-culturally" (p. 25). Since I understood the emotional nature of NICUs and consciously tried to empathize with parents, nurses, and other legal caregivers based on my previous experiences in NICUs, I approached accessing the Neonatalklinikken with humility and caution. I had spent about a month in Denmark before I contacted Betty, a nurse in Neonatalklinikken and doctoral student studying breastfeeding and skin-to-skin contact. I found Betty when I searched online for someone in Denmark with similar research interests as mine. I had her name and email address for almost three full weeks before I worked up the courage to send her an email. My "cold call" email message introduced myself, expressed my interest in her research, and asked whether it would be possible to meet to discuss an opportunity to research in her NICU. It took me three weeks of multiple email drafts, self-pep talks, and emotional duress before I acknowledged that the answer was going to be "no" until I asked. I felt so vulnerable and humbled placing myself in a position to be ignored or told "no." I did not realize then how essential that emotional labor— empathy, insecurity, vulnerability, and worry—would be or how much it would prepare me for later work. The researcher's lived experiences in health care and medical contexts are complex and important, as Powell and Takayoshi (2012) note throughout their edited collection in *Practicing Research in Writing Studies: Reflexive and Ethically Responsible Research*.

One text I encountered was especially helpful in addressing emotional vulnerability and fieldwork challenges—medical anthropologists Jordan and Davis-Floyd's (1992) ethnographic study *Birth in Four Cultures*. Jordan spent over a year in the field, assisting and finally *ipso facto* becoming a midwife to the Maya in one village in Yucatan. In the first chapter of the book, Jordan and Davis-Floyd provided an explanation for conducting a comparative study of birth in four cultures (Yucatan, United States, Sweden, and Holland). They noted the universality of childbirth, the "improve[ment] and broaden[ing] [of] our appreciation of the organization of female networks, interests, and strategies," and the changing birthing systems in various cultures (p. 5) in response to the question of why this research matters.

As Jordan and Davis-Floyd's study makes clear, the researcher's *ethos* or credibility is an essential element to gain access to a research site. Rhetoricians like Kennedy and Burke have explained the credibility of the researcher is an integral element for persuasion. Kennedy (1997), in his discussion of comparative rhetoric, claims that a person's authority is the most persuasive element across cultures and across time. More recently, Royster and Kirsch (2012) argue for "an ethos of humility, respect, and care" as "critical to achieving qualities of excellence" in research (p. 21). My experiences have taught me that humility comes from vulnerability, and that vulnerability is essential emotional labor. Teston (2012) asks how we access privileged and sensitive research sites with equally privileged and sensitive information, a question Angeli and Pigozzi also take up in this volume. I offer humility and vulnerability as requisite components to access privileged and sensitive research sites. "In most places," according to Jordan and Davis-Floyd, "[birth] is a private event, and in all places, access is restricted" (p. 119); this is most certainly the case for NICUs. Fostering identifications to augment credibility and demonstrate goodwill and empathy—with the intention that participants will consider this in their decision-making process—as integral in my approach to asking permission. The vulnerability, empathetic understanding, and caution I exhibited initially showed Betty and then Louise I respected the NICU as a sensitive and specialized space.

One passage in Jordan and Davis-Floyd's (1992) monograph helpfully discusses the implications of gaining access to field sites and the emotional labor of researching in sensitive spaces. The space referenced here is Yucatan, and Jordan's contact there is the midwife Doña Juana:

> . . . I wonder why I was so apprehensive about meeting with Doña Juana. First of all, I think, it had little to do with her but everything to do with my circumstances. I found myself in a situation where I had little control, a situation exacerbated by the fact that I knew that my ability to make sense was severely impaired. As I thought about the impending encounter, I felt that I would be operating from a position of powerlessness in which she held all the cards and I none. I wanted something from her that was extremely important to me, but I had nothing to offer in return. Furthermore, I didn't know what the local rules were for making such a request, nor did I know how to handle a potential denial.
>
> *(pp. 96–97)*

When I read this passage, I immediately recognized how I had felt at points during this research process, and especially when I initially asked permission to research in these special and specialized health care spaces. It was emotionally taxing, as our field research in health care and medical contexts can be. It was also a worthwhile reminder of being powerless and vulnerable in a situation, which helped me reflect on my role as a researcher in the field and my ethical commitment to engage with participants. It was also an important reminder of the powerlessness and vulnerabilities participants might experience and that I must be attentive to, in part through rhetorically listening with empathy and by noting microwithdrawals of consent.

Practical Suggestions for Recognizing Microwithdrawals of Consent

Rhetorical agency can be enabled by researchers. By noting Cora's closed eyes, Barbara's lack of eye contact and curtain closing, and Alice's visual deictic pointing, I sensed microwithdrawals of their consent to participate in my study to varying degrees and with differing levels of finiteness. Cora explicitly withdrew her consent to be interviewed and implicitly withdrew her consent to be observed, Barbara explicitly withdrew her consent to be observed (or viewed) and implicitly withdrew her consent to be interviewed, and Alice temporarily withdrew her consent to be interviewed.

Whole or partial, complete or temporary, more or less implicit, microwithdrawals of consent can have many forms. When a participant is informed about a study, provided an opportunity to ask questions about the study, and the participant chooses to sign the consent, we can assume at that point that she/he wants to participate. But, research with humans is complex and dynamic, and our informed consent documents should reflect this. It would be wise to include a statement akin to, "I will periodically affirm your willingness to participate in this study. For example, I might ask you if you want to take a break or stop. And you can pause or stop your participation at any time for any reason." Once the ink dries, in other words, the participant's willingness to participate might change, and we have to create spaces for participants to negotiate those changes.

Written as text, recognizing microwithdrawals seems simple enough; however, in the field, as an embodied and lived experience, how can researchers recognize microwithdrawals of consent? I offer several suggestions. Before a research study commences, I suggest casing or visiting the scene as a preparatory research practice; during research, I suggest engaging more than your visual sense; and if interviewing, I suggest familiarity with questions.

Casing the Scene

Years before I researched in any NICU, I worked in one. My previous experiences in the NICU helped to manage my expectations researching in such a sensitive research space. Because not every researcher can work in a research space before studying it, I suggest casing the scene as a preparatory research practice. Casing the scene is an exploratory research practice. It involves physically entering the proposed research space, more than likely after meeting with gatekeepers, to better acquaint yourself with the research space itself. Getting to know the noises, the actions, the environment, and other elements should better prepare you to understand the research space and the scenes you might encounter, like Edwell demonstrates in her emplaced rhetorical study (this volume). Further, acquainting yourself with the research space with the mindset that it was once new to participants, too, might help you find common ground to promote understanding, as Ratcliffe describes.

Before I embarked on research in the NICU, I cased the scene. When I first met with Betty, and after our initial two-hour conversation about their excellent Neonatalklinikken, she gave me a guided tour of the NICU. And although I did not start my research then, I did ask if I could sit in the waiting area. In a different NICU after an initial meeting with gatekeepers, years before, I asked to sit in an empty nursery and observe on the other side of a window (wearing earplugs to maintain patient privacy and limiting what I could hear). In both instances, I sought to demonstrate goodwill to the gatekeepers I interacted with, as well as familiarize myself with the environment. By doing this, I was more familiar with the space, and participants were more familiar with my presence, when I started data collection, and I was therefore better able to focus on participants. I contribute environment familiarity with being able to both practice rhetorical listening to promote understanding and foster identifications before engaging with participants.

Engaging Other Senses

While observing, I suggest engaging more than your visual sense; conversely, you can also heighten your visual sense. For example, observe aurally by closing your eyes and listening. Or observe solely visually by wearing earplugs. By attending to the aural, sensorial aspect of the NICU, I was able to recognize that when physiological monitors sounded, participants' attention went elsewhere. I recognized that if a participant's attention needed to be elsewhere, I should stop asking interview questions and be held accountable to the priority in the research space: the care of the infant. Additionally, I demonstrated mindfulness regarding *decorum*, as well as showed reflexive research practices by responding to current conditions. Being attuned to the NICUs soundscape also provided a signal that a participant might need to partially withdraw their consent to participate. During data collection in a NICU in the United States, a physiological monitor continuously alarmed, prompting the RN I was interviewing to withdraw consent through her necessary action of going to the baby's beside.

Memorizing Interview Questions

If interviewing is a data collection method in health care and medical contexts, I suggest familiarity with the questions. By being familiar with the interview questions, as well as relying on digital recordings, you can focus on participants, not the questions or taking notes. When the questions are memorized, it frees the researcher to watch for visual cues suggesting microwithdrawals of consent, like fidgeting, crossing and uncrossing legs, or no eye contact. Of course, there are many gestures that might indicate a microwithdrawal of consent. In another instance, parents I interviewed were waiting for word from an RN after their baby's minor surgical procedure. During the interview, their eyes moved to the lounge's door where the interview occurred. Given the context and their eyes gesturing toward the door, I asked if they wanted to postpone the interview. They replied now was fine, but they would go to their baby as soon as possible, suggesting the interview would end then. Recognizing the renegotiation of their participation, I helped the participants to both articulate the boundaries of their participation and to facilitate the microwithdrawal of their consent.

Acknowledging Microwithdrawals of Consent: An Ethical Research Practice

As an ethical research practice, the duty to recognize when a participant might either explicitly or implicitly withdraw consent to participate, either wholly or partially at any point during the research process, demands our attention. Explicit withdrawals, like the one I experienced in the Neonatalklinikken, are obvious and intentional: Cora stated she did not want to be interviewed. However, she also implicitly withdrew her consent to be observed when she closed her eyes and held her sleeping son. The suggestions I offer might help you to identify microwithdrawals of consent in your own research practice—a reflexive practice asking you to interrogate your approach to preparing and conducting research in health care and medical contexts.

We all have research stories. Microwithdrawals of consent exist, and I have offered advice for recognizing, by rhetorically listening, when participants microwithdraw their consent to participate in research. Erring on the side of ethical research practice by being cautious is paramount, especially in health care and medical contexts where participants might not recognize their agency in withdrawing consent—partially or wholly—once the ink has dried.

Notes

1 All names are pseudonyms.
2 For the United States site, I received approval from the health science's IRB at my university. In total, I worked with three separate human protection boards: two for Denmark and one for the United States.

References

Barton, E. (2008). Further contributions from the ethical turn in composition/rhetoric: Analyzing ethics in interaction. *College Composition and Communication, 59*(4), 596–632.

Barton, E., & Eggly, S. (2009). Ethical or unethical persuasion? The rhetoric of offers to participate in clinical trials. *Written Communication, 26*(3), 295–319.

Ericsson, P. F. (2003). *Rhetorical theory: Kairos and decorum.* Retrieved from public.wsu. edu/~ericsson/kairos_decorum.doc.

Grabill, J. T. (2006). The study of writing in the social factory: Methodology and rhetori-calagency. In J. B. Scott, B. Longo, & K. V. Wills (Eds.), *Critical power tools: Technical communication and cultural studies* (pp. 151–170). Albany, NY: SUNY Press.

Haas, C., & Witte, S. (2001). Writing as an embodied practice: The case of engineering standards. *Journal of Business and Technical Communication, 15*(4), 413–457.

Hawhee, D. (2009). *Moving bodies: Kenneth Burke at the edges of language.* Columbia, SC: University of South Carolina Press.

Jordan, B., & Davis-Floyd, R. (1992). *Birth in four cultures: A crosscultural investigation of childbirth in Yucatan, Holland, Sweden, and the United States.* Long Grove, IL: Waveland Press.

Kennedy, G. A. (1997). *Comparative rhetoric: An Historical and cross-cultural introduction.* New York, NY: Oxford University Press.

Kinneavy, J. L. (1986). Kairos: A neglected concept in classical rhetoric. In J. D. Moss (Ed.), *Rhetoric and praxis: The contribution of classical rhetoric to practical reasoning* (pp. 79–105). Washington, DC: Catholic University of America Press.

King, C.S.T., Bivens, K.M., Pumroy, E., Rauch, S, & Koerber, A. (forthcoming). "IRB problems and solutions in health communication research." Health Communication.

Lanham, R. A. (1991). *A handlist of rhetorical terms* (2nd ed.). Berkeley, CA: University of California Press.

Miller, C. R. (1994). Opportunity, opportunism, and progress: Kairos in the rhetoric of technology. *Argumentation, 8*(1), 81–96.

Powell, K. M., & Takayoshi, P. (Eds.). (2012). *Practicing research in writing studies: Reflexive and ethically responsible research.* New York, NY: Hampton Press.

Ratcliffe, K. (2005). *Rhetorical listening: Identification, gender, whiteness.* Carbondale, IL: Southern Illinois University Press.

Royster, J. J., & Kirsch, G. E. (2012). *Feminist rhetorical practices: New horizons for rhetoric, composition, and literacy studies.* Carbondale, IL: Southern Illinois University Press.

Segal, J. (2005). *Health and the rhetoric of medicine.* Carbondale, IL: Southern Illinois University Press.

Teston, C. (2012). Moving from artifact to action: A grounded investigation of visual displays of evidence during medical deliberations. *Technical Communication Quarterly, 21*(3), 187–209.

United States Department of Health and Human Services. (1979). *Ethical principles and guidelines for the protection of human subjects of research.* Retrieved from www.hhs.gov/ohrp/humansubjects/guidance/belmont.html.

Young, A. J., Kim, L., Li, S., Baker, J. N., Schmidt, M., Camp, J. W., & Barfield, R. C. (2010). Agency and communication challenges in discussions of informed consent in pediatric cancer research. *Qualitative Health Research, 20,* 628–643.

Young, I. M. (1997). *Intersecting voices: Dilemmas of gender, political philosophy, and policy.* Princeton, NJ: Princeton University Press.

9

MEDICAL INTERIORS

Materiality and Spatiality in Medical Rhetoric Research Methods

Jennifer Edwell

Keywords: emplaced rhetoric, medical rhetoric, hospital chapels, in situ, rhetorical field methods, religion and medicine

Rhetoric of health & medicine, as a subfield, has diversified the traditional targets of rhetorical study taking into account discursive interactions between health-seekers and health care providers, educational texts for health professionals, and public health discourse. As this collection demonstrates, many rhetoricians are moving beyond text-bound projects by investigating diffuse and material objects in relation to the biomedical sphere and health-seekers' lived experience. Taking seriously Greg Dickinson, Brian Ott, and Eric Aoki's (2006) claim that rhetoric scholars must "attend to the experiential landscapes in which all discourses occur," I argue for (re)envisioning the object of our study in context and as embodied (p. 42). Specifically, the methodology I advance here highlights the importance of situated—or *emplaced*—knowledge and practice within the constructed sites of medicine (including, but not limited to, clinical sites) as well as historical and cultural landscapes.

Scholars (Schuster, 2006; Fountain, 2014) have laid the groundwork for studying embodiment, materiality, and visuality in health discourse, and I expand on this research to examine how built environments organize and give meaning to the actions and actors of health care. In particular, I am adopting Dickinson et al.'s (2006) concept of "experiential landscapes" to explore the rhetorical significance of a hospital chapel. As Dickinson et al. describe, "experiential landscapes" include individuals' beliefs and knowledge (or "dreamscapes"), institutional narratives and dispositions, and geographical locales (p. 29). In effect, reimagining medicine in experiential landscapes means developing a fuller conception of the rhetorical situation of health discourse as well as medical knowledge and practices.

For example, the chapel is a distinct site within the context of the hospital, and understanding the construction and exchange of meaning between this specific site and the larger landscape can help illuminate the role of religion in medicine. This approach will require attending to the metalevel (i.e., abstracted contextualization), the history of particular built environments (including the intentions of architects and designers), and the cognitive and affective impact of emplaced discourse as well as the phenomenological encounter with the medical context.

In this chapter, I deliberate on methods of rhetorical analysis and the experience of analyzing material, spatial rhetoric through my investigation of The John M. Reeves All Faiths Chapel at North Carolina Memorial Hospital. In this case study, I highlight the rhetorical functions assigned to and experienced through different places in the hospital. Studying the hospital chapel as a place of intersecting discourses and embodied experiences provides an opportunity to expand research on medical rhetoric through an explicit focus on material, spatial knowledge and practice within medical environments. Through the discussion of my fieldwork, I explain an emplaced framework as a method of rhetorical inquiry, detailing six practices that can be incorporated into a methodology of researching medical rhetoric as emplaced.

The Materiality and Spatiality of Rhetoric

The methodology I develop in this chapter is organized around several key theoretical concepts—namely, materiality and spatiality, place and space, and experiential landscapes. To begin, I turn to Carole Blair for her work on rhetoric, materiality, and place. As Blair (1999) has explained, rhetoric is material, because "rhetoric is not rhetoric until it is uttered, written, or otherwise manifested or given presence" (p. 18). Yet the material quality of rhetoric is often ignored, neglecting the concrete, corporeal circumstances that prefigure rhetoric's epistemological function, conditions which profoundly afford and constrain meaning. In other words, beyond written and spoken discourse, the mediation of meaning occurs through a variety of material and spatial enactments.[1] Blair claims, "Rhetoric's materiality constructs communal space, prescribes pathways, and summons attention, acting on the whole person of the audience" (p. 48). Subjectivities, actions, and forms of knowledge are materialized in built environments. The convergence of material and spatial rhetoric, or emplaced rhetoric, communicates by constructing and conveying meaning through design as well as the interaction of people with and within the built environment.

Given this framework, context is not merely part of the rhetorical situation (i.e., mundane "setting"), but place is itself rhetorical. The design of buildings and other built environments construct certain kinds of actors and elicit particular actions. Consider, for example, the importance of location in distinguishing identity; my understanding of the subject position I occupy in a particular place (e.g., my parent's house versus a doctor's office) contributes to the exigency and shapes the performance of my role (daughter or patient). Thus, one of the guiding assumptions of this chapter is that the rhetorical character of health sites is fundamental in generating and sustaining medical sphere subjectivities. In health-related built environments, perhaps more than other locations, (some) bodies are especially vulnerable, open, or dependent. The roles performed in these locations anticipate and respond to this unique relation to the body.

Before describing how we might study emplaced rhetoric, I must establish my position in the ongoing debate about the distinction between place and space. Geographer Doreen Massey (1994) views space as a realm of social relations, where the "ever-shifting social geometry of power and signification" unfolds (p. 3). Place, Massey writes, is "a particular articulation of those relations, a particular moment in those networks of social relations and understandings" (p. 5). While place is often assumed to be something stable, Massey insists that the stabilization of meaning, through naming and boundary drawing, is a result of "social contest" (p. 5). Somewhat differently, geographer Tim Cresswell (2004) argues that, "Place, at a basic level, is space invested with meaning in the context of power" (p. 12). Cresswell emphasizes that this investment of meaning, through emotional attachment and social interactions, happens in material settings. For Cresswell, place denotes a more secure attachment of meaning; however, bearing Massey's critique in mind, that meaning is imposed and maintained through certain configurations of power and social relationships.

In order to make sense of the material and symbolic elements as well as the physical and cognitive experiences of a place, Dickenson et al. (2006) propose the term "experiential landscapes." The authors explain that the layout and design elements of a built environment "offer fully embodied subject positions that direct particular ways of looking" and acting (p. 30). The notion of experiential landscapes highlights the role of built environments in shaping knowledge, producing subjectivities, and prompting actions.

While the built environment may prescribe certain physical and affective experiences, not all meaning resides within the intentions of the design. Dickenson et al. write, "like the physical landscape, the dreamscape [or cognitive landscape] proffers a set of intertextual relations or 'codes' that structure the practices that occur" (p. 30). This assemblage is essential for how individuals engage with the site; yet the "effectiveness" of the site depends also on the previous experiences and expectations that individuals bring to it. Along these lines, Massey argues that, "the particularity of any place is constructed [. . .] through the specificity of the mix of links and interconnection *to* that 'beyond'" (p. 5). Thus, the condensation of meaning that gives a place its placeness is achieved through rhetorical gesturing to and invoking of things beyond the site as well as purposeful omission of other things.

The All Faiths Chapel is best understood as a place because the rhetorical capacity of the chapel is enabled by the permanence of the physical structure and ongoing recognition of the character of the site by the hospital audience. At this site, I am interested in the emplaced rhetoric, by which I mean the aspects of a place that create audiences and prescribe actions through material and spatial constructions.

Methodological Principles

Investigating the emplaced character of rhetoric entails a shift to in situ rhetorical inquiry. This method is important for the rhetoric of health & medicine (RHM) because it can reveal how medical expertise, as well as health-seekers' lived experience of health care, is fundamentally shaped by materiality and spatiality. Fountain (2014) and Schuster (2006), for example, have demonstrated the kind of insights that are possible when the critic is able to experience the embodied aspects of a rhetorical situation as well as the types of considerations that are important for in situ research at health sites. Drawing from such insights, I offer two guiding principles for investigations of emplaced rhetoric: presence and self-reflexivity.

Principle #1: Presence

Attending to rhetoric "on site" entails an embodied research experience. Blair (2001) provides theoretical and methodological direction for considering the role of the body in emplaced rhetoric. She highlights that the targets of rhetorical criticism are phenomenological in nature. When a researcher encounters an object of analysis, the researcher's experience of the context and object engages all the senses, and this proximity necessarily affects the researcher's perception of the object. Blair implores us to consider "how it is that we validate the use of reproductions in our work" at the expense of not being present and experiencing the rhetorical target in a fully embodied way (p. 276).

Thus, it is clear that the researcher must be embedded or present in order to investigate emplaced rhetoric in situ. One possible approach to doing this, put forward by Michael Middleton, Samantha Senda-Cook, and Danielle Endres (2011), is rhetorical field methods. Middleton et al. define rhetoric as constituted "through a combination of material contexts, social relationships, identities, consciousnesses, and (interrelated) rhetorical acts that produce meanings and that are coconstructed between rhetor, audience, and particular contexts" (p. 391). Rhetorical field methods requires identifying how the built environment makes rhetorical claims on audiences, observing how audiences engage or manipulate the emplaced rhetoric, and considering how such rhetoric might be practiced differently. This method combines critical rhetoric, ethnography, and performance studies. The aim is to "theorize how rhetoric constructs everyday life," including "the corporeal and aesthetic dimensions of rhetoric," by investigating how built environments are maintained and altered by actual, embodied visitors (p. 389). Middleton et al. urge researchers to unpack the "identities, relationships, and other components of *actually lived* social practice that shape how 'live' rhetorics are differently experienced" (p. 392).

In order to understand the practices of medical education, Fountain (2014) observed and joined students in their course activities in a gross anatomy lab, providing an example of in situ rhetorical inquiry. Although his project does not directly investigate the emplaced rhetoric of the lab, he illustrates the importance of materiality and embodiment for medical rhetoric. "To move beyond an exclusive focus on conventional word-based documents," Fountain writes in his introduction, "*Rhetoric in the Flesh* attends to the ways visual images and objects participate in processes of education and socialization" (p. 2). Fountain's method blended ethnographic observations, interviews, and "rhetorical analysis of displays, objects, documents, and discourses" (pp. 5, 10), including observations of students' engagement with illustrations, plastic models, and cadavers. In the lab, students are educated through "embodied rhetorical action," which Fountain defines as "the connection of objects, discourses, lived bodies, and embodied practices—an object-body-environment intertwining—that develops in participants the skilled vision that makes all technical and professional knowledge possible" (p. 15).

Fountain's study documents the way medical students engage their own bodies in visual, kinesthetic, and tactile experiences provided by the gross anatomy lab in order to learn how to see and touch the body as a physician. To make his assessment, Fountain participated in some of the learning activities orchestrated in the lab. He writes, "As I began to interact physically with the lab's visuals—the bodies, atlas images, even wall posters—I came to realize the importance of embodiment and embodied practices" (p. 11). Being in the site enabled Fountain to use his own experience as evidence, illustrating that presence is important for entering into the rhetorical situation and perceiving the dynamics of the experiential landscape.

Principle #2: Self-Reflexivity

Additionally, in situ rhetorical studies necessitate self-reflexivity, accounting for the rhetorician's body and perspective. Guy McHendry, Middleton, Endres, Senda-Cook, and Megan O'Byrne (2014) clarify the notion that fieldwork is not simply observation and conversation. Rather, fieldwork entails expectations, ideas, recollections, and the physical experience of being present. They advance the concept of "immanent participation" to account for in situ research choices, and they respond to Blair's considerations of embodiment through a focus on ethical relationships and actions. McHendry et al. write, "Immanent participation focuses on the affective dimensions of in situ research, insisting that in situ rhetorical critics analyze how people (including researchers and their co-participants in research) build affective bonds and collective subjectivities" (p. 294). Being present generates a relationship between the researcher and the site, and that relationship must prompt self-reflection and responsive research practices.

Schuster (2006) demonstrates the importance of self-reflexivity in her study, "A Different Place to Birth." Her aim is to understand "the complex constellation of mind, body, and place in the births at Baby Haven," a free-standing birth clinic (p. 11). Schuster focuses on how women's engagement with the site fosters their agency during their birthing experiences. Her method involved observations, documenting the spatial arrangement of the clinic, and interviews with women who had given birth at the clinic, all of which captured experiential perceptions of the clinic. She claims that the physical structure and features of the clinic enabled women to resist biomedically scripted birth experiences and develop counterdisourses (p. 9). In developing her method, Schuster explains, "I was faced with the challenge of balancing my own scholarly observations of a particular space with participants' perceptions of their experiences in that space as shared during interviews" (p. 5). Schuster's experience of the site provided insights, but it was different from the experience of the staff, women, and families who work or give birth at the center. This recognition is important because, without reflection on the researcher's embodied experience of the site, the description and analysis may be abstracted from the researcher's presence and, in effect, the visitor-perspective may become fictitiously generic and idealized.

Although the principles of presence and self-reflexivity can be observed across literature on in situ rhetoric, different types of places (with different kinds of audiences) will require different research choices. For example, Middleton et al.'s (2011) rhetorical field methods and McHendry et al.'s (2014) "immanent participation" advocate for the researcher to identify with and collaborate alongside the actual audience. This kind of participatory research, it seems to me, is best suited for studying established communities and relatively stable collectives in places that are part of people's "everyday" lives. For hospital staff, as well as patients and families in extended care facilities, health care sites may be places of daily life. However, for locations that are characteristically transitory, as hospitals are for many patients, the audience may not be consistent. Far from being sites of the "everyday," these locations are experienced as extraordinary. Therefore, an attempt by the researcher to isolate and emulate one particular kind of audience would be reductive. When we cannot assume a stable audience, I suggest that rhetoricians can consider how the significance of the place (meaning the stabilization and consistency of meaning in the built environment) is instantiated and transformed by the perpetually variable audience.

Practices for Studying Emplaced Medical Rhetoric

Bringing the tools of rhetoric to bear on the medical landscape invites dynamic perspectives on the meaning and construction of health, well-being, and care. However, to investigate the material and spatial aspects of medicine necessitates adapting the methods of rhetorical inquiry. Collecting this kind of qualitative data requires reading as well as listening, seeing, and experiencing. It also requires that rhetoricians be critical of how we read, hear, see, and engage with a space. What specifically might this method entail? I propose six applied practices for studying emplaced medical rhetoric. These research practices are: *Name the Boundaries, Consider the Ethical Implications, Select a Method of Experience, Frame the Questions, Find a Stance*, and *Reconstruct and Interpret*. Expanding on the literature outlined above, I will explain each practice and illustrate how it could be applied through discussion of my case study. Allowing for elasticity in method, I believe these practices can be modeled in other projects.

Case Study: The Hospital Chapel

The John M. Reeves All Faiths Chapel (see figure 9.1) is an example of an experiential landscape relevant for rhetoricians of health and medicine. The All Faiths Chapel is the main interfaith chapel in North Carolina Memorial Hospital, which is located alongside the Children's Hospital, Woman's Hospital, and Cancer Hospital. Taken together, these facilities constitute the main UNC Hospital Campus, and the medical campus is joined with the University of North Carolina at Chapel Hill. On the hospital website, the institution is describe as a "public, academic medical center operated by and for the people of North Carolina" ("About Us," n.d.). As such, individuals who experience this landscape are as diverse as the

FIGURE 9.1   The John M. Reeves All Faiths Chapel. Photo by Jennifer Edwell.

topography of this state. Staff, patients, and their families constitute a heterogeneous collective, bringing a variety of beliefs and values into the hospital.

Broadly, my research focuses on the exchange between contemporary American religion and biomedicine. Thus, I decided to study the All Faiths Chapel because the presence of the chapel within the hospital materializes belief systems and forms of knowledge that diverge from the dominant discourse of biomedicine, making it a particularly exciting case study. My experience of the site and reflexive research practices enabled me to perceive how the material, spatial composition of the site corresponded to particular subjectivities and actions. As a state institution, this hospital location also provided an opportunity to think about the significance and expression of religiosity in a pluralistic context. Importantly, the site's physical and institutional accessibility (unlike various restricted spaces within the hospital) made the project feasible.

After selecting the target of my study, my research process moved through three (rather indistinct) phases. First, I received approval from the Institutional Review Board for the Protection of Human Subjects in Research (IRB).[2] Second, I conducted fieldwork, which included interviewing a chaplain and observing the chapel over several hour-long sessions. My "data collection" focused on the chapel's architectural features, its use and function, and its position and role within the hospital. Finally, I spent time reflecting and interpreting the rhetorically significant characteristics of the chapel. Ultimately, I believe that studying hospital chapels can enrich our understanding about the role of religion in medicine as well as the transformation of religion in contexts that value cultural diversity and plurality.

Name the Boundaries

Dickinson et al. (2006) adopt Barry Brummett's notion of a "diffuse text" to explain the indistinct perimeter of material contexts (p. 29). The interaction of a specific site with its broader setting, geographic and cultural, is hazy, indeterminate, and perpetually transformed by the peculiarities of every visitor. However, the process of research entails defining the object of study, and this definition is never inconsequential. Scholars wield the power to define a place as self-contained, demarcating the borders of the experiential landscape in order to distinguish the boundaries and dimensions of a site. Likewise, Massey (1994) argues that, "all attempts to institute horizons, to establish boundaries, to secure the identity of places, can [. . .] be seen to be *attempts to stabilize the meaning of particular envelopes of space-time*" (p. 5). Therefore, studying material and spatial rhetoric requires being aware and transparent about how the target is defined.

A feminist, intersectional approach to place (one I would like to advocate) would emphasize the vectors of difference that are constructed and reiterated by a site. Accordingly, rhetorical approaches to place ought to attend to the construction, function, and deployment of individual and collective identities as well as systems of power. For example, it is important to consider how structural ine-qualities shape and compound vulnerabilities for marginalized people. Envision-ing the experiential landscape of a specific medical site in this way could reveal how access, health literacy, and quality of care issues are reified through built environments.

In kind, I found it helpful to think of the All Faiths Chapel as a diffuse text. Experience of the chapel cannot be reduced to the space within four walls because, as Dickinson et al. (2006) write, "the experience and meaning of the larger landscape (and of its attendant sites) *spill over* into specific sites" (p. 29, emphasis added). For example, in the hallway outside the chapel, framed memory quilts hang on the wall, marked with notes of loss and love for those who have died. Certainly, then, the chapel is part of a larger material and spatial discourse around loss, grief, and memory.

While the chapel must be understood in relation to places and discourses outside of this one room, I needed to demarcate the boundary of the experiential landscape for the target of my study. As a particular locale within the hospital demarcated as "interfaith," the chapel is overtly religious; however, the specific affiliation or identity of the site is rendered neutral or ambiguous (until, as I will argue, it is occupied and engaged by visitors), which is an important rhetorical move at this state institution. Yet there are other religious and spiritually demarked spaces in the hospital that afford visitors different embodied opportunities. In the cancer center, for example, there is a "Chapel and Meditation Room," which is actually two separate spaces oriented toward Christianity and Eastern faith tradi-tions respectively. I decided to focus on the main, interfaith chapel as a "pilot" of what could become a longer, broader comparative project. Also, I limited my study to the contemporary space (rather than investigating the history of chapels at UNC). In this way, I chose to prioritize the phenomenological experience of the chapel over the intentions of the architect and designers.

Consider the Ethical Implications

Doing "on the ground" rhetorical research is heavy with responsibility. In par-ticular for studies of emplaced medical rhetoric, it is important to inquire about institutional restrictions and the potential that research may involve protected population groups. Hospitals are particularly fraught with restrictions, which prompts questions about the construction of "public" space versus highly con-trolled space. Further, hospitals are certainly locations with high concentrations of acutely vulnerable people, such as the ill and injured. Reflecting on medical rhetoric as emplaced, what is the significance of accessible and cloistered spaces in the hospital? How does this geography correspond to the subjectivities of people moving through the space, including the researcher?

In order to attain IRB approval, it is necessary to consider the potential risks research may pose to human subjects.[3] Protected groups include minors, individuals experiencing diminished capacities, those with mental or physical challenges, and people who are currently pregnant. Rhetoricians can reflect on the nature of protected groups as created and transformed in different locales. For example, in the context of the chapel, the protected status of the visitors is not linked to their role as patient, family member, doctor, or nurse. Those categories are muted or dissolved in the chapel. Thus, different sites in the hospital elicit specific risks and vulnerabilities for study subjects, and protected groups (in as much as these are subject positions) exist in relation to specific places.

The IRB was an occasion to consider the ethical implications of my research, because I had to identify potential risks and explain how I would minimize them. Like other humanities scholars, some rhetoricians may not be familiar with the IRB process, and meeting this institutional requirement may challenge traditional research practices. To an extent, I believe such a catalyst for practical, moral reflection is worthwhile. Yet it is important to recognize that the values and standards of the IRB are historically and institutionally situated. Therefore, the IRB should not be the only or the ultimate impetus for moral reflection in rhetorical scholarship.

To simplify the ethical considerations of my research project for the IRB, I decided to avoid direct interactions with chapel-goers, as this might infringe on individuals' privacy in the midst of (potentially) emotional and/or physical suffering. Instead, I planned to emphasize the material aspects of the chapel with only general references to how visitors engaged with the site. Also, because the site does not have a stable collective (at least in the sense that patients are a transitory population), getting feedback from visitors would have been a significant logistical challenge. In these ways, I limited the phenomenological evidence I could gather about the experiential landscape of the chapel. The process of research into emplaced rhetorics necessarily entails deep reflection on our ethical commitments, and I sought to develop a research process that would respect people visiting the chapel and the potential pain or fear or stress they might be experiencing.

The IRB application required completing a lengthy human research ethics training course. The training and application process made me aware of many unpredictable aspects of my study, such as the identity and vulnerability of "participants" (i.e., chapel-goers). I reflected on the type of information I would collect and any risks my project might pose for participants. Then, I developed these protocols:

> The researcher will visit the chapel, documenting its material features and observing its use. If there are individuals utilizing the chapel, the researcher will not engage in verbal or undue visual contact. Observations about use of the chapel will remain general and anonymous. However, if individuals initiate conversation with the researcher, they will be made aware of the research study. Any comments will be considered strictly confidential and not included in research documentation.

Also, I created a "Guide for Observation," which included background information on the study, guidelines, and a statement of the protocols. In the background section, I explained the purpose of the study and key objectives for the observations. I used the objectives to structure the observation guidelines into three sections: physical space, use/function, and the position and role of the chapel in the hospital. Under each section heading, I provided a list of initial questions (e.g., How does the arrangement of furniture affect movement through the space?). When I conducted the observations, I printed and recorded my initial field notes on this document. On subsequent visits, I reviewed the guide and recorded my ongoing observations and reflections in a notebook.

Select a Method of Experience

Especially when the target of rhetorical inquiry is material and spatial, the researcher needs to be "on the ground" at the site. Presence, as previously discussed, is essential for this method of research, because studying emplaced rhetoric will entail a phenomenological experience. Emplaced rhetoric is not "read," but is heard, seen, and felt. However, listening, seeing, and experiencing emplaced rhetoric requires time. In the same way that a cursory reading of a text affords mostly superficial insights, it is difficult to determine the idiosyncrasies of a site quickly. It takes time to perceive rhetorically significant objects, visuals, and pathways in action.

Merely being present, however, is hardly a method of research. As scholars, it is the systematic process of gathering and analyzing information that establishes the credibility of our claims. For in situ projects, the researcher must determine what forms of evidence they will gather and what means are most appropriate. Sights, sounds, smells, textures, and other felt impressions of emplaced rhetoric could be used as valuable anecdotal evidence. Along these lines, after her review of the history of the sensorium in rhetoric, Debra Hawhee (2015) advises us to "toggle back and forth between sensation and criticism or theory" (p. 13).

As a methodological approach to studying a place and how people make meaning there, field methods can illuminate the rhetoricity of built environments, the meaningfulness of constructed sites. In an ethnographic rhetorical study, the aim might be to clarify how people's meaningful and meaning-making practices are afforded or constrained by the built environment. Additionally, one might take a reception studies approach, studying how people react or respond to a particular place. This approach might emphasize how the audience or visitor to a site is affected by the rhetorical enactments they encounter. For studies of emplaced rhetoric, presence and self-reflexivity can and should remain central imperatives; however, investigations of medical rhetoric at health care sites may need to reimagine the praxis of research. Each project will need to develop an approach that gathers information about medical landscapes with attentiveness to the health care providers and health-seekers that are working and moving inside the site.

In my study, I utilized a field methods approach. I typically conducted my observations of the chapel from a seat near the rear of the room. When the room was empty, I would focus my attention on different elements in the chapel, writing down notes and reflections. Occasionally, I would walk to different parts of the room to observe up-close an inscription or object, or to perceive the site from a new angle. When someone else was in the chapel, I tried to remain still and unobtrusive. I discreetly took notes on the amount of time a visitor spent in the chapel and how they engaged with the site. Similar to the methodology of rhetorical listening that Kristin Bivens describes in this volume, I perceived the actions, behaviors, and gestures of chapel-goers as nondiscursive expressions of their religious identification, spiritual practice, and general orientation within the chapel. My field notes are intermixed with straightforward descriptions and contemplative freewriting. I also took a number of photos of the chapel.

In addition to this method of observation and experience, I gathered information about the site through an interview with a chaplain. Initially, I contacted the Department of Pastoral Care at UNC and was connected with Chaplain Patricia Cadle. Per the IRB, I created a consent form, which I discussed with Cadle prior to the interview, and a "Guide for Individual In-Depth Interview." The guide included a statement about me, as the researcher, and the study. The interview questions focused on the arrangement, use, and importance of the chapel. On the guide, I divided the questions into five areas: background information, history of the chapel, use of the chapel, significance of the chapel within the hospital, and wrap-up questions. The interview was recorded using an audio recording app, and I transcribed portions of the interview after completing my observations.

Frame the Questions

In addition to selecting research methods, researchers must carefully reflect on the nature of their questions. Admittedly, these two practices are closely related, making any sequence somewhat artificial. However, by putting methods before questions, I mean to suggest that the ethical considerations that influence our methodological choices may predetermine (or circumscribe) the questions we are able to ask for a particular project (as Bivens and Open also demonstrate in this volume).

As I have argued, medical knowledge and practices should be understood as existing in real locations that are shaped by medicine and give shape to the content of medicine. Places of health are consequential; all built environments develop from particular design and architectural choices that are historically contingent and *kairotic*. Medical landscapes are influenced by a variety of constraints and interested parties, such as geographic locations, communities, patients, clinicians, and donors. Along these lines, we might ask: What role does location play in the composition of a health site? What are the health needs in a community, and how do these needs relate to the design of local medical landscapes? How do funding sources influence the construction of a site? Additionally, material and spatial rhetoric is phenomenological; it engages the senses, evokes affect, and registers kinesthetically. Therefore, we might ask: What do people feel or experience at a site? What do they see? What do they hear? How do they move? Asking body-centered questions matter (materially and in terms of relevancy), and rhetoricians should explore the lived experience of medical landscapes for health care providers and health-seekers.

For my chapel project, I developed a series of research questions at the outset of my study. My questions inquired about the experiential landscape of the chapel from multiple angles and prompted reflection on my own experience of the site. For example: How are hospital chapels meaningful, legible, partisan, and consequential (Blair, 1999, p. 18)? How are people being engaged (materially, visually, tactilely/kinesthetically)? Who is being engaged? What is the effect of engagement? What relationship do I, as the researcher, have to/with the site? Like most projects, my questions evolved over the course of my study.

Find a Stance

In addition to deciding on a research experience, it is necessary to decide what position or stance the researcher will occupy in relation to the site. The researcher can engage the site as a typical visitor or maintain critical distance, for instance. First visits often set an important precedent or tone for the stance of the scholar. For example, if the initial visit begins with a professional introduction to a place, then the researcher is primed by the voice of an institutional authority in their perceptions. The pathways defined by the authority are important rhetorical elements of the site and contribute to the conveyed meaning. Blair (2001) provides some important questions to ask about researchers' orientation toward a site: "Should we acknowledge genre, then, as the authorizing source of a dominant reading? Should the source of validation for a 'preferred' reading be the designer or author or speaker? Or should that validation source be an institutional authority [. . .]?" (p. 285). Conversely, moving through the site as an outsider enables a different phenomenological perspective. Determining one's stance in engaging with the site will require clarifying the aim and values of the research project.

However, the stance a researcher *chooses* might differ from the one that is *found*. The process of research, especially research that engages the body and the senses as well as the mind, will reorient the researcher. Therefore, finding a stance requires reflection and reflexivity about the experience of research.

In my case study, I did not visit the hospital as a patient, to visit a patient, or as an employee, nor did I engage in religious practice within the chapel. In these ways, my identity as a researcher enabled and reinforced a critical distance between the site and myself. This was the predetermined stance to the site that I developed as part of my method of experience.

My first visit to the chapel was also my first experience of the UNC Hospital Campus. That day, I was viscerally aware of my own discomfort in the medical context. As an outsider, all of the noises, smells, and activity verged on sensory overload. To echo Bivens (this volume), in situ research at health care sites can carry with it a unique form of emotional labor. During future visits, I found myself becoming accustomed to the scent of soap and bodies, the cadence of voices down hallways and over the intercom, and the bustling energy near the entryway. Unlike the predetermined stance described above, my stance was, in a sense, *found* "on the ground" at the research site. My unique embodied encounter with the chapel was engendered by my past experiences of religious/spiritual sites and hospitals. In retrospect, my initial anxiety stemmed from my sense of being an imposter. Since I did not look like a hospital staff person and I did not perform any ostensible religious behavior, I was concerned that someone would ask me to justify my presence. My self-consciousness waned as I began to trust that I could be in the chapel without interruption or altercation. Over time, I become confident in the inclusivity and comfortable in the freedom afforded by the chapel. Thus, my stance was influenced by the accumulation of encounters with the material objects and practices that I witnessed in the chapel, prompting continual reflexivity.

Reconstruct and Interpret

After describing the experiential landscape of a target, reflecting on the ethical dimensions of a study, developing questions, finding a stance, and gathering information through observations and other means, the researcher must begin to organize her/his findings for publication. The thick description of the site is a key moment in the composition of literature on the rhetoric of particular places. Through this description, readers are presented with a cogent reconstruction of the site that is itself rhetorical. It is important to compose a vivid, compelling reconstruction, because the persuasiveness of the interpretation is partially dependent on the reader's mental vision of the site. However, the reconstruction will necessarily be selective and partial, which reifies the researcher's position as the authority in defining the boundaries of the site. Here, again, it is crucial to reflect on the ethical, scholarly commitments that influence these choices.

After spending time in the field, I contemplated the rhetorically significant characteristics of the chapel and began to formulate my interpretation. While a full analysis is beyond the scope of this chapter, I will provide a brief reconstruction of the site and highlight a few important elements of my interpretation in order to demonstrate the final practice of studying emplaced rhetoric.

The John M. Reeves All Faiths Chapel

Upon entering UNC Memorial Hospital, one is greeted by the buzz of hospital life. People in scrubs move purposefully through the halls. Individuals in long, white coats donning stethoscope necklaces have an aura of authority. In various waiting rooms, people uneasily bounce their legs and skim magazines. Up the escalator, a sign descending from the ceiling indicates the destination.

The chapel door is located in an alcove, creating a small waiting area just off the hallway. In this nook, there is a display case. At the top of the case, visitors are welcomed to the "John M. Reeves All Faiths Chapel" in both English and Spanish. Visitors are encouraged to "enter for meditation and prayer," and they are instructed not to bring food or drink into the space. Below, a schedule of weekly and monthly services is provided. Listed first, there is a weekly "Islamic Prayer Service," and the call to prayer time is provided. Second, a "Christian, Non-Denominational Worship Service" is held every Sunday and televised throughout the hospital. Last, twice a month the space is designated for walking the labyrinth (a design element on the floor of the chapel). Each type of service is presented in a unique (and ostensibly representative) font.

The chapel is quiet and still inside. The alcove buffers noise from the hallway; the only sound is the hum of the ventilation. The chapel is bigger than the waiting room down the hall, with five rows of chairs arranged in two columns. The chairs are facing a set of opened panels, like a sliding door, revealing an ornamental tree sculpture. The tree appears to be a fruit tree with birds landing on the branches.

The front and back walls of the chapel are pale green, and the sidewalls are a soft yellow. The floor is a maze of light and dark wood, forming a labyrinth. The wooden armrests of the chairs match the large wooden table and kneeling bench, which are positioned under the tree in the front of the room. The ceiling has three layers, creating a domelike effect. Blue paint lines each tier. Although windowless, the room is brightly illuminated by ceiling lighting.

There are very few symbols in the chapel. The room is decorated with only the tree, table, labyrinth, and a compass painted on the floor near the back of the room. In lieu of symbols, the chapel contains a number of objects. Along the rear wall, there are several texts available. A display of small pamphlets, *CareNotes*, offers visitors guidance on dealing with emotional distress, coping with illness, or supporting a suffering loved one. On top of a small cabinet, a selection of religious texts are also available, including English and Spanish copies of the New Testament, the Quran, a book on "Belief and Islam," a King James Version Bible, and a Contemporary English Version Bible. A large binder lays open in front of the scriptures, and the pages are labeled "Prayer Requests." In the cabinet below, fabric mats are available.

Interpretation

The rhetoricity of the chapel is revealed through the confluence of different symbolic references and embodied, material functions. Investigating the hospital chapel within its experiential landscape requires attending to the internal complexities (i.e., symbols, objects, and visitors' physical/affective experiences) as well as the larger context of the site. Within the hospital, the chapel is a radically different kind of place than an operating room, a nurse's station, or even the waiting room. Juxtaposing these sites highlights the various functions assigned to different places in a hospital as well as suggests different sets of subjects and actions. The Intensive Care Unit (ICU) is an especially poignant example of this contrast. Jeffery Bishop (2011) explains that the ICU "is a well-demarcated space, set apart from the rest of the hospital or other institutions as a place where exceptional illness and failing physiological function meet comprehensive nursing care, ample surveillance, and extraordinary technology" (p. 112). The primary actors in the ICU are nurses, doctors, respiratory therapists, and other experts on the essential functions of the body. The life of the patient is blurred by the efficiency of machines. The spatial and material arrangement of the ICU epitomizes the assumptions and virtues of modern medicine. Under the same roof, but philosophically far afield, the hospital chapel imagines a different relationship between spirituality and rationality, ritual and intervention, life and death. Yet, the hospital chapel has many sibling referents in other like-minded contexts beyond the hospital, such as places of religious worship, spiritual sites, and other types of chapels (e.g., chapels in prisons or at cemeteries and universities).

Within the chapel, I want to highlight a few of the rhetorically significant elements. First, the tone of religious neutrality is important inside the chapel and within the larger context. At a state-funded hospital, the chapel rhetorically negotiates its religious purpose without professing an explicit, biased religious affiliation. According to sociologist Wendy Cadge (2012), contemporary hospital chapels are often "designed to be what chaplains call 'interfaith' [. . .], including either a range of religious symbols or, more commonly, none as chaplains and hospital administrators strive to create spaces they think will be utilized by a range of people, including those with no spiritual or religious background" (p. 202). The All Faiths Chapel fits this pattern. NC Memorial Hospital is the oldest section of the medical facility, and the chapel was part of the original building project. Several years ago, the chapel was renovated. Patricia Cadle, the chaplain I interviewed, described the previous look of the chapel as "very dark, [it] had an A-frame roof, kind of smelly, kind of dirty looking, [. . .] more traditional" (Patricia Cadle, personal communication, March 5, 2015). Now, the chapel is designed to be "nontraditional" through color, comfortable chairs, new lighting, a lower ceiling, and AV equipment. Additionally, the All Faiths Chapel has been designed with minimal religious specificity. A visitor expecting to see the Hindu symbol for Om, the Muslim star and crescent, the Jewish Star of David, or the Christian cross would be disappointed.

One of the only symbols in the chapel is the tree sculpture. The tree of life is a popular symbol of interfaith spirituality. Many religious traditions have used the symbol of a tree—for example, the tree of enlightenment (Buddhism), the tree of knowledge and the tree of life in the Garden of Eden (Judaism and Christianity), the tree of immortality (Islam), and the Eternal Banyan Tree (Hinduism). Each tradition offers its own variation; however, the symbols often represent the interconnectedness of the world. In this way, the tree symbolizes the ideological purpose of the All Faiths Chapel.

The spatial design of the chapel is also symbolic. Taken together, the brown floor, green and yellow walls, and blue ceiling form a landscape. When a visitor steps out of the chaotic realm of the hospital hallway, they enter an environment that reflects a utopian world. Vistors' role in the hospital, including their power or powerlessness, their knowledge or their confusion, their strength or their weakness, are somewhat dissolved here. In the chapel, visitors are positioned rightly between the ground and the sky. The layout of the room compels them to look toward the tree at the front. The emplaced rhetoric communicates order, a natural structure of life, and positions visitors in that landscape.

Although the chapel is explicitly neutral, there are objects in the room that direct visitors' religious performances toward accustomed things (especially for Christians and Muslims), but without dictating their actions.[4] During my observations, I witnessed several guests orient themselves by using the floor compass, put down a fabric mat, and pray toward Mecca. Other visitors read the Bible. Many people quietly prayed, meditated, or rested. The absence of symbols may function as an invitation or opportunity to transform the space in whatever way guests might need, enabling them to behave as though they are in a holy place.

Additionally, visitors can write in the "Prayer Requests" book. Flipping through the pages, people commonly ask for protection (for themselves or a loved one) and blessings on the hospital, staff, and patients. There are many prayers for healing. Others give thanks. Most of the short inscriptions are addressed to God or a divine higher power, and a few address the chaplain. Occasionally, there is a lengthy inscription in the form of a narrative (e.g., reporting test results and expressing uncertainty). After each page has been used, it is signed "Amen" or "Lord, hear our prayers" by a chaplain. The pages of the prayer book have never been dated. The sheer mass of the pages (easily 100 or more double-sided pages) indicates a symbolic, spiritually heterogeneous community.

Lastly, when the chairs have been moved aside, the labyrinth engages guests in a spiritual practice by encouraging contemplation as it guides visitors through the maze. According to Cadle, nurses are regular visitors on days when the chapel is arranged for walking the labyrinth. However, even for a guest who might be unfamiliar with labyrinth walking, the emptiness of the chapel invites movement.

Providing spiritual care is important to the healing mission of the hospital. In her interview, Cadle described the chapel as a reprieve from the chaos of the hospital. The hospital is envisioned as busy and chaotic, emotionally and physically exhausting. In contrast, the chapel is a "sanctuary," a place for "solitude" and "peacefulness." The psychological and emotional impact of built environments is an essential aspect of providing care that is sensitive to people's spiritual well-being. Responding to the needs of patients, their families, and the staff is the primary function of all space in the hospital. However, the rhetorical openness of the chapel may invite a reversal of the biomedical body-mind hierarchy, fostering self-care and spiritual care behaviors that are important (but otherwise neglected) to the mission of the hospital.

What's Next?

In this chapter, I have attempted to do several things. First, I provided a scholarly rationale for studying materiality and spatiality in rhetorical studies of health and medicine, including methodological principles and models. Then, I clarified six practices, exemplified by my case study, which can guide future researchers interested in doing similar work. Last, I offered a tentative interpretation of the chapel as an important medical/religious site.

As I have established, attending to material and spatial rhetoric necessitates a reconsideration of the dominant place of symbolic representations as the heart, or primary object, of rhetorical inquiry. On a fundamental level, rhetoric is knowledge or beliefs that are "manifested or given presence," as Blair (1999) claims. By contextualizing conceptual practices as extensions of prior, situated actions, we give credence to actors and actions that are eclipsed by traditional rhetorical approaches. Emplaced medical rhetoric understands actors (including doctors, nurses, patients, scientists, chaplains, etc.) and actions in their embodied, material, and spatial contexts.

Acknowledgments

The original idea for this chapter arose from vigorous discussions of place/space and rhetoric that took place during a graduate seminar at UNC-CH in 2015. I would like to thank Dr. Carole Blair for her feedback on the early development of this project as well as her ongoing encouragement. I am also indebted to my colleagues in Communications and the Department of English and Comparative Literature for many rich conversations about this paper.

Notes

1 My theoretical understanding blends a host of approaches (such as object-oriented ontology, Derrida's metaphysics of presence, Heidegger's thingness, and feminist and performance studies' notions of embodiment).
2 IRB Study Number: 15–0232.
3 For a fuller explanation of the IRB and Belmont report, see Dawn Opel's chapter in this volume.
4 In *Performing Religion in Public*, Chambers, du Toit, and Edelman (2013) explain that, "religion is not (just) a set of ethical, ontological, or theological assertions, but a dynamic, lived, and fluidly embodied set of actions, practices, gestures and speech acts at specific points in time and space" (pp. 1–2). If we accept that religions are constituted by "actions, practices, gestures, and speech acts," then can a site be religious prior to the recognition and religious actions of people? Perhaps not. Instead, places can provide arrangements that invite (or discourages) religious performances.

References

About us. (n.d.). UNC Medical Center. Retrieved from www.uncmedicalcenter.org/uncmc/about.

Bishop, J. (2011). *The anticipatory corpse.* Notre Dame, IN: University of Notre Dame Press.

Blair, C. (1999). Contemporary U.S. memorial sites as examples of rhetoric's materiality. In J. Selzer & S. Crowley (Eds.), *Rhetorical bodies* (pp. 16–57). Madison, WI: The University of Wisconsin Press.

Blair, C. (2001). Reflections on criticism and bodies: Parables from public places. *Western Journal of Communication, 65*(3), 271–294.

Cadge, W. (2012). Negotiating religious difference in secular organizations: The case of hospital chapels. In C. Bender, W. Cadge, P. Levitt, & D. Smilde (Eds.), *Religion on the edge: De-centering and re-centering the sociology of religion* (pp. 200–212). New York, NY: Oxford University Press.

Chambers, C., du Toit, S. W., & Edelman. J. (2013). Introduction: The public problem of religious doings. In C. Chambers, S. W. du Toit, and J. Edelman (Eds.), *Performing Religion in Public* (pp. 1–26). New York, NY: Palgrave Macmillian,

Cresswell, T. (2004). *Place: A short introduction.* Malden, MA: Blackwell Publishing.

Dickinson, G., Ott, B. L., & Aoki, E. (2006). Spaces of remembering and forgetting: The reverent eye/I at the Plains Indian Museum. *Communication and Critical/Cultural Studies, 3*(1), 27–47.

Fountain, T. K. (2014). *Rhetoric in the flesh: Trained vision, technical expertise, and the gross anatomy lab.* New York, NY: Routledge.

Hawhee, D. (2015). Rhetoric's sensorium. *Quarterly Journal of Speech, 101*(1), 2–17.

McHendry, G. F., Jr., Middleton, M. K., Endres, D. E., Senda-Cook, S., & O'Byrne, M. (2014). Rhetorical critic(ism)'s body: Affect and fieldwork on a plane of immanence. *Southern Communication Journal, 79*(4), 293–310.

Massey, D. (1994). *Space, place, and gender.* Minneapolis, MN: University of Minnesota Press.

Middleton, M. K., Senda-Cook, S., & Endres, D. E. (2011). Articulating rhetorical field methods: Challenges and tensions. *Western Journal of Communication, 75*(4), 386–406.

Schuster, M. L. (2006). A different place to birth: A material rhetoric analysis of Baby Haven, a free-standing birth center. *Women's Studies in Communication, 29*(1), 1–38.

10

ETHICAL RESEARCH IN "HEALTH 2.0"

Considerations for Scholars of Medical Rhetoric

Dawn S. Opel

Keywords: ethics, internet research, medical and health data

As the Internet becomes seamlessly integrated into our daily lives, so does its use for health and medical information exchange of all kinds. A growing amount of information searched for and retrieved on the Internet is related to health and medicine, with around 5% of all Google searches health-related in 2003 (Eysenbach & Köhler, 2004). The term "Health 2.0" has come to represent the myriad ways that people are using Web 2.0 (now a term to represent networked, digital technologies with web, mobile, and Cloud-sharing capabilities) for health-related purposes (Krueger, 2014). Users of the Internet may search for health-related websites, join online communities dedicated to similar illnesses, advocate for health-related causes or concerns, contribute to crowdsourced web forums or sites, and now, increasingly, track their own health through wearable or mobile tracking apps, which now number in the thousands (Kwon, 2015). Further, alongside networked communities in Health 2.0 exist new algorithmic and other computational methods of data analytics from Web 2.0 technologies. As never before, it is possible to compute and analyze patterns in the health-related behavior of millions of people. Employers increasingly incentivize—or make compulsory—their employees' participation in the collection and use of health-related data for the crafting of corporate wellness plans and other cost-saving measures (Frommeyer, 2015).

For researchers of health and medical rhetoric, life in Health 2.0 creates rich possibilities for observation and analysis, but these possibilities are rife with quandaries. Forums, boards, groups, hashtags, and communities must be regarded as vibrant, liminal spaces where people organize themselves by their affinities and afflictions. On the one hand, these changes in health information and personal connection present researchers with access to artifacts and observations in transparent ways. On the other hand, the rules for ethical conduct may seem ambiguous to researchers new to Health 2.0 contexts.

How should a researcher of health and medical rhetoric proceed in Health 2.0? This chapter offers suggestions for conducting research in networked digital contexts and how these differ from traditional physical sites of study. First, I review the history of ethics in human subjects research, tracing the move from violations and abuses with experimentation on human subjects that became the impetus for regulations and policies such as the Nuremburg Code, the Declaration of Helsinki, and the Belmont Report. I look at contemporary regulatory policies from Institutional Review Boards (IRBs) and discuss how IRBs have or have not responded to the changing nature of research with human participants in online spaces or to the use of computational tools and methods. Following a look at rules, regulations, and policies, I review recommendations from organizations committed to ethical Internet research, such as the Department of Health and Human Services Secretary's Advisory Committee on Human Research Protections (SACHRP), the CASRO Code of Standards and Ethics in Survey Research, the Association of Internet Researchers (AoIR), and the Conference on College Composition and Communication (CCCC) Guidelines for the Ethical Conduct of Research in Composition Studies. I will complete this review with legal considerations of researchers, particularly around the HIPAA Privacy Rule and modern U.S. copyright laws.

All of these published or enacted laws, policies, and statements offer guidance for the researcher of health and medical rhetoric, but ethical research does not end with a set of guidelines to universally follow. This chapter will take up how ethicists and Internet researchers from various disciplines are discussing ethics in online research, and how considerations of choice of research site, methodology, and tools for analysis factor in to ethical decision-making in Health 2.0 contexts. Using a case study of an online forum for users of home health biomedical products, I consider the ethical dimensions of a variety of Internet research methods and methodologies. The forum is a typically active discussion community centered entirely on home pregnancy test use: it is housed on a site devoted to women who identify themselves as "trying-to-conceive." By situating a discussion of the ethics of conducting medical rhetoric research online in this particular forum, I am able to demonstrate that the world of Health 2.0 gives us a staggering amount of artifacts, texts, testimonies, visualizations, data points, and quantifications to be studied. Unlike physical sites of study, these digital tools and artifacts often seem usable with little inconvenience to, or involvement of, other human beings. This case provides grounding to demonstrate how and why researchers must treat each project individually and with care, particularly with regard to informed consent, data retrieval and storage, privacy and surveillance, and methods for analysis, as each of these has its own ever-evolving ethical considerations.

Tracing the Regulation of Human Subjects Research

Contemporary academic researchers of health and medical rhetoric may begin—
and may also end—their consideration of research ethics with their institution's
review board (IRB in the U.S.) of human subjects research. Their procedures
reflect a long history—famous cases of unethical research practice that often
involved biomedical research, for example, the Nazi experiments and the Tuskegee
Syphilis Study. The most influential documents drafted in response to unethical
treatment of human research subjects include the UN Declaration of Human
Rights (1948), the Nuremburg Code (1949), the Declaration of Helsinki (1964)
and the Belmont Report (1979). These documents' themes are now often recited
in three terms: respect for persons, justice, and beneficence.

Respect for Persons

Respect for persons entails two "ethical convictions: first, that individuals should
be treated as autonomous agents, and second, that persons with diminished
autonomy are entitled to protection" (National Commission for the Protection
of Human Subjects, 1979). These convictions translate to what is frequently seen
in IRB protocols as informed consent. "Persons with diminished autonomy" are
often characterized by these protocols as persons who are young, pregnant, incar-
cerated, or disabled.

Justice

This tenet discusses the "fairness in distribution" of scarce resources and "what is
deserved" (National Commission for the Protection of Human Subjects, 1979).
Essentially, we as researchers must ask what is most fair in terms of whether
select groups get to participate and potentially benefit from research, or whether
certain groups disproportionately bear the burden of research. As Markham and
Buchanan (forthcoming) note, "This concept has been extended to include fair
access, so that persons have an equal opportunity to participate in studies that
might benefit them, as in the case of innovative methods, procedures, or therapies
in biomedical clinical trials" (p. 3).

Beneficence

The beneficence tenet posits that humans should be protected from harm in
ethical research practice. Markham and Buchanan (forthcoming) suggest that
in the United States, beneficence is approached from the perspective of a risk-
utility analysis, or weighing the potential benefit against the potential harm.
This differs, they argue, from other cultural contexts. European approaches
favor a more deontological approach, where certain basic human rights are "so

foundational that virtually no set of possible benefits that might be gained from violating these ethically justifies that violation" (citing Ess and the AoIR Working Committee, 2002).

Ethical Research After the Internet

IRBs are largely untrained and ill-equipped to handle Internet research and the changing nature of digital tools, methods, and platforms for data collection, analysis, and storage that have arrived at their doorsteps in the last ten years. As McKee and Porter (2009) note, "many review boards are either unsure of how to proceed or they apply inappropriate review criteria designed for offline research that do not apply as well—or at all—to Internet research" (p. 35). They also argue that a lack of federal regulation in this area has contributed to these discrepancies at the IRB level.

What do researchers of health and medical rhetoric in the United States have to look to for guidance as to ethical research in Health 2.0? For further regulatory guidance, the Department of Health and Human Services Secretary's Advisory Committee on Human Research Protections (SACHRP) issued in May 2013 "Considerations and Recommendations Concerning Internet Research and Human Subjects Research Regulations, with Revisions." Its purpose is to "provide a starting point for the development of FAQ and/or Points to Consider regarding the conduct and review of Internet research" (SACHRP, 2013). The document recommends that several documents and tools be developed for IRBs to be better equipped to review research involving Internet research. The section "Forms and Examples of Internet Research" begins to demonstrate the complexities associated with research on the Internet, identifying "a range of Internet research where human subjects may be involved" from scraping of preexisting information on blogs and social media platforms, to online surveys, to the Internet as vehicle for recruitment, to emerging types of research and methods (SACHRP, 2013). The document is also mindful of the Belmont Report's tenets, and provides definitions of human subjects research on the Internet, exempt Internet research, public/private information on the Internet, informed consent on the Internet, risk of harm on the Internet, online recruitment, and how deception may occur in Internet research (SACHRP, 2013).

Similarly, CASRO, or the national association representing "the U.S. research industry and those organizations engaged in the conduct, support, or education of market, opinion, or social research, often described as data analytics, consumer insights, or business intelligence," has developed a Code of Standards and Ethics that creates mandatory and enforceable standards for the ethical research of its members (Code, 2016). These standards also reflect the legacy of the Belmont Report, with sections related to privacy, confidentiality, and protection of vulnerable populations. In the "Special Considerations for Online and Mobile Research" section, the Code focuses on the "reasonable expectation" of recruitment of participants via text or mobile, and the prohibition of "surreptitious data collection methods," which include using false or misleading information to recruit participants, and gathering contact information through "subterfuge" (Code, 2016). This mirrors the SACHRP's focus on discouraging deception in online research.

The regulatory approach of the SACHRP and the CASRO Code of Standards and Ethics is meant to provide explicit guidance to those applying to IRBs, the IRBs themselves, and those working outside of IRB oversight in industry. AoIR and its Ethics Working Committee has been forward thinking, supplementing and offering considerations beyond regulatory documents. Its recommendations ensure "that research on and about the Internet is conducted in an ethical and professional manner . . . Researchers, students, ethicists, and related institutional bodies and academic organizations in the domain of Internet research may turn to these ethics documents as a starting point for their inquiries and reflection" (AoIR, 2016). Rather than a codified set of regulations, the AoIR recommendations are meant to be guidelines such that "ethical research can remain flexible, be responsible to diverse contexts, and be adaptable to continually changing technologies" (Markham & Buchanan, 2012, p. 5). The 2012 recommendations, also in line with the Belmont Report and its tenets, contain the following principles:

- The greater the vulnerability of the community/author/participant, the greater the obligation of the researcher to protect the community/author/participant.
- Because "harm" is defined contextually, ethical principles are more likely to be understood inductively rather than applied universally. That is, rather than one-size-fits-all pronouncements, ethical decision-making is best approached through the application of practical judgment attentive to the specific context (what Aristotle identified as *phronesis*).
- Because all digital information at some point involves individual persons, consideration of principles related to research on human subjects may be necessary even if it is not immediately apparent how and where persons are involved in the research data.
- When making ethical decisions, researchers must balance the rights of subjects (as authors, as research participants, as people) with the social benefits of research and researchers' rights to conduct research. In different contexts the rights of subjects may outweigh the benefits of research.
- Ethical issues may arise and need to be addressed during all steps of the research process, from planning, research conduct, publication, and dissemination.
- Ethical decision-making is a deliberative process, and researchers should consult as many people and resources as possible in this process, including fellow researchers, people participating in or familiar with contexts/sites being studied, research review boards, ethics guidelines, published scholarship (within one's discipline but also in other disciplines), and, where applicable, legal precedent (Markham & Buchanan, 2012, p. 4–5, footnotes omitted).

The AoIR Recommendations additionally identify three "major tensions/ considerations" for Internet research ethics that are pertinent to researchers of medical and health rhetoric in Health 2.0: the definition of human subjects, public versus private distinctions, and data (text) versus persons distinctions. For the AoIR Ethics Working Committee, these three areas of tension or consideration reflect the necessity of individualized, case-based approaches to ethical considerations of research on the Internet (Markham & Buchanan, 2012). Rather than an attempt to codify ethics in universals, the AoIR (as well as other leading Internet scholars who are cited heavily by their Recommendations) recommends an iterative, process-based approach that reflects on the ethical considerations unique to the contexts of each individual research study (Markham & Buchanan, forthcoming; Markham & Buchanan, 2012; McKee & Porter, 2009).

The definition of the human subject and human subjects research "no longer enjoys the relatively straightforward definitional status it once did" (Markham & Buchanan, 2012, p. 6). The manner in which review is taken up can vary dramatically across institutions, countries, and cultures (McKee & Porter, 2009; Henderson et al., 2007; Dougherty & Kramer, 2005). In a virtual environment, the lines that separate working with people versus traces, texts, audio and video, and other artifacts creates confusion as to whether a researcher is conducting research with humans at all in the manner in which their IRB may be defining human subjects. Similarly, what may be considered publicly available information by some researchers and IRBs may be viewed as private by the authors or participants in a virtual environment. AoIR noted in both 2002 and 2012 that "privacy is a concept that must include a consideration of expectations and consensus" (p. 7). In certain situations, a user may post information on a discussion forum that may be publicly viewable, but the expectation of that user was that it was intended for the audience in that forum. That user may express surprise or discomfort with the notion that this information would be used or published in another context. This is why expectation of privacy is as important as the actual privacy setting on the platform (Baym, 2013). As Nissenbaum (2010) argues, "What people care about most is not simply restricting the flow of information, but ensuring that it flows appropriately" (p. 2). Publication of information directly from a "Health 2.0" platform to a journal article may be, in some cases, an inappropriate flow of that information.

Finally, with respect to data (text) versus persons, the AoIR recommendations discuss issues of personhood, and how and when we may connect digital information to a self. Markham and Buchanan (2012) elaborate with this example: "Blogs are often considered public, published texts. On the other hand, users have described their blogs as a part of their identity, not to be treated as simply publicly accessible data" (p. 6). In another recent example, Tufekci (2014) draws attention to two journalists who wrote critical pieces about a metastatic breast cancer sufferer's social media presence, using textual selections from tweets and direct messages without permission, and without a larger awareness of the online community and conversations taking place that involve counternarratives to cancer survival. Tujeckci, who studied as a participant-observer of this community for over a year, titled her own article "Social Media is a Conversation, Not a Press Release" to draw attention to the divide between data (text) and persons in a Health 2.0 discourse community.

Other complicated issues arise from research conducted on anonymized and/ or aggregated data sets (for instance, thousands of tweets), and whether we as researchers can identify whether a person may be harmed by such research. As boyd and Crawford (2012) argue, "Big data reframes key questions about the constitution of knowledge, the processes of research, how we should engage with information, and the nature and categorization of reality" (p. 665). As people become numbers, so do the epistemological assumptions of the researcher. If the researcher can no longer visualize the person/author, does this mean that person cannot be harmed by what is reported from a data set in which their personal information is a part? boyd and Crawford (2012) argue that accountability is a better determinant for ethics than privacy when large datasets are concerned, as "Accountability requires rigorous thinking about the ramifications of Big Data, rather than assuming that ethics boards will necessarily do the work of ensuring that people are protected" (p. 673). In this way, researchers are calling for the kind of ethical decision-making processes practiced by those doing smaller-scale ethnographic work on the Internet to be taken up by those who are using the Internet to scrape large amounts of data for computational analysis, such as the collection and analysis of Twitter hashtag data using the Twitter API and a programming language such as R or Python to parse the tweets. With this method of harvesting data, the researcher may never actually read (or write about) a single Twitter handle in the files created (depending on the research question or design of the study). Does this mean that the identities of the authors of these tweets are kept private? While this may be technically be so, it does not mean that the results of the study could not be used in such as way as to compromise the privacy of those individuals, for instance if their group identity is possible to discern based on content. This is a similar question to the Internet ethnographer who must ask if, even if pseudonyms are given, whether the identity of the participant could be discovered through other means, such as by entering the participant's directly-quoted forum post into a web search engine. boyd and Crawford's accountability determinant asks the researcher to think several steps beyond what is explicit.

For those researchers of medical and health rhetoric who are members of the Conference on College Composition and Communication (CCCC), a Position Statement called Guidelines for the Ethical Conduct of Research in Composition Studies was updated in March 2015, in part to reflect more explicit language around "studies involving digital/online media" (CCCC, 2015). The Position Statement incorporates the principles of the Belmont Report as it pertains to all research in composition studies, but adds a short section on digital writing research. It has directional language to point its members who may be doing this research to McKee and Porter (2008) and to the AoIR recommendations discussed above (CCCC, 2015).

Finally, there are legal as well as ethical considerations for researchers of health and medical rhetoric in Health 2.0, particularly regarding the HIPAA Privacy Rule and modern U.S. copyright laws. While legal compliance is an important consideration in ethical research practice, *it is not the whole of ethical research practice, in much the same way that IRB approval does not mean that a researcher has always acted ethically*. In this way, language such as "surviving the IRB review" does not necessarily do a researcher any favors in creating an ethical mindset for research, particularly when the law and the regulations and policies do not yet reflect the evolving nature of research involving digital spaces and materials (Johns, Hall, & Crowell, 2004). With that caveat, health and medical researchers should have a framework for legal as well as ethical research practice, and what follows are important considerations that form a part of a much larger ethical framework for research.

The HIPAA Privacy Rule requires signed permission for a researcher to use protected health information (PHI) for research purposes, unless an exception exists. One such exemption is a waiver from an IRB (National Institutes of Health [NIH], 2004). For research conducted on the Internet, it is not likely that even individually identifiable health information falls under the category of PHI, because "individually identifiable health information becomes PHI when it is created or received by a covered entity" (NIH, 2004, para. 6). "Covered entities" include health care plans and health care providers that may transmit data electronically. Researchers should make certain they are aware of the source of the artifacts being studied, and whether they fall into the category of a covered entity. This will undoubtedly become of larger significance to health and medical rhetoricians as datasets from telemedicine and m-health become more accessible. In growing areas of medical and health care, "Concerns about confidentiality are paramount" (Goodman, 1998b). Also, it is important to be aware that the decoupling of identifying information from health data may be sufficient for legal purposes, but that this does not mean that ethical issues do not still exist. Goodman (1998b) calls attention to "group confidentiality" as an important concept, as "A population can be harmed by research on unlinked data intended to help that population" (p. 134). Many examples exist of large public health research projects involving datasets of demographic information that have both improved health care conditions for underserved populations, and simultaneously harmed groups whose genetic data now stigmatizes them (Goodman, 1998b; citing Grady, 1993; Dickens, Gostin, & Levine, 1991). This reemphasizes the vigilant commitment to reflection about ethics as recommended by the AoIR. Despite potential satisfaction of legal requirements and IRB approval by procedures such as decoupling of data, a researcher must always look to possible future harm that may be caused by the use of health and medical data.

A discussion of modern U.S. copyright and trademark law vis-à-vis health and medical research on the Internet could be the subject of a separate chapter, but it is important to recognize that there are both legal and ethical concerns involved in the use of authored works on the Internet. Some of these issues may be fairly obvious, and some may be more obfuscated to a researcher who is new to Internet research, and may not immediately connect writings such as Facebook or forum posts as authored works. Further, if a researcher is aggregating hundreds of Tweets, posts, or photos, it might not be clear that each artifact has an author. But, as McKee and Porter (2009) point out, if a researcher is "collecting online text (e.g., excerpts from blogs), downloading images, or saving audio and video files, then she is copying" and subject to U.S. copyright law (p. 53). Digital tools and platforms have made it increasingly simple to copy others' works, and as a result, researchers must look to see if they have either met the Fair Use provision or secured the permission of the original author. Use is fair, according to the provision, depending on the following:

> (1) the purpose and character of the use, including whether such use is of commercial nature or is for nonprofit educational purposes; (2) the nature of the copyrighted work;(3) the amount and substantiality of the portion used in relation to the copyrighted work as a whole; and (4) the effect of the use upon the potential market for or value of the copyrighted work.
>
> *(U.S. Copyright Office, 2008)*

Questions that a researcher must ask are whether the potential publication venue is paying the researcher for the content (if so, then not a nonprofit educational purpose), and whether the work is being reproduced in small amounts or its entirety (if the latter, more likely not fair use). Academic research does not automatically fall within fair use. It is also critical for the Internet researcher to be aware of whether the material contains trademarked intellectual property. McKee and Porter (2009) particularly note the use of screen shots to collect social media content such as Facebook walls and Twitter feeds, and whether distinctive logos, fonts, and symbols may be represented. They also note that this may not be the same sort of ethical consideration in that no harm comes to a human participant, but that some publishers may take this into consideration and require permissions. This may have financial repercussions for the researcher.

Health 2.0: A Case Study

In order to demonstrate the case-based, casuistic approach to ethical decision-making in Internet research advocated by the AoIR Ethics Working Committee (Markham & Buchanan, 2012) and McKee and Porter (2009), I will next use a case study of an online forum for users of home health biomedical products to consider the ethical dimensions of a variety of Internet research methods and methodologies. The online forum for the case study is a typically active discussion community centered entirely on home pregnancy test use; it is housed on a site devoted to women who identify themselves as "trying-to-conceive." After a description of the overall project design, I will discuss which research methods were chosen for this online space and why, how these methods factored in to the IRB review, and how other methods and methodologies would have different ramifications for ethical decision-making around research in this space.

First I will make a definitional note on methods versus methodologies and how they will be discussed here. Because the focus of this chapter is on Health 2.0 and tools and spaces for Internet research (versus research in physical spaces), I have tended to focus on *method*, what Sullivan and Porter (1997) define as "procedures, heuristics, or tools that people use for inquiry" (p. 10). As Scott and Meloncon discuss in this volume's opening chapter, method is but one of three interrelated dimensions of *methodology*, alongside ideology and practice (Sullivan & Porter, 1997, p. 11). Scott and Meloncon call for a "more explicit accounting" of our research methodologies, particularly as they relate to our ideologies and practices, because we often do not account for them as explicitly in our writing as we do method, and often these discussions lack "attention to the way that research is actually conducted in complex, messy locations that include a number of actors and ideologies" (p. 8, citing Fleckenstein, Spinuzzi, Rickly, & Papper, 2008). In this discussion of my case study, I attempt to account for all dimensions of methodology vis-à-vis ethics, and also to acknowledge that the permutation of ideologies and practices we choose may alter the ethical context for a particular Internet research method, tool, or space.

This case study, one of a series of case studies on the user experience of home pregnancy testing in the United States, reflects my own journey as a researcher to explore multiple methodologies and how each might take up this subject. The first case study I conducted was a rhetorical-cultural analysis of three brands of home pregnancy test packaging, using Schriver's (2013) information design heuristics to reveal cultural values (i.e., emphasis on the heteronormative nuclear family and childbirth as next step after testing) implicit in the marketing of the test (Opel, 2014). In the conclusion to that article, I suggest that online health forums may be a space where technical communicators and marketing professionals may research to see how users themselves negotiate their concerns for their product and ultimately work toward an ethic of care to the user (Salvo, 2001). This suggestion implied a direction for future research, and I then sought to follow my own advice to study user narratives "in a dialogic process to rearticulate how the pregnancy test experience is packaged and sold" (p. 8). With this in mind, I began exploring potential research sites.

It is at this stage when my deliberation as a researcher about methodology and ethics got comingled and indeed "messy" per Scott and Meloncon (this volume), as I attempted to design a study that reflects my ethical commitments but also is practical in light of constraints of a graduate student researcher, such as time and resources. This is an account of the ethical deliberation of this particular case. My earlier study had produced results that indicated that young and poor users' experiences were not reflected in the packaging and risk communication of the product. How would I ethically design a study in which these voices were taken into account? I went through an iterative process that reflects many of the tenets of the Belmont Report and the 2012 AoIR Recommendations (Markham & Buchanan, 2012). I knew that this demographic of user was the most vulnerable, informed consent for minors extremely difficult, and potential risk of harm from participation potentially great, due to the emotionally fraught nature of pregnancy testing, heightened when young and without access to health care. In consultation with senior researchers who believed the logistical difficulties with conducting interviews or focus groups to also be a challenge, I shifted my focus to finding a research partner, such a pregnancy test company's marketing team who may have conducted marketing research on the project. However, this was also ethically problematic for different reasons, because market research is designed to sell more tests to more affluent consumers, not to gather lived experiences to make tests more ethically designed. Finally, I located a set of extant user narratives collected online by the National Institutes of Health, and worked with an archivist at the NIH to study narratives of lived experiences of users who often reflected on test use in their youth. Still, I had research questions directly related to pregnancy test packaging and design that I wished to pursue, which why I designed a survey and sought to distribute it online. This became the case study presented here.

In this volume, messy ethical and methodological decisions such as these are rendered more visible. For example, Edwell (this volume) discusses her decision not to engage with chapel-goers when conducting a study of a hospital chapel, in part because for her, this case met the tipping point described in the AoIR Recommendations: the highly sensitive emotional state of many hospital chapel-goers—concern over the well-being of participants—outweighed potential research benefit to the researcher. In other cases, for instance, studies designed engaged in participatory methodologies (Pigozzi, this volume), the cocreation of the research project and investment by community representatives may offer a larger benefit to those vulnerable populations such that the tipping point is not met. This is an example of ethics informing methodology and vice versa.

Online Communities as Research Sites

The online community that is the site of this case study takes place on a comprehensive website devoted to resources for expectant mothers. The website is owned by an American, for-profit corporation. Alongside content created by professional writers, bloggers, and photographers on a number of different pregnancy-related themes (food, health, style, parenting), and significant amounts of advertising and sponsorship, the site hosts an active and extensive online discussion forum for trying-to-conceive, expectant, or new parents, which I will call "TTC." As of early 2016, there were hundreds of thousands of posts on the online forum in 56 active threads. The posts are accessible to the public to view, but a username and account are required in order to contribute to the discussion boards.

How a researcher approaches an online community methodologically will have implications for the ethical considerations of the research in that space. For example, for those working in online ethnography, the study of an online community is a study of the social, and the online forum is not a collection of texts, but a site of living, or an "embedded, embodied, and everyday" human practice (Markham, 2016, citing Hine, 2015). These researchers invest significant time and energy, observing in real time human behavior in online forums. In areas such as digital rhetoric, Grabill and Pigg (2012) describe an online forum as a public where "members of the public frequently perform their identities as a means for accessing and approaching the conversation" (p. 102). However, this public is limited in that it contains rhetors' "fragments of discourse" which prevent a fuller picture of participants' identities (p. 105). In their study, Grabill and Pigg perform discourse analysis on a large number of forum threads to build theory around rhetorical agency and identity in online social spaces. The differences in characterization of an online forum between these two examples affect not only which research methods and practices are used, but also the nature of the ethical decision-making that takes place, particularly around informed consent, expectations of privacy, and risk of harm to community participants. For this reason, McKee and Porter (2009) argue that an "ethical check" is necessary from outside of our disciplines when doing Internet or digital research, as "Too often as researchers (and as people) we are immersed in our own methodological and epistemological perspectives, what the rhetorician Kenneth Burke (1966) called our 'terministic screens'" (p. 44). This is even more critical in Health 2.0, where personal health information may be accessible to a researcher, yet nonetheless sensitive and published with an expectation of privacy. In order to conduct ethical research in "Health 2.0," we must iteratively reevaluate our methodologies and particularly the ideology that informs our practices and methods.

This evaluation can take place with the aid of heuristics such as that offered by McKee and Porter (2009) for informed consent, which takes into account four variables to consider: public/private nature of the information, the degree of topic sensitivity, the degree of interaction between researcher and participants, and the degree of subject vulnerability. The higher the privacy expectation and degrees of sensitivity, interaction, and vulnerability, the more necessary it is to require informed content of participants. McKee and Porter (2009) map specific methods and case studies onto this heuristic in a grid to show how each situation differs: Specifically, a participant-observer ethnographic study of a discussion group is more likely to require informed content than a rhetorical analysis of websites with published writing by patients with a particular illness (p. 97).

Survey Research in Online Communities

This case study originated as a part of a much larger dissertation project, as I mention above, in which I was studying pregnancy test users' perceptions of the packaging and design of home pregnancy tests in the United States. As a part of this study, I sought to learn how different demographics of users might perceive the test experience differently. Some aspects of the pregnancy test experience are rigorously discussed in popular media and in online communities, but the packaging and design of tests is not. As a result, I designed a short survey to administer to pregnancy test users. In deciding to recruit participants in a trying-to-conceive online pregnancy forum, I did not seek to use the space for ethnographic study, but instead saw this as the equivalent of posting a voluntary survey on a bulletin board at a physical site, such as a community center. I sought and obtained IRB approval in advance for the survey and its related procedures. These procedures included requesting permission from the forum administrators to post the recruitment script and a link to an online Qualtrics survey, and self-identifying as a researcher on the forum as way of introducing the recruitment script. The online survey included an informed consent form. The Qualtrics survey separated the informed consent from the rest of the survey, assigning a number to each survey so that identifying information was decoupled from the rest of the data in the survey.

The choice of methods, tools, and instruments reflects different goals of the researcher. For example, survey research serves a different purpose than ethnographic research of the TTC community or discourse or rhetorical analysis of their discussions. Survey research is used to "collect information" (Gurak & Silker, 1997, p. 411), not to observe human behavior or activity. For this reason, the IRB protocol for physical sites for human subjects research is readily translated to the online survey space, as the same "rules" apply. Members of the online community were asked to participate, I identified myself as the researcher, I obtained voluntarily consent, and I notified participants that they may choose to end their involvement at any time. Further, I sought to share the outcomes research with the TTC community after completion of the project. While data analysis and surveying is still ongoing, I plan to post results to the survey, as well as links to the project page on my academic website and to articles that contain these survey results. In my introductory post to the community, I also mentioned that I would later post results of the study to the forum. This attempt at transparency in academic research and scholarship is one that may be taken in the spirit of a more egalitarian relationship in which the participant community may benefit from the research being conducted (Chen, Hall, & Johns, 2004). Still, this egalitarian spirit can be much more substantially invoked in rhetoric of health & medicine research, as shown in studies conducted by Angeli (this volume) and Bloom-Pojar (this volume). Further, in Pigozzi's (this volume) participatory research study, community representatives played more direct roles in several research stages, including designing the study. To apply a participatory research methodology such as Pigozzi's to the survey instrument in my study, I might have engaged members of the TTC community as to which aspects of pregnancy testing most affected or concerned them, and then designed the survey with community input around these concerns.

Ethnographic Methods

The actual research conducted in the TTC community did not involve situated study of the community itself. But what if it had? How does ethical decision-making change if the methodology changes? First, the nature of what is studied and how the researcher engages with the online community changes with an ethnographic study. The researcher is observing (and often, participating in) a community for an extended period of time, taking field notes and often screen-shots of what transpires inside the community. The ethnographer is observing social and behavioral interaction. Such observation can generate a large number of artifacts, as the visual and textual information from a community such as TTC would be collected, observed, and analyzed. The researcher would learn various usernames and their behaviors and attributes. With TTC, the researcher would learn the trying-to-conceive narratives for each username, including observa-tion of data points such as fertility cycles, numbers of pregnancy tests taken, age, geographic location, number of children in the family, and consumer prefer-ences for fertility, pregnancy, and baby products and services. Some members of the community would maintain anonymity under a pseudonym, but many oth-ers would not, revealing their real names and locations along with these other data points.

An ethnographer by training would likely not consider this to be an exempt research study under IRB because the forum is publicly accessible. Yet because the forum requires a username to participate and become a member of the com-munity, the expectation of privacy is very high, and its members would hold the belief that the information contained within the forum would not flow outside of its forum. Additionally, due to the topic sensitivity of fertility and the vulnerability of the participants to harm if their fertility and pregnancy narratives were made known to a larger public, a researcher who sought to publish an ethnographic study of TTC should seek informed consent and seek to keep the identities of the participants confidential. If the ethnographer sought to publish screenshots of the community, efforts should be taken to redact readily identifiable information such as usernames/icons, photographs, and children's names, as well as any information subject to copyright or trademark, such as the community's logo and other social media platforms' logos and imagery.

Mixed Method to Computational Approaches

What if a researcher sought to collect all of the quantifiable data on the user forum posts for use in a mixed methods or computational study, for example, of the number of days after ovulation that users report taking a pregnancy test? A quan-titative researcher could scrape the data—increasingly, with automated tools and methods—to collect only this snippet and nothing else, placing anonymized data into a spreadsheet and analyzing thousands of self-reported numbers. This situa-tion is much less clear with regard to informed consent and privacy concerns. As

Eynon, Fry, and Schroeder (2008) argue, while IRB policies are largely based on human subject research pre-Internet, the Internet research ethical guidelines from AoIR "focus mainly on issues related to observational research in the analysis of interaction in online environments, and do not address issues of automatic data collection and large-scale analysis of online domains" (p. 23, citing Thelwall & Stuart, 2006). While AoIR and many other scholars and policymakers seek to address these emerging concerns, it is up to the individual researcher to engage in a case-by-case evaluation of the ethical considerations involved, particularly seeking to understand what harm may come to individuals or communities should patterns in behavior by a demographic group be made available, or if it is possible to trace an individual's data points back to identifying information, either from where the data is stored, or where it eventually becomes published.

Implications for Researchers of Health and Medical Rhetoric

The case study presented here only scratches the surface of what information is more and more readily available for researchers of health and medicine. Health 2.0 tools and platforms are increasingly being integrated into patient care, clinician workflow, consumer wearables, care management programs, disease management, and more (Krueger, 2014). Although an online discussion forum of home pregnancy test takers may not be the most cutting-edge digital, networked platform in Health 2.0, it provides a means for researchers from disparate backgrounds to conceive of digital spaces as more than just a site for data collection. The implications of this case study for researchers of health and medical rhetoric can be distilled to the following three suggestions:

Know Your Methodology as it Relates to the Digital

Medical and health rhetoricians may be working across a variety of methodologies with a variety of artifacts and tools. Despite the increasing versatility of researchers, particularly rhetoricians, whose "methodological mutability," or ability to borrow, adapt, and implement practices and methods across disciplines is increasingly valued (Scott & Meloncon, this volume), it is important to think about how a researcher may approach them all ideologically. As we integrate computational approaches and tools into our research methods, these must be interrogated for what kinds of beliefs they carry about knowledge, meaning making, and surveillance and privacy. IRB should not be considered a hurdle, but an opportunity among many to engage multiple stakeholders to our research and review ethical decision-making with an eye toward the human beings who may be affected, even two or three steps removed, from your data set.

Anticipate How Those Studying Internet Research May Treat Your Research Method

A considerable amount of space in this chapter is given to the AoIR Recommendations and to those ethicists and scholars who work with the AoIR Ethics Working Committee, such as McKee and Porter. This is for good reason. Regulatory bodies and policymakers are looking to these researchers to continue to provide guidance as laws, regulations, and policies are implemented. It also behooves health and medical rhetoricians to have a working knowledge of these recommendations and to understand where their own studies fall within their suggestions. The current idiosyncratic and uneven treatment of digital research by IRBs further reinforces the ethical imperative to look to specialists who are particularly mindful of the dilemmas that we as researchers in Health 2.0 currently encounter.

Treat Each Project on a Case-by-Case Basis

In this chapter, I have tried to show how choice of research subject and methodology for a particular project may alter the ethical considerations for that project. It is critical to evaluate each project as it stands rather than follow a checklist. I frequently hear researchers say, "The online forum is public, so it's an exempt study." The resources referenced in this study, from the AoIR Recommendations to McKee and Porter's (2009) mapping of principles for ethical deliberation, all show how iterative and case-based ethical decision-making in research truly is. With this particular case study, much of the ethical decision-making was conducted simultaneously with the choice of online community (TTC) and the choice of method (the survey). It was chosen in order to prevent ethical dilemmas that would be encountered with other methods and practices. Had I chosen to engage in an online ethnography of adolescent girls discussing home pregnancy testing and pregnancy decision-making, my ethical decision-making would have changed considerably: the participants become more vulnerable as minors, privacy concerns are greater as information becomes more sensitive, and my relationship with the community changes as I observe in real time.

Even if a researcher's methods and practices remain the same across study designs, it is important to evaluate ethical decision-making processes for the specific context of each new study. IRB and other regulatory bodies attempt to force researchers into yes-no binaries ("are you conducting research on human subjects?") when the reality is that each case often has complex answers to these questions. A process-based approach rather than a codified approach to research ethics will result in the kind of thoughtful decision-making required to make nuanced decisions about informed content, privacy and surveillance, and reporting. As digital environments, tools, and methods proliferate, so do the ethical concerns that arise in each Health 2.0 research project. Almost 20 years ago, Gurak and Silker (1997) issued a call to action, arguing that "technical communication scholars should begin a serious conversation about the methodological issues of conducting research in cyberspace" (p. 415). Markham and Buchanan (forthcoming) believe that 20 years of focus on regulatory models for research ethics have failed, and that "As the terrains of research continue to shift along with new technologies, it behooves researchers to consider harm from a grounded, case-by-case perspective" (p. 11). As we continue to explore health and medicine in Health 2.0, these two statements, taken together, reflect how we as researchers must ethically tread.

Acknowledgements

The author wishes to thank Dr. Alice R. Daer for her guidance in the research undertaken for this chapter.

References

AoIR. (2017). Ethics. *AoIR: Association of Internet Researchers*. Retrieved from https:/aoir. org/ethics/.

Baym, N. K. (2013). *Personal connections in the digital age*. Malden, MA: Polity Press.

boyd, d., & Crawford, K. (2012). Critical questions for big data: Provocations for a cultural, technological, and scholarly phenomenon. *Information, Communication & Society, 15*(5), 662–679.

Burke, K. (1966). *Language as symbolic action: Essays on life, literature, and method*. Berkeley, CA: University of California Press.

CASRO. (2016). Code of standards and ethics. *CASRO: The Voice and Values of Research*. Retrieved from www.casro.org/?page=TheCASROCode2014.

Chen, S. S., Hall, G. J., & Johns, M. D. (2004). Research paparazzi in cyberspace: The voices of the researched. In M. D. Johns, S. S. Chen, & G. J. Hall (Eds.), *Online social research: Methods, issues, & ethics* (pp. 157–175). New York, NY: Peter Lang.

Conference on College Composition and Communication. (2015, March). CCCC guidelines for the ethical conduct of research in composition studies. *National Council of Teachers of English*. Retrieved from www.ncte.org/cccc/resources/positions/ethicalconduct.

Dickens, B. M., Gostin, L., & Levine, R. J. (1991). Research on human populations: National and international ethical guidelines. *Law, Medicine, and Health Care. 19*, 157–161.

Dougherty, D. S., & Kramer, M. W. (Eds.). (2005). Special issue on IRBs. *Journal of Applied Communication Research, 33*.

Ess, C., & the AoIR Working Committee (2002). *Ethical decision-making and Internet research: Recommendations from the AoIR Ethics Working Committee*. Retrieved from www.aoir.org/reports/ethics.pdf.

Eynon, R., Fry, J., & Schroeder, R. (2008). The ethics of internet research. In N. Fielding, R. M. Lee, & G. Blank (Eds.), *The Sage Handbook of Online Research Methods* (pp. 22–42). London: Sage.

Eysenbach, G., & Köhler, C. (2004). Health-related searches on the Internet. *JAMA: Journal of the American Medical Association, 291*(24), 2946.

Fleckenstein, K. S., Spinuzzi, C., Rickly, R. J., & Papper, C. C. (2008). The importance of harmony: An ecological metaphor for writing research. *College Composition and Communication, 60*(2), 388–419.

Frommeyer, A. (2015, Nov. 5). A CEO's guide to group Health 2.0. TechCrunch. Retrieved from https://techcrunch.com/2015/11/05/a-ceos-guide-to-group-health-2-0/.

Goodman, K. W. (1998a). Bioethics and health informatics: An introduction. In K. W. Goodman (Ed.), *Ethics, computing, and medicine: Informatics and the transformation of health care* (pp. 1–31). New York, NY: Cambridge University Press.

Goodman, K. W. (1998b). Outcomes, futility, and health policy research. In K. W. Goodman (Ed.), *Ethics, computing, and medicine: Informatics and the transformation of health care* (pp. 116–138). New York, NY: Cambridge University Press.

Grabill, J. T., & Pigg, S. (2012). Messy rhetoric: Identity performance as rhetorical agency in online public forums. *Rhetoric Society Quarterly, 42*(2), 99–119.

Grady, D. (1993, Dec.). Death at the Corners. *Discover,* 82–91.

Gurak, L. J., & Silker, C. M. (1997). Technical communication research: From traditional to virtual. *Technical Communication Quarterly, 6*(4), 403–418.

Henderson, G., Corneli, A. L., Mahoney, D. B., Nelson, D. K., & Mwansambo, C. (2007). Applying research ethics guidelines: The view from a sub-Saharan research ethics committee. *Journal of Empirical Research on Human Research Ethics, 2*(2), 41–48.

Hine, C. (2015). *Ethnography for the Internet: Embedded, embodied, and everyday.* London, UK: Bloomsbury Academic.

Johns, M. D., Hall, G. J., & Crowell, T. L. (2004). Surviving the IRB review: Institutional guidelines and research strategies. In M. D. Johns, S. S. Chen, & G. J. Hall (Eds.), *Online social research: Methods, issues, & ethics* (pp. 105–124). New York, NY: Peter Lang.

Krueger, K. (2014, January 14). Providers, trackers, & money: What you need to know about Health 2.0. *The Health Care Blog.* Retrieved from http://thehealthcareblog.com/blog/2014/01/14/providers-trackers-money-what-you-need-to-know-about-health-2-0/.

Kwon, D. (2015, November 30). Should you take an app for that? *Scientific American.* Retrieved from www.scientificamerican.com/article/should-you-take-an-app-for-that/.

McKee, H. A., & Porter, J. E. (2008). The ethics of digital writing research: A rhetorical approach. *College Composition and Communication, 59*(4), 711–749.

McKee, H. A., & Porter, J. E. (2009). *The ethics of Internet research: A rhetorical, case-based process.* New York, NY: Peter Lang.

Markham, A. N. (2017). Ethnography in the digital Internet era: From fields to flows, descriptions to interventions. In N. Denzin & Y. Lincoln (Eds.), *The Sage handbook of qualitative research* (pp. 650–668). Thousand Oaks, CA: Sage.

Markham, A. N., & Buchanan, E. (2012). *Ethical decision-making and Internet research: Recommendations from the AoIR ethics working committee (version 2.0).* Retrieved from www.aoir.org/reports/ethics2.pdf.

Markham, A. N., & Buchanan, E. A. (2015). Ethical concerns in Internet research. In J. Wright (Ed.), *The international encyclopedia of social and behavioral sciences* (2nd ed., pp. 606–613). Elsevier Press.

The National Commission for the Protection of Human Subjects of Biomedical and Behavioral Research. (1979, April 18). The Belmont report: Ethical Principles and Guidelines for the Protection of Human Subjects of Research. *HHS.gov: U.S. Department of Health & Human Services.* Retrieved from www.hhs.gov/ohrp/humansubjects/guidance/belmont.html.

National Institutes of Health. (2004, July 8). Institutional Review Boards and the HIPAA Privacy Rule. *HIPAA Privacy Rule: Information for Researchers*. Retrieved from https://privacyruleandresearch.nih.gov/irbandprivacyrule.asp.

Nissenbaum, H. (2010). *Privacy in context: Technology, policy, and the integrity of social life*. Stanford, CA: Stanford University Press.

Opel, D. (2014, September). Social justice in technologies of prenatal care: Toward a user centered approach to technical communication in home pregnancy testing. In D. Armfield, *Proceedings of the 32nd ACM International Conference on The Design of Communication CD-ROM* (p. 8). New York, NY: ACM.

SACHRP. (2013, May 20). Attachment B: Considerations and recommendations concerning Internet research and human subjects research regulations, with revisions. *HHS. gov: U.S. Department of Health and Human Services*. Retrieved from www.hhs.gov/ohrp/sachrp/commsecbytopic/Internet%20Research/may20,2013,attachmentb.html.

Salvo, M. J. (2001). Ethics of engagement: User-centered design and rhetorical methodology. *Technical Communication Quarterly, 10*(3), 273–291.

Schriver, K. A. (2013). What do technical communicators need to know about information design? In J. Johnson-Eilola & S. A. Selber (Eds.), *Solving problems in technical communication* (pp. 386–427). Chicago, IL: University of Chicago Press.

Sullivan, P., & Porter, J. E. (1997). *Opening spaces: Writing technologies and critical research practices*. Westport, CT: Ablex Publishing.

Thelwall, M., & Stuart, D. (2006). Web crawling ethics revisited: Cost, privacy and denial of service. *Journal of the American Society for Information Science and Technology, 57*(13), 1771–1779.

Tufekci, Z. (2014, January 13). Social media is a conversation, not a press release. *Medium*. Retrieved from https://medium.com/technology-and-society/social-media-is-a-conversation-not-a-press-release-4d811b45840d#.pwdwo8bcq.

U.S. Copyright Office. (2008). *U.S. Copyright Law (Title 17)*. Retrieved from www.copyright.gov/title17.

11

NEGOTIATING INFORMED CONSENT

Bueno aconsejar, mejor remediar
(it is good to give advice, but it
is better to solve the problem)

Laura Maria Pigozzi

Keywords: participatory research, Latino, health research, relational autonomy

> You should be very surprised how many people, how many people are out there that want to speak to someone and maybe not just for little one thing, but on so many things but no one ever, ever bothers to ask them that and no one even bothers in knowing how to ask them.
>
> (Participant from the NIC Project)

Significance of Topic

I have conducted research in the local Latino community working to understand the efficacy of health communication materials. During this time, community members have expressed worry and concern over the high prevalence of diabetes within their families and neighbors. This concern is not isolated to this community; Latinos are disproportionally affected by diabetes and obesity (Cohn, Livingston, & Minushin, 2008; Vivo, Krim, Cevik, & Witteles, 2009), as well as dyslipidemia (having too high or too low lipid levels in the bloodstream), metabolic syndrome, and hypertension (Vivo et al., 2009).

In order for medical research to produce results that are generalizable for this community, as well as members of other ethnicities and races, clinical trials must intentionally include diverse participants. Certain races and ethnicities suffer disproportionately from specific diseases. In terms of drug research, drug pharmacokinetics (the interactions of a drug and the body in terms of its absorption, distribution, metabolism, and excretion) and pharmacodynamics (the effects of drugs on the body and the mechanism of their action) vary among racial and ethnic populations. Limited participation leads to limited data specific for minority populations. With the importance of trial participation in mind, I became interested in the specifics of enrolling Latinos with little to no English language ability in clinical trials, especially the process of informed consent.

A researcher has a legal and moral obligation to obtain informed consent from research participants, as discussed in the *Belmont Report* (1979), a result of hearings of the National Commission for the Protection of Human Subjects of Biomedical and Behavioral Research. The report outlines three basic principles that direct the conduct of biomedical and behavioral research that utilize human subjects: respect for persons (i.e., autonomy), beneficence, and justice. It also includes applications of these principles and provides concepts that serve to guide researchers' adherence to them. The process of informed consent operationalizes the principle of respect for persons, in particular.

While there has been much research across many fields on informed consent, little has been done to explore the process with Latino immigrants with limited or no English language skills. After a brief discussion locating informed consent within the field of bioethics, I will discuss consent as a rhetorical interaction and then describe the research project I conducted to study this process as it is understood and experienced by Latino immigrants.

Bioethics

Callahan defines bioethics as "the application of ethical theory to the dilemmas raised by the practice of modern medicine, especially those problems raised by the applications of new technologies" (as cited in Hedgecoe, 2004, p. 122). The evolution of this field has involved influences from many disciplines beginning with philosophy and theology. Jonsen explains that "theology and philosophy presided over the birth of bioethics and shaped the bioethical movement. Each brought a distinct tradition and perspective together with analytic skills sharpened by their disciplines. Together they produced an amalgam of ideas, methods, and educational structures that became bioethics" (as cited in Borry, Schotsmans, & Dierckx, 2005, p. 50). Physicians, nurses, lawyers, and, more recently, social scientists have also played consequential roles in shaping the discipline.

It is understandable, in light of the rights-based focus of the 1970s, that autonomy became a central principle in bioethics, along with the principles of beneficence, nonmaleficence, and justice (Belkin & Brandt, 2001; Beauchamp & Childress, 1979). These principles guide a normative ethic for practical decision-making based on common moral grounds, termed principlism, which retains its place as a central moral theory in the field. However, this approach is not without criticism. Charges levied against principlism include the absence of a larger moral theory (Belkin & Brandt, 2001), the lack of attention to narratives of illness (Brody, 1987; Nelson, 2004), the lack of attention to relationships, power distribution, and gender roles (Lindemann, 2006; Sherwin, 1998; Walker, 1998; Warren, 1989), and the lack of incorporation of social and cultural scholarship (Fox &

Swazey, 2008). The focus on individualism and traditional autonomy theory can be placed in opposition to a more contextualized view of autonomy, creating a tension that interferes with the integration of social and cultural perspectives into bioethics.

In an attempt to address these criticisms and place moral issues in a social, cultural, and historical context, alternative moral theories have come into use. Among these approaches are feminist ethics, communitarianism, narrative ethics, virtue ethics, casuistry, and urban bioethics. These approaches can inform a variety of humanistic and social scientific methodologies that are being incorporated into bioethical research. Turner (2003) notes that by the mid-1990s, cultural norms and ethnic differences became legitimate sites of inquiry, creating a richer context for research. The site and participants of my research reflect this advance. Additionally, I found extensions to the principlist notion of autonomy provided by feminist ethics useful in examining my research data since they allow fuller consideration of the audience's social context.

As noted by Bivens (this volume), one purpose of consent, from the view of an Institutional Review Board (IRB), is preventing potential litigation. The history of informed consent includes contributions from law and moral philosophy (among others as described in the preceding paragraphs). The law's initial involvement was concerned with the clinical use of informed consent (as opposed to consent used for research), focusing on monetary compensation for patients harmed by a physician's failure to disclose pertinent information or a disregard of patient's wishes. In moral philosophy, informed consent is concerned with respect for the autonomy of the patient or research participant (Faden & Beauchamp, 1986).

Beauchamp (2011) observes that a precise description of informed consent is complicated because two different meanings have been at work throughout its history. The first,

> is an autonomous authorization by individual patients or subjects. A person gives an informed consent in this first sense if and only if the person, with substantial understanding and in substantial absence of control by others, intentionally authorizes a health professional to do something . . . in the second sense, informed consent is analyzable in terms of institutional and policy rules of consent that collectively form the social practice of informed consent in institutional context. Here 'informed consent' refers only to a legally or institutionally effective approval given by a patient or subject.
>
> *(p. 518)*

Within the legal context, informed consent is concerned with the second sense but does little to move the concept toward the first sense. Bioethics literature maintains that it is this first sense, autonomous choice of medical patients or research participants, which must be ensured. This is the "morally best standard" (Beauchamp, 2011, p. 518) and provides a model for institutional and policy requirements of informed consent. Along with explanatory goals, my research sought to understand how best to invent a consent conference that reflects this morally best standard.

Informed Consent: An Act of Persuasion

Following Barton & Eggly (2009), I consider informed consent a process of persuasion, thus a rhetorical interaction. Lyne (2001) tells us that "To think rhetorically is to reflect constructively on the habits of representation that position people for making judgments" (p. 13). The informed consent conference positions the potential participant to take an action. Additionally, and importantly, Kleinig (2010) notes that consent is a social act and a *communicative act* that must be signified and recognized. It is the manner of recognition that I examine in my research.

Notions from contemporary rhetorical theory are useful to unpack and examine the rhetorical communicative act of the consent conference. Kenneth Burke (1969) defines rhetoric as "the use of words by human agents to form attitudes or induce actions in other human agents" (p. 41). He extends classical rhetoric's focus on persuasion with his notion of identification.[1] Identification is understood within Burke's view that language is a symbolic action; language is "a symbolic means of inducing cooperation in beings that by nature respond to symbols" (Burke, 1969, p. 43). My project looks to examine the "symbols" being used in the consent conference—how they are functioning as persuasive elements, and how they are being understood by Latino immigrants. Moreover, I examine the level of participation this population might have in the conference. For ethical persuasion to take place, the researcher needs to fully understand the needs and values of the research participants.

Segal (2005) also uses contemporary rhetorical theory to examine the medical research process, among other health interactions. She makes an observation that ties contemporary rhetoricians Perlman and Olbrecths-Tyteca's notion of a "contact of minds" to the process of informed consent: "the conditions for rhetoric include conditions for 'a contact of minds', and if these conditions are not met, then the people addressed do not properly constitute a rhetorical audience, and what is going on is not really rhetoric at all but something else: coercion, perhaps" (p. 91). This is the ethical implication.

The low rates of minority participation in human subject research is discussed in a considerable body of literature, including studies on what approaches might be best used to recruit these populations and studies on identifying and overcoming barriers to participation. Fischer and Kalbaugh (2011) report statistics from one report that estimates Hispanics represent 7.6% of all NIH research participants (p. 2217). This percentage should be put in context with the fact that Hispanics represented 17% of the total U.S. population in 2013 (Brown & Patten, 2014).

This lack of minority representation in medical trial research provided the exigency for my project. As Charleswill (2014) asserts, "The inclusion of minority populations in human subjects research may be a complex and challenging task; however, the consequences brought about by the gaps in data and information about the effects of therapeutics and other interventions on these groups are dire and of ethical importance" (p. 300). With respect to enrolling into clinical trials, Segal (2005) observes, "What frequently is thought of as 'informed,' 'shared,' or even 'consensual' decision making is actually when considered rhetorically a process of persuasion in which the parties are not, despite appearances, fully rhetorical partners" (p. 94). My research examines how the participant functions in the rhetorical interaction of the consent conference. The research question that grounded this project was: how do Latino immigrants with little to no English language proficiency understand and negotiate a clinical trial informed consent process? I explored this bioethical topic at the intersection of scientific and technical communication, rhetoric, and intercultural communication.

The bioethical ideal of informed consent is based on an autonomous individual receiving prescribed and relevant information, comprehending it, and agreeing or declining to participate. Felt, Bister, Strassnig, and Wagner (2009) suggest that this understanding of the process may be insufficient. They observe, "The framing of autonomy as informed choice that presents a narrow set of ready-made options for patients is seen as insufficient for describing and taking into account the complexities of social and historical context that contribute to patients' ways of dealing with medical encounters" (Felt et al., 2009, p. 4). In other words, persons often make decisions based on factors other than the facts before them. Consequently, one important part of this research project was to investigate just what sociocultural and historic factors might be impacting decisions made by this population.

In what follows, I describe an empirical research project I conducted at two sites in the immigrant Latino community in an urban Midwestern city. The research question reflects my training in bioethics and my ethnicity. The methodological framework reflects my philosophical underpinnings and looked to provide the participants of my project a voice they might not otherwise have on a topic of great importance to them. The methods sought to provide the participants both respect and confidentiality. Following the description of the research design, I will describe three results from this unique research design.

Negotiating Informed Consent (NIC) Project

In order to explore how Latino immigrants with little to no English-language skills negotiate an informed consent conference for enrollment into a clinical trial, I conducted a research project made up of three separate studies: the Negotiating Informed Consent (NIC) Project. This project explored Latinos' understanding of the informed consent conference considered on a broad level, including oral, textual, and visual components. This project illustrates how participatory research can provide value to a community and can reveal important insights into the community itself.

The NIC Project was participatory in that the community leaders agreed to the research questions, the research took place within the community, the participants were recruited from a community organization, and interventions were implemented at the research sites based on results from this project. I recruited participants for all three studies from two urban, Midwest Catholic parishes that served a large Latino population. Interviews and focus groups took place in the churches or their rectories, which were safe and convenient locations for the participants.

Methodology

Bueno aconsejar, mejor remdiar.[2]

Research Design

This project is a form of *participatory research*. As a Latina with training in both rhetoric and bioethics, I was committed to conducting research in the most ethical and inclusive manner available to me. I strove for the resultant epistemology to be grounded in the realities of the community. Participatory research is a methodological approach for creating knowledge in partnership and within the sociocultural context of a community. It is an umbrella term for a number of approaches: participatory action research, action research, community engagement, and community-based participatory research, among others. Such approaches are increasingly being used in health research, as they have the potential to address health disparities "by bridging gaps between research and practice, addressing social justice, and creating conditions that facilitate people's control over the determinants of their health" (Cargo & Mercer, 2008, p. 326). Viswanathan and colleagues (2004) argue that participatory research is particularly appropriate to study issues of health disparities, stating "This approach is particularly attractive for academics and public health professionals struggling to address the persistent problems of health care disparities in a variety of populations (identified by factors such as social or economic status, lack of health insurance, or membership in various racial and ethnic groups)."

In addition to grounding research processes in participants' sociocultural contexts, involving communities in participatory research can work to decrease the power differentials between the researcher and participants. Community involvement can range from "limited advisory roles in early stages (e.g., input on research priorities) to key leadership responsibilities at every stage [of the research]" (Bromley, Mikesell, Jones, & Khudyakov, 2015, p. 900). We might relate this emphasis of participatory research to Robert Johnson's (2004) concept of *audience involved*, which he contrasts to the more familiar rhetorical notion of audience addressed. Johnson explains that "the involved audience is an actual participant in the writing process who creates knowledge and determines much of the content of the discourse" (p. 93). While I was unable to involve the community in the analysis of the data, the interviewing approach I used looked to allow a degree of discussion freedom for the participants.

Within this participatory research project, I chose to use a version of the research methodology known as *grounded theory*; specifically the constructivist grounded theory methodology developed by Charmaz (2006). This is a rigorous methodology that employs the following iterative steps: data collecting, coding (initial, focused, and theoretical), memo writing, theoretical sampling, saturating theoretical categories, and finally, theorizing. The result is a unique theory specific to and grounded in the data. This methodology works well when there is a paucity of information on the phenomenon under investigation. Additionally, it allows the voice of the participants to be heard in the resulting emergent theory. In seeking to answer grounded theory's key question of "What is happening here?", I was informed by a *feminist perspective* that is attuned to how power and privilege are operating and has the goal to "make visible those lives and audible those voices that might be neglected in traditional research studies" (Lay, 2002, p. 169). Although Lay (2002) and MacNealy (1999) focus on women in their research using this perspective, I expanded this to include all marginalized people in the research (as does Sherwin, 1998).

My research could also be described as *analogue patient methodology*, which hereafter will be referred to as *analogue participant methodology*.[3] Analogue participants are research participants who are asked to imagine that they are the patient, or in this case a potential clinical trial participant, in a particular medical circumstance that is depicted in a video. "This methodology has been used in previous studies in an attempt to understand patient perceptions when an actual patient population is not available" (Blanch-Hartigan, Hall, Roter, & Frankel, 2010, p. 316). In order to explore how Latino immigrants with little to no English language proficiency negotiate a clinical trial informed consent conference, I needed a way to observe this population being recruited into clinical trials. Angeli (this volume) discusses difficulties medical rhetoric researchers often encounter gaining access to medical research sites and provides a very useful methodology, assemblage mapping. I experienced just this difficulty as I was unsuccessful in joining an existing clinical trial. I spent roughly 13 months, intermittently, attempting to gain access to enrollments in existing clinical trials with no success. The requirement that the potential trial participants be Latino with limited English language skills made locating a trial in my geographic location even more complicated. Candilis and Lidz (2010) acknowledge the difficulty of joining existing clinical trials to conduct consent research. This "piggy-backing" is difficult for a number of reasons. The original trial researchers may be concerned that their patients might be reluctant to join their trial with the additional consent research, they may be concerned that their trial is being judged, or they may be concerned about the additional burden to their patients and staff of this additional research. It is for these reasons that I adopted the use of analogue participant methodology.

A common criticism levied at *analogue participant methodology* is that it is difficult, if not impossible, to ask a participant to imagine they are suffering from a serious medical condition; therefore, their response may not be representative of an actual patient. To address this criticism, I intentionally chose a healthy patient trial as the simulation for the first two studies in this project, as it is a reasonable situation for an analogue participant to imagine. However, during the conversations that took place during these two studies it became apparent, as previously noted, that diabetes was a familiar and prevalent condition in this community. Many participants discussed themselves, family, or community members who struggled to manage diabetes. I was interested to know how the results of a medical trial simulation would impact the grounded theory and conceptual framework developed to date. At this point I was confident that participants could indeed imagine they were being enrolled into a diabetes clinical trial. Hence, Study 3 used the enrollment materials from an actual, multisite diabetes trial.

The first two studies used the materials, with permission, from a healthy patient public health trial as the simulation. Two videos were created for this simulation. The first video was a priming video, which featured the enroller (from the actual public health study), looking straight into the camera, explaining why potential participants were being asked to enroll in this trial. The enroller provided the background necessary for the analogue participant to understand the context of the simulation. In the second video the enroller, again looking directly into the camera, conducted the clinical trial recruitment conference (informed consent). The third study used the consent materials, with permission, from a diabetes clinical trial. All materials and conversations in all three NIC Project studies were in Spanish to ensure clear communication and a comfort level for the analogue participants.[4]

In interviews and focus groups, the participants and I discussed the recruitment conference after watching the videos and consulting the accompanying textual materials or, in the case of the third study, listening to a recruitment script being read and consulting the accompanying textual materials. I had prepared interview questions, although conversations were allowed to develop organically. All interviews and focus group conversations were audio recorded, transcribed, and translated from Spanish to English. The results of the NIC Project provided answers to the research questions that asked how Latino immigrants with little to no English language skills negotiate an informed consent conference. Interestingly, the results also provided a detailed conceptual framework of the sociocultural context of this community, which included information on community members concerns and anxieties. The next section explores this context.

A Sampling of Unique Results from this Methodology

Rhetorical Situation and Social Context

Quien canta su mal espanta.[5]

The conceptual framework (see Figure 11.1) summarizes the results from all three studies representing how participants negotiate clinical trial information.

Importantly, the members of this community receive and process the clinical trial information within the community's social context. Each box represents an explanatory, theoretical category that is comprised of properties and characteristics. The relationship between categories narrate the theory and answer grounded theory's question, "What's happening here?" The data from Study 3, the diabetes trial simulation, did not radically change the conceptual framework, but rather enriched and nuanced the categories. Due to the careful attention I paid to maintaining a culturally familiar, safe, and respectful environment, the participants were comfortable, open, and frank in their discussions. They provided data that not only addressed the initial research questions, but also offered a highly nuanced look at the sociocultural context in which they conduct their daily lives. This context is rich, complicated, historically bounded, and multilayered. These social factors inform individual decision-making and autonomy.

Latino immigrants in this study live in a closely-knit community, sharing a culture, language, faith, for the most part a country of origin, and the immigrant experience. Full results and discussion of this project and the above conceptual framework are outside of the scope of this chapter, but I will briefly describe a few important aspects of this sociocultural context.

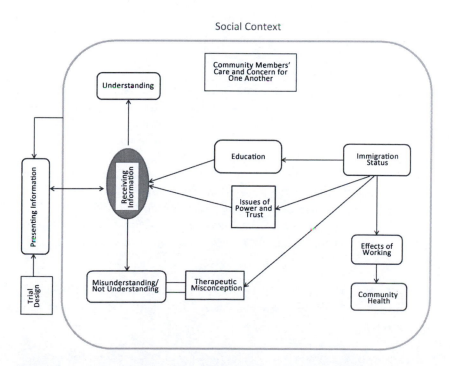

FIGURE 11.1 How participants negotiate an informed consent conference.

These community members demonstrate care and concern for one another in their shared struggles to acculturate while living with a steady sense of disquietude surrounding the immigration status of themselves, family members, or friends. An undocumented status affects all areas of an immigrant's life, limiting many potential opportunities, as discussed by one participant:

> We're very stressed about it. Because everything that's happened. The watchful groups, the immigration, the reform, police treatment, watchful groups . . . all of that affects the Hispanic community in one way or another. Even if you want to get near for a good cause, [the study] well now they're afraid and can't trust.

Many of these individuals work multiple jobs, including their roles as parents. Time spent working has resulted in poor family nutrition, a lack of physical activity, and a lack of parental supervision. The traditional family structure is disrupted and the cultural value of *familismo* is threatened by this time spent working. Community members are aware of such effects, but they do not seem to have the tools to negotiate this new reality, as explained by one participant.

> The work and money are the ambition and results in the bad things in the home. . . . And in this country where there's a lot of work, one can leave their family to come here to work to do things they shouldn't be. Also in video games, as Latinos work a lot and their kids are left with the video games, the crime. That's what happens to our people. We're rotting.

A poor diet, a result of both lack of time and lack of nutritional knowledge, affects the health of many community members. Obesity is common, which contributes to many health issues, including diabetes, a disease common in this community. Many community members do not have medical insurance since affordable medical insurance is often not available for either documented or undocumented people. Because of the expense, many are not able to receive health care on a regular basis. Some community members use natural or unconventional treatments to treat their maladies, and many rely on their faith to heal. For example, one participant explained that she takes pills that are sent to her from Ecuador along with using some creams for constant pain:

> It [pill] makes me feel better, along with some creams, and then I can work. I can work and work and work with only the aid of the cream and that pill.

The etiology of diseases such as diabetes is rooted in folk illness for some individuals, which can complicate successful treatment. The story below is a portion of one woman's narrative of her journey with diabetes, including its etiology (*susto*), noncompliance, and treatment.

> The evenings, I was assaulted. It made me very scared so I was in a state of shock (*me asusté*). So then a woman gave me two big, like this, glasses of water to drink. It's a remedy for a fright (*el susto*). But that's the worst thing that people can do when they have a fright (*un susto*).
>
> Then in the nineties, from there I came to the U.S. They told me that I was prediabetic and gave me some medicine. I thought this doctor was crazy, since I never . . . don't even come from a diabetic family. So then I was considering what the fright (*susto*) had to do with it. But since I didn't take the medicine, I decided to just leave it and started working at a fabric warehouse. I wanted to lose weight by wrapping myself with plastic, because I was big, not very big, but somewhat big. So then I started losing weight and more weight. And a coworker asked me what I was doing since I had lost a lot of weight. And I told her that I didn't know.
>
> From there she took me to the doctor. My sugar reading was at 500. . . . Right now
>
> I am taking insulin. . . . For now, I have been waking with sugar reading of 90, 105, it has not gotten any higher. But last time we had problems, it was in the 200s. So it's my opinion that frights (*sustos de corajes*) and things like that are the cause of it [diabetes].

The analogue participant in this study is describing having a *susto* and being given two large glasses of water to drink. Later she describes a problem with her husband, who we assume abused alcohol, and says she once again drank water. She believes that these *sustos* are the cause of her diabetes. This correlation between drinking water after a *susto* and diabetes is mentioned in a study that examined *susto* and soul loss in Mexicans and Mexican Americans by Glazer, Baer, Weller, Alba, and Liebowitz (2004). They found that in participants from Guadalajara, "some (12%) suggested refraining from drinking anything but eating a piece of French roll (*pan birote*) [after experiencing a *susto*]. The latter treatment was said to be important to prevent diabetes (and/or *bilis*) from occurring as a result of the *susto*" (p. 277).

In the next section I will discuss how understanding autonomy through a feminist framework provides a way to consider the social context.

Autonomy Evaluated

Del dicho al hecho, hay mucho trecho.[6]

Autonomy is the grounding of informed consent. The bioethical ideal of informed consent is based on an autonomous individual receiving relevant information, comprehending it, and agreeing or declining to participate. I am arguing that the consent process has a persuasive component, tempered by autonomy. Before enrollment, the researcher must determine if the potential participant is autonomous. Beauchamp and Childress (2009) explain that, "at a minimum, personal autonomy encompasses self-rule that is free from both controlling interferences by others and limitations that prevent meaningful choice, such as inadequate understanding" (p. 101). Dimensions of autonomy include the conditions of liberty and agency as vital.

As previously discussed, Felt, Bister, Strassnig, and Wagner (2009) challenge this traditional, principlist understanding of autonomy. They feel that individuals may make decisions on clinical interventions based on information from sources other than the information presented to them by the physician or researcher. In their study they found that patients may not be directly attending to information presented in the informed consent process and instead are relying on personal experiences, perceptions, and "imaginations" to make their decisions.

The previous section began to describe the sociocultural complexities experienced by this community. To relate this context to the principle of autonomy, I adopted Sherwin's (1998) alternative view of autonomy. Sherwin (1998) uses a feminist perspective to offer a relational approach that "allows us to maintain a central place for autonomy within bioethics, but . . . requires an interpretation that is both deeper and more complicated than the traditional conception acknowledges" (p. 44). This approach can be thought of as socially situated or contextualized. Sherwin (1998) notes that "[a] relational conception of personhood . . . recognizes the importance of social forces in shaping each person's identity, development, and aspirations" (p. 35).

Informed consent does not ensure patient autonomy; this is especially true when considering diverse, urban communities. In fact, persons experiencing oppression may be restricted to a point that "it is distorting to describe as autonomous some specific choices made under such conditions" (Sherwin, 1998, pp. 27–28). The NIC project resulted in a rich, detailed description of the community's social context (see Figure 11.1). Each of the components of that context may have an effect on an individual's autonomy. The category *Understanding* comes out of data that demonstrates an understanding of specific information presented during the simulated consent conference. It was clear that certain information was not being understood as it was intended. This is an obvious problem. More complicated are the influences of other categories on autonomy. For example, the category *Immigration Status* compiles data related to the analogue participant's status as a documented or undocumented immigrant, an overriding issue for many of the participants and one that affects the entire Latino community. A participant's actions can be restricted due to fears of calling attention to themselves and their immigration status. The category *Issues of Power and Trust* compiles data involved with concerns about confidentiality and issues of power and trust that were sparked by the simulated consent conference. Fear of deportation is at the root of most issues within this category. Respect for Persons states "that persons with diminished autonomy are entitled to protection" (*Belmont Report,* Part B. 1., para. 1). Determining the extent of protection should depend on the level of risk and the likelihood of benefit (Part B, para. 5). When working with these community members in an informed consent conference, one shouldn't assume a lack of autonomy, but should be aware of the real possibility of compromised or diminished autonomy due to their social context.

To address diminished autonomy, we as researchers might position ourselves as feminist educators and approach the conference with a flexible attitude, being prepared to tailor the information to meet participants' needs and communication preferences while also attempting to shift power dynamics and build trust. Researchers should attend to advice given by Paskett, Katz, DeGraffinreid, and Tatum (2003) who remark, "The individuals delivering the information not only must demonstrate knowledge . . . but they also must express respect, compassion, sensitivity, warmth, empathy, honesty, flexibility, and support" (p. 610).

Finally, listening to the potential participants is essential to effective communication. Bivens (this volume) provides an account of rhetorical listening that could be useful to this project. Simon & Kodish (2005), following Geerz, advise, "Rather than trying to learn about the multiple beliefs and customs of particular groups of people—an almost impossible task—we ought to listen and talk to people about their shared needs and preferences" (p. S134). Listening is one way the researcher can make a determination on the autonomy of a potential participant. For example, this project suggested that some persons in the social context described in Figure 11.1 would be adequately informed, if the conference followed the above precautions, to ethically be enrolled in the simulated trial. However, there were instances that suggested the participant was not attending to the disclosed information, but was willing to enroll because they saw enrollment as the only way they could receive medical care and be educated on diabetes. It would not be ethical to enroll this participant because he did not understand many study details including the risks and benefits of participation. And more importantly, his main reasons for wanting to participate could be addressed with clinical care and education without experiencing the study risks. Another issue that impedes full understanding of disclosed information and therefore prohibits authentic consent is that of therapeutic misconception.

Therapeutic Misconception: A Rhetorical Analysis

> *Donde hay gana, hay mañana.*[7]

Therapeutic misconception occurs when a research participant believes "that their individual needs will determine treatment, or that the likelihood of benefit is greater than is actually the case" (Candilis & Lidz, 2010, p. 338). The category *Therapeutic Misconception* in this project categorizes data that demonstrates what occurs when research participants believe or assume that their trial participation will provide them with the greatest possible therapeutic benefits, meeting their individual needs. The implications of therapeutic misconception are significant in that they effectively exclude an authentic informed consent.

There is clear evidence of therapeutic misconception in this project's data. The therapeutic misconception exhibited is the perception that trial participation has the potential to improve a family's lifestyle and potentially their future. Some believed that they would attend classes and be taught self-identified skills that could lead to better futures for their families, even if those topics had not been mentioned, as in the following participant statement:

> And that, um is important, those types of classes that would teach us better nutrition for our children, and how to give them a space, a space to do activities with them, like exercise as well as homework, or how to show interest in your children by at least asking, "How is school going for you?"

There was no mention of giving the children space to exercise or do homework. Nor was there mention of discussing communication between parent and child.

> No. It was all clear. I understood that it will all be about your activity. I think the device they'll give you will track what you eat and if you're a little overweight you'll have to be active.

In actuality, the device (a belt) was to worn by the child and tracked activity, not eating. This participant was concerned with her weight and low activity level.

There is little to no literature, to my knowledge, showing therapeutic misconception analyzed through a contemporary rhetorical framework. Burke's concept of *identification* provides a technique, an approach, to examine and explain these and other analogue participant's misunderstandings to the simulated consent conference. Kenneth Burke (1969) remarked, "You persuade a man only insofar as you can talk his language by speech, gesture, tonality, order, image, attitude, idea, *identifying* your ways with his" (p. 55).

In *A Rhetoric of Motives* (1969) Burke fully discusses identification as a necessary element in human communication that includes naturally occurring division: "Identification is affirmed with earnestness precisely because there is division. Identification is compensatory to division. If men were not apart from one another, there would be no need for the rhetorician to proclaim their unity" (p. 22). To rise above division, one can seek attributes, interests, and values in common with others.

It is not clear to me what localization efforts (culturally specific approaches) were employed in the preparation of the public health trial consent textual artifacts or consent conference script other than translation into Spanish. There was no mention of tailoring the materials to a specific population or whether they employed a recruitment approach for specific ethnic populations in the original researcher's article describing the trial (Sherwood et al., 2013). There were no localization efforts in the diabetes trial. Nevertheless, the participants perceived that the researchers were identifying with them because the topics of the trial used in the simulations were topics that held deep importance for them: their children, their diets, and their health. The values this community ascribed to these topics contributed to the analogue participants perceiving that the research-ers were intending to "help" them and their community since the researchers appear to hold similar values. This is identification through what I will term "we care" and "we will help."

Burke (1969) observes that, "A is not identical with his colleague, B. But inso-far as their interests are joined, A is identified with B. Or he may identify himself with B even when their interests are not joined, if *he assumes that they are*, or is persuaded to believe so" (p. 20, emphasis added). The analogue participants were assuming the researchers shared their values. The *ethos* of the researchers, provided by their status, may also have contributed to identification in that analogue par-ticipants may have believed that persons in their positions would only do what is in the analogue participant's best interests.

A clear source of division from the dominant culture, present for many members of this community, is the undocumented immigration status. This is a defining part of the identities of many community members. One way to examine this division is by employing another Burkian concept—that of *terministic screens*. Burke (1969) observed, "Even if any given terminology is a reflection of reality, by its very nature as a terminology it must be a selection of reality; and to this extent it must function also as a deflection of reality" (p. 45). Terministic screens determine one's reality and "direct the attention" (p. 45). Burke (1969) explained that,

> We *must* use terministic screens, since we can't say anything without the use of terms; whatever terms we use, they necessarily constitute a correspond-ing kind of screen; and any such screen necessarily directs the attention to one field rather than another. Within that field there can be different screens, each with its ways of directing the attention and shaping the range of observations implicit in the given terminology. All terminologies must implicitly or explicitly embody choices between the principle of continuity and the principle of discontinuity.
>
> *(p. 50)*

With respect to the results of this study, I have shown that the analogue partici-pants hear the presented information through the screen of their social context. The ultimate motivation for this community, the *telos* of their migration, is "a better life." "A better life" is the reason they are in this country and are confront-ing the consequences of being undocumented. The terministic screen of "a better life" directs attention to activities that work toward this goal while deflecting attention from the harsher realities of their lives. This may explain why the par-ticipants exhibited the therapeutic misconceptions they did by overestimating and misconstruing the benefits they would incur by participating in the public health trial.

Conclusion

No hay mal que por bien no venga.[8]

This project challenges the efficacy of the standard informed consent process for members of the immigrant Latino community. The research design, a form of participatory research, utilized a feminist perspective to conduct grounded theory research. Analogue participant methodology was used to employ simulations of informed consent conferences. The results work toward reducing health disparities in a number of ways.

First, the results provide insights into culturally tailored approaches to enroll community members into a clinical trial. The data also highlights the overwhelming importance of understanding the impact of a participant's sociocultural context on individual autonomy. The researcher might better ensure an individual's autonomy by approaching a consent conference as a feminist educator, not as an authority. This could work to disrupt power differentials and promote understanding since the researcher is working to connect with the individual and is probing to get feedback so confusing information can be repeated and clarified. The conference should be considered an audience-involved process.

Second, justice issues regarding inclusion highlight the need to promote trials that include immigrant Latinos, working to better generalize trial results, especially for public health issues and diseases disproportionately evident in this community. The principle of justice seeks expression in the careful consideration of who is selected to be subjected to the risks of research as well as who is included in possibly beneficial research. Some participants in this project, demonstrating issues with trust and power, expressed concern over who might benefit from the simulated trial, while others indicated that they wanted to participate in such a trial but suspected their undocumented status would prohibit participation.

Third, insights into how community members struggle with maintaining a healthy diet and taking exercise can be useful to public health providers. Many of these individuals work multiple jobs and have children. Time spent working has resulted in poor family nutrition, a lack of physical activity, and a lack of parental supervision. A poor diet affects the health of many community members. Relatedly, insights into how some community members understand the etiology and treatment of diabetes can be useful to medical providers in order to most effectively educate and treat this population. Because of the expense of medical insurance, many are not able to receive health care on a regular basis. Some community members use natural or unconventional treatments to treat their maladies, many rely on their faith to heal, and some have a poor understanding of the etiology of diseases, all of which can complicate successful treatment.

Finally, this project demonstrates how rhetorical theory and a feminist perspective can inform a grounded theory methodology, especially in recognizing and interpreting how communication is shaped by sociocultural factors. Such factors informed how community members understood the information presented in a consent conference as well the nature of their autonomy. The project offers insight into how and what consent information might be presented and what factors facilitate or restrict trial participation. In the case of this project, insight into the sociocultural context of the community works toward positioning this population as full rhetorical partners in consent conferences.

Notes

1 See Graff & Winn (2011) for a discussion on identification and communion.
2 Tr. It is good to give advice, but it is better to solve the problem. This is known as a *dicho*; a popular adage that reflects important Mexican cultural values. A *dicho* can be thought of as a form of epideictic rhetoric. In Spanish a *dicho* often rhymes.
3 This reflects the preferred term in bioethics for persons participating in a clinical trial: *participants* rather than *subjects* or *patients*.
4 Bloom-Pojar (this volume) provides an excellent discussion on translingual approaches to transcultural health practices, taking into consideration vernacular use of Spanish in health encounters.
5 Tr. He who sings frightens away his grief.
6 Tr. From the word to the deed there is a great distance
7 Tr. Where there is desire, there is the ability.
8 Tr. There is no bad that good does not accompany.

References

Barton, E., & Eggly, S. (2009). Ethical or unethical persuasion? The rhetoric of offers to participate in clinical trials." *Written Communication, 26*, 295–319.

Beauchamp, T. L. (2011). Informed consent: Its history, meaning, and present challenges. *Cambridge Quarterly of Healthcare Ethics, 20*, 515–523. http://doi.org/10.1017/S09631801110000259.

Beauchamp, T. L., & Childress, J. F. (1979). *Principles of biomedical ethics*. New York, NY: Oxford University Press.

Beauchamp, T. L., & Childress, J. F. (2009). *Principles of biomedical ethics* (6th ed.). New York, NY: Oxford University Press.

Belkin, G. S., & Brandt, A. M. (2001). Bioethics: Using its historical and social context. *International Anesthesiology Clinics, 39*(3), 1–11.

Belmont Report. (1979). *The Belmont report: Ethical principles and guidelines for the protection of human subjects of research*. Retrieved from hhs.gov/ohrp/humansubjects/guidance/belmont.html.

Blanch-Hartigan, D., Hall, J. A., Roter, D. L., & Frankel, R. M. (2010). Gender bias in patients' perceptions of patient-centered behaviors. *Patient Education and Counseling, 80*, 315–320.

Borry, P., Schotsmans, P., & Dierickx, K. (2005). The birth of the empirical turn in bioethics. *Bioethics, 19*(1), 50–71.

Brody, H. (1987). *Stories of sickness*. New Haven, CT: Yale University Press.

Bromley, E., Mikesell, L., Jones, F., & Khudyakov, D. (2015). From subject to partici-pant: Ethics and the evolving role of community in health research. *American Journal of Public Health, 105*(5), 900–908.

Brown, A., & Patten, E. (2014). Statistical portrait of Hispanics in the United States, 2012. *Pew Research Center*. Retrieved from www.pewhispanic.org/2014/04/29/statistical-portrait-of-hispanics-in-the-united-states-2012/.

Burke, K. (1969). *A rhetoric of motives*. Berkeley, CA: University of California Press.

Candilis, P., & Lidz, C. (2010). Advances in informed consent research. In F. G. Miller & A. Wertheimer (Eds.), *The ethics of consent* (pp. 329–346). New York, NY: Oxford University Press.

Cargo, M., & Mercer, S. L. (2008). The value and challenges of participatory research: Strengthening its practice. *Annual Review of Public Health, 29*, 325–350.

Charleswill, C. A. (2014). Commentary: Clinician and researcher contribution to dispari-ties in racial and ethnic minority participation in human subjects research. *Ethnicity & Disease, 24*, 298–301.

Charmaz, K. (2006). *Constructing grounded theory: A practical guide through qualitative analysis*. Thousand Oaks, CA: Sage.

Cohn, D., Livingston, G., & Minushin, S. (2008). Access, information and knowledge, his-panics and healthcare in the United States. *Pew Research Center*. Retrieved from www.pewhispanic.org/2008/08/13/ii-hispanics-and-chronic-disease-in-the-u-s/.

Faden, R., & Beauchamp, T. (1986). *A history and theory of informed consent*. Oxford, NY: Oxford University Press.

Felt, U., Bister, M. D., Strassnig, M., & Wagner, U. (2009). Refusing the information para-digm: Informed consent, medical research, and patient participation. *Health: An Interdis-ciplinary Journal of the Social Study of Health, Illness, and Medicine, 13*(1), 87–106. http://doi.org/10.1177/1363459308097362.

Fisher, J. A., & Kalbaugh, C. A. (2011). Challenging assumptions about minority partici-pants in US clinical research. *American Journal of Public Health, 101*(12), 2217–2222.

Fox, R. C., & Swazey, J. P. (2008). *Observing bioethics*. New York, NY: Oxford University Press.

Glazer, M., Baer, Weller, S. C., Garcia de Alba, J. E., & Liebowitz, S. W. (2004). *Susto* and soul loss in Mexicans and Mexican Americans. *Cross-Cultural Research, 38*(3), 270–288. http://doi.org/10.1177/1069397104264277.

Graff, R. J., & Winn, W. (2011). Kenneth Burke's identification and Chaim Perelman's com-munion: A case of convergent evolution? Studies in the new rhetoric. In J. Gage (Ed.), *The Promise of reason: Studies in the new rhetoric* (pp. 103–133). Carbondale/Edwardsville, IL: Southern Illinois University Press.

Hedgecoe, A. M. (2004). Critical bioethics: Beyond the social science critique of applied ethics. *Bioethics, 18*(2), 120–143.

Johnson, R. R. (2004). Audience involved: Toward a participatory model of writing. In J. Johnson-Eilola & S. A. Selber (Eds.), *Central works in technical communication* (pp. 91–103). New York, NY: Oxford University Press.

Kleinig, J. (2010). The nature of consent. In F. G. Miller & A. Wertheimer (Eds.), *The ethics of consent* (pp. 3–24). New York, NY: Oxford University Press.

Lay, M. M. (2002). Feminist criticism and technical communication. In L. J. Gurak & M. M. Lay (Eds.), *Research in technical communication* (pp. 165–183). Westport, CT: Praeger.

Lindemann, H. (2006). *An invitation to feminist ethics*. New York, NY: McGraw-Hill.

Lyne, J. (2001). Contours of intervention: How rhetoric matters to biomedicine. *Journal of Medical Humanities, 22*(1), 3–13.

MacNealy, M. S. (1999). *Strategies for empirical research in writing.* New York, NY: Addison Wesley Longman.

Nelson, L. H. (2004). Four narrative approaches to bioethics. In G. Khuschf (Ed.), *Handbook of bioethics: Taking stock of the field from a philosophical perspective* (2nd ed., pp. 163–181). Dordrecht, The Netherlands: Kluwer Academic.

Paskett, E. D., Katz, M. L., DeGraffinreid, C. R., & Tatum, C. M. (2003). Participation in cancer trials: Recruitment of underserved populations. *Clinical Advances in Hematology & Oncology, 1*(10), 607–613.

Segal, J. Z. (2005). *Health and the rhetoric of medicine.* Carbondale, IL: Southern Illinois University Press.

Sherwin, S. (1998). A relational approach to autonomy in health care. In S. Sherwin (Ed.), *The politics of women's health: Exploring agency and autonomy* (pp. 19–47). Philadelphia, PA: Temple University Press.

Sherwood, N. E., French, S. A., Veblen-Mortenson, S., Crain, A. L., Berge, J., Kunin-Batson, A., & Senso, M. (2013). NET-works: Linking families, communities and primary care to prevent obesity in preschool-age children. *Contemporary Clinical Trials, 36*, 544–554.

Simon, C. M., & Kodish, E. (2005). "Step into my zaptos, doc": Understanding and reducing communication disparities in the multicultural informed consent setting. *Perspectives in Biology and Medicine, 48*(1 Supplement), 123–S138.

Turner, L. (2003). Bioethics in a multicultural world: Medicine and morality in pluralistic setting. *Health Care Analysis, 11*(2), 99–117.

Viswanathan, M., Ammerman, A., Eng, E., Garlehner, G., Lohr, K. N., Griffith, D., . . . & Webb, L. (2004, August). Community-based participatory research: Assessing the evidence: Summary. *AHRQ Evidence Report Summaries.* Retrieved from www.ncbi.nlm.nih.gov/books/NBK11852/.

Vivo, R. P., Krim, S. R., Cevik, C., & Witteles, R. M. (2009). Heart failure in Hispanics. *Journal of the American College of Cardiology, 53*(4), 1167–1175.

Walker, M. U. (1998). *Moral understandings: A feminist study in ethics.* New York, NY: Routledge.

Warren, V. L. (1989). Feminist directions in medical ethics. *Haptia, 4*(2), 73–87.

12

TRANSLINGUAL RHETORICAL ENGAGEMENT IN TRANSCULTURAL HEALTH SPACES

Rachel Bloom-Pojar

Keywords: transnational; translingual; engagement; health care; Spanish; rhetoric

It was "*muy Caribe*[1]" one afternoon in a rural Dominican town about 45 minutes away from the Dominican Republic (D.R.)-Haiti border. I was working for the second summer in a row as a coordinator with a temporary health team from the United States (U.S.), and we had set up a medical and dental clinic with local residents in the town for one month. On this particular day, our medical team walked along a gravel road to make a home visit for a patient who was bedridden and in need of a consultation. I was there to help interpret and facilitate the visit. The patient was an older male, maybe 70 *y pico*[2] who had various health issues. Once we arrived, there were about six people, including the patient's wife, crowded around his double bed in a fairly small room with little light. After the patient explained his symptoms, the physician, medical students, and nursing student began to deliberate about the case in English—discussing what could be done to help ease his pain and how his future might span out with these health issues.

As the medical team conversed in English in a small huddled circle, the patient, his wife, and I quietly waited, left out of what was going on until I would begin to interpret again. I felt compelled to do something to break the barrier of silence that had been set up between the patient and the providers for that moment. Since our purpose was to spend time with him, I sat down on the side of his bed and began asking questions about his family: how many children he had, how many grandchildren, how long he had lived in the area, and so on. I began interpreting my conversation with the patient into English, and one by one the medical team turned around and joined in, alternating between discussing his family life and possible treatments for his pain. I do not remember the medications that we later brought or the instructions that I interpreted for his wife, but what I do remember is the light that emerged from his eyes as we switched from talking *about* him to talking *with* him—sitting, accompanying, and "being" with him as a whole person and not just a medical case study.

As we interacted with other patients and community members during our month-long stay, I began to notice how a rhetorical approach to health care could benefit our work and interactions in this summer program. This rhetorical approach would recognize patients as an audience, learn their exigencies and motivations, and adjust speech habits to communicate in a way that respected their values and needs. As the visiting health providers encountered the complexity of language varieties and cultural differences in this program, they began to collectively develop new rhetorical strategies that were integral to the care they would deliver.

In this chapter, I argue for a rhetorically engaged approach to studying transcultural health care, particularly in multilingual spaces. By examining one temporary health setting in the D.R., I demonstrate how a rhetorically engaged approach can serve as an entry-point for researchers in medical rhetoric to learn from the local spaces of transnational health programs. I utilize Jeffrey Grabill's (2010) methodology of rhetorical engagement to demonstrate how assembly work and supporting performances are useful ways of looking at the public work of rhetoric in health settings. This chapter also serves to problematize how we look at rhetorical engagement, and all rhetorical research in health and medicine, to account for multilingual spaces. Similar to how Bivens (this volume) argues that health care communication or communication in medical contexts should be considered cross-cultural communication, I argue that medical discourse is also inherently multilingual. This awareness challenges the assumption that researchers are working in a monolingual environment, which can be commonplace in rhetorical research that does not integrate the various voices of stakeholders in health care today. Connecting to Angeli's and Pigozzi's work on stakeholders and participatory research in this volume, I examine the rhetorical engagement that helps establish those relationships with stakeholders such as community volunteers and ad hoc interpreters. As Huiling Ding (2014) argues,

> intercultural professional communication scholarship is often ethnocentric in nature. [. . .] Moreover, the existing focus on English publications in data collection and analysis inevitably results in the unjustified preferences given to perspectives of English-speaking cultures and the exclusion of cultures where English is not a dominant language.
>
> *(p. 33)*

In this chapter, I argue that translingual approaches to rhetorical research within settings where English is not the dominant language is crucial for researching discourses of health and medicine.

Translingual Rhetoric

This study utilizes two words that may seem interchangeable but that serve distinct purposes: multilingual and translingual. Multilingual is used in this chapter to refer to spaces, groups, and interactions where multiple languages (including varieties or dialects within named languages such as English or Spanish) are used and represented by the individuals in those spaces. Translingual is used as an adjective or adverb to highlight when languages are being negotiated, crossed, mixed, and integrated for specific purposes. Within multilingual health settings, rhetorical problems often emerge amid language varieties and interpretation. In this study, participants did not just encounter English and Spanish, but also a variety of forms of Spanish. They quickly recognized a need to develop tactics to negotiate the varieties of Spanish they encountered in this program through translanguaging. Garcia and Wei (2013) explain that "translanguaging refers to *new* language practices that make visible the complexity of language exchanges among people with different histories, and releases histories and understandings that had been buried within fixed language identities constrained by nation-states" (p. 21). Not only are these fixed language identities constrained by nation-states, they are also often limited by other entities such as health care institutions and organizations. The static notion of Spanish, and especially medical Spanish, that is often taught in the U.S. is challenged by the national and regional varieties of Spanish that students and professionals encounter when traveling abroad. Thus, a translingual approach to transcultural medical rhetoric accounts for the fluidity and complexity of languages-in-motion (Guerra, 2012).

Language difference and interpretation have long been issues that health providers face with increasingly diverse patient populations, especially in light of continued migration across local, regional, and national borders today. Responding to linguistic and cultural differences represents important rhetorical activity in interpersonal health communication and health literacy. Within institutional settings, trained interpreters or interpretation services via phone are often used to ease the burden of language difference between providers and patients. However, when health providers travel to other countries and participate in temporary health programs, the use of interpreters becomes much more ad hoc in nature, requiring either local residents to take on the role of interpreter or existing members of a health team to take on the additional role of medical interpreter. Gonzales and Zantjer (2015) emphasize the benefits of examining translation practices of multilinguals that are not trained translators or interpreters, because it can provide insight into the connections between translation and localization. They utilize Batova and Clark's (2015) concept of "localization" to provide an alternative to "the one-to-one translation process" and focus on linguistic and cultural expectations and usage patterns within specific contexts (pp. 272–273). Gonzales and Zantjer make an important call for technical communicators to reconsider how they conceptualize translation work to account for the "multiple, layered, and sequenced strategies" and "the purposeful, rhetoric use and layering of these strategies" to illuminate the complex negotiations of history, culture, and language that take place in acts of translation (p. 280). This conceptualization can help us understand a translingual approach to medical rhetoric, but where Gonzales and Zantjer's definition of multilingual speakers focuses on people who are fluent speakers of more than one language, my study draws from a group of people who have varied proficiencies in speaking more than one language.

I argue that public notions of "translation" and "interpretation" in health care remain somewhat static in their classifications of language and the need to "transfer information" from "one language" to another. Translingual rhetoric functions as a part of translation work in health care, but it is a bit more complex in the ways that users adjust their own usage of language and support each other to develop rhetorical adaptability for future translingual interactions. Horner, NeCamp, and Donahue (2011) describe a translingual approach that "shifts our focus away from individuals, located on a fixed scale of competence toward 'mastery' of a reified 'target' language, and toward groups of people working in collaboration to use all available linguistic resources" (p. 288). Their fluid and collective approaches to negotiating languages draw from research in Linguistics, Second Language Studies, and Writing Studies. I take a distinctly rhetorical approach to "translingual" acts in how I examine them as useful tactics to support performances in transcultural spaces of health and medicine. Ultimately, I call for translingual rhetorical engagement in transnational health programs, a move that would encourage medical rhetoricians to participate in programs to build relationships, learn alongside practitioners and community health leaders, and identify areas where translingual and engaged rhetoric can support performances within health care.

Background of Study

The program examined in this study is run by a nonprofit organization based in Santiago de los Caballeros, D.R., called El Centro para la Salud Rural (CSR).[3] Each summer, CSR works with a private, Midwestern university to host a five-week trip for U.S.-based health professionals and students to the D.R. The summer program's purpose is to provide accessible medical and dental services to rural communities while fostering cross-cultural relationships with local volunteers who help run the clinics and host the visiting participants. Throughout the remainder of the year, CSR receives different local and foreign physicians who follow up on the referrals made by the summer program doctors and the *cooperadores de salud*[4] for each community. The *cooperadores* are leaders in each affiliated community chosen and trained by the organization to serve as the point person for the local residents' health-related concerns.

Traveling from the U.S., the summer program health team usually includes one or two professional physicians, dentists, pharmacists, and nurses. In addition, usually one or two undergraduate *ayudantes*[5] help with interpretation and work with the patient intake process. During an examination or discussion of treatment, if the student or professional encounters difficulties conversing in Spanish with the patient, s/he might call on an *ayudante* or other team members to help out with interpretation. Additionally, the *cooperadores* organized an *equipo de trabajo*[6] that helped with interpretation for the intake process as *ayudantes*, kept track of the patient list and money, and performed various other tasks to keep the clinic running.

The CSR leadership team includes one coordinator and one assistant coordinator for each *campo*,[7] who are in charge of working with the *cooperadores* in planning where and how the clinic services would be set up and where the visiting participants would live and eat during the four weeks. The coordinators also assist with facilitating daily communication and developing reflections and activities for the group to participate in together. For each community, at least one of the two coordinators needed to have advanced Spanish proficiency, specifically with an emphasis on conversational fluency in rural dialects of Dominican Spanish. The demands of the position included making house visits before U.S. participants arrived, interpreting for visiting participants with no Spanish proficiency, and making decisions to solve problems with *cooperadores* and community members— all of which require a strong command of the local language and rhetorical adaptability across languages. This often meant that coordinators had participated in previous programs with CSR or had other international experience working in Spanish-speaking countries. Before working as a coordinator with CSR, I majored in Spanish in college and served as a teaching assistant and interpreter with an undergraduate theology class in El Salvador and a high school group in the D.R.

I worked directly with the *cooperadores* before the visiting participants arrived to make plans for the program, and then we communicated on a daily basis to check in with how things were going with the visitors, the patients, and the local volunteers. As a coordinator, I worked with my assistant coordinator to plan homestays and activities for visiting health providers from the U.S. and local residents, serve as an interpreter in and outside of the clinic, and act as the primary liaison between the host community and visiting participants. Whenever local residents or visiting practitioners had questions, concerns, or needed help with interpretation, I served as a main contact person for them to approach and utilize to facilitate conversations with others who did not speak the same language or share customs with them to the end of the sentence so it says, or share customs with them. I helped manage the daily clinic activities with the *cooperadores* and moved around the various sections of the clinic and patient waiting area to ensure that things ran as smoothly as possible.

Participants

I worked with the CSR summer program in 2011 and 2012, and all interview-ees for this study worked in some capacity with my groups during those years. Generally, the summer program team for a specific community consists of about 15 U.S. participants and eight to ten Dominican volunteers, including the *coopera-dores de salud*. I completed 23 semistructured interviews with participants (n=10 Dominican and n=13 U.S.) from the two groups I worked with as a coordinator. All U.S.-based interviewees were pursuing professional degrees in health care (medicine, dentistry, nursing, and pharmacy) at the time of their participation in the program. Dominican interviewees consisted of volunteers who helped with daily clinic activities and all three of the *cooperadores* in charge of the programs held in "Buena Vista" and "Rancho de la Vaca"[8] during those years. Interviews were conducted in Spanish with all of the Dominican participants, and in Eng-lish with the U.S. participants. Interview participants represent mostly clinical staff volunteers, but the collectives that formed in and around these clinics also included patients, their families, and other community members from the town we were staying in and the nearby towns affiliated with CSR. Table 12.1 below represents interviewees for this study:

TABLE 12.1 Interviewees for this study.

#	Country of Origin	Role in Program	Buena Vista	Rancho de la Vaca
3	D.R.	Cooperador/a de Salud	1	2
7	D.R.	Ayudante	7	0
2	U.S.	Medical Student	1	1
2	U.S.	Dental Student	0	2
2	U.S.	Nursing Student	0	2
3	U.S.	Ayudante	1	2
2	U.S.	Pharmacy Student	0	2
2	U.S.	Assistant Coordinator	1	1

Data Collection

The data collection for this project relied on ethnographic methods of participant observation and interviews. Additionally, I analyzed supporting documents and presentations from the orientation week for U.S. participants to triangulate and compare findings with the experiences described in the interview data.[9]

During June–July 2012, I participated in the summer program as a coordina-tor for the second time and took observational field notes. At the request of the program director, I took all of my field notes outside of clinic hours in order to allow my focus to remain on my work as a coordinator for the group. If there were ever moments of "down time," I would jot notes about experiences to elaborate on later. Since the CSR health clinics serve various communities in the area, some of the Dominican volunteers I worked with in 2012 may have been patients or visitors to the other clinic I worked with in 2011, and vice versa. These connections were crucial to developing relationships and building my *ethos* as a successful group leader. I also made my *cooperadores* aware that I was starting a research project and that I would follow up with volunteers outside of the summer program dates about whether they would like to be interviewed about their experiences.

My previous experience with the program established some rapport with the health practitioners, but it was through our interactions in and outside of the clinic that I gradually gained their trust as someone who could provide support through interpretation and cultural brokering. My role in this program became one of "researcher-as-participant," where I was first and foremost a participant and coordinator with this program and temporary health team. Second, I became a researcher interested in exploring the rhetorical strategies that the team used to navigate cultural and linguistic differences. My role as both participant and researcher influenced the rapport I was able to develop with participants, the access I was able to gain to conversations, and the limitations that I encountered regarding when and how I could collect data.

Preparing for the data collection, I encountered various challenges that come with multi-institutional and multinational ethnographic projects. First, I encountered resistance from the U.S. institution that I was working for in conducting the research while also working in my role as coordinator. An administrator was concerned about my priorities for the research versus my daily responsibilities as a coordinator and interpreter in the program. When medical rhetoric researchers act as participants *and* observers in research sites, it is common to encounter hesitance and resistance that necessitates an explanation and plan to avoid compromising patient care for research objectives (see Angeli, this volume). The U.S. director suggested that I take field notes outside of clinic hours, and that I seek approval from the director of the organization in Santiago instead. I did gain that approval and later engaged in many productive conversations with the U.S. program director concerning feedback from my participants about the program.

Many patients were only in town for the day they visited the clinic, and I did not want to disrupt their time at the clinic with my research agenda. The director had asked that I not collect data during clinic hours. Therefore, my follow-up outside of the clinic and program was easiest with the participants I had developed relationships with: the health team volunteers. Taking field notes outside of clinic hours was another limitation to my recall of events that occurred; however, any form of field notes taken while being an active participant in a program would be somewhat delayed in order to fully participate in communicative interactions as they happen naturally in any setting. The following sections examine ways that a methodology of rhetorical engagement, and specifically translingual rhetorical engagement, enhanced the assemblage and performances of health practices during the program.

Rhetorical Engagement

Jeffrey Grabill's (2010) methodology of rhetorical engagement argues that "assembling a public and supporting performances—are essential to effective public rhetoric and fundamental to the notion that rhetoric might more usefully be understood as enabling the work of others" (p. 193). If rhetoric entails steps of assembly and support, the rhetor must have the role and ability to influence, coordinate, and/or make these steps happen. Grabill (2014) argues that this methodology "positions rhetoric as the art designed for the persistent burden of detecting shared problems, guiding inquiry, and shaping responses. It is empirical, pragmatic, and collective . . . it requires lots of individuals pulling together to do the rhetoric imagined here" (p. 259). This empirical, pragmatic, and collective approach to understanding rhetoric is crucial for a translingual approach to medical rhetoric. My application of this methodology situates it in a diverse, transnational environment that necessitates a fluid movement among languages and cultural understandings of health in order to truly detect problems, guide inquiry, and shape responses.

When I began this study, I set out to explore the messy, complicated practices of translingual literacy. I wanted to demonstrate how translingual theory could better represent the messiness of cross-language processes as they develop, rather than focusing on fluent rhetors who can easily adapt across languages and contexts. Transitioning from the focus on individual rhetors to collective action is helpful for exploring the public work of translingual rhetoric within this situated context of health communication. This perspective allows for an investigation into all of the interpreters, sponsors, and team-building efforts that enable health care to be persuasive and effective.

Research on the rhetoric of health & medicine is often inquiry into the public work of rhetoric and how publics function in health care. Lisa Keränen (2014) argues, "in a time when medicine and health play an increasingly prominent role in shaping the contours of our collective, networked and global life, we need to understand how citizens, institutions, and movements increasingly organize around biological, medical, and health matters" (p. 104). Not only is public engagement crucial to understanding how we assemble as collectives around health matters, but also the distinctly global and interconnected natures of those publics are integral to understanding how we enter and interact within them. Transnational health programs constantly rely upon the networked and public exchange of participants from different countries and cultures. These programs are often portrayed as having health providers from the global North serving patients from the global South, but recognizing the public work of community health leaders and other participants (patients, host families, etc.) in these programs will highlight the work that is done to support and sustain the assembly of people into "publics" around issues of health and illness.

I identify the "publics" in this study as "emergent collectives" (Asen, 2000) because of their temporary nature and common characteristic of collaborating across differences of race, class, power, status, and discourse. If emergent collectives in global health encounter these differences, questions of language and culture come into play with how they communicate and work together. Fraser (2007) reminds us about the challenges with

> The presupposition of a single national language, which was supposed to constitute the linguistic medium of public sphere communication. As a result of . . . population mixing . . . national languages do not map onto states . . . [and] existing states are de facto multilingual, while language groups are territorially dispersed, and many more speakers are multilingual.
>
> (p. 12)

The idea that a single national language can constitute the linguistic medium for communicating in publics does not stand as a viable option in the increasingly transnational and multilingual nature of health care today. Thus, if health practitioners are engaging in communities that are inherently multilingual, a rhetorical approach to health care must reflect the translingual moves necessary for the work carried out in these communities.

Utilizing a methodology of engagement, the work of transnational health programs can be analyzed in ways that reflect how Grabill (2010) connects the public work of rhetoric with practical, professional work in the world: "managing projects, coordinating activity, learning and using information technologies, working well with others, communicating effectively. These are the skills of assembly" (p. 205). Identifying the assemblage of a public draws attention to the process of getting to know other members of that public, spending time with them outside of work activities, and learning about their local customs and everyday lives. This engagement was important to me as a program coordinator and researcher for ethical reasons—to focus on gaining the trust of the community and facilitate working with them. The formation of this emergent collective did not just happen during our clinic hours. The local residents also helped to bring everyone together to play games, cook, and dance in the afternoons and evenings. These communal activities were essential to helping the group feel united and understand their time together to be something more than just work in a clinic. In this way, the people we lived with were not just "patients" in need of a diagnosis but also host families, neighbors, and friends.

For the context of this study, the "performances" in Grabill's second step for rhetorical engagement included medical consultations, dental procedures, patient intake, and developing rapport with patients through conversations in the clinic and social activities outside of the clinical context. To support performances, I tried to bridge communicative barriers through interpretation. As a coordinator, I walked back and forth between sections of the clinic to help interpret or check in with participants. ¡Raquel! ¡Rachel! My name was constantly called out from across the clinic for help explaining what type of pain dental patients had; how often to take certain medications; when to come back for follow-up; or whether or not we could serve any more patients that day at the clinic. My role as an interpreter, coordinator, and scholar forced me to move in between languages constantly to try facilitating understanding and promoting respect for a mixed and fluid rhetoric in our multilingual space.

As the weeks progressed, other participants became more confident in their understanding of the local Spanish dialect, and the clinic became a space of many interpreters shifting between languages to develop meaning and understanding together. They worked together to respond to problems with language "barriers," misunderstanding, and communication about health and illness. I examine the strategies of these participants as engaged rhetorical acts intended to support performances in the clinics. The following pages will describe the assembly of this group, a few of the linguistic and cultural differences that participants encountered in communicative problems, and the rhetorical strategies they developed to support clinical performances. This focus on how rhetorical strategies utilized translingual moves allows us to interrogate power, privilege, and vernacular understandings of health and illness in transcultural health practices.

Assembly

Living with host families and participating in local activities promoted the visiting participants' engagement with local community members in ways that domestic service opportunities may not. Understanding the process of the "assemblage" of a public means acknowledging that groups, relationships, and activities were very much in existence, and will continue to exist, outside of the time of engagement with this specific public. Assembly of this public was more than simply choosing the participants and *campos* for this program. There needed to be a conscious effort from all participants to acknowledge and respect each other as members of our emergent collective. Additionally, any service or outreach program that cares for the community in which it engages must consider how to get to know it first.

The assembly of a public, which is the first method of Grabill's (2010) approach to rhetorical engagement, includes three steps: "research to assemble a group in order to discern patterns of activity and their possible agencies; rhetorical assembly of ideas toward the making a Thing; and the related and always material assembly that must be gathered into any thing" (p. 201). In the context of this study, the "Thing" that was "made" was a set of health care practices that were centered around, but also extended beyond the health clinic. This application of Grabill's methodology also recognizes the multiple overlapping publics that required different kinds of assembly, but all with shared goals about public health in the local community. With visiting practitioners and students from the U.S., local resident volunteers in the clinics, host families, patients, family members of patients, community health leaders, and other local residents that we encountered all contributed to a variety of emergent collectives that engaged in discourse about health care practices in and outside of the clinics.

The assemblage of this collective began with research and preparation for the separate groups of individuals that would participate in the program. Before coming together with the local community for four weeks, the health practitioners spent one week in Santiago upon their arrival in the country for orientation. The CSR director organized this orientation week by dividing time among programming for Spanish classes, cultural and historical lessons, trips to visit museums and outreach programs in Santiago, and the packaging of medical supplies. Each morning, three different levels of Spanish classes were held for participants to familiarize themselves with conversational and medical Spanish, along with "Dominicanisms" that are present in the rural, Spanish discourse. These classes were offered in addition to the six-week course that CSR's U.S. office ran prior to the program.

The second method of assembly was the rhetorical assembly of ideas toward making our shared spaces function as a medical and dental clinic. The coordinators for each group checked in with their assigned team members to discuss preparation for immersion in the *campos*, but overall the students and professionals for all six communities integrated as one large group for the orientation week. CSR staff, coordinators, and visiting doctors used PowerPoints and printed documents to discuss topics concerning epidemiology in the country, cultural values, and running the clinics. The nursing students and *ayudantes* had meetings focused on the patient intake forms, referral forms, and other documents related to the summer health care and follow-up after the program. Once the groups embarked on their trips to work and live in the *campos*, the coordinators communicated daily with the U.S. program director to set up any clinical supply deliveries or to discuss medical, emotional, or behavioral issues that we would need to address within the group dynamics and with the local residents.

The preparation of the Dominican volunteers varied by community according to however the *cooperador/a* decided to organize it. Before the U.S. participants arrived in Santiago, the coordinators for each *campo* had their own one-day orientation with the *cooperadores* in Santiago to discuss procedures, emergency plans, and research to complete before the U.S. participants arrived. Additionally, for one weekend, the coordinators travel to their assigned *campos* with the respective *cooperador(es)* to get to know the area, visit the houses where participants would be staying, and discuss how the clinic would run with the work team. For both Buena Vista and Rancho de la Vaca, the *cooperadores* had previously hosted a summer program team and clinic in their communities. During those planning meetings, we divided our time between learning about how they ran the clinics in the years before then, and how we might make changes to improve the functionality of the clinic and integration of community. Otherwise, the CSR program director and other staff worked directly with the *cooperadores* in preparing for the program and discussing issues as they arose while the program was in session. Part of this assembly work also involved the *cooperadores* calling up community leaders from nearby towns to encourage their residents to visit the clinic and participate in the summer health program.

The third step, material assembly of the health care practices and clinic, occurred in the actions taken to create a daily schedule and set up the medical supplies, dental chairs, exam tables, and waiting area each day. Clinics were assembled in primary school buildings, and they ran from approximately 8:00 am until 1:00 pm, Monday through Friday, for four weeks. During the program, the local work team helped keep things running smoothly in and outside of the clinic. One of the *cooperadores*, José Luis, explained some of the major duties and benefits of having these local teams:

> *Se hicieron un grupo de trabajo y había un grupo de logística, había grupo de nosotros fue vamos aquí por el trabajo en todo las áreas: para limpiar la clínica, para trabajar en la cocina. . . . Todo se hecho a través de este equipo de trabajo.*[10]

Much of this organization was completed before the U.S. group arrived in the community, and the *equipo de trabajo* in José Luis's community held meetings multiple times each week to discuss daily plans for bringing the visitors and local residents together for work and social activities. Checking in to discuss planning for the clinical work and social activities positively contributed to the morale for all of the volunteers. These various roles that the work group served were also important to account for the material factors of running a volunteer health clinic.

Overall, the assembly of a public is a key method in carrying out rhetorical work and rhetorically engaged research. The assembly of this specific emergent collective occurred in various stages. First, the group assembled with designated Dominican and visiting volunteers to work as a health team in running the clinics each day. Second, each of the visiting participants lived with a host family in the community, and many of them developed a familial-type identity with the members of those households. Many host families began calling their guests "*hija/o*"[11] and/or "*hermana/o*",[12] and quite a few of the visiting participants reciprocated in calling their hosts "family," "mom/dad," and/or "sisters/brothers" depending on the composition of the household. Not all participants developed such an intimate relationship with their hosts, but the ones that did, did so regardless of their proficiency in Spanish. As a whole, the four weeks of immersion provided a constant movement of language and relationship building that enhanced the performances of the health clinic and developed connections with patients and local residents. Additionally, it is important to note that there was assembly work that happened with various individuals that came together as smaller collectives in and outside of the clinics, sometimes at the same time and other times separately for different reasons. Within transnational and translingual settings, it is crucial to recognize these overlapping collectives that form around common concerns and needs in public health work within local communities.

Gerard Hauser (1999) argues, "We belong to a community insofar as we are able to participate in its conversations. We must acquire its *vernacular language* in order to share rhetorically salient meanings" (p. 67). A translingual approach to supporting work in transnational health requires the recognition that acquiring vernacular language is crucial to participating in conversations and rhetorically engaging with a community. Matthew explains that while CSR helped provide Spanish classes and Dominican phrases, once they were in the *campo*, individuals just needed to try their best to pick out words from conversations and that

> The more and more you can sit and talk with someone, the easier it is to understand them. So I think just being down there with the Dominicans and having people who were fluent and then also having Dominicans who could kind of understand us just taking the time with people like that helped us interact better with the community.

These benefits that came from spending time together highlight the importance of assembly with this collective. Through conversations in their daily interactions, members of this collective supported each other's language development, and in turn, their translingual rhetorical adaptability.

Inquiry into the assembly of an emergent collective is crucial to the rhetorical work of supporting health care performances. Without an emphasis on this assembly, the support of performances would not easily persist over time, let alone for four weeks of cross-cultural immersion. It took both the organizational and emotional work to create a cohesive collective that could accomplish the interpretation, literacy development, and rapport building that would be crucial for serving patients and forging connections across differences. These connections, in turn, supported the development of translingual rhetorical strategies as the participants built their trust in each other and self-confidence in taking risks with languages to improve their communication during this program. Additionally, investigating the assemblage of this collective alongside the process of supporting performances highlights the complexity and messiness of translingual moves in a way that encourages development and recognizes the process, not just the product, of these performances.

Supporting Performances

Grabill's notion of supporting performances can allow researchers to see the supportive work that is needed to communicate in transcultural health spaces, and it promotes a collaborative approach to health care practices that draws from all of the collective resources of a multicultural team. As a participant in this program with no medical training, my contribution to the clinical activity was always in a supportive role: interpreting, making decisions about clinical procedures, and/or mediating understanding between individuals. Many days at the clinic, numerous people approached me asking in English or Spanish about what to do next, why something happened, and/or how to communicate a point effectively. Additionally, each team member had moments where s/he would support someone else in a performance at the clinic: holding a flashlight for the dentist, interpreting, or acting as a consult in one of the three sections (medical, pharmacy, dental). Through a variety of communicative acts, participants supported each other's performances in speaking, diagnosing, and conducting procedures. However, before developing the rhetorical strategies to support these performances amid linguistic difference, individuals needed to identify rhetorical problems they encountered. When a rhetorical problem surfaced because of differences in language, dialect, or terminology, the individuals would first need to identify the source of misunderstanding and then proceed in utilizing a specific translingual strategy to move forward in the conversation with a patient or fellow volunteer.

The Spanish language took many forms in this program. U.S. participants categorized the types of Spanish into the following five categories: *professional*, *American*, *Dominican*, *campo*, and *medical*. Dominican participants often used a binary to describe the types of Spanish for these groups: *Dominican* or *American* Spanish, or possessive pronouns such as *our* and *your* Spanish. Examining an environment where individuals define "Spanish" by various characteristics related to dialect, pronunciation, and national identity illuminates how this language is clearly not a static code. This emergent collective negotiated a variety of Spanishes, and questioned how and when they might utilize different forms in their daily interactions and health care practices. The U.S. participants who could recognize when a different form or pronunciation was being used usually had intermediate to advanced Spanish proficiency. This was also described as noticing distinct differences between what they had learned in school, or medical Spanish classes, and what they heard and spoke during the program abroad.

All of the U.S. participants tried to speak Spanish in the clinic, whether it was with a few words and pointing or attempting to hold entire conversations. Thus, there were multiple layers of Spanish interpretation, rearticulation, and pronunciation happening at any given time. Through these occurrences, a type of Spanish-to-Spanish interpretation emerged in the daily clinic activities. This interpretation entailed the volunteers negotiating different dialects of Spanish, and Dominican volunteers most often executed it. Yoel, one of the Dominican volunteers, explains, "*Yo le ayudaba a traducirle a todo los pacientes . . . A veces de inglés a español y de español a español . . . Porque no estaban impuestos a escuchar a esa lengua—escuchar la manera de hablar de los americanos.*"[13] For U.S. participants, the Dominican volunteers and their Spanish–Spanish interpretation were crucial to the success of supporting performances in our clinic. Elizabeth explains, "The first week in clinic was really difficult doing intake, because I just kept getting super tongue-tied every time I tried to ask something and . . . they would just look at me . . . then my Dominican *ayudante* helper would translate and they'd eventually get it." I began the second summer with the plan to set up the clinic similarly, asking the Dominican *ayudantes* to be available to help with interpretation, but first allowing the U.S. participants try to speak Spanish and encourage them to learn to do it on their own.

Daniel, a Dominican *ayudante*, explained how the differences in Spanish affected patient understanding in the clinic: "*Mi experiencia fue que habían muchas personas en la clínica que no entendían lo que decían ustedes.*"[14] When I asked for clarification about whether the U.S. participants were speaking in English or Spanish, he explained: "*[H]ablaban en español, pero los dominicanos no entendían bien.*"[15] Daniel and the other Dominican *ayudantes* quickly proved to be able to understand the U.S. participants' Spanish usage. While patients struggled to understand the practitioners' language use, it was immensely helpful to have younger volunteers in the clinic who were able to adapt between the Spanish of the patients and the Spanish of the U.S. participants. By working with each other and spending time together, Dominican *ayudantes* were able to familiarize themselves with the visiting participants' language use and common medical terminology used in the clinics. This led to a useful approach in the clinic in which the Dominican *ayudantes* served as "interpreters" when patients and U.S. practitioners were unable to achieve mutual understanding between their different dialects of Spanish (Bloom, 2014).

U.S. participants who worked as interpreters also encountered issues with interpreting between medical discourses: medical Spanish they learned in school and local, lay terminology for symptoms and disease. I identify this lay terminology as *vernacular medical terminology* and highlight it as part of *patient discourses of health*. In my analysis, the patient intake process was one of the areas where participants encountered the most difficulty with language difference of this kind. The intake process was set up as a dialogue between the patient and an *ayudante* or nurse to facilitate the filling out of a patient information form to prepare for the examination in either the dental or medical side of the clinic.

CSR provided patient intake forms in Spanish and informed U.S. *ayudantes* that they would use the form as an aid for orally asking the questions for documenting a patient's health history. Andrew explains how some of the terminology did not translate when having conversations with the patients: "some of the vocab that they have written out, the questions that we had to ask, were different from what . . . the patients would understand. . . . It was frustrating at times when . . . [you] have a question written for you, and you read it, and it's not being understood . . . [or] that you didn't know how else to ask it." The tension between the written terminology on the patient intake form and the oral articulation of it surfaced in the disconnect that happened between what was said and ultimately understood by patients in the clinic. Also, the participants' limited understanding of "other ways" to phrase medical history questions presented a challenge for how to move past these types of "language barriers."

Certain intake questions might include the official terminology, such as asking "*¿Tiene diabetes?*" (Do you have diabetes?), but the *ayudantes* were informed by group leaders in Santiago that it might be more common in the *campo* to ask, "*¿Tiene azúcar?*" (literally, "Do you have sugar?"). Other terms were more easily understood in a shorter form like suffering from the heart (*¿Sufre del corazón?*) rather than suffering from heart disease (*¿Sufre de la enfermedad del corazón?*). Yoel, a Dominican *ayudante*, lists some of the questions that were the same for every patient: "*como: si sufría de diabetes; si sufría del corazón; si sufría del alguna otra enfermedad, y que se iba hacer como el odontología, si a filling si empaste.*"[16] These examples show how *ayudantes* shortened formal terminology to reflect how the local residents discussed common health issues. His short code switch at the end of his response also shows how Yoel learned intake terminology in English because many times the U.S. *ayudante* would write the word "filling" in English so that the dentist knew what it was.

Another common term that created a dilemma with terminology was the word "*gripe.*" Paul explains, "In medical Spanish classes, you learn that that means 'the flu' . . . but, I came to realize this is just kind of a catchall term that meant everything's not well." Patients most often used this term when presenting cold or allergy symptoms, and U.S. participants often heard the diagnosis when they would sneeze or cough and a local resident would ask, "*¿Tiene gripe?*"[17]

Other examples of cultural differences with health terminology included when patients would refer to stomach pain as "gastritis" or answer the patient intake question about kidney problems as "*Sí,*" because of back pain. As volunteers around the clinic realized the words and questions that had different meanings between them and their patients, the health team recognized a need to approach consultations in different ways. They adjusted their language use and asked for additional clarification to ensure mutual understanding with hopes of reaching the most accurate and helpful diagnosis for each patient.

Although a few of the Dominican *ayudantes* understood English, they mainly utilized it for helping with interpretation in the clinic. The Dominican participants rarely held conversations with the visiting participants in any language other than Spanish. This provided an impetus for promoting and developing Spanish conversational skills. Thus, the integration of local volunteers in the clinics influenced conversations and language choices. When discussing the Dominican *ayudantes* who helped in one of the medical clinics, Paul explains that

> They made it very interesting to interact in the clinical setting because we couldn't always just revert to English. . . . Over the course of the four weeks that we worked with them, I did notice that we obviously grew more comfortable with them and . . . I think they, without doubt, grew more comfortable with us, and that was a very fruitful relationship and one that ended up being very beneficial for us in the clinical setting.

Both the need to challenge themselves to speak in Spanish while running the clinic and the ways participants grew comfortable with each other throughout the program were important to the collaboration that could happen in the clinic. Lisa states that the Dominican *ayudantes* "were the biggest asset to us. Like, they helped us out more than *anyone* with the language barrier . . . they allowed us to try to speak Spanish to the patient, and then once the patient was like, 'I have no clue.' They would repeat it in Spanish and it would sound the exact same thing like I said, but the patient would get it." A number of U.S. participants mentioned that it felt like the Dominican *ayudantes* would say "the same thing" but just in a different accent or a few different endings on words. Whether they were just restating phrases, or reformulating a set of words into a full sentence, their help with interpretation in the clinic was clearly a crucial component to supporting performances during the intake process.

Six out of ten of the Dominican participants, all who served as *ayudantes*, described their interest in learning English in relation to the benefits of immersion with the U.S. participants. Although many of the young residents had taken English classes in school, they explained that it was not the same as having conversations with native English speakers like their visitors in this program. Therefore, the desire for language learning also shaped relationships within the clinics while helping support performances of the *ayudantes* and nurses during the patient intake process.

By examining these interactions as performances, we can understand them as instances of ever-evolving acts of "languaging." Lu and Horner (2013) explain, "a translingual approach defines languages not as something we have or have access to but as something we do. It centers attention on languaging: how we do language and why" (p. 27). This definition resonates with the ways in which participants performed language in trying out new words and phrases that they learned from each other. Elizabeth explains how she and the other *ayudantes* would support each other's performances of language in their down time between patients:

> Each of them spoke just like a little bit of English where we would try and teach them words, and they knew how to like talk slower [in Spanish], but we also would pull out our dictionaries sometimes . . . [and] I think they were just . . . a lot more understanding of the fact that we didn't speak fluent Spanish.

With the aid of dictionaries, the *ayudantes* set up a mutually beneficial relationship by teaching each other English and Spanish as they worked together throughout the program. Joshua adds,

> In a clinical setting, when I was just trying to learn words and phrases, I would work with the other *ayudantes* and just be like, 'How do I say,

Stand here so I can measure you?' Or . . . just something very basic . . . and then they would ask me how you say that in English.

The moments of "down time" that they would have together provided space and time for developing new rhetorical strategies to perform language in new ways. The U.S. *ayudantes* were able to develop their proficiencies in Spanish by having coworkers who understood their struggles with the language. Supporting each other's language development allowed them to serve the patients better in the clinics, and by utilizing that time in between work with patients to learn from each other, the *ayudantes* also deepened their relationships with each other.

Ultimately, the act of supporting performances in these clinics aims to create connections across language and culture and contribute to what Grabill (2014) refers to as "knowledge work" as "analytical and discursive activity requiring problem-solving, abstract reasoning, and material things" (p. 249). For this specific study, that knowledge work included activities that focused on problem solving amid linguistic difference to provide health care in these temporary clinics and the negotiation of material things such as patient intake forms by various members of the collective that had "expertise" in a variety of areas. Rhetorically engaging in communities opens up spaces that challenge traditional notions of "experts" and "professionals" to identify the everyday knowledge work of emergent collectives. In my work with these health teams, I learned how these complex acts of language transfer serve as liminal spaces that can develop relationships between people, languages, and cultures.

Engaged Rhetoric Across Borders

Health care practitioners and students of "first world" nations travel across national borders each year for transnational health programs, and the complicated, temporary relationships that are established between people from different backgrounds in these programs warrant further research and reflection. Investigation into the communication practices that develop in spaces of transnational public health are critical to providing a more comprehensive look at the collaborative relationships established within emergent collectives today. If rhetoricians want to study discourses of health and medicine in transnational contexts, we must be prepared for multilingual data collection, translingual rhetorical engagement, and publication practices that reflect the multilingual nature of the sites we study. We must also consider how translingual rhetoric is negotiated in a variety of ways across dialects, discourses of medicine, and modes of communication.

Rhetorical engagement in transcultural health spaces presents an opportunity to deepen our relationships with the various stakeholders in health care. It allows us to examine the complex rhetorical work that goes into assembling emergent collectives and supporting performances in a variety of verbal and nonverbal ways. As health care practices move across any borders, they become part of new rhetorical contexts influenced by local culture, language, and health experiences. A methodological focus on entering and engaging a site and community with care can promote the assembly work that must be done to create bonds and interact with stakeholders in ways that are respectful of their values and language use.

Translingual rhetorical engagement highlights the need to examine movements across the various words, phrases, gestures, and languages that we use to express and understand health and illness. Learning from host communities and opening more spaces for their voices in dialogues may encourage health practitioners and researchers to recognize the language practices of their patients as resources in expanding their own transcultural health literacies. Conversations about health literacies and foreign language medical courses can be more inclusive to linguistic and cultural differences as resources, rather than barriers. Through these conversations, traditional "lay" terminology can be seen as an expanded vocabulary and a resource for the rhetorical adaptability of health practitioners in the increasingly transcultural and translingual work of health care.

Prioritizing learning the vernacular language practices and cultural values of host communities in transnational health programs can lead to more multilingual data collection. Additionally, encouraging more multilingual individuals to consider medical rhetoric as an area of study and profession can enable intercultural research grounded in a variety of rhetorical traditions, cultural values, and understandings of health and wellness.

Conducting research that examines rhetorical practices in constantly evolving contexts such as transnational health can help uncover the creative processes of cultivating technical skills and practical knowledge in multilingual contexts. Translingual moves in this study were not always successful and success often only came from the risks, failures, and half-understandings that often accompanies language learning and development. By examining these rhetorical acts in a predominantly Dominican Spanish-speaking context, this study gives a situated example of how rhetors negotiate language variation among varieties of Spanish, especially within transnational health settings. The negotiation of language and culture was not always neat and fluent, but when participants worked together, they found beneficial approaches to developing mutual understanding with their patients.

By working alongside health practitioners and community volunteers, rhetorical researchers can open up new spaces for collaboration and increase the potential for making research findings meaningful for the various stakeholders involved in transnational health care. By discussing the rhetorical study of language use, we must be critically reflexive about our methodologies as researchers in the rhetoric of health & medicine. What limitations come from our own language use in research sites? How do we respond to moments when we do not understand what a provider or patient has said? How can our research design explore the movements and in-between moments of connections across nations, languages, and cultural understandings of health? A rhetorically engaged methodological approach may be one starting point for developing more ethical research and active participation in using rhetoric to enable the work of others. Translingual rhetorical engagement further highlights the need to be able to rhetorically adapt and analyze data across languages, dialects, and discourses. While translingual and engaged approaches can be fruitful in the study of transcultural health spaces, we have much to learn from various non-Western rhetorical traditions and community health workers in a variety of countries. Assembling collectives with these various experts across a variety of rhetorical traditions can further inform the field about how health and illness is discussed, experienced, and cared for around the world.

Notes

1 Tr. literally "Very Caribbean." This was a term that a few of the local residents used to describe the hot heat of the afternoon.
2 Tr. "-something" or "and a bit" referring to around 70 years old.
3 Tr. The Center for Rural Health. (The name of the organization was changed for this study).
4 Tr. Health promoters.
5 Tr. Helpers. These included both U.S. and Dominican participants who helped with the initial triage of taking vital signs (blood pressure, pulse rate, etc.).
6 Tr. Work team
7 Tr. Rural town/countryside
8 These are pseudonyms for the two towns.
9 The University of Kansas Human Subjects Committee (Project #20174) approved all data collection and research methods prior to the start of this study.
10 Tr. "They made a work group and there was a logistics group, there was a group of us that came here for work in all the areas: to clean the clinic, to work in the kitchen. . . . Everything was done through this work team."
11 Tr. Daughter/ Son
12 Tr. Sister/Brother
13 Tr. "I helped translate for all the patients. . . . Sometimes from English to Spanish and from Spanish to Spanish. . . . Because they (the patients) were not willing to listen to this language—to listen to the way Americans speak."
14 Tr. "My experience was that there were many people in the clinic that did not understand what you were saying."
15 Tr. "They spoke in Spanish, but the Dominicans did not understand it well."
16 Tr. "Like: If you've suffered from diabetes, if you've suffered from the heart (heart disease); if you've suffered from any other illness, and what they were going to do like dentistry, if a filling (in English) if filling."
17 Tr. Do you have the flu?

References

Asen, R. (2000). Seeking the 'counter' in counterpublics. *Communication Theory, 10*(4), 424–446.

Batova, T., & Clark, D. (2015). The complexities of globalized content management. *Journal of Business and Technical Communication, 29*(2), 221–235.

Bloom, R. (2014). Negotiating language in transnational health care: Exploring translingual literacy through grounded practical theory. *Journal of Applied Communication Research, 42*(3), 268–284.

Ding, H. (2014). *Rhetoric of a global epidemic: Transcultural communication about SARS.* Carbondale, IL: Southern Illinois University Press.

Fraser, N. (2007). Transnationalizing the public sphere: On the legitimacy and efficacy of public opinion in a post-westphalian world. *Theory, Culture & Society, 24*(4), 1–24.

García, O., & Wei, L. (2013). *Translanguaging: Language, bilingualism and education.* New York, NY: Palgrave Macmillan.

Gonzales, L., & Zantjer, R. (2015). Translation as a user-localization practice. *Technical Communication, 62*(4), 271–284.

Grabill, J. T. (2010). On being useful: Rhetoric and the work of engagement. In J. Ackerman & D. Coogan (Eds.), *The public work of rhetoric: Citizen-scholars and civic engagement* (pp. 193–208). Columbia, SC: University of South Carolina Press.

Grabill, J. T. (2014). The work of rhetoric in common places: An essay on rhetorical methodology. *JAC: A Journal of Composition Theory, 34*(1–2), 247–267.

Guerra, J. C. (2012). From code-segregation to code-switching to code-meshing: Finding deliverance from deficit thinking through language awareness and performance. Plenary Address: *Literacy Research Association Conference.* Louisville, KY: University of Louisville.

Hauser, G. (1999). *Vernacular voices: The rhetoric of publics and public spheres.* Columbia, SC: University of South Carolina Press.

Horner, B., NeCamp, S., & Donahue, C. (2011). Toward a multilingual composition scholarship: From English only to a translingual norm. *College Composition and Communication, 63*(2), 269–299.

Keränen, L. (2014). Public engagements with health and medicine. *Journal of Medical Humanities, 35*, 103–109.

Lu, M-Z., & Horner, B. (2013). Translingual literacy and matters of agency. In A. S. Canagarajah (Ed.), *Literacy as translingual practice: Between communities and classrooms* (pp. 26–38). New York, NY: Taylor & Francis.

13

ASSEMBLAGE MAPPING

A Research Methodology for Rhetoricians of Health and Medicine[1]

Elizabeth L. Angeli

Keywords: assemblage theory, mapping practices, rhetorics of health and medicine, emergency medical services, institutional review boards

Researchers in the rhetorics of health and medicine (RHM) use a number of methodologies and methods to study their research sites. These approaches include but are not limited to textual analysis (Heifferon, 2008; Koerber, 2013; Segal, 2005); interviews (Emmons, 2010; Keränen, 2007; Lingard, Garwood, Schryer, & Spafford, 2003); focus groups (Lingard, Reznick, DeVito, & Espin, 2002; Spoel, Harris, & Henwood, 2012); and a variety of ethnographic methods, from more standard forms that focus on cultural practices (Fountain, 2014; Schryer, 1993) to forms that focus on ontologies and representation (Graham, 2015). Each approach enables researchers to see certain aspects of a research site: focus groups highlight participants' experiences with an area, observations help researchers see how participants function in a particular setting, and textual analyses draw attention to the power of the written word. Some scholars also engage a research project's larger contexts, dynamics, and stakeholders more directly (Cohen et al., 2014; Derkatch & Spoel, 2015; Kerr & Hass, 2014; Meloncon, 2013; Zoller, 2005; Zoller & Meloncon, 2013).

RHM researchers, who are trained in disciplines like rhetoric, composition, technical communication, communication studies, and English studies, often import research methodologies and methods from these disciplines to study medical sites. Yet the RHM field could do more to develop methodologies that are uniquely adapted to RHM research sites and that help researchers address challenges related to these sites. These challenges include accessing highly regulated medical institutions; following regulations, like the Health Insurance Portability and Accountability Act (HIPAA); and using protected health information (PHI) in research projects. Because RHM researchers often need to access sensitive information, they should be mindful of how they can ethically and productively navigate these research spaces.

Adding to these challenges, institutional forces can play a formative role in RHM research projects. RHM researchers typically are housed in academic institutions but conduct research in and with medical establishments (Graham, 2015; Kuehl & Anderson, 2015; Lingard et al., 2012; Teston, 2009, 2012a, 2012b). This interinstitutional work can create additional barriers when beginning and completing studies, like receiving Institutional Review Board (IRB) approval from multiple institutions. These challenges can be magnified when the guiding methodologies include qualitative research methods that are less familiar to some medical systems; some qualitative methods and tools (e.g., for interviewing) evolve as a study progresses and cannot be known at the study's start, which may make a regulating institution uneasy. In this chapter, I discuss a methodology designed to help RHM researchers collaborate with medical institutions. Primarily, I answer the question: How can RHM researchers access highly regulated research sites?

To do so, I offer a methodological framework that can be used to approach challenging, dynamic, and even unpredictable research sites, sites similar to the ones that Pigozzi and Bloom-Pojar explore in their previous chapters in this volume. Specifically, I outline concrete steps that researchers can employ when entering research sites to learn how to build relationships, which may impact the methods used in a study. I propose the model of "assemblage mapping,"[2] which is guided by assemblage theory (DeLanda, 2006). This methodology emerged as a model that helped me navigate challenges during an empirical study in which I investigated the communication practices of emergency medical services (EMS) professionals. EMS professionals include certified Emergency Medical Technicians (EMTs) at all certification levels, from basic (the entry-level certification) to paramedic (the highest level). The EMS workplace, which is inherently chaotic and unpredictable, presents obstacles to researchers and to their IRBs. EMS professionals' workplaces change because EMS professionals work wherever patients need them. These places can include patients' homes, patients' workplaces, sites of traffic accidents, the back of a moving ambulance, and the emergency department (ED) in a hospital. These places, too, are typically inaccessible for researchers because patients can be vulnerable in these situations and unable to consent to participate in research projects. IRBs and other regulating boards, like legal counsel, must protect these patients. RHM researchers, then, must strike a balance in gaining access to protected medical sites while simultaneously working within the necessary limits of IRBs, HIPAA, and other regulating entities. Assemblage mapping offers researchers a way to balance these differing needs and, in turn, to build relationships with key stakeholders.

Assemblage mapping is a process by which researchers map a project's tangible and intangible components to see how these components interact. These components include the stakeholders, communication channels, power dynamics, and shared values among stakeholders. Figure 13.1 shows an example of an assemblage map that I created early in my EMS communication research project and highlights the stakeholders involved in the early stages of the project.

Figure 13.1 offers a visual landscape of the EMS communication research project and how I initially understood its layout and the relationships involved. At the center of this map sits the researcher, in this case, me, and I am surrounded by the stakeholders, the names in boxes, who played an active role in the project's direction. To see the research landscape, I mapped my relationship with and between these stakeholders and realized that I acted as a bridge between two groups: regulatory stakeholders and my research site stakeholders. To represent this landscape, this map is split into two sections. The left section includes the regulating institutions, and the right section includes the research sites, Lochville EMS and River View Hospital. The medical director is positioned in both these sections, too, because he worked in both sites.

Figure 13.1 is one of many possible visual representations of the research process. Technical communication scholars have proposed ways to overcome research challenges by visualizing the research process, including tracing methods, mapping

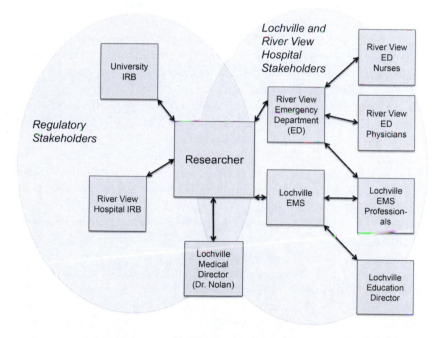

FIGURE 13.1 An assemblage map that represents early stages of the research process and the stakeholders involved in the EMS communication project at that time.

practices, communication models, and situated research practices (Porter et al., 2000; Simmons, 2007; Slack, Miller, & Doak, 1993; Spinuzzi, 2003, 2013; Sullivan & Porter, 1997). Specifically, mapping practices, like assemblage mapping, provide a graphical, nonlinear display of different points of action. In this way, a map's focal point can be recentered so that researchers can refocus a study. They then might better recognize certain connections that influence stakeholders' decisions, like approving a research project, and this information can be crucial when beginning a project. This illustration is particularly useful for RHM researchers who often work with human stakeholders and nonhuman components when conducting research, like patients, health professionals, lawyers, technology, and policies. Assemblage mapping illustrates how these stakeholders and components interact.

To present this methodological practice, I first discuss the theoretical aspects of assemblage mapping. Following this discussion, I detail the research project that led to assemblage mapping and the events with IRBs that necessitated a mapping method. The last section presents the steps to create an assemblage map and suggests uses for this research heuristic.

Assemblage Theory

Assemblage mapping grew out of assemblage theory, first fully articulated by Manuel DeLanda (2006) and building on Deleuze and Guattari's (1987) rhizome theory. Assemblage theory holds that assemblages, or "wholes whose properties emerge from the interactions between parts," facilitate networks, organizations, and processes (DeLanda, 2006, p. 5). The components of an assemblage interact dynamically, with communication acting as a stabilizing force. Assemblage theory involves understanding these dynamic relations among the components involved in an assemblage, and it asserts that entities of any size are best understood through their components. In the case of an RHM research project, these components can include hospitals, IRBs, participants, researchers, medical records, and any other items that researchers encounter. Tracking the interaction of these components can help a researcher determine how to proceed with a project (Mol, 2002).

With its focus on interactions and relationships among components, assemblage theory resembles an ecological perspective of rhetoric. In ecological rhetorical theory, as Ehrenfeld notes in this volume, agents coordinate with their environment and with one another; similarly, assemblage theory highlights this "moving into coordination" by identifying the environments—contexts—within which assemblages are located (p. 44). Assemblage mapping offers visual entry points into environments by prompting researchers to identify the dynamics involved in these relationships and the values at play.

In considering these dynamics, Ehrenfeld reminds rhetors that "[t]erms like 'ecology,' 'network,' and 'system' . . . have too often functioned as universalizing metaphors" adding that "we lack the means to theorize the power dynamics that animate [the] particularities" of these networks, ecologies, and systems (this volume, p. 44). Assemblage theory and mapping offer a way to account for the power dynamics involved in hierarchical structures, like those of institutionalized medicine, by offering a dynamic visualization system that accounts for the unique contexts in which RHM research projects are situated. By not offering a universal approach, to use Ehrenfeld's term, assemblage mapping draws on and diverts from current approaches to ecology and network theories.

To avoid a universalizing approach to RHM research sites, assemblage mapping offers questions for RHM researchers to consider as they think about the particular features and dynamics of a research site. These questions can include: What human and nonhuman components are at play? In what social, geographical, and technological contexts do these components reside? How are they connected? What values do the human components bring to the research project? How do the components interact, and what relationships emerge from these interactions? Where are the components' boundaries and points of intersection?

By grounding these questions in assemblage theory, researchers have the opportunity to situate themselves within the dynamic relations of a research project. Researchers can account for a research site's holistic contexts, that is, to see the site situated in social, technological, and geographical contexts (Wiley, Sutko, & Becerra, 2010). Seeing the research process as a social entity foregrounds the interaction of components within it, interactions that can be unpredictable. In a research project, researchers deal with a mixture of known and unknown factors. For example, RHM researchers can complete IRB documents to the best of their ability, but they may not know all the concerns that the IRB may have. The goal of assemblage mapping is to create the best possible visual landscape of a project by capturing the interaction of a research site's components.

To help frame these concepts in rhetorical theory, this focus on components' interaction can be understood through induction, deduction, and abduction. To create an assemblage map, the researcher uses induction by recognizing all the known components, including stakeholders and communication channels, and then by drawing conclusions based on observations. The researcher uses deduction to acknowledge the situational concerns and motivations under which stakeholders function and makes conclusions based on premises: "We must follow HIPAA because we believe that patient confidentiality is important." Finally, researchers use abduction to fill in unknown elements; they infer an answer based on their knowledge, observations, and best guess to take a course of action: "I know that I have to work with lawyers and that they are concerned with HIPAA. I haven't met with lawyers yet, but I should account for HIPAA when I meet with them." Assemblage maps rely on inference to help researchers identify the unknown components and find ways in which to address them.

Assemblage mapping complements current research methodologies and methods that RHM researchers employ, like focus groups, ethnography, and case studies, by turning the focus to external components, values, and power relationships that impact a research project and its methods. As Figure 13.2 illustrates, institutional forces impact RHM projects, and assemblage theory reminds researchers to acknowledge these forces. To be clear, however, assemblage mapping is not a way to collect data. Rather, assemblage mapping looks at the research process holistically, acknowledging the reciprocal relationship between a research project and the components that impact its direction. By visualizing these relationships among the researcher, research site, and research questions and methods, researchers can identify points of entry or blocks that may necessitate a shift in research questions or methods.

Figure 13.2 depicts the research project assemblage and the relationship between the internal components of a research project and the external components that influence them. The list inside the box in Figure 13.2 refers to the "internal" parts of research projects. These parts usually appear in methods sections of publications: participants, research site details, units of analysis, etc. The outside boxes represent those "external" components that impact research methods but might not appear in publications, like working with legal counsel. However, some components are both internal and external; that is, they both make up the research project and impact the project's direction. For example, participants are part of the internal components of a project, but access to participants and their availability can determine methods used. At times, too, the internal components can impact the external components, and this reciprocal relationship is represented by the two-way arrows. For example, IRBs might learn that they need to adjust their approval process based on research methods used in potentially

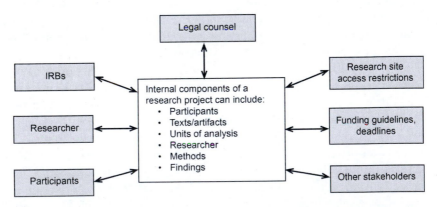

FIGURE 13.2   The EMS communication research project assemblage. Assemblage mapping draws attention to how outside components interact with the research project's internal components, which are included inside the box. The two-way arrows indicate that sometimes a project's internal components can affect the external components and vice versa.

unpredictable research settings. Scholars have called researchers to attend to these external components (Grabill, 2006; Jacobs, 2012; Sullivan & Porter, 1997; Takayoshi, Tomlinson, & Castillo, 2012). Focusing on these internal and external interactions foregrounds the "practice level" of research and the influence that these components can have on access (Grabill, 2006).

The Research Site and Methods: Lochville Emergency Medical Services

In this section, I describe my research project to demonstrate how I used assemblage mapping to identify, analyze, and address research challenges and to build relationships with stakeholders. Before I started this study, I was enrolled in an EMT-Basic class while I was a third-year PhD student studying technical communication and RHM. As a PhD student in these areas, I knew that I wanted to some kind of medical training to prepare me to work with hospitals, a calling that was solidified after I had an internship with an EMS squad two summers before I enrolled in the EMT course. During my internship and later in the EMT course, I learned about EMS communication, which prompted me to see if technical communication scholars or RHM researchers had studied the field. I learned that Roger Munger studied EMS communication and published two articles (1999; 2000), but scholarship on EMS in technical communication and RHM ended there.

This interest led me to conduct research on the communication practices of EMS professionals who were employed at Lochville Emergency Medical Services (Lochville), which became my research site.[3] Lochville provided EMS care for a midsized Midwestern county. The organization was primarily housed in one of the county's hospitals, River View Hospital. Lochville also had five locations, called squads, which were located throughout the county. Two EMS professionals were on duty at the squads daily, and some squads operated 24 hours a day, seven days a week, while others were staffed Monday through Saturday from 10am to 10pm.

Lochville employed over 40 people: a medical director, three EMS education directors, administrators, and numerous EMS professionals. The medical director, Dr. Brian Nolan, worked at River View as an emergency medical physician and oversaw Lochville's medical decision-making and EMS curriculum. EMS professionals worked under Dr. Nolan's medical license, and as such, he was responsible for the care that Lochville EMS provided patients.

Participants for this study (N = 15) included 10 Lochville EMS professionals, one River View ED physician (Dr. Nolan), two River View ED nurses, and two River View ED technicians. Participants reported having been in emergency medicine and EMS from six months to 31 years, and some participants held multiple roles in emergency medicine: two participants were former paramedics and current EMS educators; two participants worked as both paramedics and ED nurses; one participant worked as an EMT, licensed practical nurse, and was, at the time of the interview, in paramedic school; and one ED technician was also a certified surgical technician.

All 15 participants completed a survey, and 12 agreed to a follow-up interview. I interviewed participants in classrooms at the nursing school, in empty offices at the hospital, and at the squads. Participants completed surveys on their own time and returned them to me in person or by mail. In my original research methods, I planned to engage in ride-alongs where I would accompany participants as they responded to patients and observe participants' communication. I needed to alter that research method, though, as I detail in the next section.

The initial participant-observation portion of this research spanned seven months. Before this project began, I was enrolled in an EMT-Basic course, and I earned my EMT-Basic certification a few months after this project began. I conducted participant observations during my EMT course, which occurred in the EMT classroom, practice rooms, ambulances, hospitals, the locations where I met and treated patients, and during staff meetings, which were held in the EMT classroom. In staff meetings, employees reviewed skills and learned new treatment protocols. Every other month at staff meetings, Dr. Nolan conducted an audit and review of five 911 responses that Lochville completed that month. He informed Lochville staff of their strengths and weaknesses regarding medical treatment and documentation made during the response, and he discussed how the staff needed to improve their medical and documentation practices.

I worked with Lochville and completed my data collection over 16 months. This research timeline was largely influenced by Lochville's schedule and the two institutions with which I worked: the IRBs from my university and River View.

The IRB Timeline

Most researchers have their own IRB horror stories, and as researchers, we tend to share these stories in hallways, on listservs, and in our offices. Rarely are these accounts published because—frankly—readers may not need to understand or want to read the backstage work (Barton, 2004) of the research process. But the methodology I offer in this chapter was created in direct response to these important backstage narratives. These narratives shape the RHM research process, and by publishing these backstage narratives, we give credence to this heavy rhetorical work—our IRB work becomes scholarship so that we may learn from and improve it. To that end, the following IRB account has two purposes: to contextualize assemblage mapping and to inform readers who may sit on RHM researchers' tenure, promotion, or dissertation committees on why RHM research may take longer to complete than other types of research.

Phase 1: Working with the IRBs for Initial Research Approval

I knew that I was taking on a lot with my EMS communication research project. After all, I would be asking my university IRB to approve a research project that involved a researcher (me) entering patients' houses to observe medical communication, a highly vulnerable situation for all involved. To learn how to best complete the required IRB documents, I contacted my university's IRB to set up a meeting, which occurred early in Phase 1 of this project, as shown in Figure 13.3.

In November 2010, I met with two university IRB representatives, Sally and Lisa. As I told them about my project, I saw concerned looks develop on their faces. They told me that I would need approval from their IRB and River View Hospital's IRB that housed Lochville because I was a member of both institutions: I was a university student, and I was a researcher and student at the hospital and Lochville. Sally and Lisa were most concerned that I follow HIPAA guidelines, but they were confident that the university IRB would approve my research as long as two things happened: 1) The hospital's IRB needed to approve my project first, and 2) The hospital IRB needed to provide the university IRB with written documentation that I would follow HIPAA guidelines. Sally and Lisa advised, though, that I submit my IRB documents to the university as soon as possible so they could begin reviewing the project and offer feedback. Feeling confident, I left our meeting to call River View's IRB.

Contacting River View's IRB proved more challenging than I had thought. My university advised me to call the hospital directly. When I called the hospital, the operator said, "We don't have a review board. I'll connect you to Human Resources." Not surprisingly, no one at Human Resources knew what I was talking about. I realized that the cold call route was not getting me anywhere, so I emailed my university's IRB. After a few forwarded messages, I received the contact information for River View's IRB administrative assistant, April.

I emailed April immediately. She forwarded my request to Dr. Jessica Holden, the head of River View's IRB. April quickly advised me that I would need a River View physician to sponsor my project. At this point, I did not know any physicians

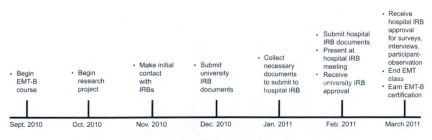

Phase 1: Seven Months

FIGURE 13.3   Phase 1 of the research project's timeline.

at the hospital. I was only in contact with my EMS teacher, Ben, about this project. Frustrated and unsure of where to turn, I emailed Ben who directed me to Dr. Brian Nolan, an ED physician and Lochville's medical director. Ben mentioned that Dr. Nolan was interested in improving communication, so he would find my project interesting; this interest became one of our shared values. After an email, some face-to-face conversations in the ED, and a phone conversation, Dr. Nolan confirmed that he would happily sponsor my project. I didn't realize it at the time, but this serendipitous interest in EMS communication was crucial to this project's success, and it fueled our collaborative efforts to gain IRB approval.

With Dr. Nolan's sponsorship in place, I submitted my university IRB documents the first week of December 2010, and I forwarded them to April at River View. She told me the hospital IRB would meet on January 28, 2011, and for them to even consider my project, the university IRB needed to approve the project first; the hospital would defer to the university's decision. I informed her that the university IRB would approve my project only if River View would approve it first; the university would then defer to the hospital's decision. I was in a catch-22: Both IRBs would defer to each other, but one IRB had to approve the project first.

After a few more emails, the university IRB agreed they would review—and hopefully approve—the project first. By this point, it was mid-January 2011, and I wanted to meet River View's January 28 IRB meeting deadline. I learned that my university IRB application needed some revision, such as accounting for how I would report any patient abuse that I could potentially observe. Dr. Nolan helped me with this and other revisions, and I resubmitted the application to the university.

While waiting for the university's decision, I emailed April on January 21 to double check River View IRB's submission requirements, seven days away from their IRB meeting. On January 26, April replied and included a list of submission requirements, requirements I had not seen before. As I read those documents, I learned that River View's IRB needed my documents two weeks prior to the January 28 meeting date. Quickly realizing that I was not going to make the January 28 deadline (I still did not have university approval), I asked April for the next meeting date: February 18, 2011. Needless to say, I was frustrated and feeling a bit hopeless at this point, but I continued working to meet the new deadline.

Despite my best efforts, I still did not have university approval at the end of January. To add to the delays, the university was closed for two days due to winter weather. April advised that I wait for the February 25 meeting. So, I had until February 18 to submit all my documents and gain university IRB approval. Thankfully, I received approval from the university IRB on February 9, giving me time to submit my documents to the hospital IRB before our February 25 meeting.

As I prepared for that meeting, April suggested that I attend the River View IRB meeting to present my project. The Board "usually has questions," she said. Her suggestion caught me off guard because I was used to academic IRB reviews—quietly submitting my documents, letting them speak for themselves, and receiving revision and approval letters by email. I agreed to attend, and I prepared my presentation with the following goals: to receive approval to distribute surveys, conduct interviews, and ride along with participants on 911 responses after my EMT class ended on March 26.

On the snowy morning of the hospital IRB meeting, February 25, I arrived at 7:00 am, 30 minutes before the meeting's start time. I saw the IRB director, Dr. Holden, and she told me what to expect during the meeting and showed me to the meeting room, a large conference room complete with a continental breakfast. I poured myself a cup of coffee and asked Dr. Holden where I should sit. She pulled out a chair and said, "Right here, next to me"—at the head of the table. As 7:30 am drew closer, the Board filed in: lawyers in formal suits, nurses in scrubs, physicians in lab coats. Dr. Holden called the meeting to order, and she introduced me to the Board. They shuffled their papers around, looking for my proposal that they read prior to the meeting. Once everyone had my proposal out, I presented my research project. Some Board members looked at me as I talked while others read along. I could not get a good feel for my audience, which made me uneasy.

After my presentation, Dr. Holden opened the floor to questions. One Board member leaned forward on the table and paged through his notes. From his white lab coat, I gathered that he was a doctor. "I don't see why we have to review this," he commented as he casually tossed my proposal on the table. He was talking to me and Dr. Holden. "This project doesn't involve collecting blood or performing medical procedures. You're just listening to people talk. How is that research?" he asked. I replied, "In my research field, observing people communicate is research. Scholars need IRB approval for it, and our data includes surveys, field notes, and transcripts from audio-recorded interviews." Satisfied with the answer, he sat back in his chair, waved his hand, and said, "Fine with me." Other Board members were concerned with how I was going to protect patient information. I told them that it is common practice in my field to change participants' names and even genders to protect them. They seemed satisfied with that answer, too.

I then asked the Board if I could participate in ride-alongs after my EMT course ended. The members paused; some looked ok with the ride-alongs until one Board member grew concerned: "What happens if you're on an ambulance observing communication and the patient goes into cardiac arrest?" She continued, "Will you just continue taking notes and observing?" Other Board members chuckled. "No," I replied, a bit offended at her assumption. "At that point, I will be a certified EMT. I of course will put down my notebook and start compressions or do whatever the medics need me to do. I will not compromise patient care for a research project."

In response, another Board member and physician, Dr. Williams, said that I could ride along because I would still be a student—a student at the local university. He had forms that I needed to complete, which he would email me. The meeting ended shortly thereafter. I left, and the Board continued their work.

Two days later, I still had not heard from Dr. Williams about the forms, so I followed up with him through email. He eventually wrote back, saying that he forwarded my ride-along request to the state compliance office. This news took me by surprise; no one mentioned the state compliance office at the meeting. But I waited. With my ride-along request submitted to the state compliance office, the hospital IRB approved my initial request to distribute surveys, conduct interviews, and continue participant observation. I began collecting that data. The ride-along approval process took months to sort out, and this is where Phase 2 began (see Figure 13.4). I was still feeling frustrated and disheartened because I thought that I addressed all the concerns leading up to the IRB meeting. I started to realize that these concerns were our shared values: The Board, compliance office, hospital, and I valued the same things, like patient privacy, but we approached our values from different positions. These different positions were in part the result of power dynamics: The Board held advanced degrees in law and medicine whereas I was working on my advanced degree in English and an EMT-B certification.

Phase 2: Waiting for (and Receiving) Waiver of Informed Consent

Part of my frustration stemmed from the seemingly moving parts involved in my project and the power dynamics that started to influence both my project and my ability to build relationships with stakeholders. Specifically, the hospital's lawyers became involved after the February 25, 2011 hospital IRB meeting. Through Dr. Nolan, I learned that Dr. Williams worked closely with the hospital's legal department; he held an important executive role in the hospital. "Well, that explains the compliance office," I thought. Once the lawyers became involved, the approval process slowed to a crawl, as one might imagine. I realized I was in over my head now that I was dealing with lawyers, and at this point, I revisited the assemblage map that I created in Figure 13.1 to create the map below in Figure 13.5, which includes shared values among the stakeholders.

Figure 13.1 did not include hospital lawyers because I did not know that I would be working with them. I learned about these stakeholders through my

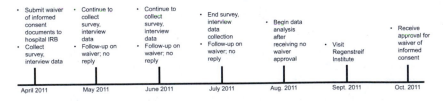

Phase 2: Seven Months

FIGURE 13.4 Phase 2 of the research project's timeline.

other stakeholders, like Dr. Nolan. Instead of working with the lawyers directly, I worked with physicians, like Dr. Williams, who spoke to the lawyers on my behalf. The map in Figure 13.4 helped me see how I could communicate with these stakeholders, and it laid out the concerns they had. I included—as best as I could—how the stakeholders connected to me and to one another by mapping communication channels. For example, I knew that Dr. Williams was forwarding my emails to the state compliance office and lawyers, so I was connected to them through Dr. Williams. Therefore, I remained mindful of those audiences as I typed my emails, ensuring to use words that reflected shared values like "HIPAA" and that appealed to medical credibility by signing my name "Liz Angeli, EMT-B" once I passed the state exam in early March 2011.

Figure 13.5 represents more than just communication channels, though. These communication channels also represent levels of access, with email being the lowest level of access and face-to-face the highest level of access. From this particular study, face-to-face communication meant the stakeholders had time to meet with me, and in medicine, time can reflect a stakeholder's level of interest: Higher levels

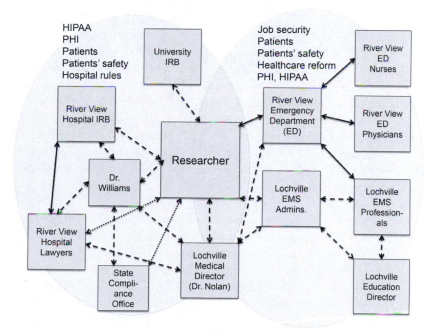

FIGURE 13.5   Research assemblage map created between Phases 1 and 2. Dashed lines represent communication via email, phone, or face-to-face. Dotted lines represent that they communicate with one another through another stakeholder. Solid lines represent a combination of email/phone/face-to-face communication and communication through another stakeholder.

of access can reflect higher levels of interest and commitment. Knowing that communication channels reflect access, I created the assemblage map in Figure 13.5 to help me identify which stakeholders could access other stakeholders.

In the beginning of April 2011, I was unknowingly preparing for another seven months of waiting, as shown in the timeline presented in Figure 13.4. Dr. Williams and I emailed and spoke on the phone quite a bit at this point. He learned through the hospital's attorney that I needed to be a student at the hospital's nursing school to do ride-alongs, but at this point my EMT class had ended. I emailed Dr. Williams, purposely identifying our shared values: "Does it help that I'm a certified EMT? Or that I'm researching medical communication?" His reply read something along the lines of, "I'm sorry, but the lawyers and I see no way around this situation."

Determined to find another way, I revisited my assemblage map in Figure 13.5. I saw that I lacked connections to the key stakeholders: the lawyers and state compliance office. Dr. Williams connected me to them, but he had just informed me there was no way forward. I then saw that Dr. Nolan also was connected directly and indirectly to these stakeholders, and he had a higher degree of power in this situation because he was a medical doctor who worked at the hospital. I wanted to investigate these connections further. From our conversations, I learned that Dr. Nolan shared values with other stakeholders, including patient safety, PHI, HIPAA, and hospital rules. He differed from other stakeholders, however, in that he was openly committed to my project's success, helping me identify roadblocks and pathways around them. To better understand his role in my project, I placed him at the center of a new map and focused on what I could learn about the communication he used to communicate with the stakeholders. Figure 13.6 was the result.

I quickly learned that Dr. Nolan was the best way to communicate with Dr. Williams, the hospital lawyers, and the state compliance office because he could communicate with them through multiple channels: email, phone, and face-to-face. I called him to talk about moving forward. He emailed and called the lawyers, including me in email replies and forwards. In one of these emails, the lawyers wrote, "It certainly helps Liz's case that she is an EMT-B," but they needed more information: How would participants give me consent on the ambulance? How was I going to use the information I learned? Participants were unable to give me consent because of their vulnerable positions, and I continued to stress that I was interested in how Lochville EMS professionals, not strictly patients, were communicating. The lawyers suggested an alternative. I could ask them to approve a waiver for patient consent, which would allow me to ride along with Lochville without having to ask patients for their consent to observe communication.

The lawyers wanted to meet Dr. Nolan and me face-to-face to discuss the waiver in early April 2011. Dr. Nolan forwarded me this meeting request on April 7, 2011, when I was at a conference. I saw the email between conference

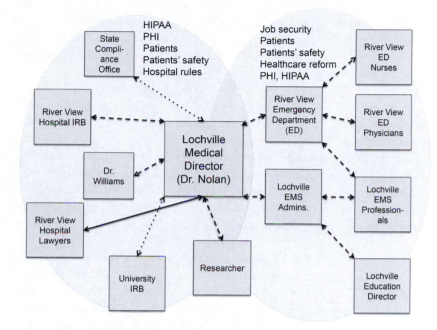

FIGURE 13.6   Assemblage map that places the medical director at the center. This map illustrates how he interacted with other stakeholders. Dashed lines represent communication via email, phone, or face-to-face. Dotted lines represent that they communicate with one another through another stakeholder. Solid lines represent a combination of email/phone/face-to-face communication and communication through another stakeholder.

sessions, and I immediately went back to my hotel room to call him. I sat on the bed, bracing myself for a logistical nightmare. I could not make the face-to-face meeting. Then I remembered my map in Figure 13.6 and realized that maybe I didn't need to attend because I was not connected to the lawyers. My research landscape showed that Dr. Nolan played the strongest role in my project at that point. He was my strongest advocate, and as a medical doctor familiar with medico-legal concerns, he was in the best position to work with the lawyers. I would have to trust him with my project.

Dr. Nolan sounded exasperated on the phone, and who could blame him? The two of us had been working for weeks to address this waiver-of-consent roadblock. On top of that, Dr. Nolan worked full-time in the ED and served as Lochville's medical director. He was by no means obligated to help me. Because I was out of town, Dr. Nolan offered to speak with the lawyers again on my behalf, and he asked me questions on the phone to help him prepare.

Our efforts paid off. Once the lawyers spoke with Dr. Nolan, they agreed that a waiver of informed patient consent would suffice. They asked me to write an informed consent waiver request to the hospital's IRB. I wrote to Dr. Holden, head of the hospital IRB, to update her about the development. She said that I would receive a "positive reply" once she received my request. After reading that email, I was relieved but thought, "That seems too easy." And it turned out that my suspicions were correct.

On April 11, 2011, I sent my waiver request to the hospital IRB. I did not hear anything after emailing it to Dr. Holden and April, her assistant. I waited. I sent emails during the summer. I called. I heard nothing back. By this point in my project, I learned that patience was a good characteristic to display, so I waited and hoped that someone was working to approve my forms. I continued to collect data through surveys and interviews, and I attended staff meetings, thinking that I would be approved to get back on the ambulances by July. But by August 2011, I figured that the hospital had not decided to approve my request and just failed to let me know, so I continued working as if ride-alongs were not part of my research methods.

As I continued working, a unique opportunity presented itself. In September 2011, I was conducting secondary research on emergency medical documentation and learned about the Regenstrief Institute, a health care research organization whose mission was to deliver effective health care and to reduce medical error (Regenstrief Institute, 2015). Their researchers were studying electronic medical records (EMRs), and I contacted them to learn more. I visited the institute to interview an affiliate scientist and emergency medical physician, Dr. John T. Finnell. We spoke about EMRs and how this shift in form would affect EMS. He asked me if I wanted to shadow him in the ED to see how EMRs worked in action. I took him up on his offer and spent one shift shadowing him in his emergency room, which served as a main emergency room for the local EMS crews. Although this experience was not part of my original data collection, this experience in a busy ED augmented my understanding of EMS communication. In that way, it helped me fill in some gaps in knowledge that I was hoping to address through ride-alongs.

Finally, in October 2011, I sent another email to Dr. Holden, head of River View's IRB. Instead of hearing back from her, I received a reply from her assistant April. April had planned to get my approval letter signed at the July Board meeting, but she was out of town. She remembered this upon seeing my email and, three days later, scanned me a signed approval letter that authorized ride-alongs— seven months after I had started this process.

Then my graduate advisor and I were confronted with the next challenge: my graduation timeline. I was on the job market that year and set to graduate in May 2012. If I started ride-alongs in mid-October 2011, knowing full well that I would be going on campus visits and writing my dissertation, I could jeopardize my graduation date. We decided that I needed to focus on graduating, and I continued as I had been: conducting research and writing as though I did not plan on ride-alongs. Although I was not able to return to the ambulances, I turned to my field notes, sketches of assemblage maps, and saved emails from my experience with the two IRBs to make sense of the past 16 months, my experiences, and my data.

As I sorted through these research artifacts and reflected on my interactions with the IRBs, I was left with questions: Do other rhetoricians of health and medicine confront similar obstacles in their research processes? How can my project help other researchers in this situation? I turned my attention to the methods and guiding principles I used in this project, including ways to account for relationship building, shared values, and power dynamics. I aimed to augment the conversation about research methodologies in RHM settings; assemblage mapping was the result.

Working with Research Sites: Steps for Creating Assemblage Maps

It is difficult, if not impossible, for researchers to identify every barrier they may encounter. To address this challenge, assemblage mapping offers a unique characteristic: its dynamic, shifting nature. Researchers can modify the map as they learn more about their research site. This section presents steps for how to create an assemblage map.

You can complete the following steps with pen and paper or with Word, Power-Point, Pages, Keynote, or InDesign (Figures 13.5 and 13.6 above are examples of completed assemblage maps). As you move forward into a project, modify the map as needed. I break up the steps here in three parts: steps 1–5 (component parts), steps 6–8 (power dynamics), and steps 9–11 (mapping the assemblage). I show an example of steps 1–8 before presenting steps 9–11.

Steps 1–7 ask you to create two tables: one table identifies the stakeholders, shared values, and communication channels (i.e., the component parts; see Table 13.1), and the second table identifies power dynamics involved with each stakeholder (see Table 13.2). These tables will be used to generate the assemblage maps, which are outlined in steps 9–11.

Part 1: Steps for Creating the Table of Component Parts

1. Write a list of the components that you think make up your research project. The components can include people, places, policies, technologies, shared values, and communication channels.

    *   This list of components will become the stakeholders, values, and communication channels that will make up your map. In the examples I provide here, I am examining my research project (whole), which is made up of interacting stakeholders (parts of the whole).

- You can add information throughout the process. If you don't have all the information you need, place a question mark in the accompanying table cell, conduct research, and add the learned information to the table.

2. Create a table with three columns and at least five rows to start (you can add or remove rows as needed; see Table 13.1 for an example). In the three columns, insert these three headings:

   - Whom does my project involve? (stakeholders)
   - What will the stakeholder value? (values)
   - How can I communicate with the stakeholder? (communication channels)

3. Identify the stakeholders in your list. Then, place them in a table under a heading, "Whom does my project involve?"
4. Identify particular values the stakeholders may have; these values may be in your list from step 1, or you may need to add them. Consider words or phrases that you've heard people use at the IRB or at the research site. Add these values to the "values" column.

   - For example, which stakeholders might be concerned with HIPAA regulations? PHI? Are there policies you listed in step 1 that stakeholders could be concerned with?

5. Identify the communication channels that you can use to contact each stakeholder, such as email, phone, video, or face-to-face meetings. If you cannot contact a stakeholder directly, list who can contact them for you. List these channels in the "communication channels" column.

Table 13.1 below represents steps 1–5 of my own EMS communication research project, and this table eventually led to the assemblage map in Figure 13.5. In this table, I included myself as "researcher," but I left the values and communication channels open. Although you will bring your own values to the research project, it is important at this stage to pay attention to the other stakeholders' values. In turn, you will most likely begin to value the same things. For example, in my map, patients are not a separate stakeholder of the map; they are part of the values because they were not research participants. As such, IRBs, regulating boards, and my research participants (Lochville EMS professionals and River View staff) valued patients and their safety. This value permeated my research project approval process, and rightly so. As such, patients became part of our shared values.

Part 2: Steps for Creating the Table of Power Dynamics

6. Next, create a second table with two columns and enough rows to represent all the stakeholders (see Table 13.2 for an example). This table will include the power dynamics of the research project. Label the table columns "The

TABLE 13.1 List of component parts (steps 1–5) for the assemblage map in Figure 13.5.

Whom does my project involve? (stakeholders)	What will the stakeholder value? (values)	How can I communicate with the stakeholder? (communication channels)
Hospital IRB	HIPAA, PHI, patients, patient safety	Email, phone
Hospital lawyers	HIPAA, PHI, patients, patient safety, hospital rules	Email, through Dr. Nolan and Dr. Williams
State compliance office	HIPAA, PHI, patients, hospital rules	Through Dr. Williams
Dr. Williams, hospital IRB member and affiliated with hospital lawyers	HIPAA, PHI, patients, patient safety, hospital rules	Email, through Dr. Nolan
Dr. Nolan, Lochville medical director, River View ED physician	HIPAA, PHI, patients, patient safety, job security, health care reform, improving EMS communication	Email, phone/text, face-to-face
Emergency department (ED)	HIPAA, PHI, patients, patient safety, job security, health care reform	Through medical director
ED nurses	HIPAA, PHI, patients, patient safety, job security, health care reform	Through medical director, face-to-face
ED physicians	HIPAA, PHI, patient safety, job security, health care reform	Through medical director
Lochville EMS administrators	HIPAA, PHI, patients, patient safety, job security, health care reform, improving EMS communication	Through medical director, email, face-to-face
Lochville EMS professionals	HIPAA, PHI, patients, patient safety, job security, health care reform	Email, phone/text, face-to-face, through medical director, though EMS
University IRB	HIPAA, PHI, patients, patient safety	Email, phone, face-to-face
Researcher (me)		

TABLE 13.2 List of potential power dynamics between stakeholders and me that influenced relationship building. Gender is based on pronouns stakeholders used in discussions (i.e., Dr. Nolan referred to himself by "he," "him," and "his"). Education level is based on titles stakeholders used and on informal conversations I had with stakeholders. I do not include race here except my own because I did not ask about stakeholders' races, and I do not want to assume the races of my stakeholders.

The Project's Stakeholders	What power dynamics do I need to be aware of? How are we similar and different?
Researcher (me)	Female; white; college degree, advanced degree, working on PhD; an EMT student with limited medical experience; mid-20s; not from the town; affiliated with the university but will be moving after I graduate (town-and-gown divide); a researcher; no affiliation with the hospital
Hospital IRB	Unsure of gender makeup but at least two females serve on the Board; higher levels of medical training than I have; college and advanced degrees; unsure of age range, but some members older than I am
Hospital lawyers	Unsure of gender makeup but at least one male serves as counsel; high levels of medical training; advanced degrees; older than I am
State compliance office	Unsure of gender makeup and age; have the final say in approving my project; made up of lawyers who are interested in protecting the hospital and patients
Dr. Williams, hospital IRB member and affiliated with hospital lawyers	Male; high levels of legal and medical experience; advanced degrees; older than I am; represents the lawyers who are interested in protecting the hospital and patients
Dr. Nolan, Lochville medical director, River View ED physician	Male; high level of medical experience; advanced degrees; older than I am
Emergency department (ED)	Unsure of gender makeup but more males in positions of power; high levels of medical experience; advanced degrees; older than I am; town-and-gown divide and may not trust me as a researcher
ED nurses	Unsure of exact gender makeup but more females than males; high levels of medical experience; all have college degrees, some may have advanced degrees; younger and older than I am; town-and-gown divide and may not trust me as a researcher

The Project's Stakeholders	What power dynamics do I need to be aware of? How are we similar and different?
ED physicians	Worked with three males and one female; high levels of medical experience; have advanced degrees; older than I am; town–and–gown divide and may not trust me as a researcher
Lochville EMS administrators	All male; high levels of medical experience; high school diploma, at least one has college degree; older than I am
Lochville EMS professionals	Unsure of exact gender makeup but more males than females; high levels of medical experience; high school diploma, some have college credit/degree; younger and older than I am; town–and–gown divide and may not trust me as a researcher
University IRB	Unsure of gender makeup but worked with two females; less, same, or more medical experience than I have; same or higher level of education than I have

Project's Stakeholders" and "What power dynamics do I need to be aware of? How are we similar and different?"

7. List the stakeholders in the "Stakeholders" column.
8. Consider the relationships at play in your project and include them in the "Power Dynamics" column. This step includes naming the power dynamics involved, which can include, but are not limited to, gender, race, education level, and age. Although you may not map these dynamics, they are helpful to identify how stakeholders may see you in relation to themselves and to the project.

Part 3: Steps for Mapping the Tables

9. Think about and note how the elements listed in the tables connect to one another. Make notes as you answer these questions:

   • Which stakeholders interact and communicate with one another, and how?
   • What values do stakeholders share?
   • How are the stakeholders connected? Does one person connect all the stakeholders together?

10. Map the research assemblage, the stakeholders, and their values using the first table you created (see Figures 13.5 and 13.6 for examples):

   a. Place the primary stakeholder that you want to focus on in the middle of your blank document, like "researcher" or "medical director." Circle or box it.

    b.   Place other stakeholders around the primary one, grouping stakeholders who are related or may share values.

    c.   Enclose the grouped stakeholders with a circle or circles to represent shared values. These circles will create boundaries that visually group together stakeholders with shared values.

    d.   List the values in the circle to map the larger forces at work. You might even map the power dynamics in these circles, too.

11. Link the stakeholders together with arrows to indicate communication channels. The arrows can be single- or two-headed arrows to indicate one- and two-way communication. You also can format the lines to represent different communication channels as Figures 13.5 and 13.6 show.

To help complete steps 1–11, you might start by brainstorming answers to these questions:

- What stakeholders will I interact with?
- How will these stakeholders understand my research?
- How can I talk about my research based on how they will understand it? What words should I use or avoid?
- Do these stakeholders interact with other stakeholders I might speak with?
- How might technology influence my message?
- Do I know someone connected with the institution who could advise me?
- What values will the stakeholders have regarding my project?

Figures 13.5 and 13.6 offer two examples of the assemblage maps that I created to help me navigate this project. In Figure 13.5, I mapped the research assemblage from four months' worth of interactions with the project's stakeholders, including the elements in Table 13.1 above. Figure 13.5 illustrates the communication channels and values that influenced each stakeholder in the larger assemblage. In Figure 13.6, I placed the medical director at the center. Midway through this project, I wanted to learn how he could help me connect with stakeholders that heavily influenced my project, like the lawyers. By seeing how he was connected to the other stakeholders and by reflecting on the power dynamics that could influence our relationship (see Table 13.2), I could see how I was indirectly connected to and better positioned to interact with other stakeholders. I learned, too, about areas I needed to research further, i.e., the connections between the hospital IRB and lawyers and how the connection impacted the project.

Although an assemblage map is intended to help improve the research process, the process can be frustrating, challenging, and time consuming. To prepare yourself for a large project that involves many moving components, consider the following preparatory steps:

1. Write and practice a 30-second elevator speech that you may need to share with stakeholders. This speech should succinctly but accurately describe your research plan. Explain your project plan in plain language, i.e., remove any field-specific jargon like "activity theory" or "multimodal composing practices." You could include shared values in this speech, too, like "patient safety" or "communication practices."
2. Find at least one person within the institution who is interested in and cares about your research topic. For example, the medical director was my point person because we shared a value: improving EMS communication.
3. Save all documents—paper, electronic, even something written on a napkin.
4. Take careful notes during all phone calls and meetings. If you cannot take detailed notes, consider alternative methods such modified grounded theory (Teston, 2009) or observational heuristics (Teston, 2012a), both of which help researchers capture complexity through checklists and freehand sketching. After meetings, you also can audio record your notes and transcribe them later.

As stated before, assemblage mapping involves balancing your needs as a researcher with those of the institutions with which you are working. This methodology can help researchers remain mindful of this balance and act accordingly. When faced with research roadblocks, use assemblage maps to find alternatives, but be mindful that you might need to accept roadblocks instead of working around them. Be flexible. If you force your project too much and stick to your original plan, you may miss other opportunities, including connecting with someone who is willing to help you. In other words, let *kairos* play a role in your project.

Conclusion

In this chapter, I have proposed assemblage mapping as a methodology for RHM researchers, and it can also be a useful activity for graduate student researchers. Students may find it helpful if they share their assemblage maps with other students. Similar to reading drafts of academic papers or research study notes, students can see how other researchers approach institutional research, and they can receive feedback from their colleagues. Likewise, researchers can share their assemblage maps with stakeholders to see if they have overlooked potential stakeholders, shared values, communication channels, or power dynamics.

As an emerging field, RHM needs methodologies to guide our research projects. These projects often involve research sites and variables that challenge research timelines and access, and discipline-specific methodologies can help address these issues. Assemblage mapping offers a way to proceed by creating a visual landscape of the RHM research process, acknowledging the important role of relationship building and interaction among stakeholders, values, and power dynamics that impact the process.

Notes

1 This research was funded in part by grants from the Purdue University Research Foundation and Towson University's Faculty Development and Research Committee.
2 In this chapter, I use the terms "mapping" and "map" to refer to a visual heuristic tool rather than a geographical description (see Brizee, 2015; Simmons, 2007; Sullivan & Porter, 1997 for descriptions of mapping as visual heuristic tools).
3 This research received IRB approval. Per IRB review, HIPAA, and informed consent form guidelines, participant and organization names of Lochville EMS and River View Hospital are pseudonyms.

References

Barton, E. (2004). Discourse methods and critical practice in professional communication: The front-stage and back-stage discourse of prognosis in medicine. *Journal of Business and Technical Communication, 18*(1), 67–111.

Bloom-Pojar, R. (2017). Translingual rhetorical engagement in transcultural health spaces. In L. Meloncon & J. B. Scott (Eds.), *Methodologies of the rhetoric of health & medicine* (pp. 214–234). New York, NY: Routledge.

Brizee, A. (2015). Using Isocrates to teach technical communication and civic engagement. *Journal of Technical Writing and Communication, 45*(2), 134–165.

Cohen, E. L., Vanderpool, R., Crosby, R., Noar, S. M., Bates, W., Collins, T., . . . Casey, B. (2014). 1–2–3 Pap: An HPV prevention campaign to reduce cervical cancer in Eastern Kentucky. In G. L. Kreps & M. J. Dutta (Eds.), *Reducing health disparities: Communication interventions* (pp. 158–177). New York, NY: Peter Lang Publishing.

DeLanda, M. (2006). *A new philosophy of society: Assemblage theory and social complexity*. New York, NY: Continuum.

Deleuze, G., & Guattari, F. (1987). *A thousand plateaus: Capitalism and schizophrenia*. New York, NY: Continuum.

Derkatch, C., & Spoel, P. (2015). Public health promotion of "local food": Constituting the selfgoverning citizen-consumer. *Health: An Interdisciplinary Journal for the Social Study of Health, Illness, and Medicine, 21*(2), 154–170. doi:10.1177/1363459315590247.

Ehrenfeld, D. (2017). Ecological Investments and the circulation of rhetoric: Studying the "Saving Knowledge" of Dr. Emma Walker's social hygiene lectures. In L. Meloncon & J. B. Scott (Eds.), *Methodologies of the rhetoric of health & medicine* (pp. 41–60). New York, NY: Routledge.

Emmons, K. (2010). *Black dogs and blue words: Depression and gender in the age of self- care*. New Brunswick, NJ: Rutgers University Press.

Fountain, T. K. (2014). *Rhetoric in the flesh: Trained vision, technical expertise, and the gross anatomy lab*. New York, NY: Routledge.

Grabill, J. (2006). The study of writing in the social factory: Methodology and rhetorical agency. In J. B. Scott, B. Longo, & K. V. Wills (Eds.), *Critical power tools: Technical communication and cultural studies* (pp. 151–170). Albany, NY: State University of New York Press.

Graham, S. S. (2015). *The politics of pain medicine: A rhetorical-ontological inquiry.* Chicago, IL: University of Chicago Press.

Heifferon, B. (2008). Pandemics or pandemonium: Preparing for avian flu. In B. Heifferon & S. C. Brown (Eds.), *Rhetoric of healthcare: A new disciplinary inquiry* (pp. 51–74). Cresskill, NJ: Hampton Press.

Jacobs, G. (2012). Troubling research: A field journey through methodological decision making. In P. Takayoshi & K. Powell (Eds.), *Practicing research in writing studies: Reflections on ethically responsible research* (pp. 331–348). Cresskill, NJ: Hampton Press.

Johnson, N. R. (2017). Infrastructural methodology: A case in protein as public health. In L. Meloncon & J. B. Scott (Eds.), *Methodologies of the rhetoric of health & medicine* (pp. 61–78). New York, NY: Routledge.

Keränen, L. (2007). "Cause someday we all die": Rhetoric, agency, and the case of the "patient" preferences worksheet. *Quarterly Journal of Speech, 93*(2), 179–210.

Kerr, A. M., & Hass, S. M. (2014). Parental uncertainty in illness: Managing uncertainty surrounding "orphan" illness. *Journal of Pediatric Nursing, 29*(5), 393–400.

Koerber, A. (2013). *Breast or bottle? Contemporary controversies in infant-feeding policy and practice.* Columbia, SC: University of South Carolina Press.

Kuehl, R. A., & Anderson, J. (2015). Designing public communication about doulas: Analyzing presence and absence in promoting a volunteer doula program. *Communication Design Quarterly, 3*(4), 75–84.

Lingard, L., Garwood, K., Schryer, C. F., & Spafford, M. M. (2003). A certain art of uncertainty: Case presentation and the development of professional identity. *Social Science & Medicine, 56*(3), 603–616.

Lingard, L., McDougall, A., Levstik, M., Chandok, N., Marlee, M. M., & Schyer, C. (2012). Representing complexity well: A story about teamwork, with implications for how we teach collaboration. *Medical Education, 46*(9), 869–877.

Lingard, L., Reznick, R., DeVito, I., & Espin, S. (2002). Forming professional identities on the health care team: Discursive constructions of the "other" in the operating room. *Medical Education, 36*(8), 728–734.

Meloncon, L. (2013). Visual communication in environmental health: Methodological questions and compromises. *Communication Design Quarterly, 1*(3), 34–37.

Mol, A. (2002). *The body multiple: Ontology in medical practice.* Durham, NC: Duke University Press.

Munger, R. (1999). Prehospital care narratives: A time for reflection and professional growth. In J. M. Perkins & N. Blyler (Eds.), *Narrative and professional communication* (pp. 151–166). Stamford, CT: Ablex.

Munger, R. (2000). Evolution of the emergency medical services profession: A case study of EMS run reports. *Technical Communication Quarterly, 9*(3), 329–346.

Pigozzi, L. M. (2017). Negotiating informed consent: Bueno aconsejar, major remediar (it is good to give advice, but it is better to solve the problem). In L. Meloncon & J. B. Scott (Eds). *Methodologies of the rhetoric of health & medicine* (pp. 195–213). New York, NY: Routledge.

Porter, J. E., Sullivan, P., Blythe, S., Grabill, G. T., & Miles, L. (2000). Institutional critique: A rhetorical methodology for change. *College Composition and Communication, 51*(4), 610–642.

Regenstrief Institute. (2015). *About us.* Retrieved from www.regenstrief.org/aboutus/.

Schryer, C. (1993). Records as genre. *Written Communication, 10*(2), 200–234.

Segal, J. (2005). *Health and the rhetoric of medicine.* Carbondale, IL: Southern Illinois University Press.

Simmons, W. M. (2007). *Participation and power: Civic discourse in environmental policy decisions.* Albany, NY: SUNY Press.

Slack, J. D., Miller, D. J., & Doak, J. (1993). The technical communicator as author: Meaning, power, authority. *Journal of Business and Technical Communication,* 7(1), 12–36.

Spinuzzi, C. (2003). *Tracing genres through organizations: A sociocultural approach to information design.* Cambridge, MA: MIT Press.

Spinuzzi, C. (2013). How can technical communicators study work contexts? In J. Johnson-Eiola and S. Selber (Eds.), *Solving problems in technical communication* (pp. 262–284). Chicago, IL: University of Chicago Press.

Spoel, P., Harris, R., & Henwood, F. (2012). Healthy living: Metaphors we eat by? *Present Tense: A Journal of Rhetoric in Society,* 2(2).

Sullivan, P., & Porter, J. E. (1997). *Opening spaces: Writing technologies and critical research practices.* Westport, CT: Ablex Publishing.

Takayoshi, P., Tomlinson, E., & Castillo, J. (2012). The construction of research problems and methods. In K. Powell & P. Takayoshi (Eds.), *Practicing research in writing studies: Reflexive and ethically responsible research* (pp. 97–122). Cresskill, NJ: Hampton Press.

Teston, C. B. (2009). A grounded investigation of genred guidelines in cancer care deliberations, *Written Communication,* 26(3), 320–348.

Teston, C. B. (2012a). Considering confidentiality in research design: Developing heuristics to chart the un-chartable. In P. Takayoshi & K. Powell (Eds.), *Practicing research in writing studies: Reflections on ethically responsible research* (pp. 303–326). Cresskill, NJ: Hampton Press.

Teston, C. B. (2012b). Moving from artifact to action: A grounded investigation of visual displays of evidence during medical deliberations. *Technical Communication Quarterly* 21(3), 187–209.

Wiley, S. B. C., Sutko, D. M., & Moreno Becerra, T. (2010). Assembling social space. *The Communication Review,* 13(4), 340–372.

Zoller, H. M. (2005). Health activism: Communication theory and action for social change. *Communication Theory,* 15(4), 341–364.

Zoller, H., & Meloncon, L. (2013). The good neighbor campaign as a communication intervention to reduce health disparities. In G. Kreps & M. Dutta (Eds.), *Reducing health disparities: Communication interventions* (pp. 436–456). New York, NY: Peter Lang.

14

MEDICALIZED MOSQUITOES

Rhetorical Invention in Genetic Engineering for Disease Control

Molly Hartzog

Keywords: rhetoric of science, rhetorical invention, *topoi*, boundary objects, genetic engineering

Mosquitoes, to the majority of U.S. citizens who come in contact with them, are often thought of as a nuisance—a disruption to backyard summertime barbeques, but (relatively) easy to control with window screens, bug spray, tiki torches, and citronella candles. Of course, in many other areas of the tropical and subtropical world, mosquitoes are considered more than a nuisance; they are a threat to one's health and livelihood. Mosquito control efforts, in all areas of the world, have mostly involved pest-deterrent strategies to minimize human-mosquito contact. These include technologies like insecticides and bed nets. However, insecticide resistance in mosquitoes is a growing concern, on top of the known adverse health and environmental effects of insecticide use. Additionally, bed nets are not always successful for reasons of access, human use error, and the presence of daytime-biting mosquitoes. For these reasons, medical experts are turning to alternative pest management techniques, like genetic engineering, to minimize or eliminate the need for pest-deterrent strategies. These techniques, in a nutshell, alter the mosquito on a molecular level to either prohibit the mosquito from carrying and transmitting the target pathogen, or to restrict the mosquito in reproducing, thus decreasing the population of the target species. Reframing mosquito control in this way leads medical researchers to think of the mosquito as a technology of medical *intervention*, rather than a target for *elimination*. Thinking of the mosquito as something that can be manipulated and exploited to prohibit transmission of disease requires a very different rhetorical framework than thinking of the same organism as something that needs to be eliminated, or at least deterred from human contact. The former, thinking of the mosquito as a technology, might fall within the purview of rhetoric of science and technology (RST); the latter, thinking of the mosquito as a vector of disease, might fall within the purview of rhetoric of health & medicine (RHM). Each of these traditions of rhetorical scholarship are related, but also stand on their own merit. In my research on mosquitoes, I have found myself bouncing between the two areas of scholarship, depending upon the way in which I am framing the mosquito in my research questions.

In her annotated bibliography of RHM scholarship, Eberhard (2012) argued that RST has been one "access point" to studies in RHM. Earlier, in another review of RHM, Segal (2005) argued that rhetoric of health & medicine "is now at a place analogous to the place of rhetoric of science over twenty-five years ago" (p. 312). This place, she details, is the position of borrowing "rhetorical" work from a range of other fields that may or may not explicitly identify as rhetorical in order to build a canon of work that more fully distinguishes RHM as a field of inquiry. While division is sometimes helpful for creating new opportunities for research, as it has done for RHM, these same divisions can inhibit other opportunities of research that reside between the two spaces. In this chapter, I explore the intersections of RST and RHM using the case study of genetically modified mosquitoes. The case study itself demonstrates the interdependence of these two fields of inquiry—the genetically modified mosquito (a product of experimental scientific research, a subject of RST) is one response to the exigence of vector-borne diseases (an issue of public health, a subject of RHM). Additionally, this case study is positioned to respond to Keränen's (2011) call for "biocriticism" and Prelli's (2013) call for studies in rhetorical invention. This study examines discursive formations around the malaria mosquito to show how the mosquito is cross-conceptualized in two respects: 1) a vector of human disease, and 2) a technology of medical intervention. I borrow the concept of "boundary objects" from sociology to understand how researchers are working around the rhetorical constraints of the malaria mosquito, constructing and reconstructing it for different purposes.

In the following section, I provide an overview of the concept of boundary objects and its use in RST. Next, I outline some of the rhetorical constraints of defining species, drawing from literature in history and philosophy of science that addresses "the species problem" in the sciences. Following this, I analyze a proposal for the sequencing of several species of mosquitoes for malaria research, as well as a series of research papers on the distribution of malaria mosquitoes around the globe. In conclusion, I argue that understanding the mosquito as a vector of disease leads directly to understanding the mosquito as a medical technology. I argue that the boundary object of the mosquito, connecting the discursive formations of disease to those of medical interventions, could serve as a productive metaphor for understanding intersections between and doing research in the boundary between the RHM and the RST.

Boundary Objects, Boundary Work, and Science

Understanding organisms as species, and understanding a species as belonging to genus, a genus to a family, and so on, are practices of definition and classification. In the context of defining and classifying organisms, these are practices of identifying specific boundaries for one organism, or a set of organisms. It is no surprise, then, that the notion of the boundary object was developed out of a study of species and their function in museum research. The term boundary object was introduced by Star and Griesemer (1989) in their study of the work of Joseph Grinnell and Annie Alexander in Berkeley's Museum of Vertebrate Zoology.[1] They define boundary objects as

> those scientific objects which both inhabit several intersecting social worlds . . . *and* satisfy the informational requirements of each of them. Boundary objects are objects which are both plastic enough to adapt to local needs and the constraints of the several parties employing them, yet robust enough to maintain a common identity across sites. They are weakly structured in common use, and become strongly structured in individual-site use. These objects may be abstract or concrete. They have different meanings in different social worlds but their structure is common enough to more than one world to make them recognizable, a means of translation. The creation and management of boundary objects is a key process in developing and maintaining coherence across intersecting social worlds.
>
> *(p. 393)*

Star and Griesemer offer this notion as a mechanism to explain how cooperation occurs despite the heterogeneous nature of scientific work. They argue that consensus is not a requirement to achieve cooperation. Boundary objects, instead, provide points of stabilization among different social worlds, enabling members of these worlds to cooperate and collaborate. Boundary objects are both adaptable and rigid. They create boundaries between different social worlds in their exchange while also bridging these social worlds together. They both originate within different social worlds but are also exchanged between social worlds and adapt as they are exchanged.

Boundary objects, like *topoi*, provide places to generate new ideas. While *topoi* describe the relations between things, boundary objects are the things themselves; *topoi* are used for identifying, defining, and arranging these objects. Therefore, the exchange of a particular boundary object will evoke a plethora of inventional *topoi*. Narrowing focus on a few of the *topoi* that the object evokes can help a rhetor identify the relevant features of a boundary object in relation to an exigence. This is a recursive process—through identifying the boundaries of a centralizing boundary object, a rhetor is also refining her exigence. Elsewhere, this process has been called boundary work.

Boundary work, as it was first developed by Gieryn (1983), is the demarcation of science from nonscience; this involves defining what science *is* as well as defining what science *is not*. This concept has been widely used in rhetorical studies to describe the rhetorical work involved in demarcating boundaries in order to accomplish work (e.g., Miller, 2005). Wilson and Herndl (2007) take a different approach to boundary work by considering it alongside the concept of boundary objects in a way that "encourages an integrative rather than a demarcation exigence" (p. 132). What they are advocating here is an expansion of the idea of "boundaries" into "shared social, organizational, and discursive spaces" (p. 131). While Star and Griesemer's original idea of boundary objects also emphasizes how cooperation can occur among different social worlds with different interests, what Wilson and Herndl do for boundary objects is refine what can easily be an overused metaphor by opening the space of the "boundary" for rhetorical investigation. Opening this space brings into question how the object is defined and classified, or what *topoi* are used to describe its place in a specific rhetorical situation. It then becomes the work of the rhetorician to not only identify boundary objects and trace their exchange, but also to question what the object *does* for the conversation in different situations.

There is a wealth of literature in the history and philosophy of science on debates concerning species concepts and taxonomy. Much of this debate has involved demarcation and conflict in identifying the best possible means of defining and classifying organisms. In other words, these debates have engaged in boundary work for the purpose of creating boundary objects, objects that then become the subject of scientific research. The following section provides a brief overview of these debates and their rhetorical significance for defining species. By way of surveying the rhetorical nature of defining species, this section also provides an introduction to "tree thinking," or thinking of organisms in terms of their evolution, how they are related and change over time.

Species Concepts and Evolutionary Thinking

For many centuries, classification was established as an exploratory means of observing the natural world. Prior to Darwin's work on evolution, this was easy, as species were primarily understood to be stable, created, and unchanging entities. There was no need to question what makes a pigeon a pigeon, because it was understood to have always been a pigeon. This understanding lent itself to ideas like the *scala naturae* that put species on a hierarchy based on their affinity to a singular deity (Pietsch, 2012). The goal of this type of classification was to illustrate harmony and creation (Mayr, 1982). It was based on the idea of essentialism, which argues that organisms have an essence (or *eidos*) that is identifiable and classifiable: the pigeon's pigeoness is a type of birdness, and so on.

Darwin's evolutionary theory created a number of rhetorical problems for science. Under this theory, species are understood to be changing, dynamic entities that do not have clear, well-defined boundaries. However, the need for a stable system of communication requires that researchers agree upon, if only temporarily, a universal definition of specific species. In *Origin*, Darwin problematized the issue of species and thus their classification by illustrating how organisms exist on a continuum rather than as discretely compartmentalized (and created) entities (Ghiselin, 1969). Darwin's novel way of looking at species is a result of his novel method for conducting work in natural history. He borrowed from geologists a way of looking at the earth chronologically, that is looking at past events as explanatory devices for present phenomena (Ghiselin, 1969), such as earthquakes forming the mountains of Chile, or volcanoes forming atolls. Darwin's theory of evolution by natural selection looked at the history of a "species" to explain its current development.

Darwin's theory of evolution created a difficult rhetorical problem. In order to persuade others of the mechanisms of evolution by natural selection, Darwin had to use the prevailing species concept of the time (species as stable, created entities). However, his theory debunked this very notion (Beatty, 1992). According to Beatty, Darwin resolved this dilemma by "formulat[ing] his position in terms of the evolution of what naturalists call 'species' and 'varieties,' . . . but [Darwin] was also able to communicate and defend a position concerning the undefinability of those terms" (p. 239). Darwin did not undo the species concept; rather, he proposed a process for the development of species. This enabled him to show the lack of distinction between what naturalists call "species" and "varieties." In fact, Darwin did not seem very concerned with a definition of the concept at all, according to Beatty (1992): "Darwin felt that natural history would be liberated by abandoning the search for [a definition of 'species']—liberated in particular from the constraints of nonevolutionary thinking built into pre-Darwinian definitions of the term" (p. 243).

Darwin added the idea that these classifications were relations of degree and time, not of parts. In other words, he shifted the conversation to draw from different *koinoi topoi*. Despite his desire to keep the definition of species fluid, Darwin did not believe that species did not exist; to make this claim would prevent one from seeing any evidence for evolution. We need species to understand evolution, but we need them to be fluid in order for the theory to hold true (Winsor, 2013). This idea, though, puts classification in a quandary. When species change, grading into one another, it becomes difficult to impose boundaries without recognizing a certain degree of artificiality. In fact, it even becomes difficult to discuss what we recognize as "species" (Ghiselin, 1969).

Classification should be both a way of communicating with the natural science community and a source of invention—it should tell us something about the natural world (Mayr, 1982). This tension between the need for a stable communication system, and for our system of communication to reflect evolutionary theory was the spark of the "taxonomy wars" that, interestingly, did not gain full steam until the mid-20th century. It was around this time that the work of Willi

Hennig, considered the "father of phylogenetics," gained popularity. Phylogenetics attempts to illustrate a tree of life that reflects the actual ancestry of organisms through the principle of maximum parsimony, which states that the most plausible tree will involve the fewest possible splits. However, the problem with using phylogenetics to create a system of classification is that as new data are discovered about species, the tree of life may potentially be entirely reconfigured, making it a very unstable form of communication. In other words, phylogenies are always working hypotheses, not stable categories (Benton, 2000).

My reason for including this detailed (yet still brief) overview of species concepts and taxonomy is to demonstrate the rhetorical problems presented by evolutionary theory. Under this theory, species are understood to be changing, dynamic entities that do not have clear, well-defined boundaries. Nearly a century after Darwin, a system of taxonomy based on his theory, called phylogenetics, gained purchase in the wider scientific community as a valuable model for thinking. This type of thinking, now often referred to as "evolutionary thinking" or "tree thinking," involves considering an organism in terms of its membership in a species, that species' relationship to other species, and its development over long stretches of time and many generations.[2] In the following section, I explore one specific case that demonstrates the tension between "tree thinking" and the need for a stable system for communication.

The Consequences of Classification on Mosquitoes and Malaria

These debates about classification in biology are not merely debates over our choice in terminology or how we choose to organize species like we organize books in a library. These choices have direct consequences for the way research is conducted. The case of vector-borne diseases and pest management provides apt illustrations of the kinds of consequences these decisions bring to bear. The following analysis is based on a white paper that proposed the sequencing and further research on 13 specific mosquito species known to transmit malaria, and three research articles (published as a sequence) that provide reports on the distribution of known vectors of malaria. I perform a close reading of these texts in order to understand the warrants for defining and classifying specific species of mosquitoes as "malaria mosquitoes," specifically in terms of traits that define their "vectorial capacity," or ability to serve as a disease vector. As I demonstrate below, rhetorical invention in malaria research is constrained by the complex taxonomic status of the species that are known to transmit the disease.

Malaria-transmitting mosquitoes provide an interesting example of evolutionary development. There are approximately 500 known species in the *Anopheles* family. All mosquitoes that transmit malaria are in the *Anopheles* genus, but not all *Anopheles* mosquitoes transmit malaria. To be specific, only ~30 species are currently known to transmit malaria. Furthermore, those species that transmit malaria are not necessarily closely related. From an evolutionary perspective, this seems counterintuitive. Generally speaking, species that share similar attributes are generally assumed to be related. However, this line of thought assumes that such attributes or traits only evolve once. When looking at vectorial capacity in mosquitoes, phylogenists would conclude that this ability must have evolved more than once. Figuring out why and how this ability has evolved then becomes a central question to malaria control efforts. Once it is known how vectorial capacity evolves, geneticists can then develop a method of intervention to disrupt disease transmission that is applicable to all malaria vectors.

Collectively, these constraints of the *Anopheles* family tree serve as the warrant in a white paper that calls for the sequencing and comparative genome analyses of 13 anopheline mosquitoes (Besansky et al., 2008). This paper was compiled by the *Anopheles* Genome Cluster Committee, a group of 13 scientists from universities at Cambridge, London, Liverpool, Yale, Pennsylvania, and others, chaired by Nora Besansky at Notre Dame. According to an email published in an appendix to the paper, this paper was shared over a professional email list in May 2007 to solicit endorsement from the wider scientific community in order "to assess the size and strength of the community of potential users of these sequence data" proposed in the paper. In just two weeks' time, the authors indicated they received support from over 70 scientists.

The authors divide the 13 proposed species into three tiers. Tier 1 includes *An. Arabiensis, An. quadriannulatus, An. merus, and An. epiroticus* (formerly *An. sundaicus* species A), which were chosen because they are considered "the species most closely related to *An. gambiae*," which is widely considered the most important malaria vector (p. 9). Tier 2 includes seven additional species that represent the "most evolutionary diversity" present within the subgenus that is represented in tier 1, with divergence times ranging from 10,000 years ago to 40–50 million years ago. Tier 3 represents species the authors consider to be "outgroups" respective to malaria transmission; these species extend evolutionary divergence up to 100 million years ago. In this proposal, the authors are using a form of tree thinking to make the case for research on these 13 species—each tier branches out from the previous, with relatedness to *An. gambiae* serving as the "anchor" for the project. This particular species is actually referred to as a "species complex" that "comprises seven formally recognized species that vary considerably in vectorial capacity, from the nominal *An. gambiae*, considered the world's most important malaria vector, to its non-vector sibling *An. quadriannulatus*" (p. 2).

Given that malaria-transmitting mosquitoes are not necessarily closely related, determining how vectorial ability has evolved becomes a central point of concern. The importance of vectorial capacity in anopheline mosquitoes can be summarized in two important points provided by the authors:

> First, because vectors from different complexes are not closely related, at least some of the underlying vector traits arose independently multiple

times in different lineages. Second, the presence of both vector and non-vector species in the same species complex implies either rapid loss or rapid gain of "vector traits". Thus, at least some of the genes that are associated with vectorial capacity—whether involved in immunity, host-preference, or some other physiological or behavioral response—are likely to be rapidly evolving rather than highly conserved over long evolutionary distances. In particular, genes associated with behaviors like preference for human blood meals, selection of anthropogenic breeding sites, or preference to rest inside human dwellings, all of which represent 'use of' the human environment, are likely to be very recent evolutionary adaptations that postdate human cultural innovations such as the development of agriculture and animal husbandry that enabled the human populations to reach high and stable (i.e. non-nomadic) densities.

(p. 3)

While these authors are fighting against the usual line of thought that "species with similar attributes must be related," the underlying assumption in their reasoning for choosing these 13 species for genomic analysis is that vectorial capacity must evolve for similar reasons or in a similar manner. This could turn out to be yet another constraint, given that there is clearly no "one size fits all" approach to understanding anopheline mosquitoes. In the paragraph following the above quotation, the authors make this assumption a bit more explicit:

The traits that impact a mosquito's role in malaria transmission are known, in principle. They include susceptibility of the mosquito to the parasite throughout the entire sporogonic stage, and mosquito population density, longevity, and bloodfeeding behavior. Acquisition of genome assemblies for the mosquito species highlighted in this proposal is critical for understanding the genetic basis for these traits.

(p. 3)

The authors here are building to the conclusion that once the evolutionary basis of these traits is understood, we would be able to apply this information across different species, closely related or not. This is quite explicitly stated in the conclusion of the paper:

The entire community of vector biologists and parasitologists who are seeking novel solutions for controlling malaria will benefit from the availability of additional anopheline genome sequence data. *An. gambiae* represents *the* model organism for the study of malaria vector biology and control. Our ultimate goal is to extract from its genome information that will expedite development of new malaria control methods, both chemical and genetic, that will alter vectorial capacity.

(p. 10)

To work around the constraint that vector species of malaria are not nicely grouped together on a phylogenetic tree, these authors are proposing to use a different form of tree. The authors are essentially proposing to use *An. gambiae* as the "trunk" and branch out from there using vectorial capacity rather than common ancestry as the connective thread. While I do not intend to discredit this line of thinking, I do wish to bring attention to the new set of constraints (whether enabling or restricting) that accompany it. As I mention above, this line of thinking assumes that vectorial capacity traits evolve for the same reasons and in the same way across species, albeit at different times. Should this be accurate, we would then have a control technique that would be transportable, or applicable to all vectors, thus, theoretically speaking, eliminating the spread of disease. While the broader malaria research community has recognized that *eradication* of the disease may be an unattainable goal, it seems that these researchers are still holding out hope for this outcome.

Understanding the important role of vectorial capacity in malaria control research helps to situate a more recent project that focused on mapping the distribution of known malaria vectors. This project was published as three research papers that focus on malaria vectors in the Americas (Sinka et al., 2010b); Africa, Europe, and the Middle East (Sinka et al., 2010a); and the Asia–Pacific region (Sinka et al., 2011). The authors explicitly state the goal of this series of three articles in the final article on the Asia–Pacific region:

> This article concludes a project aimed to *establish the contemporary global distribution of the [dominant vector species] of malaria.* The three articles produced are intended as a detailed reference for scientists continuing research into the aspects of taxonomy, biology and ecology relevant to species-specific vector control. This research is particularly relevant to help unravel the complicated taxonomic status, ecology and epidemiology of the vectors of the Asia–Pacific region. All the occurrence data, predictive maps and EO-shape files generated during the production of these publications will be made available in the public domain. We hope that this will encourage data sharing to improve future iterations of the distribution maps.
>
> *(Sinka et al., 2011, p. 1, emphasis added)*

In these articles, the authors focus on mapping the distribution of known malaria vectors in each of these three regions. Vectors are mapped based on biting habit (inside or outside), feeding habit (human or animal), biting time (day, dusk, night, dawn), prefeeding resting habit (inside or outside), postfeeding resting habit (inside or outside), larval sites (light intensity, salinity, turbidity, movement, and vegetation, natural, artificial or man-made). The options listed are not mutually exclusive; for example, *An. albimanus* is both anthropophilic and zoophilic, meaning it feeds on both human and nonhuman animals. Additionally, some of these species don't differ at all based on these descriptors; for example, *An. albimanus* shares the exact same characteristics listed as *An. aquasalis*, and is only different from *An. albitarsis* in that *An. albitarsis* has some evidence of endophilic postfeeding resting habit, meaning that the species has been known to rest inside human habitats after feeding.

The authors choose to focus on these characteristics because they encompass the behaviors that they believe affect the disease transmission cycle, and thus provide some insight into vectorial capacity. Focusing on behaviors that are connected to disease transmission enables scientists to explore where those behaviors can be manipulated or disrupted to break the transmission cycle. What this does not consider is the role of humans, nonfeeding related habits of the mosquito, or the biology of the malaria pathogen. Given that these reports were published in *Parasites & Vectors*, the intended audience is entomologists and experts in related fields. The other aspects of the general ecology of malaria transmission would be relegated to experts in other fields such as epidemiology and virology.

Working from the perspective of vectorial capacity, there are major taxonomic constraints in malaria control. The authors of the mapping projects identify "species sympatry," meaning two species that cohabitate but do not interbreed, as one such constraint. The assumption with species sympatry is that the two species were once a single species and at some point in the past diverged. To help work around this constraint in mapping dominant vector species, the authors propose "an overview of the life history characteristics (bionomics) of vector species pertinent to epidemiology and control" (Sinka et al., 2010b, p. 2). Bionomics, the authors explain,

> highlights DVS [dominant vector species] behaviour and life-history characteristics that are relevant for mosquito control, but also clearly indicates *the marked behavioural plasticity* of each species. The influence of human behaviour such as insecticide use, environmental disturbance to a greater or lesser extent, or host activities in the evening and night also drive local variation in species bionomics. Moreover, concerns regarding species identity also add to the uncertainty in categorising species behaviour and thus local, expert knowledge must be consulted when interpreting or acting on the data summarised here.
>
> *(Sinka et al., 2010a, p. 20, emphasis added)*

The authors here point to the use of species as boundary objects quite explicitly. The authors are choosing those characteristics that they see as relevant to malaria control for this particular audience of mosquito experts, but indicating flexibility in the transmission-related behavior of each species, thus flexibility in how they are defined by this community. Related to the constraint of species sympatry is the concept of "species complexes" that encompass a group of closely related, morphologically indistinguishable species, which may occur in sympatry (but not interbreeding) yet still display behavioral differences that could confound any control efforts that ignore their bionomics and epidemiological importance.

Moreover, even amongst those species that are not members of a complex, behavioral differences are common depending upon location, such that a species can be considered a primary vector in one area but of secondary or no importance elsewhere. The correct identification of any vector implicated in malaria transmission is key to successful control (Sinka et al., 2011, p. 2).

Here we see that these boundary objects remain rigid in their evolutionary relatedness, but flexible in the behavioral characteristics that are related to vectorial capacity, enabling the authors to demarcate species of interest (those that transmit malaria) and behavioral characteristics of interest (those related to malaria transmission to humans). Given their goal of mapping species distribution based on these characteristics, the authors identify one major constraint that impacts their results. Discussing interventions that limit human–mosquito contact, such as insecticides, repellant, and bed nets, the authors write:

> These interventions are often deployed without a detailed understanding of the distribution, species composition and behaviour of local vectors. This complicates impact monitoring, the appraisal of arguments for more holistic integrated vector control and evaluation of the potential of novel vector control methods. Distribution maps can also be applied to gauge the importance of emerging insecticide resistance among the DVS of Africa. In contrast to Africa, the European and the Middle Eastern region contain areas with low to no malaria transmission. Despite this, the existence of *Anopheles* species with the capacity to transmit malaria is often highlighted as providing the potential for the re-introduction of malaria.
>
> *(Sinka et al., 2010a, p. 2)*

Related to this constraint of the impact of current pest control strategies is the constraint of insecticide resistance. This is a major ongoing issue in many pest control initiatives, mosquito and otherwise. These authors conduct some explicit demarcation boundary work to justify their exclusion of insecticide resistance:

> The bionomics summary of each species is included to accompany the predictive maps as the success of interventions and control methods . . . in reducing malaria transmission is closely related to the behavioural characteristics of the local DVS [dominant vector species]. This review does not, however, include detailed information relating to insecticide resistance. This was a purposeful omission as it would not be possible to do full justice to this highly dynamic and important aspect of the DVS within the space confines of the current work. Moreover, insecticide resistance is being addressed in detail by other groups, including those at the Liverpool School of Tropical Medicine and the Innovative Vector Control Consortium (IVCC).
>
> *(Sinka et al., 2010a, p. 4)*

Additionally, the authors point to another constraint involving human development that they were also unable to consider in their review:

> Moreover, in an increasingly changing environment, deforestation, the implementation of new irrigation programmes and expanding agricultural development can rapidly alter the composition of the local mosquito fauna, and subsequently influence the control methods required.
>
> *(Sinka et al., 2011, p. 3)*

In sum, the authors of this series of articles addressing the global distribution of dominant vector species of malaria employ strategies of boundary work to demarcate a certain set of behavioral and taxonomic characteristics that they see as relevant to the control of malaria, thus creating an operational (if not comprehensive) definition and classification of the dominant vector species. Sinka et al. attempts to identify patterns in these plastic aspects of the mosquito behavior that are common among all malaria vectors in order to identify an appropriate intervention strategy to disrupt the transmission cycle. These issues are particularly salient in the authors' analysis of vector species in the Asia-Pacific region:

> Simple, universal species-specific statements regarding the biology of these vectors are nearly impossible due to the locational diversity in behaviour and sympatric distributions of sibling species that contributes to a level of complexity not seen amongst the DVS of other regions. Here we have indicated the *behavioural plasticity* and *locational variation* in species behaviour where possible, and also where known and suspected species complexes exist. However, *until the taxonomic situation is resolved*, the behaviour of many of these DVS will remain unclear.
>
> *(Sinka et al., 2011, p. 32, emphasis added)*

Conclusion

This chapter explored the rhetorical form "mosquito" takes in the discourse on pest control research for malaria. Considering the mosquito as a boundary object and investigating the boundary work that scientists engage in to define this object reveals some of the inventional strategies that are used in malaria research. The mosquito moves from being considered an object to be eliminated to an object that facilitates its own control. As defined by Star and Griesemer (1989), boundary objects are objects that are both robust enough to retain a common identity across different boundaries, and plastic enough to be adapted to local needs. In the world of molecular control of malaria, scientists are defining the malaria-transmitting *Anopheles* mosquitoes by a specific set of behaviors related to the blood-feeding cycle and, by extension, malaria transmission. These scientists are using a form of tree thinking that pushes against the assumption that "organisms with similar attributes must be related," by using *Anopheles gambiae* as the "anchor species" for legitimizing research on other malaria-transmitting species. Because not all vectors of malaria are closely related, and not all closely-related mosquitoes transmit malaria, these scientists are required to make the assumption that vectorial capacity evolved more than once. It then becomes critical to understand *how* and *why* this particular trait evolved in order for scientists to develop a strategy that would be applicable to all species that carry the malaria pathogen. This shift from studying *that* mosquitoes have vectorial capacity to *how* and *why* this trait evolves is the critical shift I wish to point out with this study. This is a significant conceptual shift involving the repositioning of the mosquito as *cause* to the mosquito as *means*. Importantly, this conceptual shift creates a new terministic screen, one that potentially ignores the role of human biology, pathogen biology, and environmental variables.

The complexities around the taxonomic status of the dominant vector species (DVS) of malaria pose significant constraints to rhetorical invention. In the case of malaria research, the inventional framework provided by evolutionary theory falls short because the species that are known to transmit malaria are not closely related. This constraint led researchers to employ a variation of tree thinking that uses the special *topos* of vectorial capacity in place of "evolutionary relatedness" to develop a system for organizing and prioritizing species of interest to malaria researchers. This replacement enables the researchers to not only formulate a stable method of communication about dominant vector species of malaria, but also to continue to use evolutionary thinking as a method of rhetorical invention. To put this back into the terms of boundary objects, evolutionary relatedness remains rigid to create a stable method of communication, and the behaviors related to vectorial capacity become the plastic features that adapt to the local needs of the area or species of study. In this way, malaria researchers are using points of tension between their practical needs as researchers and the theoretical framework of evolution as productive sites of rhetorical invention. The complex taxonomic status of malaria vectors created the exigence for developing an alternative *topos* of invention: vectorial capacity.

This *topos* of vectorial capacity bridges two contrastive conceptualizations of the mosquito: 1) as a vector of human disease, and 2) as a tool for disease control. The *Anopheles* mosquito is employed as a boundary object in this research community, defined by the characteristics that are seen as central to the transmission of human disease, the same characteristics which are exploited to create a genetically modified mosquito that will stop the transmission of disease. This *topos* of vectorial capacity, then, leads directly from understanding the mosquito as a vector to understanding the mosquito as a technology of medical intervention. Exploring this path from the discursive formations of disease to discursive formations of medical interventions, and vice versa, could be a productive line of inquiry in both RHM and RST. Following this path from disease to medical intervention could make the boundary between the two areas a productive space of rhetorical inquiry in and of itself, leading scholars to new assumptions and approaches to rhetorical problem solving.[3] Rather than thinking of the two areas as simply "interrelated," or one as an "offshoot" of the other, conceptualizing the boundary as a productive space could help us formulate strong identities for each field and simultaneously understand when and where the two can productively inform each other and work together to address health issues.

Notes

1 See Nathan R. Johnson (this volume) for a fascinating use of the concepts of boundary objects and boundary work to develop an infrastructural approach to rhetoric of health & medicine. Much like my own case study, Johnson shows how objects are transformed into classification systems used for health care intervention strategies.
2 Entire textbooks (e.g., *Tree Thinking: An Introduction to Phylogenetic Biology* by Baum and Smith [2013]) and journals (e.g., *Trends in Ecology and Evolution* [*TREE*]) are devoted to promoting this type of thinking.
3 In this volume, David R. Gruber similarly calls for a productive boundary space between the "rhetoric of neuroscience" and the "neuroscience of rhetoric."

References

Baum, D. A., & Smith, S. D. (2013). *Tree thinking: An introduction to phylogenetic biology*. Greenwood Village, CO: Roberts.

Beatty, J. (1992). Speaking of species: Darwin's strategy. In M. Ereshefsky (Ed.), *The units of evolution* (pp. 227–246). Cambridge, MA: MIT Press.

Benton, M. J. (2000). Stems, nodes, crown clades, and rank-free lists: Is Linnaeus dead? *Biological Reviews of the Cambridge Philosophical Society*, 75(4), 633–648.

Besansky, N. J., Ashburner, M., Carlton, J. M., Coetzee, M., Collins, F. H., della Torre, A., . . . Wirtz, R. (2008). *Genome analysis of vectorial capacity in major anopheles vectors of malaria parasites*. Retrieved from www.vectorbase.org/projects/genome-analysis-vectorial-capacity-major-anopheles-vectors-malaria-parasites.

Eberhard, J. M. (2012). Rhetoric of health & medicine. *Present Tense: A Journal of Rhetoric in Society*, 2(2). Retrieved from www.presenttensejournal.org/volume-2/an-annotated-bibliography-of-literature-on-the-rhetoric-of-health-and-medicine/.

Ghiselin, M. (1969). *The triumph of the darwinian method*. Berkeley, CA: University of California Press.

Gieryn, T. F. (1983). Boundary-work and the demarcation of science from non-science: Strains and interests in professional ideologies of scientists. *American Sociological Review*, 48(6), 781–795.

Keränen, L. (2011). Addressing the epidemic of epidemics: Germs, security, and a call for biocriticism. *Quarterly Journal of Speech*, 97(2), 224–244. doi:10.1080/00335630.2011.565785.

Mayr, E. (1982). *The growth of biological thought: Diversity, evolution, and inheritance*. Cambridge: Belknap Press.

Miller, C. R. (2005). Novelty and heresy in the debate on nonthermal effects of electromagnetic fields. In *Rhetoric and incommensurability* (pp. 464–505). Retrieved from http://www4.ncsu.edu/~crmiller/Publications/MillerParlorPress05.pdf.

Pietsch, T. W. (2012). *Trees of life: A visual history of evolution*. Baltimore, MD: The Johns Hopkins University Press.

Prelli, L. J. (2013). The prospect of invention in rhetorical studies of science, technology, and medicine. *Poroi, 9*(1). doi:10.13008/2151–2957.1164.

Scott, J. B., Segal, J. Z., & Keränen, L. (2013). The rhetorics of health and medicine: Inventional possibilities for scholarship and engaged practice. *Poroi, 9*(1). doi:10.13008/2151-2957.1157.

Segal, J. Z. (2005). Interdisciplinarity and bibliography in the rhetoric of health & medicine. *Technical Communication Quarterly, 14*(3), 311–318.

Sinka, M. E., Bangs, M. J., Manguin, S., Coetzee, M., Mbogo, C. M., Hemingway, J., . . . Hay, S. I. (2010a). The dominant Anopheles vectors of human malaria in Africa, Europe and the Middle East : Occurrence data, distribution maps and bionomic précis. *Parasites & Vectors, 3*(1), 117. doi:10.1186/1756-3305-3-117.

Sinka, M. E., Bangs, M. J., Manguin, S., Chareonviriyaphap, T., Patil, A. P., Temperley, W. H., . . . Hay, S. I. (2011). The dominant Anopheles vectors of human malaria in the Asia-Pacific region: Occurrence data, distribution maps and bionomic précis. *Parasites & Vectors, 4*(89). doi:10.1186/1756-3305-4-89.

Sinka, M. E., Rubio-palis, Y., Manguin, S., Patil, A. P., Temperley, W. H., Gething, P. W., . . . Hay, S. I. (2010b). The dominant Anopheles vectors of human malaria in the Americas: Occurrence data, distribution maps and bionomic précis. *Parasites & Vectors, 3*(72), 1–26.

Star, S. L., & Griesemer, J. R. (1989). Institutional ecology, "translations" and boundary objects : Amateurs and professionals in Berkeley's museum of vertebrate zoology, 1907–1939. *Social Studies of Science, 19*(3), 387–420.

Wilson, G., & Herndl, C. G. (2007). Boundary objects as rhetorical exigence: Knowledge mapping and interdisciplinary cooperation at the Los Alamos National Laboratory. *Journal of Business and Technical Communication, 21*(2), 129–154.

Winsor, M. P. (2013). Darwin and taxonomy. In M. Ruse (Ed.), *The Cambridge encyclopedia of Darwin and evolutionary thought* (pp. 72–79). New York, NY: Cambridge University Press.

15

EXPERIMENTS IN RHETORIC

Invention and Neurorhetorical Play

David R. Gruber

Keywords: brain, computational, ecological, experiment, invention, multi-plicity, neurorhetoric

Rhetoric and related fields continue to explore and expand ecological perspectives inclusive of the body, affect, and materiality (Rice, 2008; Blackman, 2012; Rickert, 2013; Hawhee, 2015). Such efforts foster engagement with biological and neurobiological research. Scholars in neurorhetorics, for instance, have pursued a "neuroscience of rhetoric" that evaluates the potential for new brain findings to contribute to rhetorical theory (Jack, 2010; 2014; Mays & Jung, 2012; Gruber, 2013, 2014a; Littlefield, 2015). These engagements compliment Felicity Callard and Desmond Fitzgerald's (2014) recent call for the social sciences to "look to the neurosciences" for a future of experimental research and to craft new "entanglements" (p. 6).

Rhetoricians studying the biomedical sciences have examined research and even entered labs to engage the matter/s of life. Celeste Condit (Bates et al., 2003; Condit et al., 2002), for instance, teamed with a genetics lab and published cross-disciplinary, collaborative papers. T. Kenny Fountain (2014) conducted a multiyear study of anatomy labs, examining how medical students approach and think about the use of cadavers. Scott Graham (2015) reviewed neuroimaging and pain diagnosis, hearing from both patients and doctors. Despite the compelling nature of these various interactions with the body and biomedical communities, rhetorical scholars have for the most part avoided dipping into the experimental.

Hesitations to fashion formal experiments in rhetoric come with good reasons, of course. As a field, rhetoric has not been interested in simplified, staged settings. Following Aristotle's analysis of political speeches before crowds and, much later in the 20th century, Kenneth Burke's analysis of the psychological effects of mythical images and vocabularies mediating in situ human interactions (Burke, 1969, pp. 202–224), scholars' interests tended to follow suit. Discourse in action, set in specific times and places, not only offered a chance to experience rhetorics firsthand but left a record upon which scholars could test, tease, and sometimes torment those familiar concepts of the rhetorical tradition—audience, purpose, arrangement, etc. Setting up a lab or forming a controlled experiment, as in the neurosciences, for instance, would not only be a move beyond the training and probably the comfort of most rhetoricians, but could sit uncomfortably with roles in which rhetoricians are already somewhat welcome: 1) developing theories of science and medicine, including how such areas are practiced, socially negotiated, and then communicated to the public, and 2) helping scientists and medical professionals to communicate their findings to the public.[1]

More than this, rhetoricians have a longstanding commitment to the rhetoricalness of the world. As Barbara Biesecker and John Louis Lucaites (2009) explain, once "the signified in any given case" is made "the retroactive effect of the situated circulation of signifiers themselves," then the entire world is "necessarily rhetorical" (p. 7). In seeing the world as composed both with *and against* materiality and seeing the body itself as both signifying *and asignifying* materiality, the world becomes "rhetorical" but also "other than" the circulation of signifiers. The body, as Richard Marback (2008) notes, must be "given its due" (p. 46). Accordingly, experimental settings might make more known and offer an alternative approach to constructing understandings of material interactions; experimental approaches hold the potential to participate in, as Graham and Herndl (2013) puts it, a "postplural rhetoric of science," which brings multiple ontologies into appearance through different means of "touching" and does not presume things to be in alignment with discourses or circulating symbolic compositions.

In this chapter, I want to consider how the study of the body and affect might compel the rhetoric of science and medicine to transform in experimental directions. Rhetorical scholars, I contend, have no a priori reason to sit satisfied with analyzing how the body has been scientifically composed in medical arenas in advance of rhetorical theorizing. There are rhetorical questions and theoretical inquiries that cannot draw on the existing research of the biomedical sciences to find an answer. At the same time, turning to experimental protocols might prove valuable when a rhetorical analysis of biomedical discourses exposes distinct areas of discontent; rhetoricians may find remedy in collaboration and revised approaches to scientific materiality directly informed by rhetoric. The case studies reviewed in this chapter bring this latter point to the fore.

With that noted, building a cross-disciplinary team and/or redesigning hands-on practices is not always a straightforward matter. Yet, it is also, importantly, not tantamount to adopting a simplistic logical strategy of suggesting that because more of X (the body, affect, etc.) is now desired, therefore Y, experimental approaches are needed. Rather, experimental entanglements, I hope to show, prove their own value in specific times and places, just as the neurosciences have value on their own grounds and can certainly offer new insights or avenues of exploration to rhetoric when rhetoricians are open to considering them and when the questions being asked prove relevant.

The full impact of what it means to confront materiality in rhetoric may not yet be fully absorbed in the field, but implications for methodological pluralism loom large, especially at a time when methods are expanding and nonsymbolic and asignifying effects and affects occupy the minds of so many rhetoricians (e.g., Muckelbauer, 2007; Rivers, 2014; Hawhee, 2015; Rice, 2015). Perhaps, the balanced question for now is whether specific experimental approaches fitting to the rhetoric of science and medicine can be developed and shared with colleagues having a different expertise and can be pursued without leaving behind what rhetoricians do best. Before answering this, we might remember rhetoric's longstanding connection to science. Randy Harris (2013) points out that Aristotle pursued a "scientific" approach, Gorgias discussed the physiological effects of persuasion, and Kenneth Burke probed "universal structures" of signification (pp. 1–2); consequently, Harris notes that science bubbles within "our very disciplinary origins" (p. 1). Taking his comments as inspiration for further investigation into experimental approaches, I explore what an experimental rhetoric within the sciences of the brain (within a neurorhetoric) might be. I actively pursue the *experimental*—a term I intentionally use with productive ambiguity to mean both scientific experiment and playful, new ways of working—with the brain sciences.

In particular, I aim to show how rhetorical scholars can exercise what they already know and stay grounded in "real-life" situated analysis, as well as continue to study texts when appropriate, while still stretching outward to the environments where experiments benefit more traditional modes of rhetorical inquiry. In doing so, I explore two neuroscience-rhetoric projects as case studies. The first forges a textual, rhetorical critique of neuroscience literature and then builds a partnership with researchers in the cognitive neurosciences to develop a new brain scan experiment and reshape foundational premises based on rhetorical insights. The second remediates a set of neuroscience findings through algorithmic, computational means with the aim of visualizing different interpretations of that finding amid neuroscientific debate; the project aims to see what might surface through alternative practices, bringing different textual interpretations of the brain to life insofar as a viewer experiences them as artistic visualizations. I review the methodological procedures of each in reference to its aims and outcomes, discussing constraints and affordances. I also discuss the two projects together because they both engage the brain sciences but also demonstrate a principle of practical play and collegial mutuality in forging experimental approaches to questions of rhetoric.

Ultimately, I argue that a neuroscience of rhetoric can be, and would benefit from being, a *neurorhetorical performance* seeking *invention* and residing at the corner of play and experimentation. Here, following scholars like Andrew Pickering

(1995), Annemarie Mol (2002), and Scott Graham and Herndl (2013; 2015), I advocate a move from seeing neuroscience (and biomedical science more generally) as a representational enterprise that unveils a singular material reality to a collaborative process that performs material—and many possible/plural—realities. In so doing, I intend to show not only how the social and symbolic are embedded in neuroscience research processes such that rhetorical scholars can analyze how neuroscience is made and legitimized, but also push toward the notion that rhetorical scholars can and have already started to pursue new, exciting forms of joint research practices through play and experimentation, practices that expose alternative material realities ultimately benefitting both neuroscience and rhetoric.

I take Callard and Fitzgerald's (2014) claim about the immense importance of "the science of life" seriously. However, I do not reify an epistemological hierarchy with the science of life illuminating the way for humanities inquiry; instead, I situate rhetorical scholars as contributors and engineers[2] amid a future opening to transdisciplinary collaborations and mixed methods. This effort compliments Keränen's (2013) call for rhetorical scholars to examine "artifacts" and "material practices," and it corroborates Graham's (2015) call to give attention to ontology. However, I want to emphasize here the unpredictability of building with others in unfamiliar environments, in not following a particular discursive method with a set of defined steps (find X type of text, look for Y discourse, connect to an old concept in rhetoric, etc.); rather, I celebrate stepping out to follow a meandering path—inquiry as experimental activity. My reasoning is similar to Stephen Ramsay's (2011) when he asks Digital Humanities scholars to build and to directly engage the dirty material processes of digital media. Likewise, I herein assert the role of experimental design and hands-on play with a medical and scientific apparatus as a legitimate mean to approach materiality rhetorically. If we cannot expect a Digital Humanist to be ignorant of programming languages, clueless about algorithms, and unfamiliar with the technical processes happening behind the screen, what might we then expect of rhetorical scholars critiquing scientific epistemologies and commenting on ontologies in the rhetoric of science and medicine? In this volume, Molly Hartzog's examination of the mosquito body as a technology of medical intervention and Nathan Johnson's attention to infrastructures of science and medicine underscore the importance of engaging structures, layouts, processes, and practices. Indeed, if rhetorical analysis is now, more than ever, tied to medical machines, diagnosis charts, patient record systems, as well as the physical structure of bodies and the affective experiences of patients, then working alongside of and getting right "inside the scenes" of science and medicine is essential.

At the same time, we need a workable and balanced approach to what Scott and Meloncon (this volume) describe as a "vast array" of "multilayered" discursive-material practices in science and medicine. Noting that critiques of reductionist tendencies in the sciences may at times clash with experimental approaches to the body and affect only intensifies the importance of discovering a new, open and imaginative approach that builds from rhetoric's sense of self and yet avoids abrogating the need for experiments in rhetoric. Consequently, I herein advocate a type of rhetorical building that aims to blend disciplinary boundaries not only because rhetoric pursues interaction and methodological pluralism at a time when scholars lend (perhaps ever greater) agency to bodies and practices, but because this way of moving pushes past a stifling division between (perceived) scientific and rhetorical enterprises.

A key clarification is useful here. Focusing on the conceptual and practical spaces in between disciplines is not a reification of the kind of limited invention solely attentive to "perspectives of or about science" as advocated by Lawrence Prelli (2013) in his article about invention in the rhetoric of science and medicine. He remains strongly rooted to "the identification, analysis, and criticism of commonplaces" and is focused almost entirely on texts and discourses (pp. 2–3). Instead, I advocate what John Muckelbauer (2009) calls "rhetorical invention," the search for a pragmatic middle space between old dualities and dialectical negations. That is to say, I search for productive avenues of conceptual and methodological change in rhetoric within a hands-on, conceptually challenging if not fun-loving, approach to neuroscience, one that actively advances rhetorical insights just as it avoids concretizing contributions of researchers or propping up traditional disciplinary and epistemological hierarchies. The projects examined in this chapter demonstrate "the movement of change" in a playful, joint "style of engagement" that works to overcome any easy negation of neuroscience as "an Other" (see Muckelbauer, 2009, p. 7), building pragmatic ways for rhetoric to "respond differently" to the world (p. 13).

Project 1: Experimenting with the Social Processes of Neuroscience

In a five-year-long transdisciplinary project, rhetorical and literary studies scholar Melissa Littlefield, along with team members from the social sciences and the neurosciences, planned and performed an experiment—a kind of reexperiment—using functional magnetic resonance imaging (fMRI) scans in an effort to uncover areas of the brain that might be active during a truth-telling task. The collaboration was inspired by Littlefield's study of "the lying brain" in her 2011 book of that same title. What clearly troubled Littlefield early on was the overly simplistic isolation of "truth" or "deception" in previous fMRI studies. From her reading, experimental conditions did not capture the immense complexity of social life, that is, the ways and means by which people compose different variations and degrees of lies given rhetorical evaluations of social relations, stakes, and values.

In exposing the false and "ideal conceptualizations of objectivity and value neutrality" tied to fMRI studies, Littlefield (2011) argued for a rhetorical perspective, a recognition that science is "subjective, invested, situated, and imbricated with/in culture" such that brain-based lie detection never was a simple matter (p. 10).

Indeed, she went further, arguing that methodologically the body determined to deceive in neuroscience experiments was one already "integrated within discourses" (p. 11). To make the case, she showed how lie detection devices proliferated as a solution to interrogation and followed from a symbolic history wherein the emotional or reactive body was one that deceived (p. 14). The discourses surrounding more traditional lie detection devices inculcated, she argued, the goal of developing an easily readable code based on "emotional inscriptions" associated with "anxiety, fear, and guilt," which informed brain-based studies seeking to detect "truth" or "deception" (p. 16). To move beyond those discourses and complicate experimental studies seeking simple codes for deception, Littlefield sought collaboration with a broader research team that might compose a new brain-based experiment, which could itself, hopefully, expose how experimental conditions in the neurosciences played into dominant discourses of a deceptive body.

In terms of the intellectual process that paved the way for the study: Littlefield's initial rhetorical reading of neuroscience research about lie detection—inherently a discursive critique built on the semiotic, social constructivist intellectual resources of scholars such as Foucault and Haraway (Littlefield, 2011, p. 8–13)—resulted in reflection on how one might approach a brain science that is, as Andrew Pickering (1995) states, a "mangle of practice" tied to technologies, resources, and discourses (p. 3). This led Littlefield to plan a brain experiment methodologically acceptable to the cognitive neurosciences. The trick, of course, was to work across disciplines and to produce experimental results able to forge an exigence from previous studies while simultaneously questioning those studies' foundations. If "telling the truth is inherently a social construct," and "not a simple cognitive task" (Littlefield et al., 2014, pp. 553–554), then fMRI brain mapping should be able to show social evaluations being made in the corresponding areas of the brain, that is, if the experimental conditions allowed for such nuances to emerge from truth-telling tasks.

Littlefield's critique of the neuroscience literature and the methodologies employed, which sought to detect deception independent of realistic social circumstances and independent of an evaluation of others who might uncover or not uncover the liar, eventually did result in an experiment showing that "'truth' is not a simple or singular variable"; truth-telling conditions "range from simple truth to social truth and beyond" (p. 6). By all accounts, Littlefield and colleagues succeeded, publishing about the project in both *Frontiers of Human Neuroscience* (2014) as well as *Social Studies of Science* (2013). Yet, the project did not reach publication without difficulty.

As noted in their 2014 article, the researchers encountered "experimental politics" regarding "right" and "wrong" ways to go about brain research. Feeling self-consciously aware of the expectations and desires of different disciplines, they also developed what they described as a "*ressentiment* of collaboration" (p. 701). Undeniably, then, the project proved taxing and emotionally difficult. In addition, as Littlefield expressed in her 2013 paper presentation at the Society for the Social

Studies of Science, she subsequently faced the real possibility that she had inadvertently advanced brain-based lie detection, a field that she retained significant hesitations about with respect to its deployments and agendas.

The emotional and practical difficulties of prolonged neurohumanities/neurorhetorical collaboration cannot be overlooked. Yet, Littlefield and colleague's experiment and eventual publications are worth reviewing and celebrating for at least two reasons. First, the end-publications provide strong examples of a rhetorical, textual achievement that meaningfully builds an exigence from the existing neuroscience literature and argues persuasively from and for a new kind of experimental arrangement, adding social, situational evaluations into conceptions of "lying." With the experiment and the publication, the team essentially redefines a "lie" in neuroscientific terms as something that might adapt to everyday circumstances given local conditions and interpersonal dynamics. On this level, the project is a complex and daring rhetorical success story. Second, the project should be regarded as an achievement for its mode of inventive transdisciplinary practice, which is to say for its playful experimental approach.

Although the project did not always sound "fun" by most accounts, it pursued an imagination forged from the insights that scholarship in the rhetoric of science and medicine generated. It took the next step and injected (for lack of a better metaphor) some of the best scholarship from rhetoric of science into the brain sciences. As both a scholarly and creative endeavor—that used neuroscience methods to rhetorically revise neuroscience methods in lieu of rhetoric—the project deserves recognition for its movement from the comforts of textual rhetorical critique at a distance to fully engaged intervention amid cross-disciplinary partnership.

We might also consider the project in terms of more formal definitions of "play": if play is a something done by active agents through a "set of rules" within an "imaginary situation" and which exists "outside of ordinary life" (see Gray, 2013, p. 1; Vygotsky, 1967, p. 10), then the revised fMRI experiment, although quite serious, more basically enacted the rhetorical imagination to bring to life a new frame for neuroscience research. Situating Littlefield's project this way centers the doing and focuses attention on rhetorical possibilities—what can be done when established, scientific, experimental methodologies are put into conversation with a rhetorical perspective and then actively reimagined "outside of ordinary life" and remade accordingly.

With respect to play, the lingering question, however, is whether the *means* of such experimental play could be valued as much as the ends. Playful activity is often characterized by the sheer value of the performance; things are done without much concern for the ends but merely for the joy of the means (Gray, 2013). Of course, this is not always the case, as James Schirmer (2013) notes when equating the classical rhetorical concept of *techne* with play by suggesting that play is not completely wild and open-ended but flexibly guided, founded on history, and composed through specific processes while remaining open to variable interpretations (p. 150). In both cases—play as celebrated for the joy of performance and for the ability to shape a compelling performance—Littlefield offers a success story.

Even without such an impressive endpoint, rhetoricians, I believe, should applaud the methodological means—the particular sets of neuroscientific technologies and transdisciplinary practices engaged in Littlefield and colleague's brain scan experiment—both for the enactment of the performance and the skill (*techne*) in shaping the performance. The way that they centered the social and the environmental in the adopted fMRI brain scan methods in order to see if any new results might complicate existing discourses is inherently a rhetorical act and a methodological achievement with or without a publication. Valuing the intersection of neuroscience and rhetoric that Littlefield's team crafted herein fronts an attitude of negotiation and a "let's see what happens" mindset at a point when more rhetorical scholars seem to want to engage the brain sciences.[3]

Thinking about approaching a new methodology as a "playful" activity decenters the ends and seeks a form of "rhetorical invention"—what Muckelbauer (2009) calls "an affirmative sense of change" derived from breaking boundaries and eliding dichotomies (pp. 8–13). Such invention pragmatically ignores disciplinary constructs of proper-improper/familiar-foreign methods. Rhetorical invention focuses, instead, on the processes of recomposition and the everyday practices that dismantle rigid divisions. In rhetorical studies of science and medicine, adopting the stranger (estranged) scientific methodologies—or useful aspects of them—that seem to construct objectivity to defend singular visions of materiality enfolds intellectually with the insight that rhetorical scholars are themselves subjected to "confirmation and falsification" (Depew & Lyne, 2013, p. 6) and builds from a history where "rhetoric has always lent itself to interdisciplinarity" (Depew & Lyne, 2013, p. 14). But more directly with respect to rhetorical invention: an "affirmative sense of change" remembers both that science is rhetorical and that rhetoric is invested in materiality while being itself always as wildly multiple and ecological as the material world.[4]

One simmering contention may be that Littlefield's project of adopting—more accurately, reperforming—established, disciplinary scientific methods privileges or concretizes an epistemological hierarchy with the neurosciences at the top. However, when seen as the playful activity of rhetorical invention, the project unravels a hierarchy with the unabashed assurance that an "in between" space can be made and that rhetoricians can be instigators of newness. Because Littlefield recognizes that science is social and symbolic as well as material and practical, her team displays the confidence that rhetoric, as a field area, has much to offer and can meaningfully engage the (neuro)sciences.

A *neuroscience of rhetoric* embracing such an attitude and approach foregoes a situation where neuroscience is directly and forcefully applied to rhetoric or rhetorical theory. In like manner, a *rhetoric of neuroscience* refuses to be content with/after rhetorical criticism. The __X__ *of* __Y__ formula dissipates, transforming into a thoroughly *neurorhetorical* engagement because it composes *rhetorical invention in between conceptual and applied spaces.*

Project 2: Performing Interpretations of Neuroscience

For over two years, media artist Daniel Howe and I took as our focus and directive Muckelbauer's (2009) notion of rhetorical invention as we pursued a computational project visualizing interpretations of a neuroscience finding about "mirror neurons." In seeking to blend conceptual, disciplinary spaces (rhetoric and media arts and neuroscience), we explored mirror neurons (MNs) through remediation. The goal was to visualize and contrast MN interpretations in a creative way and, thus, to bring MNs to life as algorithms and to see them anew. Prior to detailing the nature of the project, however, it is useful to briefly provide an overview of the neuroscience of MNs.

These neurons—according to Vittorio Gallese (2003), Marco Iacoboni (2009), and the other neuroscientists who popularized them (Di Pellegrino et al., 1992; Rizzolatti & Craighero, 2004)—are said to act as little "mirrors in the brain"; they are special kinds of neurons theorized to internally simulate the visual environment and, thereby, aid in the understanding of other people's actions (Di Pellegrino et al, 1992; Gallese, 2003; Iacoboni, 2009). Subsequently, MNs have been tied to linguistic and emotional processing (Gallese & Goldman, 1998; Wicker et al., 2003) and have been employed in numerous fields ranging from phenomenology (Lohmar, 2006) to dance therapy (Berrol, 2006) to group psychotherapy (Nava, 2007; Pisani, 2010; Schermer, 2010). Often mentioned within discussions of "mirroring" other people's body movements, MNs have been invoked as a neurological basis of attention disorders and empathetic functions (Staemmler, 2012; Winters, 2008). Yet, MN findings from the cognitive neurosciences have also come under intense scrutiny (Csibra, 2007; Hickok, 2009; Jacob, 2008; Lingnau et al., 2009), and MNs may not perform any "mirroring" function at all, but rather may be predicting actions (Michael, 2009; Hickok, 2014). Still, multiple articles validating "mirroring therapies" in Group Psychotherapy, in particular, have turned to MNs both to legitimize existing practices (Foulkes, 1964; 1975; Pines, 1981, 1982) and to invent new forms of therapy focused on body language (Schermer, 2010).

Our computational project—called "Gesture/Language/Mirror"—took MN findings from the cognitive neurosciences as inspiration for a new algorithm that matched gestures across actors performing transcripts from group therapy sessions. The algorithm functioned by detecting changes in hand and body position in prerecorded videos of therapy interactions. The project involved several videos of different actors (playing therapy patients), each video lasting roughly 15 minutes in length (see Figure 15.1). One video served as a "driver" that played in real-time and caused the others to "jump" and display the closest matching gesture.[5] The result was a fragmented narrative stream, a kind of chopped up story told only

FIGURE 15.1 Gesture/Language/Mirror—Therapy Performance Session, 9/2015, courtesy of D. Gruber.

through mirrored gestures. When a match was found, sounds from both the driver and the matched video across all screens were heard. For example, on video screen one, a male actor/patient cupped his hand to his ear and light-heartedly said, "I called her on the phone . . ."; at the same time, another actor/patient on video screen two made the same gesture when recalling a haunting story and said, "I can just hear his voice." At one point, a patient shook fists in frustration, saying, "I'm thinking, like, punch you in the head," while another balled fists in nervousness, saying, "I feel all tense."

Prior to filming, actors were given the preselected therapy transcripts half an hour in advance. The actors performed them from memory with improvisation allowed to embody the character emerging from the transcripts. The short time of exposure to the transcripts ensured a level of immediacy in performance, theoretically producing gestures closer to those that might appear in real therapy sessions. During the filming, one researcher sat behind the camera as a role-play therapist, mirroring the actors' body language without their conscious knowledge of the mirrored performance, mimicking what group therapists might do in conducting actual "mirror therapy" sessions. Group therapist Malcome Pines (1982; 1998), for example, advocates using body language to call attention to a patient's identifications, annoyances, and disconnections. For him, "The therapist acts as the mirror . . . by his interventions and interpretations" (p. 29). Likewise, Victor Schermer (2010) mirrors body language in group therapy, arguing that a mirrored image "is always an immediate reproduction simultaneous with the time frame of the observer at the moment he perceives it" and, thus, forces internal reflection (p. 217).

Along the way, we developed several algorithmic iterations for the project, accounting for the fact that MNs changed as they were debated in the neurosciences—being called the "foundations of human civilization" by one neuroscientist (Ramachandran, 2009) and a "myth" by another (Hickok, 2014). This caused scientific descriptions of "mirroring" processes in the brain to vary over time. Exploring these dramatic differences suggested new possibilities for algorithmic play and invention and allowed us to call attention to difference and disagreement within the neurosciences. Further, the algorithms inspired by different interpretations became an experiential and artistic way to probe possibilities for mirroring and human identification.

Two dominant computational iterations eventually emerged. The first was based on early mirror neuron theories, which interpreted MNs as a "direct matching" mechanism between the motor areas of two different brains (Gallese et al., 1996; Rizzolatti, Fogassi, & Gallese, 2001). The idea was that monkeys, and presumably humans as well, simulated each other's body movements through the same MN mechanisms and, thus, felt similarly, or, at least, they might have sensed what it was like to be the other monkey/person from within a neurobiologically similar production. Researcher Gerben Rotman and colleagues (2006) explained that view of MNs this way: "The direct matching hypothesis posits . . . when people observe action, they implement covert action plans that, in real time, match the action plans executed by the actor" (p. 1358). This direct matching hypothesis informed the development of an algorithm that would "directly" match body movements across video inputs. The computer screen acted as a metaphor for the motor system of the brain. The processing programming language divided the screen into tiny computational boxes wherein movement across any number of those boxes would be directly compared. This resulted in a program that checked for the same directional movement of the same speed across the same boxes of the screen from two or more video inputs.

Later MN explorations, starting with Ferrari et al. (2005), Oberman et al. (2005), and Dapretto et al. (2006), revealed that different people may have different qualities, arrangements, or amounts of MNs in a broader MN system. Studies also found that MNs do not fire all the time but seem to only fire in response to specific kinds of goal-directed actions (Umilta et al., 2001). In other words, MNs only fired when a person watched another person do something like eat food or drink coffee, but MNs did not fire when someone was moving arms or hands for no apparent reason (Tai et al., 2004). This generated increasing emphasis on the "Action Understanding Theory" of MNs (Rizzolatti & Craighero, 2004; Nelissen, Luppino, Vanduffel, Rizzolatti, & Orban, 2005), which proposed that MNs were primarily responsible for helping people to understand what others *intended* to do.

Building an algorithm that took "Action Understanding" as its inspiration, we then added a database of gestures from the video inputs. The database took into account the limitations of MNs insofar as MNs did not fire every time a similar movement was detected but only in response to specific gestures; in our project, a gesture had to be "recognized" by the computer system. Experimenting with the algorithm in this way allowed us to see MNs and thus to craft a point of entry for rethinking MNs.

Creatively, the new algorithm solved the three problems previously encountered. First, calling up gestures from a database allowed for better gesture matches, since similar movement using the direct matching method produced many questionable "matches" (i.e., hands thrown across the same screen areas were not necessarily formal "matches"); using a database, the "matches" could be identified and more closely related. Second, the experience of watching the new version created more reflective space for the viewer. In the previous version, the matching system created a bombardment of noise and images due to the high number of matches. Finally, the revised algorithm better reflected the phenomenological experience of everyday life, since, of course, people do not always "mirror" others nor identify with body movements nor always care about what others are intending to do. Indeed, the immense number of fast matches spinning in the first algorithm added to doubts about that particular interpretation of MNs.

Overall, the project was a computational means to explore and expand MN interpretations without any tie to scientific realities related to computational neuroscience. Using computation as an artistic tool—not as a scientifically valid brain simulation—the project located a visual/computational way to think about the embodied experience of mirroring as well as to perform neuroscience interpretations and allow viewers to think through all of the issues and possibilities. The project, we felt, achieved this goal by showing what was and what was not being mirrored as a result of the different algorithms, in terms of bodies, moods, attitudes, affects, and topics. By watching the gesture matches in real-time, viewers could reflect upon the differences or consider whether the algorithm seemed to "get it right" or discover whether something was missing with respect to human experience and/or neuroscience research.

In the end, we felt that the project highlighted what was not mirrored just as much as what was mirrored. Watching the algorithm locate so-called "gesture matches" troubled the notion that two similar body movements ever related in precisely the same way to the environment, to a social situation, or to affect-laden psychological experience. Visual inputs were, themselves, somewhat empty. In other words, the stories told in the therapy setting *felt* so different even though the bodies were matched and looked so similar. "Gesture/Language/Mirror" called attention not only to how bodies shifted with audience and purpose and environment but how embodiment and phenomenological experience were contextual and shifted on a different, if not occasionally intersecting, plane of existence with body language.

The project also probed the extent to which bodily "mirroring" described "identification" among bodies. Because a substantial body of scholarly literature has tied MNs to sympathy and empathy—often crucial components or characteristics of identifying with others—the question of whether a computer could properly "mirror" bodies and then illicit strong feelings in a participant who watched the videos proved relevant (see Staemmler, 2012; Ramachandran, 2009; Winters, 2008; Wicker et al., 2003). The result was uneven. Seeing many kinds of mirroring—of different extents and in different alignments with various emotional utterances—suggested that algorithms cannot always do the human work of instigating the human feeling of connection and, perhaps, also hinted at the possibility that scholars can forge more complex notions and illuminate a hidden plural in concepts of mirroring and identification.

From a rhetorical standpoint, the plural hides in Kenneth Burke's (1969) well-wrought concept of persuasion as "identification" (pp. 19–24). The project suggested phenomenological, experiential diversity within identification, questioning the singular "one-as-one" formula embedded in "persuasion as identification." Two bodies that "match" and "mirror" did not necessarily identify nor always appear "consubstantial" in the same way (Burke, 1969, p. 21). The outward signs exhibited when one feels identification with another can be complex and multiple, just as the outward bodily signs of making a "goal-directed" gesture said to signal MN firing can be multiple (Umilta et al., 2001). Seeing, for example, a person fill a cup of water could express the intention of empting a pitcher just as much as the intention of drinking the cup of water.[6] Gesture circulates in multiplicity—enacting multiple entwined configurations—with intentionality, mirroring, and identification.

In matching individuals in the videos based purely on body movements and not on specific experiences in a conversation, the algorithm, surprisingly to us, directed attention to the messy complexity of the whole affair. The emotions and affects of the matched gestures sometimes demanded care, comfort, and attention on the part of the viewer, just as the gestures sometimes elicited disregard, discomfort, and inattention. Crossing legs, rubbing eyes, pointing to the sky, shaking fists, all exhibited degrees of intensity and became performances more or less persuasive—and differently persuasive—with respect to thinking screens alike or with respect to feeling for the individuals on screen. In this way, the project highlighted an expansive gray area of mirroring, intention, and identification—a range intimately tied to an inventive body sensing the world, actively "becoming affective" (Gruber, 2014b, p. 156) in a (co)production of reactive life.

Ruminating on these connections led me to revisit David McClelland's (1987) explanation of "motive" as not always existing consciously and often appearing to be variable in kind and strength (pp. 591–593). Here, human "motive" as a "natural incentive" rests not only at the intersection of biology and symbolicity but becomes varied and variable over time (p. 591). Identification, herein, reorients toward multiplicity as Burkean identification is inherently linked to motive insofar as "bridging a distance" is the ultimate human motive, as Bryan Crabel (2009) argues. In line with the computational project's visualizations, bodies engaged in similar actions do not provide a neat pathway to understanding meanings nor to feeling similarly, as some MNs theorists have previously asserted (Gallese et al., 1996; Rizzolatti et al., 2001). Indeed, upon revisiting McClelland and putting his work into conversation with the "Gesture/Language/Mirror" project and with Crabel's identification as "distance," I developed new skepticism with respect to the prospects of an "ultimate human motive" and became suspicious of a singular, all-inclusive notion of "identification" writ large, which seemed more an analytical convenience than a material reality. At the very least, I am now stirred to consider many shades or bodily expressions of these concepts. What proves striking in all of this is that computational and neuroscientific engagement did not upend the importance of rhetorical situatedness even while neuroscientific theories of "mirroring" provided the platform from which I could play and in playing question concepts in rhetorical theory.

The spaces in between disciplines herein come to the fore. Rhetorical exploration of processes of identification, upon seriously engaging bodily matter, cannot disregard what other fields and similar conversations happening in those fields can bring into view. The claim does not necessarily mean that hiring a neuroscientist or developing a novel experiment is always the best way forward. But the "Gesture/Language/Mirror" project tries to demonstrate that experiments in rhetoric can draw on available resources to discover new conceptual and practical spaces in between many fields, which can then add to rhetorical theory and criticism.

Conclusion: Inventing Ways Forward

If the social sciences and the humanities must "entangle" with the science of life, as Callard and Fitzgerald (2014) claim, then simple knowledge-sharing activities and applications of one field to another risks reifying disciplinary conventions and may well miss what rhetorical invention has to offer. Seeking new realities through imagining possibilities that surge out from within one's own field strives, at an intellectual core, to break down a dichotomy sustained by one field listening to, applying, and/or critiquing another. Accordingly, the subfield of neu-rorhetorics must move beyond the either-or currently embedded in the proposi-tion that it mutually enact a "rhetoric of neuroscience" wherein neuroscience is read rhetorically or a "neuroscience of rhetoric" wherein new neuroscience findings are applied to rhetorical theories (see Jack, 2010).[7] The movement from cross-pollination to the in between space of rhetorical invention is needed. An in-between calls out for a different kind of engagement, an experimentation that plays and seeks after new appearances of things from a place of rearrangement and contribution.

Any concept of collaboration or "entanglement," no doubt, raises real chal-lenges. No one denies tangible fears that transdisciplinary projects will start heroi-cally and then eventually flounder with no place, no legitimization, no funding, and no publication. These fears are real. They will materialize for many projects and end beautiful imaginations. However, the case studies detailed in this chapter, I believe, offer hope and direction.

Littlefield's reexperimentation demonstrates the usefulness of more traditional rhetorical readings to the neurosciences as well as evidences how methodologies, in being appropriated, can be recomposed to promote new in-betweens. The space of imagination activated through a spirit of rhetorical invention takes as its starting point existing disciplinary formations and then finds its own way, as Lit-tlefield did with the reimagination of truth-telling tasks that became social and situated and, ultimately, much more interesting. My project with Daniel Howe demonstrates how remediation and creative performance might expose dueling rhetorics at play in the neurosciences and spur questioning about the object of discussion. The project does not so much strive to directly comment on sci-entific realities as use existing debates to motivate new concepts of mirroring and (rhetorical) identification. It is a philosophical intervention through the arts hoping to invent alternatives and combine rhetoric, media arts, and cognitive neuroscience.

Both projects share rhetorical theorists building things and undercutting any prefabricated idea of disciplinary hierarchies that might discourage experimental (in both senses of the word) projects. By centering rhetorical invention and work-ing out from the insights of rhetoric, the field maintains a solid sense of itself even as it approaches new areas and practices directly informed by the sciences of life. Indeed, in building from existing insights and yet playfully pursuing a positive sense of change to perform new ways of thinking and doing with other fields, rhetoric rewrites itself without artificially estranging itself.

Here, a call to embrace what might be termed playful, wild, or messy meth-odological pluralism is not to overlook how multiple approaches change what is seen, how it is seen, how it is written, and why. If neuroscience is, as Little-field points out, "subjective, invested, situated, and imbricated with/in culture," then so is rhetoric. The ideological dimension cannot be discarded in favor of sheer newness. Yet, for rhetorical scholars existing, for the most part, in tight and collegial communities, face a risk—both of insulation and of strict adherence to the realizations of the semiotic turn and to textual analysis even in cases of embracing or confronting materiality. However, rhetorical invention, as Muckelbauer (2009) outlines it, demands more. He argues that "actual change" cannot be an endless continuation of tradition nor a simple refusal of the past, but a practical engagement, aligning itself with "repetition with a difference," feeling a tension with past formations, yet altering interactions (pp. 145–146). On this point, Muckelbauer quotes Carolyn Miller (2000) who sees innovation not as a total break with the past but as a situated development that must "occupy the border between the known and the unknown" in order to be "rhetorically useful" (p. 141). The discussion resonates with Nathan Johnson's observation on page 75 in this volume that "minor changes can make a big difference," both in the infrastructures that he analyzes but also in the approach that rhetoricians might take.

As a "mangle" (Pickering, 1995), rhetoric, like science, will change along with new technologies, practices, and environments. Its traditions, approaches, and methods will mutate. Of course, as Lawrence Prelli (2013) notes, "What distinguishes RSSTM [Rhetoric Studies of Science, Technology, and Medicine] is a rhetorical approach" (p. 6); however, that "approach" need not be singular, qualitative, or exclusively focused on the discursive. The neurorhetorical projects detailed in this chapter point the way toward hands-on activities originated for exploration and intending to invent possibilities for rhetoric and for neuroscience without letting either fall to the wayside or block the way. If there remains any lingering question of whether the field of rhetoric will be ideologically or pragmatically swamped by newer, domineering, or illustrious methods from the sciences of life, the question is already at odds with the situated change inhabiting the in-between of rhetorical invention.

Notes

1 These purposes were first observed by Gross (1994).
2 I use the word "engineers" here in place of something like "innovators" to emphasize the pragmatic planning and building inherent to rhetorical invention.
3 This statement is made from recognition of the Neurorhetorics Seminar featured at the 2015 RSA Summer Institute as well as from the growing body of scholarship that discusses bodies and affect now being produced.
4 Here I inherently draw from the insights of multiple ontologies theory in rhetoric and in science and technology studies (STS), which asserts that many "realities" are brought into appearance over time and through different ways of "touching" (see Mol, 2002).
5 The "driver" video alternates such that each video/patient acts as the driver during the exhibit.
6 In the conclusion of his 2009 article, Gregory Hickok makes a similar observation regarding the ambiguity surrounding the notion of "intention" in the neuroscience literature, and I believe the computational project reinforces the problems of that ambiguity.
7 I make this argument more fully in a study of how scholars in phenomenology have interacted with the neurosciences (Gruber, 2016).

References

Bates, B. R., Templeton, A., Achter, P. J., Harris, T. M., & Condit, C. M. (2003). What does "a gene for heart disease" mean? A focus group study of public understandings of genetic risk factors." *American Journal of Medical Genetics, 119A,* 156–161.

Berrol, C. F. (2006). Neuroscience meets dance/movement therapy: Mirror neurons, the therapeutic process and empathy. *The Arts in Psychotherapy, 33*(4), 302–315.

Biesecker, B. A. and Lucaites, J. L. (2009). Introduction. In B. A. Beisecker & J. L. Lucaites (Eds.), *Rhetoric, materiality, and politics* (pp. 1–160). New York, NY: Peter Lang.

Blackman, L. (2012). *Immaterial bodies: Affect, embodiment, mediation.* London, UK: Sage.

Burke, K. (1969). *A rhetoric of motives.* Berkeley, CA: University of California Press.

Callard, F., & Fitzgerald, D. (2014). The entanglements of interdisciplinarity: An interview with Des Fitzgerald and Felicity Callard. *Theory, Culture & Society.* Retrieved from http://theoryculturesociety.org/the-entanglements-of-interdisciplinarity-an-inter view-with-des-fitzgerald-and-felicity-callard/.

Crabel, B. (2009). Distance as ultimate motive: A dialectical interpretation of *A Rhetoric of Motives. Rhetoric Society Quarterly, 39*(3), 213–239.

Csibra, G. (2007). Action mirroring and action interpretation: An alternative account. In P. Haggard, Y. Rosetti, & M. Kawato (Eds.), *Sensorimotor foundations of higher cognition: Attention and performance XXII* (pp. 435–480). Oxford, UK: Oxford University Press.

Dapretto, M., Davies, M. S., Pfeifer, J. H., Scott, A. A., Sigman, M., Bookheimer, S. Y., & Iacoboni, M. (2006). Understanding emotions in others: Mirror neuron dysfunction in children with autism spectrum disorders. *Nature Neuroscience, 9*(1), 28–30.

Depew, D. J., & Lyne, J. (2013). The productivity of scientific rhetoric. *POROI, 9*(1), 1–21.

Di Pellegrino, G., Fadiga, L., Fogassi, L., Gallese, V., & Rizzolatti, G. (1992). Understanding motor events: A neurophysiological study. *Experimental Brain Research, 91,* 176–180.

Ferrari, P. F., Rozzi, S., & Fogassi, L. (2005). Mirror neurons responding to observation of actions made with tools in monkey ventral premotor cortex. *Journal of Cognitive Neuroscience, 17*(2), 212–226.

Fitzgerald, D., Littlefield, M. M., Knudsen, K., Tonks, J., & Dietz, M. (2014). Ambivalence, equivocation and the politics of experimental knowledge: A transdisciplinary neuroscience encounter. *Social Studies of Science, 44,* 701–722.

Foulkes, S. H. (1964). *Therapeutic group analysis.* London, UK: George Allen and Unwin.

Foulkes, S. H. (1975). *Group-analytic psychotherapy: Method and principles.* London, UK: Gordon and Breach.

Fountain, T. K. (2014). *Rhetoric in the flesh: Trained vision, technical expertise, and the gross anatomy lab.* New York, NY: Routledge.

Gallese, V. (2003). The roots of empathy: The shared manifold hypothesis and the neural basis of intersubjectivity. *Psychopathology, 36*(4), 171–180.

Gallese, V., Fadiga, L., Fogassi, L., & Rizzolatti, G. (1996). Action recognition in the premotor cortex. *Brain, 119,* 593–609.

Gallese, V., & Goldman, A. (1998). Mirror neurons and the simulation theory of mind reading. *Trends in Cognitive Sciences, 2*(12), 252–254.

Graham, S. S. (2015). *The politics of pain medicine: A rhetorical-ontological inquiry.* Chicago, IL: University of Chicago Press.

Graham, S. S., & Herndl, C. (2013). Multiple ontologies in pain management: Toward a post-plural rhetoric of science. *Technical Communication Quarterly, 22*(2), 103–125.

Gray, P. (2013). Definitions of play. *Scholarpedia, 8*(7), 30578. Retrieved from www.scholar pedia.org/article/Definitions_of_Play.

Gross, A. (1994). The role of rhetoric in the public understanding of science. *Public Understanding of Science, 3*, 3–23.

Gruber, D. (2013). The neuroscience of rhetoric: Identification, mirror neurons, and making the many appear. In J. Jack (Ed.), *Neurorhetorics* (pp. 37–53). London, UK: Routledge and Rhetoric Society of America.

Gruber, D. (2014a). Mirror neurons in a Group Analysis hall of mirrors: "Translation" as a rhetorical approach to neuro-disciplinary writing. *Technical Communication Quarterly, 23*(3), 207–226.

Gruber, D. (2014b). The (digital) majesty of all under heaven: Affective constitutive rhetoric at the Hong Kong museum of history's terracotta warrior exhibit. *Rhetoric Society Quarterly, 44*(2), 148–167.

Gruber, D. R. (2016). Reinventing the brain, revising neurorhetorics: Phenomonological networks contesting neurobiological interpretations. *Rhetoric Review, 35*(3), 239–253.

Harris, R. A. (2013). Rhetoric of science meets the science of rhetoric. *POROI, 9*(1), 1–12.

Hawhee, D. (2015). Rhetoric's sensorium. *Quarterly Journal of Speech, 101*(1), 2–17.

Hickok, G. (2009). Eight problems for the mirror neuron theory of action understanding in monkeys and humans. *Journal of Cognitive Neuroscience, 21*(7), 1229–1243.

Hickok, G. (2014). *The myth of mirror neurons: The real neuroscience of communication and cognition.* New York, NY: W. W. Norton.

Iacoboni, M. (2009). *Mirroring people: The science of empathy and how we connect with others.* New York, NY: Picador.

Jack, J. (2010). What are neurorhetorics? *Rhetoric Society Quarterly, 40*(5), 405–410.

Jack, J. (2014). *Autism and gender: From refrigerator mothers to computer geeks.* Champaign, IL: University of Illinois Press.

Jacob, P. (2008). What do mirror neurons contribute to human social cognition? *Mind & Language, 23*(2), 190–223.

Keränen, L. (2013). Inventing the future: The rhetorics of science, technology, and medicine [Special issue]. *POROI, 9*(1).

Lingnau, A., Gesierich, B., & Caramazza, A. (2009). Asymmetric fMRI adaptation reveals no evidence for mirror neurons in humans. *Proceedings of the National Academy of Sciences, 106*(24), 9925–9930.

Littlefield, M. M. (2011). *The lying brain: Lie detection in science and science fiction.* Ann Arbor, MI: University of Michigan Press.

Littlefield, M. M. (2015). From handwriting to "brain" writing: Graphology and the neuroscientific turn. In S. I. Dobrin (Ed.), *Writing posthumanism, posthuman writing* (pp. 214–233). Anderson, SC: Parlor Press.

Littlefield, M. M., Fitzgerald, D., Knudsen, K., Tonks, J., & Dietz, M. (2014). Contextualizing neuro-collaborations: Reflections on a transdisciplinary fMRI lie detection experiment. *Frontiers in Human Neuroscience.* Retrieved from http://journal.frontiersin.org/article/10.3389/fnhum.2014.00149/full.

Lohmar, D. (2006). Mirror neurons and the phenomenology of intersubjectivity. *Phenomenology and the Cognitive Sciences, 5*(1), 5–16.

Marback, R. (2008). Unclenching the fist: Embodying rhetoric and giving objects their due. *Rhetoric Society Quarterly, 38*(1), 46–65.

Mays, C., & Jung, J. (2012). Priming terministic inquiry: Toward a methodology of neurorhetoric. *Rhetoric Review, 31*(1), 41–59.

McClelland, D. C. (1987). *Human motivation*. Cambridge, UK: Cambridge University Press.

Michael, J. (2009). Mirror neurons and social cognition: An extended simulationist frame-work. In H. W. de Regt, S. Hartman, & S. Okasha (Eds.), *EPSA philosophy of science: Amsterdam 2009* (pp. 217–226). New York, NY: Springer.

Miller, C. (2000). The Aristotelian *topos*: Hunting for novelty. In A. G. Gross & A. E. Walzer (Eds.), *Rereading Aristotle's Rhetoric* (pp. 130–146). Carbondale, IL: Southern Illinois University Press.

Mol, A. (2002). *Body multiple: Ontology in medical practice*. Durham, NC: Duke University Press.

Muckelbauer, J. (2007). Rhetoric, asignification, and other: A response to Diane Davis. *Philosophy & Rhetoric, 40*(2), 238–247.

Muckelbauer, J. (2009). *The future of invention: Rhetoric, postmodernism, and the problem of change*. Albany NY: State University of New York Press.

Nava, A. S. (2007). Empathy and group analysis: An integrative approach. *Group Analysis, 40*(1), 13–28.

Nelissen, K., Luppino, G., Vanduffel, W., Rizzolatti, G., & Orban, G. A. (2005). Observing others: Multiple action representation in the frontal lobe. *Science, 310*(5746), 332–336.

Oberman, L. M., Hubbard, E. M., McCleery, J. P., Altschuler, E. L., Ramachandran, V. S., & Pineda, J. A. (2005). EEG evidence for mirror neuron dysfunction in autism spectrum disorders. *Cognitive Brain Research, 24*, 190–198.

Pickering, A. (1995). *The mangle of practice: Time, agency, and science*. Chicago, IL: University of Chicago Press.

Pines, M. (1981). The frame of reference of group psychotherapy. *International Journal of Group Psychotherapy, 31*(3), 275–285.

Pines, M. (1982). Reflections on mirroring. *Group Analysis, 15*, 1–26.

Pines, M. (1998). *Circular reflections*. London, UK: Jessica Kingsley Publishers.

Pisani, R. A. (2010). Malcolm Pines' contribution to group analysis. *Group Analysis, 43*, 328–336.

Prelli, L. (2013). The prospect of invention in rhetorical studies of science, technology, and medicine. *Poroi, 9*(1), 1–11.

Ramachandran, V. S. (2009). The neurons that shaped civilization *Tedtalk*. Retrieved from www.ted.com/talks/vs_ramachandran_the_neurons_that_shaped_civilization?language=en.

Ramsay, S. (2011). On building. *Stephen Ramsay Blog*. Retrieved from http://stephenramsay.us/text/2011/01/11/on-building/.

Rice, J. (2008). The new "new": Making a case for critical affect studies. *Quarterly Journal of Speech, 94*(2), 200–212.

Rice, J. (2015). Pathologia. *Quarterly Journal of Speech, 101*(1), 34–45.

Rickert, T. (2013). *Ambient rhetoric: The attunements of rhetorical being*. Pittsburgh, PA: Pittsburgh University Press.

Rivers, N. (2014). Tracing the missing masses: Vibrancy, symmetry, and public rhetoric pedagogy. *Enculturation*. Retrieved from http://enculturation.net/missingmasses.

Rizzolatti, G., & Craighero, L. (2004). The mirror-neuron system. *Annual Review of Neuroscience, 27*, 169–192.

Rizzolatti, G., Fogassi, L., & Gallese, V. (2001). Neurophysiological mechanisms underlying the understanding and imitation of action. *National Review Neuroscience, 2*, 661–670.

Rotman, G., Troje, N. F., Johansson, R. S., & Flanagan, R. J. (2006). Eye movements when observing predictable and unpredictable actions. *Journal of Neurophysiology, 96*, 1358–1369.

Schermer, V. L. (2010). Reflections on "reflections on mirroring." *Group Analysis*, *43*(3), 214–227.

Schirmer, J. (2013). Techne as play: Three interstices. In R. Colby, M. S. S. Johnson, and R. S. Colby (Eds.), *Rhetoric/composition/play through video games* (pp. 149–160). New York, NY: Palgrave Macmillan.

Staemmler, F. M. (2012). *Empathy in psychotherapy: How therapists and clients understand each other*. New York, NY: Springer.

Tai, Y. F., Scherfler, C., Brookes, D. J., Sawamoto, N., & Castiello, U. (2004). The human premotor cortex is "mirror" only for biological actions. *Current Biology*, *14*(2), 117–120.

Umiltà, A. M., Kohler, E., Gallese, V., Fogassi, L., Fadiga, L., Keysers, C., & Rizzolatti, G. (2001). I know what you are doing: A neurophysiological study. *Neuron*, *31*, 155–165.

Vygotsky, L. S. (1967). Play and its role in the mental development of the child. *Soviet Psychology*, *5*(3), 6–18.

Wicker, B., Keysers, C., Plailly, J., Royet, J. P., Gallese, V., & Rizolatti, G. (2003). Both of us disgusted in *my* insula: The common neural basis of seeing and feeling disgust. *Neuron*, *40*(3), 655–664.

Winters, A. (2008). Emotion, embodiment, and mirror neurons in dance/movement therapy: A connection across disciplines. *American Journal of Dance Therapy*, *30*(2), 84–105.

INDEX